THIS IS HOPE: GREEN VEGANS AND THE NEW HUMAN ECOLOGY

Finally! A MUST READ for anyone seeking a practical planetary path from the current trajectory of death and desperation to one that truly engages and embraces hope for all species. This book provides a pioneering path for those who truly want to be the change we want - and need - to see in this world. As we collectively experience this never-before era of one species empowered to make it or break it for all, we now have HOPE to survive together. As a scientist in wildlife management and conservation, I can attest to tragically ridiculous and archaic methods that continue to be used (mis)manage wildlife and plant species for human ignorance and greed rather than for the planet and successive generations. *This Is Hope* incorporates the best and the brightest of science while allowing for the potential of humanity - in an emerging planet of interspecies coexistence and survival.

Toni Frohoff, Ph.D., Wildlife Behavioral Biologist, TerraMar Research and Author, *Dolphin Mysteries* and *Between Species*

We are at the precipice where human existence and that of all other species is in doubt. Can we commit to a course of action in time to stop the loss of biodiversity, while increasing human prosperity? In *This Is Hope*, we realize that our old way of thinking about our place in the world must change. Here you will find not just another explanation of where we have gone wrong; but also that we have the power to create the world all of us would hope for ourselves and future generations.

Brenda Peterson, author of *Build Me an Ark: A Life with Animals* and *Animal Heart*

In *THIS IS HOPE* Will Anderson proposes a unifying and comprehensive approach to stop the loss of ecosystems and biodiversity and to end the wanton abuse of wild and domesticated nonhuman animals (animals). It's essential for people with different agendas but often overlapping goals to talk *with*, not *at*, one another, and make every attempt to come to agreeable solutions concerning our inevitable interactions with ecosystems, species, and especially *individual* animals. This is no easy ask. However, Anderson covers most of the issues with which deep ecologists, environmentalists, species and animal rights activists, students of human ecology, vegetarians, and vegans are concerned. In this ambitious and heartfelt book a wide range of people will find common ground and a shared language for developing and implementing a unified approach to bring an end to the wanton redecoration and destruction of landscapes and to end the egregious harm to individual animals for which humans are uniquely responsible. Globally, there are many passionate people who care deeply about the world in which we all live, so as we attempt to expand our compassion footprint and rewild our hearts we need to step out of comfort zones and think and act out of the box. Whether you agree or disagree with Anderson here or there is of little concern for this book will make you think deeply about a large number of issues that are closely connected—although at first glance this might not seem to be the case. I learned a lot from reading *THIS IS HOPE* and I'm sure you will as well.

Marc Bekoff, Ph.D., University of Colorado; author of many books including *The emotional lives of animals, Animals matter, Wild justice: The moral lives of animals*, and *The animal manifesto: Six reasons for expanding our compassion footprint.*

This is Hope: Green Vegans and the New Ecology is thoughtful and thought-provoking. In this comprehensive and well-researched book, Will Anderson weaves together the impact our behaviors have on the web of life, without leaving loose ends. As a vegan, somebody with a comparatively light footprint on the planet, I appreciated the reminder that when I buy non organic vegan products I poison the Earth and thereby the animals. That may be what Anderson does best — he challenges us to do better. I liked the challenge and know that other readers will too.

Karen Dawn, author of *Thanking the Monkey: Rethinking the Way We Treat Animals.*

This is Hope is filled with well-documented insights, eloquently expressed, into the causes and conditions of the malaise that is spreading over the Earth and afflicting all of its occupants as a result of the human desire to coerce the planet to conform to our will and our will alone. Ironically, our drive entails a death wish that can be seen not only in the extinction of other species but in the destruction of the ecological systems and networks upon which all beings on Earth, including ourselves, depend and into which all of us are integrated, for better or worse. As terrible as species extinction is (I have often thought of what it must be like for a creature to experience being the last of its kind, like the last Dusky Seaside Sparrow who was so uncaringly reported in the news media as having drowned in "its" water cup at the zoo and whose death as a species was said to matter only because of what it could portend for humans) – as terrible as species extinction is, I say: equally terrible and in some ways worse is the endless proliferation of animals to fit the procrustean beds of global industrial agriculture, experimental research and all of the other human horrors that not even death can rescue them from being forced to endure in endless rebirths of an agonized Phoenix. Apathy or Empathy, Apathy or Action: These are the questions that confront us and that are affirmatively addressed in *This is Hope*. This book presents its solid conceptual arguments in lucid prose while evoking the experiences of actual beings who, once you have lived with them in its pages, you will never again be able to forget or abandon for "someone else" to care about.

Karen Davis, PhD, is the President and Founder of United Poultry Concerns, a nonprofit organization that promotes the compassionate and respectful treatment of domestic fowl, and the author of *Prisoned Chickens, Poisoned Eggs: An Inside Look at the Modern Poultry Industry*, *More Than a Meal: The Turkey in History, Myth, Ritual, and Reality*, and *The Holocaust and the Henmaid's Tale: A Case for Comparing Atrocities*. http://www.upc-online.org. http://www.upc-online.org/karenbio.htm.

This is Hope: Green Vegans and the New Human Ecology

How We Find Our Way to a Humane and Environmentally Sane Future

First published by Earth Books, 2012
Earth Books is an imprint of John Hunt Publishing Ltd., Laurel House, Station Approach,
Alresford, Hants, SO24 9JH, UK
office1@jhpbooks.net
www.johnhuntpublishing.com
www.earth-books.net

For distributor details and how to order please visit the 'Ordering' section on our website.

ISBN: 978 1 78099 890 9

U.S. Library of Congress number: 2012913233

A CIP catalogue record for this book is available from the British Library.

Design: Stuart Davies

www.ThisIsHopetheBook.com

Email: will@thisishopethebook.com

Printed and bound by CPI Group (UK) Ltd, Croydon, CR0 4YY

This is Hope:
Green Vegans and
the New Human
Ecology

How We Find Our Way to a Humane and
Environmentally Sane Future

Will Anderson

EARTH

BOOKS

Winchester, UK
Washington, USA

Earth gave me everything and everyone, my parents, my partners who made life meaningful, friends who celebrated it with me along the way, and individuals from other species who etched their contributions to the holiness of life into my soul.

Writing this book took more time and effort than I had imagined. It required endless patience from my persevering partner, Hal. Others have dedicated their lives, sometimes in prison, for selfless service to humanity so that we may end the horrors we create in the lives of individuals from other species. I dedicate this book to those who care, to the 7 billion humans who inhabit this world, to ecosystems, and to the individuals of all species whom we hope not to harm or lose forever.

Acknowledgments

I thank those who helped me wade through this immense subject area. Though I alone am responsible for any errors or omissions, and they may or may not subscribe to all of what I have written, my gratitude in no particular order goes to Laurel Ornitz (editor), Laura Lee Bennett (editor), Mark Palmer, Marc Bekoff, Toni Frohoff, Debra Durham, Jo Coring, Lynn Leque, Tami Drake, Pamela Ziemann, Sharon Young, website designer Michael Jaworski and my many friends who made suggestions to improve this book. I'm grateful to everyone at John Hunt Publishing / Earth Books. Your professional support and skills have made my message accessible.

Thank you Sightline Institute, Humane Research Council, Above the Fold/Environmental Health News, National Public Radio news, Care2 Causes, and Grist for alerting me to a number of sources I cite.

CONTENTS

Preface

While sitting in a Seattle pizza restaurant in 1968, I took off my leather belt, woven leather ring, and my cherished leather sandals. After I put them on the table, I sat there, pondering the story behind their making. In this raw reality, I suddenly understood who had owned the skin before I paid a stranger to turn him or her into leather. In my mind's eye, I finally saw an expressive individual from another species in full color with a face, a body, and a life. What had I done to the original owner? This was an easy decision.

I resolved to stop wearing body parts taken from others. The more I acknowledged their nonhuman identities, the more my own identity was transformed. It was a strong mental and emotional event that later unfolded to become a life-altering process.

A year before this, I had realized that I was presenting myself consciously as a vegetarian. I was not proselytizing to anyone; I just felt "vegetarian." I quietly told individuals from other species, more in thought and "vibe" than spoken word, that I was not a meat-eater. I would consciously act like an herbivore at peace and move more slowly and deliberately in the world as one should do when in the presence of wildlife. This evolved into a growing awareness and appreciation for the beauty of trees, flowers, insects, and eventually, ecosystems. It felt good.

Unexpectedly, I was a person with a new identity. I loved being in the presence of other sentient beings and feeling happy because they reminded me that I was no longer a threat to them. I felt lighter within. And more at peace.

Many of us have gone through this awakening. We understand this is important not because it is about us, but because it is about others. We work to inoculate our communities with this experience because we understand that this dietary and lifestyle transformation of relationships with sentient species, non-sentient species, and ecosystems must be our new ecological identity, our species' place in the world. We are working and hoping against the odds that enough people will realize this. Perhaps we are unsure of what empathy and compassion can accomplish. But we shouldn't be.

Change is a process, not often an event. I have learned that this single transformation, from omnivore to vegetarian and later vegan, was just a beginning. There was much more to understand about the other life-and-death consequences of my actions. And I started asking different questions.

How can we live intimately with our domestic animal companions in our homes and then deny they share similar experiences and states of being as we do? We understand, and appreciate *their* rich experience of living a life. How is it then that we refuse to see individuals of farmed and hunted species in the same light? Why do we think it is logical and appropriate that we have loving, humane relationships with some, and brutal, murderous relationships with others who have the same capacities to experience happiness and suffering as do our companions?

As we feel the presence of our companion cats, dogs, rabbits, birds, horses, and others, we are given this great chance to remain steadily conscious of the wildlife and ecosystems around us, near and far—the coyotes in the city and the wolves in the forest—and be reminded of the presence and condition of biodiversity.

What do spiders, snakes, and plants experience that would direct my behavior to their special needs? And what of plants that send chemical signals when they are under physical attack, signals that create measurable responses in other plants?[1, 2] Why do we think we have the right to ignore precaution and caring as we run road graders over Earth's skin? The most adaptive, and ethical response for our species is to assume everyone, everywhere can suffer and that all have a right *not* to suffer at our hands. Earth does not have to prove her innocence to be protected. That is all I personally need to know. Will it be enough for you?

I have witnessed the near tripling of Earth's population since I was born,[3] the loss of ecosystems and species, the unspeakable malice we inflict on others, and the searing reality of human poverty in many places on our planet. While working on campaigns to stop our cruelty toward wild and domestic species and the decline of ecosystems, I found that these issues are connected. Our responses to them are woefully inadequate because we are failing to challenge our beliefs and behaviors that cause this harm.

If we are to succeed in our own survival and protect the ecosystems that give us life, our response has to be comprehensive, not piecemeal. The name I have given to that response is *the new human ecology.*

Introduction

Our human ecology is the expression of everything we do and is represented by every interaction we have on Earth. Broadly, it consists of the multitude of relationships we have with other people, other species, and our physical environment. For human ecologists, it is the science and study of our interrelationships with our environment. As author and human ecologist Gerald Marten notes, the term *human ecology* has a long history, diverse interpretations, and many applications.[4] My intent in *Hope* is to describe the unsustainable harm we cause with our current human ecology, how the new human ecology will stop that harm, and how we get from one to the other.

In *Hope*, we are not studying our human ecology; instead, we are creating our *new* human ecology intentionally. It requires us to make several fundamental changes in our behavior, not just one or two that we prefer.

Our *current* human ecology is characterized by a worldview that asserts we have dominion over all the Earth. It believes that Earth is here for our purposes and that all other species are below and inferior to us. This is the human-centered, or anthropocentric, perspective. The current human ecology is the cause of our human overpopulation, our overconsumption of resources, the poverty of ecosystems and people, and our disregard for the rights of individuals from other species.

The *new* human ecology I am proposing replaces the current human ecology. The new human ecology incorporates and expands upon *deep ecology*—a term and idea developed by Norwegian philosopher Arne Naess. It recognizes that all species, individuals of those species, and their ecosystems have intrinsic value. This is the biocentric perspective. Deep ecology is explicitly present throughout the new human ecology and missing from the current human ecology. The new human ecology seeks to achieve Seven Results that we create by changing our behavior. Those results include reducing our population, increasing social and economic justice, reclaiming lands for restoring ecosystems to the extent possible, and establishing a sustainable vegan human ecology. All seven are described in chapter 2.

You will not see hunters, fishers, or animal agriculturalists (those who raise livestock) in the Seven Results. Those behaviors are cruelly inappropriate and unsustainable. They do not support a sustainable physical and moral survival for us, and they are no longer adaptive to ecosystems. In their place we have created neo-predation. *Neo-predation is produced every time we lay down a highway, every time another one of us is born and physically occupies habitat, every time we add greenhouse gasses to a warming atmosphere, and every time we consume material goods and services that impact ecosystems.* This neo-predation creates similar harms that the hunters, fishers, and animal agriculturalists produce but without our firing a shot, setting a hook, or partaking in any part of animal agriculture.

I want to be clear here. The new human ecology does *not* endorse the type and degree of neo-predation we see today. We have to reduce all forms of the neo-predation I describe throughout *This Is Hope*. It is as unsustainable and inhumane as hunters, fishers, and animal agriculturalists are. Our task is two-fold: end hunter, fisher, and animal agriculture predations and sharply reduce our neo-predations.

The current human ecology insists we can be two kinds of predators at the same time. It believes the Earth can support hunters, fishers, and animal agriculturalists *and* neo-predation simultaneously. The new human ecology insists there can be only neo-predation and that its environmental harms and cruelties must be reduced immediately. But by definition, when we address our human ecology, no issue sits in isolation from the others.

Because of its comprehensive consideration of human relationships to all else, changing our human ecology addresses multiple issues simultaneously from a consistent value and belief system. The issues include our environmental impacts, our relationships to individuals from other species, the false promises of fish and wildlife management, our overpopulation, the poverty found in social and economic injustice, and the environmental communities' beliefs about the omnivore movement and animal rights.

Now that our individual and collective environmental impacts reach distant ecosystems, we must consider our relationships with the entire Earth in the decisions we make. There is a need for a globalized human ecology. We must understand that we do not get to choose what we must accomplish here; our choices are defined by what ecosystems require of us. We *do* get to be creative about it.

Because the Earth needs us to reduce harm, and because humans, individuals from other species, and ecosystems suffer unnecessarily and beyond our comprehension, our human ecology has to have a moral foundation woven into and interpreted though diverse cultures that live in diverse ecosystems. E. O. Wilson, preeminent biologist, author, and Harvard University research professor, describes our environment as "a membrane of organisms wrapped around Earth so thin it cannot be seen edgewise from a space shuttle, yet so internally complex that most species composing it remain undiscovered."[5] If we agree that we have a moral responsibility to protect this membrane where all known life exists, what have we done so far? We have flipped the turtle on his back.

Instead of us adapting to ecosystems, we have altered them so much that ecosystems are now trying to adapt to us. Ironically, in our blind efforts to thrive, it is unlikely we will be able to live with and adapt to the tattered ecosystems we are creating. We quite literally may not be able to live with ourselves. The fate of all species, including ours, comes down to who we have become and now, who we choose to be. We are arrogantly out of control and a threat to all life on Earth, not because it is our destiny, but because we have chosen to be so.

In *The Bridge at the End of the World*, James Speth, Dean of Forestry and Environmental Studies at Yale University, wrote, "Nothing—not national or international laws, global bioreserves, local sustainability schemes, or even 'wildlands' fantasies—can change the current course.... the extinction crisis—the race to save the composition, structure, and organization of biodiversity as it exists today—is over, and we have lost."[6] He is referring to the biological diversity of the planet that, as E. O. Wilson reminds us, exists on three levels: ecosystems, organisms, and genes.[7] Our current human ecology, is killing biodiversity at all three levels. Much has been lost, and perhaps we have already fallen too far to change Speth's belief that we are too late. But as long as we are willing to try and ecosystems are healthy enough to recover what is recoverable, we still have a chance to salvage what is left.

The new human ecology is ready to replace the current human ecology. The issues of environmental crises, the plight of humans and individuals from other species, the flood of our human population, social and economic justice, species extinction, economic systems that cannibalize natural capital—what we consider to be *resources*—and political freedom and stability are knotted together. They come as a single package. Whenever we address any one of them, we must address all the others. All of them can be considered as expressions of our human ecology. Human cultures and societies are interdependent as never before. The new human ecology must transcend cultural diversity and its entrenched personal and institutional beliefs.

For instance, there is nearly universal agreement that child labor, human trafficking for the sex trade, female genital cutting (FGC),[8] "honor" killings of women, incest, sexual abuse, torture, and slavery are wrong. Now we need a universal consensus about standards of decency toward ecosystems, individuals from other species, and Earth. We cannot do this unless we end carnism. The term *carnism* was coined by psychologist Melanie Joy:

> Neither carnivore or omnivore expresses the beliefs beneath the behavior ... I have chosen to employ the terms carnism and carnist to the ideology of meat production/consumption and its proponents ... By naming the belief system which underlies the acts of meat production and consumption we are better able to acknowledge that slaughtering nonhuman animals for human consumption is not a given but a choice; a choice that is based upon an ideology in which the domination and exploitation of other animals is considered a natural human privilege.... The naming of carnism is another step toward nonhuman animal liberation; it enables vegetarianism to challenge not only the practice of meat production and consumption, but also the ideology upon which such acts stand. In this way, the primary objective of vegetarianism becomes not simply the eradication of meat-eating, but the abolition of carnism.[9]

Joy continues in her book, *Why We Love Dogs, Eat Pigs, and Wear Cows,*

This system dictates which animals are edible, and it enables us to consume them by protecting us from feeling any emotional or psychological discomfort when doing so. This system teaches us how to *not* feel. The most obvious thing we lose is disgust, yet beneath our disgust lies an emotion much more integral to our sense of self: our empathy.[10]

The result, Joy notes, is our losing empathy and gaining apathy. I will explore how this loss has consequences for ecosystems and the fractured foundation of today's environmental community.

Holmes Rolston III, the father of environmental ethics and a patron saint of many environmentalists and biologists, allowed for suffering caused by humans against other species as long as it did not stray beyond limits defined by what happens in nature herself. He believed that when we cause suffering as we extract resources, we are "... simply follow[ing] nature." He noted in 1988, "The relevant question is not simply [philosopher Jeremy] Bentham's 'Can they suffer?' but 'Is the human-inflicted suffering excessive to natural suffering?'" For domesticated species, he noted, "We can add that where pain in agricultural or industrial animals has also become pointless, because they too have been removed from the environment of natural selection, humans have a duty to remove that pain, as far as they can. With that we do not disagree, but this extended ethic is a duty of benevolence, not one of justice."[11]

My point is not to take Rolston's views from decades ago and thaw them out now, but rather to note that the rights of other-than-human individuals and species has been a concern of environmental philosophy far longer than today's environmental community seems to care to remember. Again, Ralston:

A citizen has a *legal* right to vote, assigned in laws. But we also think that *natural* rights exist, regardless of law. Innocent persons have a natural right not to be killed no matter whether they have court access.... Few legal rights have been assigned to animals ... so animal rights would seem to be natural rights. No 'bill of rights' exists to give legal status to them; perhaps one should.[12]

In *This Is Hope,* we eliminate our excuses for the ill treatment of ecosystems and individuals from other species, wild and domesticated. This is not benevolence, it is justice.

To this day, there is an evolving, and utterly unsatisfying, ping-pong game between leading ecologists, deep ecology thinkers, and animal rights philosophers. Philosopher Tom Regan observed, "... although we can count on deep ecologists such as Sessions and Devall [leading deep ecology proponents Regan described as "applauding" hunting] to add their voices to those of reformists and abolitionists in some cases, they emerge as defenders of the status quo in others."[13] As I will explain later, the animal rights platform is equally inconsistent.

In that debate, there is still much to consider about our lack of moral behavior toward individuals from other species and ecosystems. Get close to their suffering and ecosystem destruction and I guarantee it will overwhelm you intellectually and emotionally. That is certainly the case with me as I struggle between outrage and calm, despair and hope, data and heart.

In the chapters that follow, I explore why the environmentalist, and more so conservationist, messages neglect to tell us the whole story of what we have to do to save Earth from us. Environmental and other nonprofit communities and ecosystem management agencies are unwilling to challenge the outdated carnist hunter, fisher, and animal agriculturalist models embedded in our current human ecology. Unintentionally, they are conspiring with our personal resistance to change; this makes our wholesale failure to save much of anything more likely.

Perhaps a reminder is in order about how thoroughly cultural worldviews blind us to carnism. In *Raising Steaks*, Betty Fussell, food writer and meat enthusiast, reports her practices as if comatose:

But it's the beef I'm here for, the primal experience of the carnivorous American omnivore, sinking fingers and jaws into a chunky two-inch-thick shell steak cut from a 15-pound short loin of prime Black Angus, dry-aged 38 days. The loins are grilled on spits over roaring flames to produce a crust as black as a merry-widow corset, protecting a bordello-pink interior, sliced on cutting boards by big men wielding knives, and finally dipped in a finger-licking sauce of butter, drippings, and Worcestershire sauce. Away with the effeminacy of serrated knives and foppish forks. It's every caveman for himself, clasping his meat like a hunk of mastodon, gnawing flesh that resists seductively before it yields, squirting fluids red with blood and fat over my hands and down my chin to the anomalous apron below. We are one in our carnal desire.[14]

Fussell is describing the act of eating the flesh of sentient beings (and it seems, sex) and the cultural beliefs supporting it. That is carnism. She goes on a bit more about sopping up those body fluids with bread and triple-shots of alcohol, a band that plays the traditional song, "A Bicycle Built for Two," and everyone jumping to their feet to sing "God Bless America." Though in an American setting, this is just one example of how the cultures of carnism that exist throughout the world are deeply embedded in human societies. This same carnism is embedded in today's faddish omnivore movement.

Omnivores are lethal barriers to sustainability. Those who endorse it, as author Michael Pollan has done in *Omnivore's Dilemma*,[15] are intent on making carnism seem sustainable and just when it is not. Environmental organizations and the professions of fish, wildlife, and ecosystem management also are corrupted by the idea that omnivorism is sustainable.

Adopting a new human ecology means we deconstruct and reconstruct much of what we are doing. Vegan human ecology, for instance, is an entirely new realm for science, conservation biology, environmental and species rights organizations, and ecosystem management agencies. We will change the world they work in and insist they change their manner of doing business as well. In a relatively short time we will release marine ecosystems from our predatory fisheries and return cropland currently dedicated to growing animal food back to ecosystems. In the United States, 80 percent of the corn and 22 percent of wheat is grown for "livestock" food. Some 75 percent of the soybean crop in the United States goes to feed them.[16] Corn and soybean crops occupy a combined 145.2 million acres of U.S. habitat.

Our global human population topped 7 billion late in 2011. We add nearly 80 million more people every year. Ecologist Joel Cohen notes that "In absolute numbers, putting the first billion people on Earth took from the beginning of time to about 1830."[17,18] At today's rate, we are adding at least 1.0 billion people every 12 years.[19] So while we have exploited ecosystems to increase our numbers, it is a heartbreaking fact that billions of people still do not have adequate shelter, fair wage employment to pay for their fundamental needs, access to potable water and sanitation, adequate medical care, education, or hope. The new human ecology can change this, too. Our conscious and unconscious decisions create the moment-by-moment increase or decrease of harm. Our human ecology is inextricably linked to the increase or decrease of sustainable happiness. It starts with us and ends with us.

In *Hope,* I will focus mostly on how our vegan human ecology will profoundly change the world. I will include other aspects of our human ecology more generally such as social and economic justice and the growth of our human population because they are essential to our survival and the new human ecology I am advocating. They are not less important than the vegan human ecology, but they need less explaining because some are accepted as near universal goals already while others, like our population, are inevitable. I will also spend considerable time in the latter chapters to review wildlife and ecosystem management agencies because they control most of our relationships with ecosystems and individuals from other species. What they do reflects our core values and attitudes toward them. My goal is to convince you that a comprehensive revision of our current human ecology needs to produce Seven Results.

I am aware, and more than a little self-conscious, of how much I am trying to take on, given that our human ecology is such a vast, all-encompassing subject. I do it out of necessity as best I can but that is why you will read more about some subjects than others. I strive to cite reliable sources, though the data on some issues will differ somewhat from one source to another. International institutions like the United Nations and the World Bank, scientists, and specialists have difficulty trying to measure things like the number of poor living on $1.25 per day[20] or how much of the Earth's biological output we are consuming. There are sometimes disagreements between experts and between agencies that may spin the information on progress or the lack of it because of the measuring problem and the constant change in the human and Earth's condition. Though the data sources may differ within an acceptable range, this makes no difference in their meaning; their value is in their power to make us understand what the trends demonstrate, what we stand to gain and lose, and the short time we have to accomplish our tasks.

I will ask you in the last chapter to create the Seven Results, bundled together as the new human ecology. If this book is simply another layer of information that you read but do not act upon, then you and I will have failed because we did not change our behaviors, our relationships, and our human ecology. This book is about *doing*.

Dave Foreman, environmentalist and co-founder of the Rewilding Institute, cited the revered conservationist Aldo Leopold in his book *Rewilding North America / A Vision for Conservation in the 21st Century*:

> One of the penalties of an ecological education is that one lives alone in a world of wounds ... An ecologist must either harden his shell and make believe that the consequences of science are none of his business, or he must be the doctor who sees the marks of death in a community that believes itself well and does not want to be told otherwise.[21]

For me, Leopold is describing the same pain that afflicts those of us who feel the plight of impoverished and suffering people and the suffering of individuals from other species, wild and domestic. We see and feel it wherever we turn, in the poverty caused by unjust economic and social systems, in animal agriculture, in research labs seeking cures for human diseases, much of which caused by our lack of self-care, in the destruction and killing that goes on in oceans and lakes, the hunting and trapping in forests and prairies, even in the sky where migrating birds are shot as they seek rest in national wildlife refuges. *This pain does not overwhelm us as much as it provokes us to act.*

Hope is about joyous change. When we acknowledge and accept responsibility for not just our own lives, but also those we impact, we are motivated to remember our altruistic potential, and the good we have accomplished and continue to do. What follows are my observations, reporting, and reflection about how we might adapt to an enormously changed world. It requires billions of us to figure out how to achieve our personal new human ecology. This is not the complete story; that will be written by you. But, ecologically, we must become a new species.

There is one thing that will not change: We must work endlessly and passionately to live up to our avowed claims that we are an evolved, spiritually aware species. My task here is to gain your consensus that we will create Seven Results that represent a comprehensive new human ecology. We have never experienced Earth in its present condition before. Our hope lies in how we respond.

New Human + Human Ecology = New Human Ecology

Part I:

The Past Has No Future

Chapter 1:

Current and New Human Ecologies

… my gamble is not that the public can't handle the truth, but that given the truth we can ask people to be genuinely heroic and rise to the occasion in a way that humans never have before. That runs counter to the view that we can just appeal to self-interest, and the profit motive, and corporations will lead us to the Promised Land. You all go down that road as far as we can go. But I don't think at the end of that road you will find anything like sustainability, decency, and fairness.[22]

—David Orr, Professor of Environmental
Studies and Politics, Oberlin College

Through our personal cultures, tools, institutions, emotions, technologies, spiritual practices, population trends, economies, sciences, worldview beliefs, and countless individual actions, our choices weave and create our history, legacy, and destiny on this planet. When natural systems had the upper hand, our behavior had to adapt to them so we could survive. Our adaptation often meant that we altered ecosystems to meet our needs. Over time, we altered so many ecosystems that we began exceeding their capacities to replace what we take from them. Humankind is exerting overwhelming hydraulic forces upon ecosystems large and small, upon their physical structures and living matter, from cell to organism to entire species, upon every vital process, including the gaseous composition of our atmosphere and climate itself.

As we adapt to ecosystems by altering them, they in turn shape our social, cultural, and technological responses. This is the dynamic inter-action created by the choices we make and how ecosystems respond to us. Our human ecology evolves, or is supposed to evolve, as a sustainable response to a changing environment. But before I go more deeply into these issues, I want to review a number of findings and statements of belief proposed by others.

In his book, *Human Ecology, Basic Concepts of Sustainable Development*, author Gerald Marten defines the field as "the study of how human social systems relate to and interact with the ecological systems upon which they depend."[23] This definition is closest to the one that interests me but with this caveat: As I use it in this book, the *new* human ecology is not a study; it is our intentional construction of a human ecology of relationships. Human ecology is our platform for change. It is here that we advocate for deep reforms in our relationships with all the individuals from other species and people we cohabit with on Earth. We achieve reform by changing our behavior. We must cure the diseased *current* human ecology that threatens the survival of ecosystems and us. Evidence of our failed current human ecology is overwhelming, spans many cultures, and is documented throughout this book.

Norms of human behavior vary between the cultural human ecologies spread across the geography of our planet. Besides adapting to external, local environmental variations, we know that cultures can influence or dominate one another through conquest. Simple contact between cultures has the same effect; ideas and beliefs have always been in competition. Cultures now are far less isolated. They were arguably more unique in their past isolation than today thanks to accessible transportation, trade economies, and communications media. While cultural uniqueness remains, the ecosystems they adapted to are changing rapidly, mostly because of us. Yet, our cultural human ecologies have not responded to the needs of the environment in ways that would help diminish our impacts, much less attain sustainability. Instead, we have chosen to hasten environmental decline.

Our species' signature ability to adapt is rapidly changing the ecosystems of other species. When these changes exceed their evolutionary abilities to adapt, we say they are caught in an ecological trap. In "Ecological and evolutionary traps," the authors include these examples. Leatherback turtles eat jellyfish. Because human trash, plastic bags in this instance, look like jellyfish, the turtles swallow them. With their intestines blocked, the turtles slowly die. They do not have the evolutionary experience of living with the sudden appearance of our plastic trash. Nor do they have an ability to escape the fishing nets and longliner fishing hooks we drag through the oceans. Because of these evolutionary traps we created for them, their endangered populations slide closer and closer to extinction.

Grassland birds evolved by "nest[ing] in habitats with low vegetation structure." When they see our pastures and crops that, evolutionarily, are the right height, the birds nest, thinking it is ideal habitat. That is until mechanical harvesters remove the vegetation, such as hay, and crush what remains of the nests. The newly hatched grassland birds never fly.[24]

We are creating an ecological trap for ourselves as well. As we diminish the capacities of ecosystems that support us, we fail to recognize the extent of the dangers we have created for ourselves. Perhaps we have lost our appreciation of what adapting to our environment does for us: It allows us to live.

The current human ecology worked for a time, at least for some populations of our species. Sometimes our populations lived within the carrying capacities of ecosystems. There were fewer humans extracting ecosystem services—clean air and water, pollination, nutrient cycling, food, shelter, and biodiversity are a few[25]— from mostly local environments. Though we were still able to wreak havoc and cause species extinctions in the past, it was a time when our ability to affect ecosystems was far less than now.

In part, that was because we relied upon human and then domesticated animal energy while we harnessed our future to technologies like the oxen-drawn plow. As our abilities and technology advanced, we spread like a flood across the planet. Once we captured fossil fuel and nuclear energy, our power made it easier for us to decimate entire ecosystems. Our power continues to grow. A United Nations' "Millennium Assessment" reflected that

Nearly two thirds of the services provided by nature to humankind are found to be in decline worldwide. In effect, the benefits reaped from our engineering of the planet have been achieved by running down natural capital assets [natural capitol is the resource base of ecosystems we rely upon]. In many cases, it is literally a matter of living on borrowed time.[26]

For sound reasons, we are beginning to feel foreboding and ill at ease because so many things are going terribly awry on a massive scale within ecosystems. The immense disparity between the poor and the overly wealthy, between the fed and unfed, and the decline of native species as invasive species thrive, are all painfully obvious. Recent catastrophes like earthquakes, tsunamis, tornados, droughts, cyclones, and fires remind us of how ecosystems determine our fate just as we are determining theirs. We see clear signs that the Earth is reeling from our demands, and we can easily imagine an inescapable, terrible collapse of ecosystems and societies. Anyone taking the time to look knows the issues we must face are immense. The complexity and scope of our unsustainable human ecologies is increasing. There are more questions than answers about our future. Some of us feel powerless while others choose denial.

To make our denial easier, those of us who are economically secure can live in perfect oblivion, distracted by a blanket of material wealth with all the possessions, services, experiences, and leisure that are at our command. We also may live within a worldview or religious belief that emphasizes *the next life* and discounts or denies the importance of what is happening to ecosystems and other species. Individuals from other species quickly become the nonhuman outcasts we exclude from our immediate circle of compassion. However, behind the curtain, behind every aspect of our existence, there exists a world of vanishing and injured ecosystems. When we impact them and they impact us in return, the importance of our actions becomes a moral responsibility as well as a matter of survival.

Two Human Ecologies

In *This Is Hope,* I compare the outcomes of two human ecologies; one is tragic, the other full of promise. I will continually expand the details about our *current* human ecology to illustrate how we are living inappropriately, cruelly, and unsustainably at present. The current human ecology is what we have already done and continue to do. It is unsustainable, unjustifiable, becoming more and more politically unstable, employs unjust economic systems, is ecologically destructive, inhumane, and unfair to humans in the distribution of health, wealth, and justice. It is obsolete and has been for a long time.

I will focus on the most destructive aspects of the current human ecology. One of them is our hunter, fisher, and animal agriculturalist identities; they are no longer useful to us or appropriate for our relationships with other species and ecosystems. These identities come from outdated worldviews that encourage dominion, anthropocentrism, human overpopulation, excess and unsustainable consumption, and cruel, hierarchical injustice stemming from our disregard for individuals from other species and ecosystems. We are *stuck* in this current human ecology. It is cemented into our political, social, economic, and religious institutions and powered by the inertia of our habits, cultural customs, and thoughtless personal behavior.

The new human ecology recognizes that all species have innate value. I often will make reference to *species rights* to expand upon the concept of *animal rights,* a term I will avoid using most of the time. There are several pitfalls in using the limited concept of animal rights that I will describe later in the book. For the moment, know that species rights are not dependent upon *sentience,* the ability to experience psychological and physical states of being. The sentient can enjoy and they can suffer. However, the sentient depend upon the non-sentient for those experiences and rights. They need ecosystems, the homes where their experiences are created. I also prefer to use the term species rights because once we do that, we can compensate for our lack of understanding about where sentience begins in other species.

Species rights in its most abbreviated form is simply the right to exist. Species rights enables us to approach our human ecology in a context that reflects all species' dependence upon ecosystems for health and life. If we limit our considerations to the animal rights of the sentient, they will be doomed because when we kill the non-sentient, we destroy the ecosystems of the sentient. That creates suffering and ends their right to exist. But with their fundamental rights secured, we can then map out a human ecology that will respond to each species' unique needs and innate value.

I believe the new human ecology can win our hoped-for future: human prosperity and sustainability, social and economic justice, species rights, stopping the loss of biodiversity and healthy ecosystems, and achieve a smaller, sustainable human population that enjoys access to more equitably distributed resources. The new human ecology is our comprehensive approach to adapting to today's Earth.

Mega, Presence, and Economic Predation

There are three unique ways we are preying on species and ecosystems: *mega* predation, *presence* predation, and *economic* predation. Collectively, this is our *neo-predation*. This is a relatively new development that exceeds what we normally think of as predation. When we see our environmental impacts more precisely as neo-predation, we can better understand where change has to come from in our behavior. The concept we have been using is *environmental impact*; it has been useful for understanding our roles in ecosystems but falls short of describing what other species are experiencing at our hands, and how we are creating impacts as predators in ways we should not be ignoring.

First, our predation is *mega* because of our immense human population: 7 billion people now and rising. Second, we create *presence* predation because we occupy habitat; the space we take up with our activities denies species their physical spaces in ecosystems as we exclude them with our noise, structures, and activities. We take exclusive control of space that is habitat for others. Third, our *economic* predation is linked to our consumption of goods and services and is the cause of environmental impacts. All three—mega, presence, and economic predation—kill individuals from other species and ecosystems. This neo-predation exists independently of the types of predation we normally think of: hunting, fishing, and animal agriculture. Neo-predation is unsustainable at today's level by itself without adding on hunter, fisher, and animal agriculturalist predations. Both are out of control.

The new human ecology responds by stating that we cannot be hunter, fisher, and animal agriculturalist predators and neo-predators at the same time.

Most of us create these two types of predation today:

- We create the first predation when we choose to continue as top-of-the-food-chain carnists who are consumers of products coming from hunter, fisher, and animal agriculture sources.

- We create the second predation as neo-predators because billions of us are consuming increasing levels of material goods and services that impact other people, other species, and ecosystems.

Together, these predations have displaced, destroyed, and altered individuals from other species and ecosystems everywhere on Earth.

This is going to be difficult to change because our habits, economic systems, and resource management institutions favor the continuation of hunter, fisher, and animal agriculture models of predation. With our endless appetites, we have become increasingly voracious and ferocious predators, far more so than our ancestors were. In denial of who we have become, we hold onto believing the hunter, fisher, and animal agriculture forms of predation are our identities, that it is *in our genes* and cultural traditions, and therefore inescapable. And we do it on a massive, unsustainable scale.

The impact of this dual predation upon the living planet is staggering, wantonly destructive, and unbelievably inhumane. We do not appreciate the impact that we create with our two types of predation. People in developed and emerging economies impose this dual predatorship upon the Earth most, though disproportionately so between rich and poor. All of us are tied to this entirely new and infinitely greater neo-predatory machine that has displaced our historic ecological niche roles as hunters, fishers, and animal agriculturalists. We have become, inescapably, neo-predators who consume entire ecosystems in the blink of an eye. The new human ecology seeks to end the hunter, fisher, and animal agriculture human ecology model and greatly reduce the impacts of neo-predation through you. For new human ecology advocates, the current human ecology is already dead.

Disrespect for a Whale

In 2010, a 37-foot male gray whale swam into the shallow waters off of

West Seattle, Puget Sound, Washington. It was not long before he took his last breath. A necropsy did not reveal the cause of death, but he was in poor nutritional condition.[27] What was found in that whale's stomach is a sad testament to our neo-predation upon other species. The Cascadia Research Collective scientists report,

> The animal had more than 50 gallons of largely undigested stomach contents consisting mostly of algae but also a surprising amount of human debris including more than 20 plastic bags, small towels, surgical gloves, sweat pants, plastic pieces, duct tape, and a golf ball.[28]

We do not consciously intend to be predators when we become careless. But the trash in that gray whale's stomach came from us. We flush household cleaning supplies and leftover pharmaceuticals down the drain as if it does not return to an ecosystem. Our lawn chemicals migrate into the water and wildlife downstream. Did those objects in this whale's stomach and the historic accumulations of industrial toxins in Puget Sound kill or contribute to the death of this young gray whale? Cascadia Research reports, ... there was no clear indication [debris] had caused the death of the animal. It did clearly indicate that the whale had been attempting to feed in industrial waters and therefore exposed to debris and contaminants present on the bottom in these areas.

As neo-predators, it was not for our lack of trying to kill him. We destroyed his habitat, and reduced his chances to live. I have lived within in the Puget Sound watershed for 15 years, and if I am not yet a whale killer, I know that through my mega, presence, and economic predation, I soon will be. I already have killed countless individuals from other species and damaged our shared ecosystems without partaking in hunting, fishing, or animal agriculture. It is predation nonetheless.

Wood we take for furniture and houses is cut from forest plantations that have no tolerance for bears and biodiversity. Look at the inner parts of celery and lettuce. When we see small granules of dirt, we do not see the valley where the soils came from hundreds if not thousands of miles away from where we live. When we buy fruit and flowers from other continents, we have removed water (it's in the fruit and plants) and the nutrients from the soil while often adding pesticides and herbicides. This is our neo-predator footprint in ecosystems there. If we choose to eat farmed shrimp, we destroy 45 percent of Thailand's coastal mangroves. If we pay for shrimp caught at sea, we support a fishery that has one of the highest levels of discarded bycatch in the industry.

Our human ecology has become a voracious furnace. It runs 24 hours a day. Its mega, presence, and economic industries never sleep; we are always present. Through our neo-predator use of natural resources to build, heat, and cool our overly large homes, provide extravagant personal transportation, eat resource-heavy food, create countless material goods and services, and even while eking out a survival life of poverty, we destroy habitat and the species who had lived here as surely as attacking them with heavy artillery. We can slow and then stop this unsustainable juggernaut. But it requires us to change our human ecology.

The harmful relationships we have created with ecosystems and individuals from other species through our current human ecology are endless. So are the opportunities to improve them.

Pushing on Human Ecology

The subject of human ecology has become somewhat generic and has been used to describe a number of subjects. University degree programs offer human ecology programs of study focused on workplace environments, nutrition, health care, designing built structures and their spaces, fabrics, gerontology, ergonomic furniture, and even home economics ("women's studies"), according to one source.[29] The Society for Human Ecology[30] and similar organizations appear to focus mostly on how cultures interact with their environments. If the primary role of human ecologists is to study human ecology, then it may be too much to ask them to purposely create a new one, which is what I am attempting to do.

Human ecologists help us understand our historic and current human ecosystem relationships and outcomes. However, they appear professionally sensitive about challenging other cultures that live unsustainably and practice cruelty. They muffle criticism while our species continues down culturally parallel roads to self-destruction. Perhaps human ecologists are too often anthropocentric instead of biocentric. Perhaps they believe to a fault that it is not their purpose to challenge our radical current human ecologies and behaviors head-on if it means questioning all cultural practices that threaten Earth, our supremacy, and our being the reason why all else exists. Fortunately, there are exceptions.

Visionaries

There are human ecologists, animal behaviorists, and environmentalists who are deeply troubled about our relationships to individuals from other species and ecosystems. In *Human Ecology Review*, a publication of the Society for Human Ecology, and other publications, Marc Bekoff regularly alerts us to our behavior toward other species. Bekoff is a cognitive ethologist, someone who studies animal behavior in natural environments.[31] He worries,

> Rather than take a doomsday view that the world will not even exist in 100 years if we fail to accept our unique responsibilities, it is more disturbing to imagine a world in which humans and other life coexist in the absence of any intimacy and interconnectedness. Surely we do not want to be remembered as the generation that killed nature.[32]

Ecologist and philosopher Mick Smith[33] writes about an issue that many human ecologists still neglect:

> Modernity's predominantly carnivorous culture ensures the unquestioning reproduction of its values and practices.... Today, industry and gastronomy combine to make farm animals little more than a standing reserve of meat products ready for consumption.[34]

Others see our task clearly. Thomas Berry, a Catholic priest, ecologist, and author of *The Dream of the Earth* wrote,

This task [ending environmental destruction and human poverty] concerns every member of the human community, no matter what the occupation, continent, ethnic group, or age. It is a task from which no one is absolved ... [It] reaches out to all the living and nonliving beings of the earth, and in some manner out to the distant stars in the heavens.[35]

Bekoff, Smith, and Berry are describing our relationships to others, the results of our human ecologies. A new human ecology must sufficiently heal the relationships we have with the rest of life on Earth. It must be broadly effective in solving monumental problems in our current human ecologies. Above all, it must recognize that the power to affect change glows within billions of us. People across cultures act on evidence and are capable of a universal response. I am convinced of its possibility. We will not find a human ecology model already in existence. Our ancestors did not have to adapt to the ecosystems we live in today, so our adaptation, our human ecology, will be different. At every moment, we make choices that either support our survival or ensure its end. For all of us, this is new terrain.

The Obstacle to Our Survival

Our innate resistance to change threatens our efforts. How we respond to challenges depends on how the messages about them are crafted and whether or not solutions are described at the same time. One research study found that "The scarier the message, the more people who are committed to viewing the world as fundamentally stable and fair are motivated to deny it...."[36] That is a problem. If I describe how bad our human ecology has become, I take the chance that you will deny the need for us to make wholesale changes in our lifestyles.

For instance, the Humane Research Council found in their study, "Advocating Meat Reduction and Vegetarianism to U.S. Adults," that "Almost 8 in 10 say that they are 'not at all likely' to ever give up eating meat entirely" because the idea frightens them. They also believe it would be unhealthy.[37] Resistance to the changes we are required to make in order to continue living on Earth, the resistance itself, threatens us and the biosphere. We need to understand the true gravity of our situation, but it *is* scary. The scarier it gets, the worse our response may be.

We understand that a positive message is more appealing than the negative news, and we see that most of us prefer the comfort of gradual adjustments to solve problems rather than abrupt changes that challenge us. That is the conundrum we face. We keep thinking about change from an anthropocentric platform where we see only the superficiality of our own short-term interests. That will work well for, say, selling new Microsoft software, but not for the revolution that ecosystems need from us.

Our comfort zone regarding the alterations we must make in our human ecology must be based on a biocentric consideration about what the Earth's living systems and other species need from us. If they need change from us immediately, then that must be the nature of our response. If we complain day and night that living humanely and sustainably is too stressful to consider, we, especially the poor, will also suffer. Or, we can think about telling elephant matriarchs that we are too uncomfortable with rapid changes in our lifestyles and will let them suffer from the ravages of human-induced drought, loss of habitat, and deadly conflicts because of our own overpopulation. We can forget about caring about the seals and polar bears who are dying because we have melted their ice. And we can tell ourselves that we did not care enough for the current generation of friends and families we have and those that may follow.

I cannot spin the information about the ill health and decline of Earth's living systems and what we inflict on others. Everyone is relying on us to do whatever it takes to preserve life no matter how intimidating it gets. It can only be about us, if it is *not* about us.

Lumps

As a survival instructor in the Air Force, I took my students on a several-days-long field exercise. Especially in winter, the aircraft crew was severely tested by nature in the culmination of their training. It was during the icy winter wilderness months that instructors quietly and "affectionately" referred to our students as "lumps." The expression reflected the students' reluctance to leave the warmth of the fire. To keep the flames and fire's warmth going, they had to walk away and into the cold, deep snow to get more wood. It made sense to keep the fire going, but the students were exhausted and cold; they often stood around like "lumps." They expected others to take the initiative despite knowing what had to be done. Sometimes the fire would cool and only then would they, ranked from airman first class to colonel, find the motivation to gather more wood. By then, everyone was chilled. The fire had dimmed. It was too feeble to dry out the wet new wood that was soaked by winter's moisture. Not only was the fire less than optimal, burning wet wood produces a lot of smoke, if it burns at all. Instead of a clear, hot fire, acrid gray plumes wafted about stinging everyone's eyes, sinuses, and lungs.

If the highest-ranking officer of the class made a rule that anyone not collecting their fair share of firewood would be denied the warmth of the fire, lumps turned into solutions. As each person went out into the cold and snow and brought wood for himself, he also brought it for the group. Everyone gained a quality fire to stay warm and dry, two requirements for survival. We are acting like lumps today all over the world. We know what needs to be done, but do not want to experience the temporary discomforts and challenges of changing our behaviors to properly maintain Earth, the source of our comfort and our survival.

Homo Sapiens Express

We have given ourselves a proud title: *Homo sapiens*. It translates to wise or knowing human. How are we living up to that standard so far? Early humans used an estimated 0.1 percent of the productivity of their local ecosystems. When we converted land ecosystems into agricultural production, the carrying capacity of that land increased a "thousand-fold" for our purposes and supported larger human populations.[38] When we took control, the costs of that increase were paid by the original ecosystems and species. Carrying capacities for native species was reduced or eliminated as our activities took their places. They declined; we increased.

There were about one billion people on Earth in 1850.[39] Today, in 2012, we are 7 billion. The U.S. population has more than doubled since 1950.[40] What have we done to Earth's living ecosystems to get to where we are today? Global carbon dioxide (CO_2) emissions from fossil fuel burning in 2008, a major cause of global warming, were 40 percent higher than in 1990, with a three-fold acceleration over the past 18 years.[41] The World Meteorological Organization estimates that CO_2 in the atmosphere was nearly constant at around 280 parts per million (ppm) for 10 thousand years. The 2011 average rose to 391.57 ppm by year's end.[42] By March 2012, it was 393.88.[43] Using data from Mauna Loa Observatory in Hawaii, the organization CO2Now reports it was 395.77 ppm three months later this June.[44] Organizations such as 350.org are using the best available science to tell us we must quickly reduce it to 350 ppm if we are to avoid the worst effects of global warming.

While we are busy taking 20 to 30 percent of the freshwater on the planet for irrigation,[45] agriculture assaults the quality of ecosystems on several additional fronts. Ecologist David Pimental estimates we are losing some 75 billion tons of soil each year due to erosion. We have a hard time imagining what that pile of dirt would look like but we understand the consequences: "soil is being lost 13–40 times faster than the rate of renewal and sustainability."[46] No soil, no food.

As we strip the land, we do the same thing to the oceans. Their fate is ours. When 42 percent of shark and ray species in the Mediterranean are threatened with extinction, we have a measure of our current human ecology.[47] The International Union for the Conservation of Nature (IUCN) estimates that "21 percent of all known mammals, 30 percent of all known amphibians, 12 percent of all known birds, 28 percent of reptiles, 37 percent of freshwater fishes, 70 percent of plants, and 35 percent of invertebrates assessed so far are under threat." By "known," they are referring to 45 thousand species they have assessed so far.[48, 49] However, there are an estimated five to 30 million species on Earth and we do not have a clue about most of them.

The oceans must be a lonely place for many whale species since we decimated most of their populations worldwide. Biologists Scott Baker and Phillip Clapham calculated that, in the twentieth century alone, more than 2 million whales were killed by the (then) Soviet Union in just the southern hemisphere. We nearly eliminated an entire trophic level, a link in the food chain, from the marine ecosystems of the Earth.[50] We are perpetuating the same crime against other species all over the world.

What more will we demand from Earth? If we passively accept the projection that there will be 2.3 billion more people by 2050,[51] it means we will need to produce 70 percent more food.[52] How can we justify expanding our demands when, already, as the World Bank explains,

Today, as much as 50 percent of the earth's ice-free land surface has been transformed, and virtually all land has been affected in some way by such processes as co-adapted landscapes, climate change, and tropospheric pollution. Much of this change is a direct conse-quence of land uses: approximately 40 percent of land surface is in agriculture (including improved pasture and co-adapted grassland), which accounts for nearly 85 percent of annual water withdrawals globally and surpasses nature as the principal source of nitrogen emissions; ...[53]

Avoiding Past Behavior and Future Tragedy

Our ancestors were challenged to live sustainably or die, just as we are today. This is not a new issue. While we are hoping to avoid the largest collapse of human societies in all of human history, we can learn from our ancestors. They flourished or died from the choices they made.

Several authors have looked at cultures that span human history to find what our ancestors did right to succeed and what they did wrong before they failed and died. Those examples tell us what the new human ecology has to accomplish, and avoid. Their findings are similar though described in their own terms and perspectives. More important, their conclusions are complementary, not exclusionary.

We start with scientist and author Jared Diamond in *Collapse/How Societies Choose to Fail or Succeed.*

"The processes through which past societies have undermined themselves by damaging their environments fall into eight categories, whose relative importance differs from case to case ...[bullet points added]:

- deforestation and habitat destruction, soil problems (erosion, salinization, and soil fertility losses),
- water management problems,
- overhunting,
- overfishing,
- effects of introduced species on native species,
- human population growth,
- and increased per capita impact of people....

The environmental problems facing us today include the same eight that undermined past societies, plus four new ones:

- human-caused climate change,
- buildup of toxic chemicals in the environment,
- energy shortages,
- and full human utilization of the Earth's photosynthetic capacity."[54]

In *Rewilding North America*, environmentalist Dave Foreman uses these criteria "to describe seven ecological wounds to the land:

- Direct killing of species;
- Loss and degradation of ecosystems;
- Fragmentation of wildlife habitat;
- Loss and disruption of natural processes;
- Invasion by exotic species and diseases;
- Poisoning of land, air, water, and wildlife;
- Global climate change."[55]

Author Thomas L. Friedman, in *Hot, Flat, and Crowded*, updates us with his identification of the "five key problems that a hot, flat, and crowded world is dramatically intensifying. They are:

- the growing demand for ever scarcer energy supplies and natural resources;
- a massive transfer of wealth to oil-rich countries and their petro-dictators;
- disruptive climate change;
- energy poverty, which is sharply dividing the world into electricity haves and have-nots;
- and rapidly accelerating biodiversity loss, as plants and animals go extinct at record rates."[56]

Friedman estimates that our rising human population is linked to the extinction of a species every 20 minutes. His response is a thoughtful proposal he calls "Code Green," a plea to act now.

In *The Sustainability Revolution,* Andres R. Edwards describes "... three crucial issues in ecological sustainability:

- short-term versus long-term perspective;
- piecemeal versus systemic understanding of the indispensability of ecosystems for the viability of human existence;
- and the concept of built-in limits to the human impact that ecosystems can sustain."[57]

They and others are calling for us to wake up, examine our conduct, think systematically, and establish guidelines to guide our behavior. Primatologist Jane Goodall and ethologist Marc Bekoff refer to "The Ten Trusts" (also the name of their book) that we must establish between ourselves and individuals from other species. The first trust they list is "Rejoice that we are part of the animal kingdom."[58] In another encouraging call for change, James Speth writes in *The Bridge at the End of the World*, "The solutions of the New Sustainability World and the Social Greens World point positively beyond today's situation to the new vision and new worldview that are needed."[59] Like Al Gore, Lester R. Brown, and the environmental community in general, with few exceptions little is said about the enormous suffering by individuals from other species. That, too, must guide us.

Otherwise, all of these authors are correct. Twelve problems, seven ecological wounds, five key problems, three crucial issues, Ten Trusts, and new worldviews that can inform us about what works in human ecology and what does not. We can infer that they seem to agree in general, but excepting The Ten Trusts, they all neglect the extreme violence we press upon the individuals from other species. The unnecessary suffering we inflict upon them is as important to our human ecology as all else. A new human ecology must address each of these threats to human and other species' existence. I have attempted to sum them up broadly as Seven Results.

Chapter 2:

The Seven Results

Ecology is often assumed to announce the end of modernity—the final breakdown of modern confidence, the settling up of accounts between exploited nature and an exploitative society. Ecology exposes the disasters caused by the excesses and limitations of the modern: pollution by two centuries of industrialism; over-population supported by technological advances and driving them in turn further forward; viruses and bacteria renewed by the medical science that was meant to destroy them. Meanwhile, another ecological 'lesson' is that factory farming has finally warped our relationship to what remains of the countryside ...

—George Meyerson, *Ecology and the End of Postmodernism*[60]

We have seen what has not worked across several cultures and ecosystems. To avoid their mistakes and disasters, the new human ecology must achieve the minimum Seven Results.

1) Healthy, intact ecosystems that dominate the global landscapes and seascapes and require little to no human intervention:

Aside from their intrinsic value and beauty, ecosystems provide us with life-sustaining services such as food, clean water, a balanced atmosphere, medicines, pollination, seed dispersal, flood control, nutrient recycling and redistribution, raw materials for durable goods and housing, biodiversity, habitat for individuals from other species, climate regulation, personal renewal, and spiritual inspiration. Ecosystems have their own needs. They cannot stand to be fragmented. To maintain their abilities, ecosystems need all the species that have evolved together and have formed complex, interdependent relation-ships; these relationships provide ecosystems their stability. Ecosystems have limited and variable carrying capacities for how many humans they can support.

They always have limits to the demands we can successfully place upon them. Those limits must not overwhelm what I call ecosystem supremacy; we establish ecosystem supremacy when we prioritize ecosystem integrity and dominion over human excesses. We strive to maintain the self-regulating mechanisms of ecosystems. By that I mean ecosystems should not be made dependent upon constant human intervention to maintain intrinsic, original services, processes, and abundant biodiversity required for their health. Where restorative intervention is required for the short or long term, we must ensure we are not increasing or perpetuating unnecessary dependence upon our interventions. To the extent possible, we are looking to recover First Ecosystems as best as we are able, knowing we will not regain all or even the majority of what we have removed forever from Earth. Our abilities and means to achieve ecosystem recovery depend upon the size of our human population, our values, knowledge, technology, and most of all, the human ecology we choose.

2) A vegan, organic, and humane consumer lifestyle oriented to sustainable efficiencies and relationships:

In the new human ecology, animal agriculture dies, and botanical agriculture (plants) provides 100 percent of our nutrition. Our vegan, organic, and humane lifestyle consumes far less of our shared resource base, is more environmentally friendly, and infinitely more humane. If tied to a reduction in our populations, it can be sustainable.

Our vegan human ecology reduces greenhouse gasses by 18 to 51 percent.[61] Scientists Robert Goodland and Jeff Anhang report that when carnists become vegans, we "... can achieve quick reductions in atmospheric greenhouse gases [and] also reverse the ongoing world food and water crises." They calculated that consuming 25 percent less animal products worldwide by 2017 "... would yield at minimum a 12.5 percent reduction in global anthropogenic GHGs, [greenhouse gas] emissions." Goodland was the chief environmental adviser at the World Bank Group for 23 years. Anhang served as an environmental specialist at the World Bank Group's International Finance Corporation.[62]

The estimated number of *head* of livestock chewing on Earth varies. The Food and Agriculture Organization of the United Nations (FAO) puts the range at 21.7 billion to 50 billion.[63] Animal agriculture accounts for 70 percent of all agricultural land used.[64] Between 22 to 26 percent of Earth's ice-free surface is grazed by livestock. A vegan human ecology changes everything. Grazed ecosystems and croplands dedicated to producing animal products for human consumption will be released for as much recovery as is possible. Habitat fragmentation is reduced and we end the killing of large predators on behalf of livestock and hunting interests. A vegan, organic, and humane consumer lifestyle stops the global fishing industry's disgraceful bycatch of 653,365 marine mammals every year (considered a low estimate), including 307,753 cetaceans (whales and dolphins) and 345,611 pinnipeds (seals, walrus, and sea lions).[65] We stop the pollution and waste that is inescapable in animal agriculture. Water, petrochemicals, and other resources used to produce animal products will be conserved.

Organic does not mean humane. According to Grist.org, "the USDA has not seen fit to demand that organic dairy production is pasture-based ... [which is] fully exploited by Dean Foods and Aurora Organic, the dairy giants that together produce more than half of U.S. organic milk."[66] Weighed against the destruction a carnist lifestyle produces, the objective measuring of veganism wins.

Organic veganism is the single most effective step we can take toward sustainability. It transforms our human ecology immediately. We "go vegan" for the same reason we "go organic." The benefits to our health are well documented. Going vegan is infinitely more effective in reducing harm and increasing sustainability for ourselves and ecosystems than going organic alone.

Taste for traditional foods is something we acquire from our cultural and social environment. Over the span of our lives, the foods we eat become full of meaning and attached to memories. Carnist omnivores ignore the facts and do terrible things to satisfy their learned preferences for particular food flavors, textures, and colors. Even when these learned preferences are shown to be massively destructive and cruel beyond compare, people still resist changing them. Vegans break through this carnist barrier every day. Our vegan human ecology profoundly improves every relationship we have with individuals from other species and ecosystems. As we end our use and abuse of ecosystems and individuals from other species, we become *Homo sapiens* vegan.

3) Social and economic justice for all with transparency in public and corporate institutions:

What is poverty? As described by the World Bank,

> Poverty is hunger.... lack of shelter ... being sick and not being able to see a doctor. Poverty is not having access to school and not knowing how to read. Poverty is not having a job, is fear for the future.... Poverty is losing a child to illness brought about by unclean water. Poverty is powerlessness, lack of representation and freedom.[67]

Social and economic justice include the right to shelter, freedom of spiritual practice, medical care, free and fair elections, freedom of speech, employment at a living wage, sufficient untainted food and water, access to education, unfettered media supported by the general public, and the pursuit of happiness measured in part by access to increasing equitable per capita resources. In addition, our ecosystems must provide food free from toxic contamination, support our health, and provide for us a reasonable quality of life sustainably. Many aspects of this justice hold true for all species. Clean air, water, soil, freedom from persecution, and access to open space and wilderness within ecosystem integrity and supremacy are human rights, and the rights of all species.

But the responsibilities are ours. For us, consumption of resources must be made more equal across the globe. As much as 95 percent of humanity has seen their per capita income rise over several recent decades. However, the increases were unevenly distributed. "From 1970 to 2010 per capita income in developed countries increased 2.3 percent a year on average, compared with 1.5 percent for developing countries."[68] Some of us must reduce consumption while others increase it. Wealthier economies must increase their investments into poorer ones dramatically.

The wealthy must not create volatile food prices by irresponsible consumption or market manipulation. Even small changes in food costs drive hundreds of millions of people into or out of poverty. Children leave school when food is made unaffordable; what little family money there is must be used for food first instead of books, school supplies, and school uniforms. Rising food prices since mid-2010 have dragged an estimated 44 million more people back into poverty.[69, 70, 71] The 2010 World Bank Report said this about hunger and poverty:

> ... For very poor people, reducing consumption from already low levels even for a short period has severe long-term consequences. Higher food prices during 2008 alone may have increased the number of children suffering permanent cognitive and physical injury due to malnutrition by 44 percent.[72]

As of 2009, poverty was killing 8.1 million children under five every year. That is an "improvement" over 2006's 12.4 million.[73] The 2012 Report focused on violence and how it denies 1.5 billion people the security they need to maintain and improve their lives.[74]

When people and governments are poor, there is little if any ability to protect ecosystems, provide for transportation of crops to market, access to seeds, fertilizer, technology, and organic agricultural alternatives. Severely impoverished people are not empowered people who can easily oppose dictatorial regimes, fight corruption, regulate resource use, or maintain health. Still, research has revealed that despite struggling with basic needs, "citizens of poorer nations are just as concerned about environmental quality as their counterparts in rich nations."[75]

4) An immediate negative human population growth based on natural attrition:

There are too many people. The United Nations projects that by 2050 there will be 9.3 billion people on Earth.[76] We have made the egregious mistake of defining Earth's human carrying capacity as the maximum number of people possible while accepting minimal populations of other species, expected extinctions, and wholesale devastation of habitat. That is not sustainable, and if we believe in the intrinsic value of other species and ecosystems, it is not moral behavior. What is our sustainable human population from this biocentric perspective? Estimates vary.

Somewhere near the middle is anthropologist Jeffrey K. McKee's opinion. After stating that human population is the leading cause of extinctions, he asked, what "... would it take before every country in our database demonstrated a reduction in threats to at least one or more species of mammals or birds? The answer is ... approximately 3.4 billion [people] would accomplish this goal."[77]

Anthropologist J. Kenneth Smail believes Earth's long-term sustainable population is 2 to 3 billion.[78] Some feel the sustainable population is much higher, though there is little said about what Earth would lose in the process. Opinions go as low as 500 million.[79] How would we reduce our numbers?

In *The World Without Us*, author Alan Weisman referred to a study by Sergei Scherbov and others. They found that if every fertile woman had only one child, "our current 6.5 billion human population [2007] would drop by one billion by the middle of this century."[80] They note that if we were able to maintain the one-child average until 2075 there would be 3.43 billion humans, and by year 2100, there would be 1.6 billion. If ecosystems remained stable to the end of this century despite our unsustainable depredations, sustainability seems attainable. That is a big *if*. The organization "How Many People" estimates that "Every year about 135 million people are born and 55 million people die ..."[81] If there were no births at all anywhere on Earth, the annual natural attrition would be 55 million fewer people per year. But of course, we are still choosing to add nearly 80 million every year.

Every child born, no matter how sacredly perceived, is another unsustainable demand upon ecosystems and a threat to all species' survival. It is still extremely difficult for us to accept pregnancy, birth, and children in those terms. But in the emergency we face, Scherbov's one-child solution is the least we can do until our population drops significantly. Zero population growth is meaningless until our populations decline substantially.

The *Washington Post*[82] published an article on attitudes about population and how it is connected to climate change. The reporters found that many environmentalists and political leaders did not want to be interviewed, not the Sierra Club, not President Obama's administration, and not a UN representative. Impoverished citizens would be insulted worldwide, the UN official warned, because they consume far less than people in wealthy economies do. Tell the wealthy to stop having so many children instead. What was the report these leaders were asked to comment on? A 2009 paper titled "Reproduction and the carbon legacies of individuals." It found that "In the United States, each baby results in 1,644 tons of carbon dioxide, five times more than a baby in China and 91 times more than an infant in Bangladesh. ... child-bearing was one of the most fateful environmental decisions in anyone's life."[83] Excess population neutralizes our efforts to live sustainably.

On a lighter note, there is a webpage for the Voluntary Human Extinction Movement (VHEMT).[84] Their motto is "May we live long and die out." However we feel about the issue, adding 2.3 billion more people to ecosystems and our personal space by 2050 is insane. As environmentalist and author Paul Hawken pointed out, there are 1,000 times more people today than there were 7,000 years ago with each of us consuming 100 to 1,000 times more resources than our ancestors did.[85] Negative population growth does more than any other population policy to support sustainability. Do not go to bed without this result.

5) Economic systems that are ecologically sustainable and restorative, enable social and economic justice, are moral and humane, and operate within the new human ecology.

The economic systems we live in today require endless growth to function. Many people believe this nonstop growth is possible through improvements in technology and efficiencies of production. Others understand that endless growth is neither possible nor desirable. Not knowing what else to do, growth advocates continue to ignore the limits of the Earth's carrying capacity for human activity. The new human ecology endorses the Steady State Economy proposed by the Center for the Advancement of the Steady State Economy (CASSE).[86] Leading proponents, Brian Czech and Herman Daly, have written this brief description:

> The most distinctive trait of a steady state economy is stable size. A steady state economy undergoes neither growth nor recession.... it

has constant populations of people (and therefore 'stocks' of labor) and constant stocks of capital. It also has a constant rate of 'throughput' —i.e., the energy and materials used to produce goods and services.... there are limits to productive efficiency imposed by the laws of thermodynamics and therefore limits to the amount and value of goods and services that may be produced in a given ecosystem. In other words, consistent with the ecological principle of carrying capacity ... there is a maximum size at which a steady state economy may exist. Conflicts with wildlife conservation occur long before a steady state economy is maximized. By 'constant' we do not mean absolutely unchanging at the finest level of measurement. We mean mildly fluctuating in the short run ... but tending toward a stable equilibrium in the long run....[87]

Ecologically sustainable and restorative economic systems must have goods and services that are priced to protect ecosystems and people. Pricing today does not include the costs of protecting ecosystem services such as climate stability, clean air, unpolluted water, soil integrity, biodiversity, and a livable wage. In *The Ecology of Commerce*, author Paul Hawken observes that "Markets are superb at setting prices, but incapable of recognizing costs." This is keenly evident, for example, when we change the innate value of sentient beings (their natural order of value) into an economic order of value. We slaughter lambs and pigs as if their value is by the pound and ignore all else about them. Our economic systems rest on the foundations of ecosystems. Reminding us that we are nowhere close to finding sustainability, Hawken continues, "If every company on the planet were to adopt the best environmental practices of the 'leading' companies ... the world would still be moving toward sure degradation and collapse."[88] Our economic system mediates our survival. For most of us, we suffer or die without an income that flows from our economic systems. We will do anything to keep that lifeline, including our continued destruction of ecosystems.

If we could personally experience the impacts our purchases have upon other people, ecosystems, and individuals from other species at the very moment of purchase, I believe we would stop the worst of our consumer behavior. Consumption can feel innocent while we enjoy the pleasures it gives us. But that pleasure has to be weighed honestly by our empathy, compassion, and the innate value of ecosystems and all species. We must not allow or contribute to economic systems that cannibalize ecosystems and extract suffering as a byproduct of production.

6) An increase in empathy, love, and compassion toward all beings and ecosystems:

Empathy, love, and compassion are essential to our human ecology. The Golden Rule means that we will treat others as we want to be treated. In the new human ecology, *others* includes individuals from other species, species, ecosystems, and people. We defend them all. We love them all.

Whom and what we choose to love, or not love, determines whom and what we nourish, or destroy. Empathy, love, and compassion inform us about our rights and responsibilities. The relative rarity of love in the current human ecology is demonstrated by our lack of compassion and respect for individuals from other species. Ecosystems die for the same reasons.

Economist and author Jeremy Rifkin believes that we are transforming ourselves into a global empathic biospheric consciousness, an "Empathic Civilization."[89] We can make that possible. As we participate in creating the details of the new human ecology, delve deeper into its translation and application to science, technology, our lives, and relationships, we are reminded that our personal responses matter.

7) Appropriate, sustainable, and equitable consumption of goods and services:

This is where our economic systems interface with ecosystems. This is where we protect or harm. Appropriate, sustainable, and more equitable consumption of goods and services removes barriers to social and economic justice. We do not know yet if we, the haves, will be willing to reduce our gross consumption enough to become sustainable. Though I do not always feel like an over-consumer, I see how quickly my recycling, non-recycling, and compost baskets fill. There are many ways to measure our consumption. We can quantify the resources we consume, the CO_2 we expel into the atmosphere, the number of sentient beings we harm, the health of ecosystems, and the disparities found between rich and poor. We control every one of those outcomes.

Noted advocate for nonviolence and the environment Satish Kumar hoped, "If we can treat nature nonviolently, then the same spirit will permeate in the human world.... Poverty is violence, and it is caused by the economics of violence."[90] We cooperate as consumers to make this happen.

As we work to improve our lives, we should consider how we improve, not harm, the lives of others in distant ecosystems and cultures. They matter. Our consumption should not be so ravenous that we make it impossible for other people to afford food, or live in a healthy ecosystem. We can change our appetites for excess consumption. We can feel prosperous whenever the quality of life for others is achieved as a product of ours. Over-consumers, at least a billion of us, are called upon to decrease consumption now.

The Synergy Factor

Every one of the Seven Results is related to the rest. For instance, growing human populations increase the chances they will destroy the carrying capacities of ecosystems. Impoverished ecosystems then deepen human poverty. This stresses social stability and chances for economic and social justice. In a downward spiral, poverty destroys the ecosystem, and the defeated ecosystem can offer only greater poverty. If we fail to solve a single issue—population, poverty, ecosystem destruction, sustainable consumption—all Seven Results are threatened.

There is absolute joy in what we are accomplishing. Environmentalists, human welfare and population policy advocates, advocates for justice, and crusaders for species rights are already supporting a portion of the new human ecology. Each of our missions is connected to the others. Yet we are failing to see the other results all of us and all organizations are ultimately responsible for.

We evolved rightfully integrated into ecosystems, but Earth does not need us. As we are behaving now, she would be better off without us. In addition to biodiversity loss and its companion, declining ecosystem health, we have severely interrupted the processes of evolution and natural selection. They gave us a richly endowed and absolutely beautiful place to love. I thank God for creating Earth's fullness and utterly phenomenal functioning that transcends anything we can claim about ourselves. To me, the whys and hows of our existence are a metaphysical mystery. But whatever our beliefs, we need humility, renewal, and a reformation of our species' character.

Limiting Factors: Do as I Say, or the Tree Dies

A tree needs ecosystem services and structure to survive. These include

- the physical support and nutrients provided by soil and the organisms in it,
- a narrow range of exposure to solar energy,
- sufficient space,
- water in just the right amount,
- a specific range of tolerable ambient temperature,
- an atmosphere containing a favorable mix of gases,
- the decomposers, bacteria and fungi, to recycle nutrients so they are available throughout the ecosystem,
- and other species with whom the tree has beneficial and detrimental relationships, such as insects and seed-spreaders like birds and mammals who hone the tree's evolution.

Like the tree, we need the biosphere. It provides all of these things for us. An inadequacy or absence of even one environmental necessity causes us to weaken, wither, and die as if we were trees. The tree is woven into the ecosystem and the ecosystem into the tree. So are we.

Interconnected

Into coastal streams and rivers, salmon swim from the sea, spawn, and then die high on the slopes of mountains. After their death comes decay. It releases rhythmic contributions of nitrogen and other nutrients to the ecosystem and an entire food web. In this way, salmon corpses nourish the trees that shade their watery birthplace, keeping the stream cool enough for young salmon survival. When those salmon trees die or are blown down, their trunks fall into streams. There, their wet woody circumferences solidly divert the main force of the stream's current and provide stillwater areas where salmon eggs are protected from being scoured away.

On the Pacific coast of British Columbia, Canada, spawning salmon carry within their bodies toxic chemicals. These toxins accumulated from the food chain they ate from while at sea. As they push upstream into the mountain ecosystems where their lives began years earlier, they bring these substances with them. Then, grizzly bears eat them.

In "Persistent Organic Pollutants in British Columbia Grizzly Bears: Consequence of Divergent Diets," researchers report that salmon "deliver" 70 percent to 90 percent of several toxic chemicals "found in salmon-eating grizzly bears, thereby inextricably linking these terrestrial predators to contaminants from the North Pacific Ocean."[91] Those relationships, between the salmon, the trees, the bears, and their unbelievably complex ecosystems, are like the Seven Results. They each make the others possible. We are working to detoxify human behavior.

Tropical forests experience a net global loss of 2 to 3 percent of forest canopy cover every year. They once cooled ecosystems. In their absence, warmth-loving insects like mosquitoes who carry malaria, West Nile virus, and dengue fever are increasing. One study found a 200-fold higher rate of mosquito bites to people in areas deforested by 80 percent or more compared to areas cleared 30 percent or less. Clearing forests also releases vast amounts of GHGs that warm the atmosphere. With this global warming, Lyme disease, carried by ticks, moves northward. We can expect more movements of disease because it has already been documented that Hantavirus, the plague, cholera, E. coli, salmonella, and childhood diarrhea from Peru to India to Europe to Botswana are diseases correlated with El Nino, the Pacific Decadal Oscillation, and other conditions of higher temperature and humidity. We cut trees in excess, the temperature rises, and insects and the diseases they carry spread to us and other species.

Our future depends upon ecosystems. They will live or die with the choices we make. We are the single largest cause of accelerating environmental decline. Without the innocence of salmon swimming to the mountains, we knowingly deliver the poison of our own demise. Our social fabric, freedom of choice, and the measure of our morality are determined by how we treat our ecosystems and the individuals therein. Our current human ecology is like a weapon we are directing at ecosystems. If we do not change, ecosystems will continue to unravel beyond our species' ability to adapt to them. In that process, we will bring down many other species with our own. It all depends on what we do next.

In the chapters that follow, I report and describe the outcomes of our current human ecology. I then propose and advocate we adapt this universal new human ecology model that fits Earth's needs. Advocating for a standard set of human ecology practices and calling upon other cultures to adopt them at the required rate is unavoidably controversial. But that is nothing compared to our present radical, insane behavior, nothing compared to ecosystem death, nothing compared to the collapse of our societies and perhaps civilization itself. Our first responsibility is to look not at other people, but ourselves. This is an emergency. It requires us to rethink who we are, change our perspective and worldviews, and trade in some of our most cherished behaviors for better ones so we can live more honest, abundant, and happier lives. That is the *what we must do*.

Our new human ecology is an overdue adaptation to today's ecosystems. Let's step back a moment and examine what we see and feel through our personal norms. They live under the roof of our flawed worldviews.

Chapter 3:

Our Worldviews, the Problems They Create, and a Profile of Where They Have Taken Us

It is our contention that various religious and cultural worldviews have helped shape traditional attitudes toward nature. Indeed, as Larry Rasmussen[92] observes, from a worldview there emerges a method for action, from a cosmology there arises an ethics. These are inextricably linked. By presenting various worldviews, we hope that a broadened context for a new ecological ethics will be created. Without such a comprehensive context of restraint and respect, the exploitation of nature and its resources will continue unchecked.
—Mary Evelyn Tucker and John A. Grim, *Worldviews and Ecology: Religion, Philosophy, and the Environment*[93]

Killer Views

What we believe about the world, its nature, our place in it, and our purpose here, informs our behavior and shapes our relationships with ecosystems, people, and other species. If we believe nonhuman animals are simple and not complex, are not like ourselves, are here for the purpose of serving our whims and manufactured needs, are less than us, beasts, commodities to be sold, bought, and killed, then with that worldview belief we will treat them as a means to an end, and without question, subservient to humankind. If our worldview tells us there is a hierarchy of species wherein the *lower* life forms, other species, are here to serve the needs of the apex life form, conveniently, humans, then we can see where the current human ecology of dominance and unrelenting exploitation gets its validation.

Worldviews determine how we deal with all things that come our way. In *Deep Ecology*,[94] Bill Devall and George Sessions write, "A dominant worldview (or social paradigm) is the collection of values, habits, and norms which forms the frame of reference for a collectivity of people, such as a nation." After listing five "elements"[95] of a worldview that lock in our beliefs, perceptions, and the actions we take in response to our external environment, they observe, "There are rarely public debates about the general assumptions of the worldview."[96] This is the debate we must have.

If we believe ecosystems have no meaning or purpose without us, then we will be more likely to convert these sacred, complex systems to serve our narrow purposes even if it means destroying them before we understand their miracles. We are doing that now. We are inclined to blow up coral reefs, weaken the gene pool with trophy and other recreational hunting, cruelly warp wildlife populations and their ecosystems with wildlife "management" to fit human desire, kill sentient beings by neck-snaring them, drown and trap individuals from other species for their furs, clear-cut forests, club seals, blame marine mammals for the human destruction of fish populations, poison land, water, and wildlife with agricultural and other industrial toxic chemicals, fire missiles into whales, let mine wastes leach their poisons into watersheds, allow bottom trawl fisheries to scour the living seabed, imprison exotic, environmentally impoverished wildlife species in zoos and aquaria, let military forces fill the oceans with harmful noise, and drive species to extinction. And we do this while our economic systems are failing to provide the majority of people on Earth a decent life. Instead, we usurp ecosystems until they no longer exist as living institutions of beauty and nourishment for all species. We do it all, willfully using our various worldviews as excuses to behave badly.

This did not happen overnight. What our ancestors believed at the dawn of agriculture some 10 thousand years ago still affects our worldviews today, at least for Westerners. Author Jim Mason expanded on this idea in *An Unnatural Order*, writing,

Controlling—and alternately battling—nature is ... so deeply ingrained in us that we are rarely conscious of it.... we have the eyes, ears, hearts, and minds of agriculturalists .... if you are a Westerner you are imbued with the culture of the farmer and it determines virtually everything you know and think about the living world around you.[97]

For me, author Matthew Scully describes another worldview we inherited when he writes,

> ... it is about time the Nimrods and Dr. Deers and Christian gentlemen hunters and Safari Clubbers of the world ... explained to us where on earth they got this idea of dominion as a relentless, merciless merchandising and pillaging of our forests and their inhabitants.[98]

We are immersed in these variations of worldviews from birth to death. Through the lens of our worldview, we project our consideration of what has worth and what does not. By that reckoning, we demand the lives of other species and the services of the entire, living Earth, for our purposes. Worldviews are the foundation for our beliefs, but they evolve.

The concept of speciesism is an example. American legal scholar Gary L. Francione defines speciesism as

> The use of species to justify the property status of animals is *speciesism* just as the use of race or sex to justify the property status of humans is racism or sexism.... If we apply the principle of equal consideration to animals, then we must extend to animals the one basic right we extend to all human beings: the right not to be treated as things.[99]

Speciesism directed at wildlife has equally disastrous consequences for ecosystems. The recognition of speciesism is spreading, but it comes from a different worldview.

Our survival requires that we understand sustainability and what it takes to maintain ecosystem integrity. That is not the hard part; changing our worldview is. We do not tolerate challenges to our core worldview beliefs very well. It will be no exception when we are urged to leave the current human ecology behind in order to grow into the new one.

Global Norms as Blindness

Norms are the generally accepted consensus of shared beliefs, values, and the way we should behave. What we believe without question as *normal* is the norm. Our political, economic, and social systems, as well as our individual and group behaviors, operate within norms. Though invaluable for everyday life, our norms also create bias in what we understand about what we see and how we think.

Our families, our communities, and our cultures give us norms of behavior and belief to abide by. If we see and think only from within our personal traditions and cultures, we lose opportunities to examine whether or not our human ecology of relationships is appropriate, reasonable, or in tune with the needs of ever-changing ecosystems and other people. But cultures and beliefs do change. They must because they are obliged to remain adaptable to ecosystems.

If we refuse to step out of the bubble of our personal norms, we have no way to compare our normal behaviors and understanding to more objective standards. We become prone not to understand what our behavior means from the perspectives of other individuals belonging to other species. How can we notice anything wrong?

Self-awareness is a lifelong work in progress. It does not help that we have been living too deeply within a limited and shared shoebox of norms. Equally blind, we can do something terribly wrong in unison, as a culture, nation, or species, and not realize it. Without reflection and objectivity, without a willingness to understand larger perspectives other than our own, especially those of ecosystems and individuals from other species, wild and domestic, we will remain unconscious to what we are doing to them. We will not have reasons to care or change.

During a necessary solo protest decades ago at the blessing of the fleet in St. John's, Newfoundland, I was surrounded by a large, hostile crowd. Unlike myself, they were there to see fishers who were about to go to the ice and brutally club thousands of young harp seals to death. This was not the brightest thing for me to do but it provided me with an "Aha" moment. Before being taken away and put into protective custody by the Royal Canadian Mounted Police, an older woman yelled at me that killing seals was no different than slaughtering chickens, and

I ate chickens didn't I? Well, I had not since 1968. Still, I was struck that she made a no-questions-asked leap from one act of cruelty to the other. Her cultural worldview wove together her belief in the relationships between humans and two very different species. It approved of both the bashing of two- and three-week-old harp seal pups in view of their mothers and the slitting of chicken throats in full view of other chickens. Both species were there, it seems, for the killing. That was her norm.

Unexamined, anthropocentric worldviews corrupt us. They hinder us from seeing the reality of what we do. If we are ever going to get out of the mess we have created as a species on Earth, we must look to larger perspectives and norms that are more inclusive of people and individuals from other species. Former large-scale animal agriculturalists like author Howard Lyman and his wife, Willow Jean, have gone through life-altering worldview conversions. Awakening to the fact that livestock are sentient individuals from other species, he wrote,

> I am a fourth-generation dairy farmer and cattle rancher. I grew up on a dairy farm in Montana, and I ran a feedlot operation there for twenty years. I know firsthand how cattle are raised and how meat is produced in this country. Today I am president of the Vegetarian Union.[100]

The Lymans tour the world sharing their message, as are other farm families profiled in the moving documentary *Peaceable Kingdom, The Journey Home*.[101]

Converting from carnist to veganist requires a change in worldviews and norms that allows for seeing sentient species as individuals on the farm and in the wild. They have emotional lives, physical needs and drives, and rights to live with fullness and longevity we would hope for ourselves. If we do not understand and believe this, our killer worldview will destroy everything. Our norms about dairy products do this.

Dairy Me Not

From the beginning of our domestication of other species and agriculture some 10 thousand years ago,[102] the animal agriculture industry has become a phenomenally large and powerful business. Its environmental impacts come from the billions of lives we have chained to our purposes.

We produce and consume dairy by taking total control of mothers and offspring from another species. The goal of dairy is to get these individuals revved up to the maximum milk production in the shortest time with the least downtime for the least cost. This model is used throughout animal agriculture. As if this industry's colossal size were not enough, interwoven business alliances grow dairy's kingdom. It is hard to tell the producer from the wholesaler from the retail seller. Pizza sales in the United States provide an example.

According to postings on the World Dairy Business Blog, pizza accounts for 25 percent of cheese consumption in the United States "... representing more than 2.5 billion pounds of cheese annually and more than 25 billion pounds of milk used each year."[103] As part of the Dairy Checkoff Program,[104] a marketing and partnering effort to increase sales of dairy products, dairy producers teamed up with Domino's to increase lagging pizza sales and cheese. The American Legends line of Domino's Pizza uses 40 percent more cheese than regular pies. Dairy's Checkoff Program invested $12 million over two years while Domino's was "four to five times" that. With the pizza's higher cheese content, dairy producers hoped to achieve additional "cheese sales [of] more than 10 million pounds of cheese annually, using more than 100 million additional pounds of milk."

Dairy has other alliances. They include "McDonald's, BURGER KING, Wendy's, Pizza Hut, Starbucks Coffee Company, Yoplait, General Mills, and others."[105] McDonald's coffee drink, McCafe, consists of up to 80 percent milk. McDonald's spent a reported $1 billion dollars for remodeling and new equipment for this line and $100 million per year in advertising.[106] This is a fraction of the 9 billion pounds of cheese made from almost half of the U.S. milk supply each year. About a billion gallons of ice cream are produced from milk.

Liquid milk constitutes the minority share of production. Two-thirds of calves' milk produced in the United States is used for dairy products instead of liquid milk.[107] Where does this flood of milk come from? Millions of cows who are artificially inseminated to bear calves. The calves are slaughtered. We take their mothers' milk. The mothers are slaughtered.

About 25 percent of school meals are pizza.[108] Starbucks Coffee Company's new line of Vivanno Smoothies is expected to use "more than 3.7 million pounds of whey protein, requiring more than 550 million pounds of milk annually."[109] Try ordering a soy mocha coffee at a Starbucks Coffee Company store in Seattle. You will be penalized 60 cents extra for it—kudos that it is organic. I am charged a similar penalty in every coffee shop I visit. I find it strange there is a surcharge applied for avoiding the environmental costs and inhumane sourcing of milk. Why not instead tax the calves' milk that produces so much harm and use that income to pay for the soy, rice, almond, and other alternatives? The dairy industry controls the market.

Dairy's messaging saturates our awareness. The marketing power of the dairy industry dwarfs the educational efforts of the vegan community. Still, a lot is being accomplished by vegan volunteers who partially offset a lack of financial resources. Operating on a low-budget grassroots campaign, Vegan Outreach volunteers have passed out over 9 million vegan and animal issues–related brochures since 1994, often at colleges.[110] But the rivers of calves' milk continue to flow into the human diet.

We have seen the trucks on our highways and peered through their slatted sides. Perhaps you have seen their cargo: cattle, chickens, goats, and pigs. The cows likely are in the semi-truck trailer because they are no longer productive enough to pay with milk for their right to live. They are going to slaughter. Those nonhuman individuals are hurtling toward a violent death while on the same highway we drive to our own, kinder destination. Every one of them is an individual whose life experience is as real as ours. Cows are not empty, blank-minded beings. They are sentient and able to feel fear and distress. Some are injured before and during transport. While trying to stand in a moving vehicle, they are blasted by hot, wet, cold, mouth-drying 50 mile-per-hour wind.

They stand in their own waste and cannot drink water to slack their thirst nor eat to sate their hunger. U.S. federal law (49 USCS § 80502) regulating such matters allows this transport up to 28 hours before a five-hour rest is required.[111]

Cows' calves fare no better. They are usually taken from their mothers not long after birth and slaughtered a few days to six months later. The emotional distress to mother and calf at forced separation is an ingredient in the dairy product, as is their slaughter. Sadly and ironically, much of the food given to the calf after being forcibly removed from his mother and her milk is whey and other byproducts from the cheese industry. This *replacer* food is used because milk products sold to humans are more valuable under an economic order of value than the calves' need and enjoyment of mother's milk and nurture under a natural order.

Some veal production operations[112] pride themselves as state-of-the-art caregivers of calves. They have eliminated the dreadful close-confinement veal stalls. There, calves are tied in place and denied enough space to turn around or even groom themselves. In its place, the state-of-the-art, self-described progressive operations feed the weeks-old calves with mechanical devices meant to replace their nurturing mothers; the mechanical feeding and other practices are intended to reduce stress. The motherless calves are grouped by age, so there is no adult-calf socialization, but they appear to have larger spaces with far more freedom of movement than we have come to expect from animal agriculture.

A Canadian company, Delft Blue Farms, tells us,

> The veal industry's support for the dairy industry goes beyond the purchase of surplus dairy calves. It also buys large amounts of milk by-products. … In order for the dairy industry to thrive, a cow must give birth to produce milk. A bull calf is born 50 percent of the time.[113]

Bull calves are the source of veal. Delft Blue Farms works with and through their U.S. partner, Provitello.

Provitello ("Committed to Innovation Through Technology and

Compassion") informs its website viewers and uses the Delft Blue Farms language nearly word for word:

> Typically, animals are not bred specifically for the veal industry.... 'Veal production is limited by the number of calves,' says Bartelse [owner]. But in western New York the supply seems almost limitless."[114] Provitello's home page continues: "Basing calculations on USDA figures of 120,300 cows in seven northwest New York counties ... there are 50,000 to 60,000 bulls available for veal if dairies average 40 to 45 percent bull calves.[115]

Looking at their website videos, I am struck cold by the mechanization of the calves' lives. Provitello wants me to believe that nurturing is what they are all about as they reduce stress to gain higher veal output. This business would like us to believe there is nothing moral left to consider. The industrialization of these calves means they get an artificial heat source instead of a mother's warm body and cleansing, comforting tongue. They are not licked and not nurtured to meet needs that evolved over the millennia. Some female calves, heifers, of high milk producers will be replacements for their mothers. They rotate through the dairy system, quickly become *spent*, and then slaughtered. *Spent* is the dairy industry's perception of cows who no longer produce enough milk to pay the expense of keeping them alive.

Under natural conditions, the calves would suckle six to 10 times per day for a year. In commercial conditions, the mothers' maternal drive is left wanting year after year as their calves are dragged away after giving birth. This is a profoundly sad statement about how animal agriculture will always be blind and insensitive to the deep needs of the individuals they use to make money. This is a corrupted relationship imposed upon another species. This, too, defines animal agriculture.

Where calves' milk comes from and at what cost to sentient beings is easy to determine with the right worldview. Though a very few cows will be kept for 10 or more years, their average lifespan in the dairy business is four or five years out of a natural lifespan of 20 years plus.[116] Dairy cows are artificially inseminated (AI) to give birth year after year. This is forced, rape-like *freshening*. The resulting birth after a nine-month pregnancy starts the mother's lactation for nine to 12 months. This is the time when calves' milk is taken for pizza, cheese, yoghurt, whipping cream, butter, and glasses of milk. No new calves, no milk. As fellow mammals, you would think we would figure that out.

I have gone to livestock auctions and have seen what spent really means. The bleak mental image of spent dairy cows in their pens is something I cannot shake from my mind. They had been moved once again, this time to the auction I attended. Separated from any remaining relationships they may have had with other cows, they were sold by the pound for slaughter. These particular cows were gaunt and obviously malnourished. They were undoubtedly depleted of calcium, caused by so many pregnancies. They looked exhausted, like cast-off objects of our uncaring worldview; they were dispirited inmates with their heads hung very low, as if suffering in their return from losing a war. Spent dairy cows account for 17 percent of the U.S. meat supply.[117]

Less than a hundred feet away were the calves. The skeletal mothers in the auction pens may not have been the ones who gave them life. The auction staff paraded the calves in a semi-circle inside the auction ring as bidders in working attire looked on from the stands. The calves startled at the amplified auctioneer's voice. Prodded sharply with sticks into and out of the auction ring, many slipped on the sawdust and concrete floor when they made sharp changes in direction as the bewildered do. After auction, they will be trucked to the next indecency. These serial, countless crimes are paid for by the consumers of dairy products.

Websites like Dairy Farming Today[118] use slick language that camouflages the cows' experiences. Down to the last person, these factory farmers want us to believe that what they do is good and just. As I would wish if I were in their shoes, they need to believe in the rightness of dairy. Considered normal within the current human ecology, the dairy and veal industry, as well as the people buying their milk and flesh, do not see or want to see the suffering and injustice they raise and purchase.

For the industrial dairy sector, it helps to be a powerful player capable of controlling public perceptions and behavior through advertising. Advertising is meant to manipulate us and it works. Few people care enough to end their drinking of calves' milk, eating yoghurt and cheese, and spreading butter because "Happy Cows" campaigns and "Got Milk" messaging leave cows defenseless to the ravages of a carefully cultivated human demand.

Though they try to be different enough, smaller scale farming operators do the same harm in their manipulation, control, and killing of cows, calves, and cattle. The small producers market themselves as *family* and present an image that belies the facts. They want to appeal to a subsector of dairy consumers. *Portrait of a Burger as a Young Calf*,[119] written by journalist Peter Lovenheim, reports on small dairy production after working with family-farm operators. The young calf under Lovenheim's keen observation was a male born of a dairy cow. He was raised for meat instead of veal or immediate slaughter. This is an exception to standard practice. If you have lingering support for dairy, read this calmly presented book and then ask whether this industry can ever reduce its evil content.

The norms of animal agriculture consistently accept routine cruelty. For decades, I ignored the insufficiency of my vegetarianism. I had left my dairy consumption intact even after I ended my use of meat, then leather, and then eggs.

Taking Responsibility

"Willed ignorance" is a concept I first encountered in Jeffrey Moussaieff Masson's introduction to his book *The Face on Your Plate: The Truth about Food*. Willed ignorance is a technique of denial. Willed ignorance means just what the phrase describes: It is the act or state of purposely turning away from a truth we do not want to face. We do not want the responsibility of acting on the information before us that might require we change our behavior, and our relationships, even though our actions are objectively indefensible and immoral. We use it in animal agriculture and we use it in environmental destruction. We use it to deny what we are doing to Earth and individuals from other species.

I could claim ignorance in my 1968 beginnings as a vegetarian, certainly willed ignorance for a long time after that, and cruel laziness years later. None of that excuses me from the fact that I killed and harmed many, many individuals from other species at arm's length even after I knew the consequences for them. I eventually discarded dairy in no small part because of the brilliance of alternative foods that have grown in variety, nutrition, and flavor. While some oppose these processed foods, and raw food advocates appear to be well ahead of the rest of us, these food companies have moved vegan human ecology forward. Access to alternatives grows every day for at least 1.1 billion of the Earth's most affluent people. Where the climate allows, alternatives to nutrition from animal agriculture has the same potential in impoverished regions. Worldviews and cultural norms are obstacles to overcome in both cases.

Cows are highly social. If given a chance, they will develop preferences about whom they hang out with and avoid. However, their relationships with others of their kind are broken by constant culling. About a third of the dairy cow population is killed every year. Dairy creates other relationship breakers: when cows are segregated into groups when pregnant, after giving birth, and when *drying off*, the period when they are rested for a few months. Then dairy starts the cycle again. In the United States, dairy is subsidized with our federal taxes. Price support for milk means the dairy animal agriculturalists will be paid a guaranteed minimum price per hundred pounds of milk the cows produce. There are a number of similar programs that buy up excess dairy products and make exporting them easier.[120] Tax-paying vegans contribute to dairy atrocities.

We are all responsible for the slaughterhouses where these sentient cow and calf beings see, hear, and feel the last moments of their experience. In *Slaughterhouse*, author Gail Eisnitz interviews Dave Carney, a USDA meat inspector for nearly 20 years. "'It's as if they're not even killing animals. They're disassembling them ... quite often uncooperative animals are beaten, they have prods poked in their faces and up their rectums, they have bones broken and eyeballs poked out....'"[121] I will leave it to your imagination about what else Eisnitz describes.

We do not need dairy products. We can release dairy cows and their calves from the hell we have created for them. Our children do not need calves' milk and they do not deserve to be made into unwitting co-

conspirators, consumers of this travesty.

Elsewhere, dairy is a relative newcomer. The Chinese government has pushed dairy consumption intensively for the past several decades. From a *Los Angeles Times* article, we learn that "Milk is not part of the traditional Chinese diet ... and many arc repelled by the smell of dairy products. Chinese sometimes complain, in whispers, that Westerners smell like cheese." (I once worked at an isolated ski lift on a mountaintop in Germany. I ate lots of cheese, and in fact, could smell the difference in my body odor.) Chinese leadership understood that dairy could become a business with the right marketing about their children needing milk to grow as tall as Westerners. There were about 100 thousand dairy cows in China in 1949. By 2008, there were 14 million.[122]

Whenever and wherever we try to alleviate human poverty and suffering with increased animal agriculture, we shift human misery into the backs of sentient individuals from other species. Human populations continue to grow. And as more people grow wealthier, demand for animal products soars. With the multiplier of our billions of fellow human beings consuming, taking, and killing other sentient species, we suck the life out of Earth. We show the same disregard for cows as we do for ecosystems.

We take the fertility of Earth and cow alike and then abuse them without feeling. We take as if there were no rules, no moral codes of conduct required of us. We destroy without need and create untold suffering on farms and in ecosystems. The cow and her calf suffer like the goose whose mate was shot by the hunter, like the orangutan whose forest we destroyed, like the bear we displaced with our house. This is the consistency of our behavior.

Many of us have responded with veganism. This is actually a vegan human ecology. It attends to the cow and her calf and ultimately to every species on Earth. The new human ecology challenges anyone who believes becoming a dairy and egg-consuming vegetarian is humane and an environmental godsend. Vegans drink almond milk, hemp milk, rice milk, and soymilk. We call dairy milk accurately for what it is: *calves' milk*. Never just "milk." Language that clarifies calves' milk for what it is, is our ally. Never forget who pays the price.

Worldviews and norms must change. We can expect strong denial and resistance to what the new human ecology requires about our core beliefs and behaviors. The new human ecology defines our justifiable place on the planet, describes our relationships with all others, and through them how we get better at being human. The revised world-views and embedded norms of the new human ecology require behavioral changes that are among the most sensitive and close to defining who we are, individually and culturally. We have histories and lifetimes of associating current human ecology behaviors with pleasant memories and sensations: eating, buying, and consuming, driving, travelling, sex, career, skill identities, parental identities, having families, and religious beliefs.

In the next chapter, I will hold up a mirror that will help us remember what our worldviews and norms have created. We are behaving badly toward ecosystems, each other, other species, and individuals from other species. A look at our reflection more closely should motivate us to change how we live.

Chapter 4:

The Bullet Points at Our Hearts

The Human Development Report features a new multidimensional poverty measure that complements income-based poverty assessments by looking at multiple factors at the household level, from basic living standards to access to schooling, clean water and health care…. About 1.75 billion people in the 104 countries covered by the MPI—a third of their population—live in multidimensional poverty—that is, with at least 30 percent of the indicators reflecting acute deprivation in health, education and standard of living. This exceeds the estimated 1.44 billion people in those countries who live on $1.25 a day or less.

—The Multidimensional Poverty Index (MPI)
Human Development Report 2010/Media Release[123, 124]

Our worldviews and our human ecologies that flow from them create measurable outcomes. Our progress in ending poverty, our relationships with other species, and the state of ecosystems reveal both the healthy and sick parts of our human ecology. Those indicators are interdependent. For instance, we can temporarily reduce human hunger but destroy ecosystems in the process. Finding a balance between human presence, a quality of life for us and other species, and the requirements for healthy ecosystems requires a human ecology that can make it possible.

Hope will not *happen*; we must create it and also make sure we do not stand in its way. After looking at Earth from the perspectives of our species and other species, we can cite evidence for both good trends and bad. However, like the limiting factors for the tree I described earlier, creating a majority of positive trends will not keep us alive. It takes only one failure, like a tree without water, or sun, or soil, to destroy us or at least undo all the good we otherwise accomplish. Which big-picture negatives alone can cause our downfall? The rising cost of food and the political instability it causes? Climate change that is well underway? A human population that grows so large that ecosystems collapse under its demands? The indicators are dynamic; some are changing for the better, others are getting worse. We have to pay attention closely because our future depends on them. Here are a few bullets aimed at our hearts.

Humanity

In September 2000, 139 nations pledged that the Millennium Development Goals (MDGs) would be achieved by year 2015. The United Nations Development Program (UNDP) established several benchmarks to measure progress. UNDP continuously refines its methods to understand the progression or regression of the global human experience. There is both progress and disappointment. Hunger can be reduced one year and then increase the next.

From the 2011 MDG Report, we learn that the global poverty rate was expected to fall below 15 percent by 2015, though unevenly across the world.[125, 126] Poverty was defined as earning less than a specific PPP, Purchasing Power Parity, which is what a unit of money buys in local economies. This PPP poverty is expressed in U.S. dollars at $1.25 per day. By this measure, UNDP believes there will be fewer than 900 million people in poverty by 2015.[127] The World Bank pegs it at 833 million. That is far better than their estimate of 1.4 billion people who were living in extreme poverty in 2005.[128] Additionally, the World Bank wants us to remember that in 2011 there were 2.5 billion poor people subsisting on the U.S. equivalent of two dollars or less per day.[129, 130] Neither goal would be acceptable for ourselves.

For the poor, poverty reaches into every aspect of their lives. Though over 1.8 billion people "gained access to an improved drinking water source between 1990 and 2008,"[131] ... "more than 2.6 billion people [are] still lacking access to toilets or other forms of improved sanitation."[132] As a result, women are exposed to rape as they walk at night to latrines or, along with over one billion people, have no choice but open defecation.[133] For a person living in Niger, Africa, poverty means living "26 fewer years, to have 9 fewer years of education and to consume 53 times fewer goods than a person born in

Denmark."[134]

Human population growth works against every improvement gained for the poor. It causes social and economic injustice. According to the Population Reference Bureau (PRB), we are adding around 83 million humans to Earth every year.[135] The estimates vary from source to source. PRB anticipates world population will reach 8.1 billion in 2025.[136] Projecting the human population into the future is a difficult task and often revised. The U.N median projections are 9.3 billion by 2050 and 10.1 billion people by 2100.[137] The populations that are consuming the most are generally declining in number at the moment, leaving most of the population growth to the developing and sub-developing regions of the world. It is anticipated that the U.S. population will grow from 310 million to 439 million by mid-century[138] while Africa's doubles.[139]

Also on our report card:

- Kenneth Weiss writes in the *Los Angeles Times* that "If global population were to grow by less than a billion by midcentury, instead of by more than 2 billion, as expected, it would be the equivalent of cutting as much as 29 percent of the [GHG] emissions reductions needed by 2050 to keep the planet from tipping into a warmer, more dangerous zone. By the end of the century, it could cut fossil fuel pollution by 41 percent."[140]

- As of the end of 2010, conflict and persecution displaced some 43 million people worldwide.[141]

- Since 1990, "… literacy rates have risen from 73 percent to 84 percent... In general, children in developing countries learn far less than children schooled for the same number of years in developed countries.... [they score] on average about 20 percent lower on standardized tests—about a three-grade difference."[142]

- About 2 billion rural people, many of them poor, rely on 500 million smaller scale farms. The Food and Agriculture Organization (FAO) reports that "Small-scale farming constitutes about 80 percent of African agriculture, producing largely staple foods."[143]

Every gain, every human success, everything we have comes from ecosystems. We cannot end human poverty in the midst of impoverished ecosystems.

Other Species: Wild

Earth's wondrous ecosystems and individuals from other species deserve being on our report card.

Western Winter Wrens sing highly structured songs that reflect the dialect of the neighborhoods where they grew up. At 36 notes per second, each song can consist of some 300 notes. Researcher Donald E. Kroodsma found one Western Wren with 30 song types.[144] Above the wrens and us, 3 billion to 6 billion insects pass directly overhead in a summer month.[145]

> Every year, an enormous migration takes place in Western Europe. Millions of moths fly for days, riding wind currents southward in the fall and north in the spring. Scientists thought these insects were simply blown to their destinations, but ... The moths actually select the fastest wind currents, and even change course to shorten their trip. ... 'The moths select the altitude where the winds are fastest,' says entomologist Jason Chapman. ... and bats know all about them. Bats in the American Southwest suddenly swarm half a mile up into the sky. 'The reason they're going up there is that there is a huge migration of moths coming in and out of Mexico into the Southern states,' he says, 'and the bats were taking advantage of this ... .'[146]

Like these moths, each insect has a complex natural history. Paper wasps remember individual other wasps for at least a week. They recall the wasps' unique face markings from the past encounters even after meeting many different other wasps.[147]

Like the skies above us, we live as if unaware of life below the water that covers 70 percent of Earth's surface. How often do we think about elephant seals who dive to 5,000 feet and stay submerged in the dark for up to two hours?[148] Do we interrupt our thoughts to remember that six of the seven species of marine turtles are endangered?

Perhaps that is why we accept the fishing industry's long history of rampant destruction. In 2000, an estimated 50,000 marine turtles were killed as bycatch, which is to say they are caught accidentally, carelessly, along with the intended species. The turtles died after taking baited hooks into their mouths.[149] That is a biological and moral crime but the carnage continues. According to a suit filed by the Center for Biological Diversity, nearly 1,000 sea turtles were caught on longline fishing hooks between July 2006 and December 2008 in the U.S. portion of the Gulf of Mexico alone.[150] Small-scale, community-based fishing (artisanal) can be as destructive given that increasing populations of people live at the shore. From one studied area in Baja California Sur, Mexico, researchers estimated that between 1,500 and 2,950 endangered loggerhead turtles were killed every year there as bycatch from small-scale fisher activity.[151]

Freshwater fish in some areas fare no better. "More than a fifth of Africa's freshwater species are threatened with extinction ..."[152] while "... 38 percent [of] European freshwater fish species are threatened with extinction and 12 are already extinct ..."[153]

If we cannot relate to songbirds, moths, bats, elephant seals, turtles, and fish enough to stop their extinctions, can we do better in our relationships with nonhuman primates? The short answer is no. Twenty-nine percent are threatened with extinction.[154] The western lowland gorilla population "has been decimated by the commercial bushmeat trade and the Ebola virus. Their population has declined by more than 60 percent over the last 20–25 years."[155] Because of habitat destruction from logging and the expansion of palm oil plantations, the Sumatran orangutan is critically endangered and the Bornean orangutan, endangered.[156] Orangutans are shot as pests as their habitat is cleared. Their Indonesian forest homes may be reduced by 98 percent by 2022,[157] just 10 years from now.

After being separated from their mothers in Burma, three- and four-year-old wild Asian elephants are captured, broken, and then sent to either the logging industry or to some 300 tourist trekking camps in

Thailand or similar operations elsewhere. They are brutalized physically and psychologically during the captures of mothers who are often killed while protecting their young. Each tourist camp chains 10 to 80 elephants to offer unsuspecting tourists the thrill of a lifetime, for the lifetime of the elephant.[158] Reports about their training where they are *broken* will break your heart.

Across the span of wild species, we see the results of our current human ecology. Of the 738 Mexican and North American reptile species studied by IUCN thus far, 90 are threatened with extinction.[159] Plants are faring no better; of 12,043 species studied, 8,447 are threatened with extinction. Millions more species, still undiscovered and still unstudied, are threatened with extinction, facing extinction, or are already extinct due to human impacts.

Other Species: Animal Agriculture

The development of animal agriculture did not stop the slaughter of wildlife. It allowed our population to grow and as it did, the slaughter increased. We replicate the violence and suffering of species in the slaughterhouse that we wage against species in the wild. Just as effectively, we kill wildlife whenever we alter ecosystems for the sake of growing food for livestock and for grazing.

Feeding grain to the species we have bound over to animal agriculture is a notorious waste of resources. In the United States, *industrial* meat requires as much as 35 units of fossil fuel energy for every 1 unit of food energy produced.[160] This is a foolish way to create food. About 2 percent of soy is dedicated to direct nutrition in the United States. Each non-vegan consumes over a ton of grain every year, most of it by eating grain-fed individuals. Livestock eat seven times more grain than people living here. Total livestock weight in this country is about five times that of the U.S. population.[161]

In 2010, red meat production in the United States totaled 49.2 billion pounds. This represented the remains of more than 34.4 million cattle, 878,600 calves, 110.3 million hogs, and 2.46 million sheep, 93.1 percent of them lambs and yearlings.[162] Goats, bison, ducks, turkeys, and exotic species are additional fare for our appetites. Farm animals are not protected by federal welfare laws excepting in transport and, often ineffectively, during slaughter.[163] Exempted are the chickens and other birds who represent more than 90 percent of the individuals slaughtered in the United States.

The global scope of animal agriculture is hard to comprehend. According to the World Preservation Foundation, we use 67 billion farm animals to produce meat, much of it coming from species we use to produce milk and eggs after they are no longer deemed productive.[164] Getting an exact count is difficult, but many organizations assume the number hovers at 50-plus billion.[165] This does not include those individuals killed on fur "farms" and the countless individuals we call hunted wildlife. Add to their toll the many billions of fish and "sea food" individuals from other species whom we consume.

When the World Bank estimates that livestock production uses over "two-thirds of the world's surface under agriculture, and one-third of the total global land area,"[166] they are describing the fact that these terrestrial ecosystems are controlled by tens of billions of our domesticated livestock. They are invasive species. The people of Argentina take 12,000 cattle to the Liniers Market in Buenos Aires every day. Some cattle started their lives in grasslands, were auctioned, and then slaughtered. Another 8,000 eight-month-old cattle weighing 400 pounds are taken to feedlots. While there, they consume 150,000 pounds of high-protein corn each one of those days. Three months later, they reach 600 pounds, considered the optimal weight for auction and slaughter. The general manager of the feedlot says a third of the 15 million *head* slaughtered each year in Argentina now pass through feedlots, up three-fold from 2001.[167]

In the developing world, there are 700 million people depending upon farmed animal species for up to 40 percent of their household income. Globally, "livestock account for only 1.5 percent of global gross domestic product, but provides food and income for a billion of the world's poor people."[168] While not all people currently have alternatives to livestock and artisanal fishing, billions of us do. We are the engine behind an immense animal agriculture industry that subjects a mind-numbing number of individuals from other species and ecosystems to suffering and destruction.

Earth

Earth is on our report card. It is impossible to exaggerate the depth of our environmental impacts and unjust treatment of individuals from other species. Since our response has to be equal to those excesses, I dare not minimize how much we have to change our current human ecology. If we want to avert the worst disaster in all of human history, we cannot continue the same human ecology and expect a different outcome. In developed economies, we have to reduce our per capita greenhouse gas emissions 80–95 percent by 2050[169] to reduce the severity of global warming already underway. Yet, global warming is only part of our problem. We are not facing a single disaster, but a multitude. This is not a time for willed ignorance.

Marine phytoplankton are the foundation for oceanic ecosystems. They are responsible for about half of Earth's net biological primary production (NPP), the almost entirely plant-based conversion of sunlight into food energy. Researchers have observed marine phytoplankton declining in "eight out of ten ocean regions."[170] There are natural cycles of phytoplankton abundance, but it appears warming surface waters are associated with a much longer downward trend, declining about 1 percent per year. This is bad news for marine species that starve as easily as we do. If the trend continues, we are all at risk.

The GHG carbon dioxide (CO_2) that traps atmospheric heat and warms the planet is also absorbed by the oceans. As it dissolves in seawater, the carbon dioxide increases the acidity of the water, making life difficult or impossible for many species. In acidified water, calcium becomes less available to a wide array of organisms, including corals, those that require strong shells to survive, and the aforementioned plankton. Acidification also affects the way sound travels in water. If you are a marine mammal who depends upon communicating over long distances, the acoustic properties of your communications medium, saltwater, are vital. Since the industrial revolution that developed roughly from 1760 to 1850, oceanic acidity has increased about 30 percent.[171, 172]

In his book *Our Choice/A Plan to Solve the Climate Crisis*, Al Gore pointed out how the effects of climate change would impact the agricultural output of many countries by 30 to 50 percent.[173] If we believe in eradicating the abject poverty of billions of humans, we must alter the course of climate change.

Planets

Our average standard of living increased a mere 100 percent over 4,000 years until the invention of the steam engine in 1712. At that point we began applying non-animal energy to industry. Three hundred years later, we have taken over the planet.

We are demanding more than what Earth can replace after we consume her resources. In 2001, researchers estimated we were using 1.2 planet's worth of "productive hectares." A hectare equals about 2.471 acres of land. Assuming "ecological footprints are often compared to the 11.4 billion productive hectares on Earth," they predicted that by 2015 our ecological footprint would grow to 18.1 billion hectares, or 1.6 planets.[174] We are right on schedule.

It is now 2012. The Global Footprint network estimates we are consuming "the equivalent of 1.5 planets to provide the resources we use and absorb our waste. This means it now takes the Earth one year and six months to regenerate what we use in a year." To clarify our unsustainability, they let us know when "overshoot day" arrives, "when humanity's demand on nature exceeds the biosphere's supply, or regenerative capacity." If current trends remain unchanged, "we will need the equivalent of two Earths to support us" by the 2030s.[175]

According to the Population Reference Bureau, we were already using 1.6 planet's worth of NPP in 2009. They observed that "About half the world lives in poverty."[176] That is the sobering "big picture."

These bullets aimed at our hearts are glimpses into the state of life on this planet. They have to penetrate our minds as well. They have to mean something to us. While global warming, greenhouse gasses, and carbon "footprints" grab our attention, we should not forget that they are symptoms of larger issues. Population, justice, carnism, and unsustainable consumerism are some of them. We have abandoned biocentrism in favor of a human-centered worldview and value system, anthropocentrism. Unless we return to biocentric solutions, we will continue our unjustified conduct toward nature. The widest perspective we can apply in our attempts to see a way forward, one that tells the whole story, is to look at our human ecology.

Given the seriousness of the threats we have created for ourselves, you would think finding consensus for a new human ecology would be straightforward. While we *can* create the Seven Results, it requires a consistent, underlying worldview that is sustainable, biocentrically inclusive, compassionate, empathetic, ecologically humane, and socially just. We can drop the tortured reasoning we use to justify our killer worldviews and the bad behavior that flows from them. We do not have to be in denial of what really needs to change.

Chapter 5:

Perspective/Views of the View

One afternoon a student observing chimpanzees at the Gombe Reserve took a break and climbed to the top of a ridge to watch the sun set over Lake Tanganyika. As the student, Geza Teleki, watched, he noticed first one and then a second chimpanzee climbing up towards him. The two adult males were not together and saw each other only when they reached the top of the ridge. They did not see Teleki. The apes greeted each other with pants, clasping hands, and sat down together. In silence, Teleki and the chimpanzees watched the sun set and twilight fall.… The chimpanzees who watched the sundown with Geza Teleki were not unique.

—Jeffrey Moussaieff Masson and Susan McCarthy,
When Elephants Weep: The Emotional Lives of Animals[177]

A Vital Perspective

Carnism is deeply embedded in cultures. It still rules human behavior. Carnist culture is a norm that runs so deep it is nearly invisible. That invisibility hinders the best of us from seeing how carnism is at the center of what ails Earth and us. It causes hunger in ways we would not necessarily expect.

Hunger is caused by a number of factors. For one billion planetary citizens, rising food prices make it impossible to get sufficient nutrition. In addition, transportation and communication infrastructure, political stability, sufficient investment in people, a social safety net, access to clean water, clear title and access to arable land, access to agricultural technology and tools, and the carrying capacities of ecosystems are factors that contribute to hunger. Many species are going hungry because of us. We can end our carnism but it will not, by itself, end world hunger for them or us. It will, however, make an immense difference. Compared to plant foods, animal agriculture and its products create a disproportional addition to greenhouse gases and thus global warming.

We also live in a global market where, for instance, international demand for grain creates rising and falling food prices at home and overseas. A large portion of that market is controlled by carnists who consume an unnatural amount of grain that is invested in meat, cheese, milk, and eggs. Additional uses of grain, such as biofuel production, create price competition between us who are overly fed and those who struggle to eat.

The FAO predicted in 2008 that "Biofuel production will utilize an estimated 100 million tones of cereals (4.7 percent of global cereal production) ..."[178] As ethanol production increases in other countries, food prices for meat, dairy, sugar, soybeans, and rice are affected.[179] The global grain market responded to the ethanol industry's purchases by increasing food prices. Poor harvests, increasing human populations, civil strife that disrupts agriculture, unwise economic policies, corrupt governments, and changing climates are additional players. They all influence the price of food.

In 2010 Russia, a heat wave, drought, and 26 thousand fires destroyed 26 percent of their wheat crop. Because they normally export one-third of the world's wheat, this loss contributed to rising food prices people had to pay around the world, including the people of Mozambique who rioted in response.[180] Our increasing human population also increases demand and the price of food. Described by Paul Roberts in his book, *The End of Food*,

> In any given year, 4 million of Kenya's 31 million people go hungry, and in bad years [drought] ... that number can easily double.... population has climbed from 8 million in 1960 to 40 million today, the country must import nearly half of its grain, and even then, nearly half of its people are food insecure—nearly double that in 1980.[181]

Droughts, floods, and political upheavals set the table for the poor. Biofuels and farmed species fed with corn and soy affect people at and beyond where the crops are grown. The United States exports meat and grain to those who can pay for it. Prices rise and fall for reasons.

Researchers have found that there is 80 percent likelihood that the Russian heat wave was statistically linked to climate change.[182] The riots in Mozambique and the ongoing severe drought in Kenya become more likely elsewhere as increasing concentrations of GHGs warm the planet. Most of the world's people will not escape the consequences of global warming. While wealthier economies have the assets to partially counter climate change threats, least developed economies, especially where food is imported extensively, will suffer the most. It was the hottest Moscow month in 2010 since weather statistics were first recorded 130 years ago.

Many NGOs (non-government organizations) refuse to associate their organizations' mandates to establish human sustainability, maintain biodiversity, and create a world without hunger with a call to end carnism. The elephant in the room is the absence of a worthwhile discussion about the suffering of domestic and wild individuals from other species condemned to be human food. It should unite us instead of divide us. If we the affluent are unwilling to demonstrate the benefits of a vegan human ecology, we should not expect others to listen.

Transoceanic

The government of Brazil has collaborated with corporations to decimate vast areas of the Amazon rainforest basin. In the forest's place, they grow monocultures of soybeans that are fed to cattle there, in Europe, and elsewhere.[183] Joining this corporate destruction of ecosystems are newly arriving subsistence farmers. These smaller scale farmers find thin, poor soils on cleared land that are quickly depleted after a few years of cropping. They are forced to move on to virgin forest or attempt grazing cattle on the sparse remnants. When large predators retreat because they have lost their habitat to farms, they may attack livestock to survive. For that, they are killed.

When ecosystems are decimated, it does not matter what corporations or who commits the crimes. New roads, mining, promise of a better life, and the settlements that result all push the frontiers of destruction. As the populations of indigenous people grow, so does their need for food. Their slash-and-burn food plots are given less time to rest before being reused. Without time to regenerate, the soil becomes less productive. The people move up to steeper slopes, slashing, burning, and planting where erosion is more prevalent. Making matters worse, the desperately poor who move out of the cities and into the forests often encroach on indigenous peoples' lands.

Decades ago, I flew in a small commercial airliner over West Africa. As we lifted off the corrugated metal runway dimly lit by generators behind the small restaurant/bar/baggage area and into the dark skies, I looked down and saw the Earth on fire. Over what must have been thousands of square miles, the land burned brightly on an otherwise night-dark land. I was told it was the season for burning before planting crops.

The land still burns, world population has doubled since my flight, and change is speeding up. A Transoceanic Highway nearing completion runs from Brazil's Atlantic Ocean seaports of Rio de Janiero and Santos for 3,400 miles through the Amazon Basin, through the Peruvian rainforests, then over mountains, terminating at Pacific Ocean seaports in Peru. The highway cuts open the belly of many ecosystems. Indigenous species, like red blood, pours from the wound. A flood of new people are arriving full of hope for a new life. In Peru's Amazon Basin, virgin rainforest is being annihilated by gold miners. They cut the trees, some over a thousand years old, burn the remaining slash, and then pump powerful jets of water into the bare earth and wash away the soil up to 50 feet below the former forest floor.[184] In their quest, they first alter the ecosystems abutting the highway. Then they move deeper into the habitats of species, abetted by secondary roads.[185] Development along the Transoceanic Highway has exploded even before its official completion. Loggers, hunters, settlements, livestock to feed the settlers, and the presence of people whose activities extract and diminish, not add, biodiversity, have arrived. Brazilian government policy is to grant land to anyone clearing it.

Some of the human inhabitants who lived there prior to this new influx were heavily dependent upon harvesting Brazil nuts. The new settlers illegally cut down those and other trees and planted the land with papaya, bananas, and additional cash crops, excluding the indigenous peoples. A series of reports by National Public Radio's

Lourdes Garcia-Navarro and John Poole[186] profile this lawless region where corruption and violence prevail. Many newcomers are poor. They are intent on turning these ecosystems into sustenance and perhaps relative wealth. One farmer interviewed stated he had killed 10 endangered jaguars to protect his pigs, cattle, and chickens. The natural order of the Amazon Basin became an economic order in a heartbeat.

While we wish prosperity for other people, we must not ignore the costs that tear apart ecosystems. Billions of us are scraping off the living surface of the planet. Our excesses flatten any chance we might have to make things right. *Ecosystem or people* is not a choice we should be making. But that is exactly our effect on the planet because we have a cancerous current human ecology. We act as if ecosystems will forever pay the price of our follies. We have already done to the U.S. tallgrass prairies what the people of South America are in the process of doing to the Amazon Basin, what people are doing to the landscapes, seascapes, and atmospherescapes around the world. Less than 4 percent of the original tallgrass prairie remains in North America; another source cites 2 percent. Kansas harbors 80 percent of that small fraction.[187, 188]

When people do get access to land and financing for seed, tools, technical education, and more consistent access to food and water, will they stay with the current human ecology, or learn about the new? Will the people extracting life out of Amazon Basin ecosystems blindly move up the food chain of carnists and eat increasing amounts of meat and dairy as part of an unsustainable lifestyle they see the wealthiest one billion people gorging on? We need to show the world by example that the vegan new human ecology makes sense.

From Fertilizer to Poverty

Fertilizer has induced farmland to increase botanical (plant) agriculture productivity more than ever thought possible. It has helped alleviate hunger for billions of people. When researchers learned how to create fertilizer synthetically from natural gas, agricultural output exploded. But it also means we are now the largest contributor of nitrogen to the biosphere. When applied to the vast acreage required to feed animal agriculture, one of fertilizer's downsides becomes visible as oceanic dead zones.

More than 70 percent of the Mississippi basin's botanical agriculture yield, most being corn and soybeans, is grown to feed livestock. This watershed area extends from Montana to Minnesota to Ohio and Louisiana. Soil, livestock sewage, and manufactured fertilizer are transported off this land by rain, wind, and melting snow. Contaminants flow from stream to river to ocean from mile after square mile of corn and soybean fields and large Concentrated Animal Feeding Operations (CAFOs). They are transported down the silty Mississippi River into the Gulf of Mexico. Along the way, this excess nitrogen fertilizer and animal waste fuels explosions of plant life. Eventually, algae and other organisms die and sink to the seafloor in the Gulf. As this organic matter decomposes, it depletes oxygen in the water.

Dead zones are where everything or nearly everything dies after the oxygen is depleted. Entire marine ecosystems suffocate. The dead zone in the Gulf of Mexico is the size of Massachusetts. Simon Dinner writes in the periodical *Global Environmental Change* that the dead-zone-producing fertilizer flowing to the Gulf of Mexico would be cut by over half if humans adopted a vegan diet. He concluded that the dead zone in the Gulf would disappear.[189] Imagine if we could test his conclusion and watch how much the land, rivers, and the Gulf of Mexico would respond to our vegan human ecology.

Earth is pockmarked with more than 400 oceanic dead zones of our doing. They affect 245,000 square kilometers[190] and double in number every 10 years. In 2006, a dead zone formed to cover 1,200 square miles of ocean off the coast of Oregon where 80 percent of the water column was affected. The seafloor was carpeted with dead fish and invertebrates who suffocated. This is one of the few documented instances where a dead zone occurs naturally and cyclically.[191]

Naturally does not take into account an important detail: Climate change alters weather and wind patterns that strongly influence the strength and direction of oceanic currents. A change in the currents that bring oxygenated water into potential dead zones can be disastrous to marine life. Those currents also mix warm water at the surface with cold water upwelling from the depths. The distribution of temperature influences which species are present and can determine the composition of the entire food web.

This is just one way animal agriculture impacts ecosystems and the viability of our future. First, agricultural runoff creates dead zones that harm ecosystems. Second, animal agriculture's GHGs add significantly to global warming. Global warming alters the wind and water currents that normally bring oxygenated water into dead zones. The same GHGs emitted from animal agriculture that warm the atmosphere melts glaciers and Arctic and Antarctic ice shelves. This melted water is fresh, not salty. The added freshwater alters the ocean's salinity, especially nearshore. Because freshwater is less dense than saltwater, it lies on top. This increased layering of ocean water, combined with changes in weather and wind patterns, may further affect major oceanic currents. Since these currents distribute cooler and warmer waters around the globe, they influence weather patterns that impact the yields of food crops. This cycle of destruction started in the agricultural fields and returns there. Animal agriculture is responsible.

GHG-spewing burger-eating carnists are changing oceanic currents and weather patterns a hemisphere away. They determine crop yields, grain prices, and the prevalence of hunger. With dead, climate-ravaged soil, it will do little good to own or till land that is dry, hard-baked pan. From oil to meat to cars, a growing segment of humanity is enriched while ecosystem health and biodiversity declines. More and more of us gorge ourselves in midst of insufferable poverty where at least 48 percent of humanity lives on less than two dollars per day.[192, 193]

The neo-omnivore movement is proposing a wholly unsatisfactory and unworkable response to these issues. They deny the extent to which we must change our behavior and foolishly cling to the current human ecology that idolizes meat. They deserve special consideration.

The Most Important Dilemma: Problems with Flawed Choices

A popular movement in food culture deserves attention from the perspective of human ecology. Its proponents describe themselves as omnivores. Like all omnivores, they choose to eat both plant- and animal-sourced food. However, these omnivores call for tweaking, not ending, carnism to make it acceptable. They oppose some critical excesses of industrial agricultural practices and ill-considered consumer behavior, but do not challenge the appropriateness of carnism itself. Switching to locally sourced, organic, grass-eating cattle meat over the grain-fed industrial animal product is the kind of change that leaves them satisfied. These reformed omnivores allege their dietary choices are environmentally sustainable and humane. There is no foundation to either claim.

Michael Pollan is perhaps the most popular omnivore reformer since his book *The Omnivore's Dilemma* was published in 2006. A professor of journalism and skilled writer, he performs an important public service because he draws millions of people into thinking about agriculture and how we choose the food we eat.[194] He brings more people to the table, so to speak. Tragically, he and the reformed omnivore movement that responded to his messages remain stuck in a current human ecology that is neither adaptable to ecosystems, thus unsustainable, nor moral in its treatment of individuals from other species. I will refer to them simply as omnivores from here on.

Pollan rallies us to consider our food choices. He shares his discoveries about the absurdities of industrial corn production and its connections to factory farming. He rallies to the dangers of monocultures and pesticides. This is great stuff. I recommend his books. But it is not long before his carnist worldview becomes evident in the aberrations and biases found in some of his most important presumptions and conclusions in *Omnivore's Dilemma*. He falls short of doing justice to the great questions he raises about our food choices.

In *Dilemma*, Pollan uses inappropriately applied terms and unfounded concepts about ecology, ecosystems, animal behavior, the motivations of vegans and vegetarians, and the few philosophers he chose to represent them. And after a few perfunctory acknowledgments about their good intentions, he becomes unpleasantly dismissive of vegans and vegetarians.

The first clue to the book's conclusions arrives quickly on the initial pages of *Omnivore's Dilemma*.

"But in the end," Pollan writes,

this is a book about the pleasures of eating, the kinds of pleasures that are only deepened by knowing.... Many of these species have evolved expressly to gratify our desires, in the intricate dance of domestication that has allowed us and them to prosper together as we could never have prospered apart.[195]

With one broad stroke of his personal and deeply anthropocentric worldview, he dismisses humanity's history of horrific treatment of billions upon billions of sentient beings and ecosystem losses long before factory farming existed. He asserts that this "intricate dance" has been beneficial to the sentient species farmed for their meat because they now exist in large numbers. This author considers they are "prospering" when we artificially induce their short productive lives that "gratify our desires" but gives no accounting of their innate value. Population equals good in this simple equation. He asks us to believe the absurdity that all of the suffering and abuse we have rained upon them would be—if choice were possible—the choice domesticated individuals from other species would make just so they could now exist in the billions.

Norm Phelps, author and founder of the Society of Ethical and Religious Vegetarians, pulls back the curtain on similar unexamined worldview assumptions about our relationships with domesticated species.

Unsupported by evidence, the 'volunteers for death' theory is a self-serving justification for modern-day animal slavery and slaughter projected backward in time so it can masquerade as legitimate scholarship. It is the interspecies equivalent of claims that African slaves were happy in their servitude because it spared them the risks and uncertainties of freedom.[196]

As Phelps is reminding us, if Pollan's criteria were applied to human slaves, we would see it as racist. When it is applied to other species, it is called speciesism.

Peter Singer, philosopher and author of *Animal Liberation* (whom Pollan castigates), and Jim Mason, journalist, environmentalist, and attorney, who with Peter Singer wrote *Animal Factories,* take exception to Pollan's use of this argument as well. In *The Way We Eat,* they remark, "Pollan is surely not asserting that any individual animal ever consciously made a bargain with, to, for example, trade her eggs or milk, or even his or her flesh, for a year or two's food and protection from predators."[197]

Pollan's dancers always intended to use the lives of these species for their own purposes, not to benefit the eaten for their own sake. Livestock are not making mutual bargains as he asserts. He narrowly, and I believe wrongly, interprets this as biological *mutualism,* which means both species benefit from the relationship. Does he believe these are benefits for the other species? We distort their ancestral genetics and leave them with such artifacts as huge cow udders prone to painful disease and turkeys bred for white-meat breasts that grow so large they are unable to walk; we induce growth rates in poultry that painfully overload their hearts and lungs;[198] we remove offspring from cows to the deep, emotional distress of mother and calf; often days after birth, we butcher those calves; we kill young cattle, pigs, and sheep (lambs) within months to a few years after birth and deny them the experience of a natural lifespan; we diminish or eliminate altogether their quality of life; we deny them their natural behaviors, including nurturing; and we sever their social lives time and again. This is not mutualism and not prosperity.

Cattle and the other domesticated animals he considers have a wild ancestry. That we vanquished their ancestral cultures, communities, knowledge, languages, roles in ecosystems—their entire species' identity, ecology, and quality of life—is not calculated in what Pollan terms a mutualistic "dance." How can Mr. Pollan say Holstein dairy captives are prospering when they are killed at five years of age, on average, instead of living out their natural lifespan of 20 years and more? His inappropriate use of the term *mutualism* is useful to the storyteller but a fiction in the argument Pollan wants us to believe. We are not dancing with other species. They did not evolve "expressly to gratify our desires." This is about domination, opportunism, exploitation, and the elimination of their species' ancestral genetic attributes and free will. We commandeered their evolution.

His next book, *In Defense of Food,* continues this theme but accurately calls our relationship with livestock *symbiotic* instead. That biological term can be used to describe a wide range of relationships, from mutually beneficial to parasitic. We have shaped these individuals to produce and be food for us. Along the way, we removed much of their ancestral adaptive abilities for normal ecosystem survival. They have little to no control of where they are, what they eat and drink, when and how they mate (artificial insemination), their relationships with others of their kind, or even when they empty their udders. If Michael Pollan ever taps you on the shoulder asking for a dance, run like hell.

If you do not, this is what can happen. He will be as dismissive and unfeeling for you as he was for the individuals in his book. Toward 534, a young steer named after the number on his ear tag, he turned a blind eye. Pollan bought 534 to document what he already knew would be a steer's short, barren, industrialized life. A social, intelligent being, 534 had experiences that undoubtedly included attempts at bonding with others of his kind. Those bonds were shredded by animal agriculture's customary practices. The rancher-humans forcibly took him from his mother, shuttled him from one group of stranger-steers to another, and then drove him to an industrial feedlot.

After standing idle and distant while 534's innate needs were denied to his short life, this is the observation Pollan gives his readers:

> As I gingerly stepped toward him the quiet shuffling mass of black cowhide between us parted [Pollen's steer was now at the feedlot], and there stood 534 and I, staring dumbly at one another. Glint of recognition? None, whatsoever. I told myself not to take it personally; 534 and his pen mates have been bred for their marbling, after all, not their ability to form attachments.[199]

Dilemma reports very little contact between him and 534 prior to that moment. Pollan's observation in a feedlot helps us understand at least some of how his worldview is constructed, how he sees this meat unit, number 534, and how he will perpetuate the myths he needs to remain an omnivore.

Doing further harm to our understanding, he does not accurately report our connections and our relationships to ecosystems through food choices. He writes, "*The Omnivore's Dilemma* is about the three principal food chains that sustain us today: the industrial, the organic, and the hunter-gatherer."[200] Though sharing some similarities with food chains, the first two are at best methods of production with the third being methods of acquiring food. Claiming that hunter-gatherers are a food chain instead of a method of procuring food is an idea I hope readers will see as obviously misapplied.

Give Us Our Daily Food Web

When Pollan applies an ecological term like *food chains* to organic and industrial methods of food production, he is comparing plots of land under agriculture to nonagricultural food chains that occur in ecosystems. In botanical agriculture, one can plant and harvest rice by hand (nonindustrial), then use pesticides and herbicides, and thereby not be organic. Those are aspects of production. They are not food chains. A cropped field is a very narrow view of the larger biological world. Food chains describe the interconnectedness of food energy flowing through species but farms are not the same as the ecosystems they are embedded within.

If we start thinking that farms are the beginning and end of our food chain, we drift from more traditional references of complex food chains that occur in ecosystems. Though intensely altered, an agricultural field is still embedded in an ecosystem. If we believe Pollan's proposal that agricultural fields or agriculture itself are representative of stand-alone food chains (his industrial and organic idea), I believe the inevitable result will be a disconnect between what Pollan thinks our food chain should be in agricultural systems instead of what ecosystems need from our food chain choices. Even if he is peaking metaphorically, this is dangerous. All of our food choices must provide the best possible outcomes for ecosystems. In fact, we will see in a moment what happens when *Omnivore's Dilemma* refers to a farm as being a complete ecosystem that ends at the fence line. They do not end at the fence line. He forgets to write that the fences themselves are damaging to ecosystems.

It is at this biocentric ecological level, and within the context of ecosystems, where we must make our dietary decisions. Ignore that, and we will get a Pollan set of omnivore *answers* that are insufficiently adaptive to ecosystems and unsustainable. In a biocentric choice, individuals of all species have intrinsic value. Telling of his human-centered perspective, intrinsic value is sorely lacking throughout *Dilemma*.

For instance, Pollan advocates nonindustrial meat, dairy, and egg consumption at some lowered level that easily satisfies his industrial, organic, and hunter-gatherer faux food chain. But when measured biocentrically instead of anthropocentrically, we see the omnivores' destructive effects on native species and ecosystems. It is here that we can see livestock for what they are, invasive species.

Omnivore's Dilemma rightly decries feedlots, educates us about many insane aspects of our food production system, reminds us of the injustices perpetuated upon the botanical farmers through public policy, worries about the degradation of soil, helps us understand how cow stomachs work, and describes his ideal of animal agriculture. But Pollan also encourages readers to swallow statements like "In fact, when animals live on farms the very idea of waste ceases to exist; what you have instead is a closed ecological loop—what in retrospect you might call a solution."[201] He was referring to a specific type of small-scale farm, Polyface Farm.[202] It is an effort by Virginia farmer Joel Salatin and his family to be sustainable, if not kind. This is a comment one visitor sent into United Poultry Concerns:

> I toured Polyface on a sweltering day. Chickens were in tiny cages with tin roofs in the beating sun, panting like mad. The cages were located over manure piles the birds were supposed to eat larvae from. Rabbits were kept in factory-farm conditions in suspended, barren wire cages. There was no sign of freedom or compassion for these animals.[203]

When Pollan calls Polyface a closed system that ends at the fence line is overstated at best, and from an ecosystem perspective, false. That is perhaps the inevitable outcome when food chains are defined non-biocentrically as industrial and organic production on farms, and hunter-gatherers procuring food away from farms.

A farm's land remains part of and continues to interact with the host ecosystem, no matter what activity occurs. Farming or no farming, it just interacts differently depending on what is happening on the land and in the air and water. We can remember that all farms were once naturally evolving habitat. They are now fragmented, fenced ecosystems, multiplied hundreds of millions of times in animal and non-animal agricultural plots girdling the Earth, but part of ecosystems still. In addition, remember because I repeat it enough, grazing cumulatively uses up to 26 percent of Earth's arable land "while feed crop production requires about a third of all arable land." Similarly, remember that livestock accounts for 20 percent of terrestrial animal biomass. That is a monumental amount of habitat removed and invasive species introduced. Animal agriculture is an immense, unnecessary contribution to the loss of ecosystems. Omnivores are at its core.

In a summary of *Livestock's Long Shadow*, the FAO "recommends a range of measures to mitigate livestock's threats to the environment" that include "… land degradation … greenhouse gas … emissions … water pollution … biodiversity loss …"[204] Through us, our vegan new human(e) ecology does far more than "mitigate" those disasters; we are eliminating them. No fuss and no mess with a vegan ecology.

As the FAO further reminds us,

> The sheer quantity of animals being raised for human consumption also poses a threat of the Earth's biodiversity. ...and the land area they now occupy was once habitat for wildlife. In 306 of the 825 terrestrial eco-regions identified by the Worldwide Fund for Nature, livestock are identified as "a current threat," while 23 of Conservation International's 35 global hotspots for biodiversity'— characterized by serious levels of habitat loss—are affected by livestock production.[205]

There are alternatives to the type of animal agriculture Pollan promotes, alternatives available at the command of at least a few billion people who are economically and environmentally able to access them. The meals he prepares to demonstrate his food chains and his flimsy effort as a vegetarian described in *Dilemma* hide the bigger problems of carnism. Pollan stopped at the same fence line where he said ecosystems began.

Food chains describe the procession of species, one consuming another. They are complex biological relationships that never leave ecosystems. If a lion eats you, then you are part of her food chain, as is what you ate. When a sea lion consumes a fish, he occupies a place in a food chain. That place is called a *trophic level*. Below the sea lion in his food chain are fish who may have eaten smaller fish; that creates another place in the food chain, or trophic level. Smaller fish may have eaten phytoplankton or zooplankton, and zooplankton ate phytoplankton. All are trophic levels in a food chain.

The primary producers, the foundation of our and most species' food chains, are able to convert organic matter, usually by photosynthesis, into useable food for primary consumers. In the oceans, zooplankton are primary consumers of phytoplankton, the primary producers. On land, examples of primary consumers are plant-eating insects and herbivores like deer. They are consuming the primary producers, plants. At every point in a food chain from phytoplankton, to zooplankton, to smaller fish, to larger fish, to sea lion, to shark, each step is a trophic level. Humans are capable of being primary, secondary, tertiary, and onward consumers. It can get more complex, and often does.

In the phytoplankton to sea lion food chain I just described, food chains can overlap into complex food webs. Food webs reflect how food chains overlap. Farmers try their best to keep their crops from other species' food chains and webs by applying herbicides and insecticides, planting genetically modified crops, or as we all want, use organic practices to accomplish the same things. The farmers do this because they are responding to the ecosystem trying to take back habitat in which the crops are growing. Here is an illustrated figure of a food web consisting of many overlapping food chains shared with us by David

Opposite: "A partial food web for the Scotian Shelf in the Northwest Atlantic off eastern Canada. Species enclosed in rectangles are also exploited by humans. This food web is incomplete because the feeding habits of all components have not been fully described. Further, all species—including some of the marine mammals—do not spend the entire year in the area." Reprinted with permission from Lavigne (2003).[206]

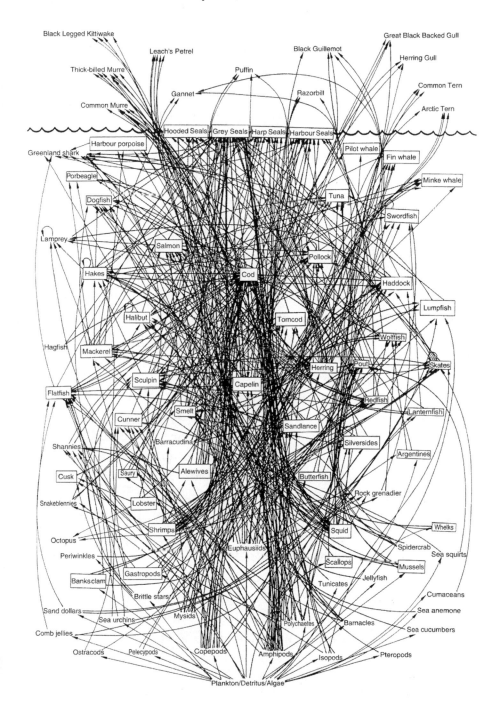

Lavigne, PhD. You need only follow a few connections to see how food chains must not be described as industrial, organic, and hunter-gatherer.

Not shown in the illustration is that a few species are able to chemosynthesize their nutrients in places like deep sea volcanic vents. It is important also to remember the decomposers, the fungi and bacteria that break down the detritus, the organic matter that remains after the deaths of other species, so it is available for uptake by others. This is nutrient recycling.

Vegans are primary consumers of primary producers, plants. Vegan human ecology means we eat low on the food chain. Many of us are vegan for environmental reasons. We see the fields where our food is grown as part of the ecosystems that also belong to other species, not just our own. We do not eat fish because they come from other species' food chains and webs. They are impacted by our decision to eat fish or not and it has nothing to do with industrial, organic, or hunter-gatherer methods of production and procurement. We are most concerned about our ecosystem niche and how it affects all other species.

The closer we are to eating primary producers, plants, the more energy and resource-efficient we become. That is because energy is lost during respiration, metabolism, and locomotion. So the lion who ate you in my earlier example got only a fraction for the food value you consumed over your lifetime. Cattle eating corn return a small fraction of the corn's energy and nutritional value as meat, as Pollan recognizes. If we graze millions of invasive cattle who displace wildlife, we cannot avoid profound outcomes for our human ecology, ecosystems, and wildlife management. When we eat lower in our vegan food chain, there is far less impact upon ecosystems than any case of animal agriculture Pollan envisions. Methods of production and procurement are important, but they do not inform us sufficiently about the most important decisions we must make about our food.

Cross Pollination

Pollan declares that he intends to take the "approach [of] the diner as a naturalist might, using the long lenses of ecology and anthropology," while employing "the shorter, more intimate lens of personal experience."[207] My charge is that he cannot do this without evaluating his choices from a more thorough consideration of ecological, as a naturalist would, and anthropological outcomes. This includes examining more deeply the legitimacy and appropriateness of carnism itself and whether being an omnivore within today's ecosystems is a moral and survivable human adaptation to Earth.

He makes an appealing argument for us to reduce some of the environmental impact involved in animal agriculture, but cannot bring himself to stop it altogether. Instead, Pollan romanticizes our human history of carnism in general, and hunting and other cultural practices in particular. The traditions he defends are destroying the planet. He cannot claim to look at this issue thoroughly as an ecologist might, nor make a credible claim of waxing anthropological given his unexamined impacts, like the GHGs spewing from omnivore choices, upon other people geographically distant from his dietary choices. This "short lens ... of personal experience" strikes me as being nothing more than an extension of his own cultural, anthropocentric wet blanket that he drapes over the entire enterprise.

Omnivore's Dilemma needed to include, at minimum, a studied comparison of carnist omnivorism to an alternative vegan human ecology. Bypassing that need allowed him to retreat to where his personal traditions live. Pollan's central theme is that we face a dilemma about how we choose our food in the midst of plenty. It can be addressed with a basic knowledge of vegan, organic, whole foods nutrition. Instead of a fair, side-by-side comparison of omnivorism to veganism, he chose to describe vegetarians, who also have more to ponder about dairy, leather, and eggs, and by inference vegans, as urban eccentrics wholly detached from "the real world." He never wavers in his allegiance to carnist omnivore culture and the world-views that support it. Whether he likes it or not, his undeniable story-telling craft has bolstered food epicureans and their enabling chefs, gluttons who treat him as an icon. There is a communications media happy to grant all of them absolution for the destruction and suffering omnivore choices create.

A telling critique of *Omnivore's Dilemma* comes from B.R. Meyers, contributing editor for *The Atlantic* at the time, in his book review titled "Hard to Swallow." He wrote:

> For centuries civilized society took a dim view of food lovers, calling them 'gourmands' and 'gluttons' ... They were even assigned their own place in hell ... force-fed for eternity.... [F]ood writers' hostility to the very language of moral value and Pollan's use of language [is] to side step and diminish people like you and me who are calling out for different answers to the questions *Omnivore's Dilemma* raises.[208]

Although he proscribes "eat mostly plants," Pollan distances himself from advocating a vegan diet even in the face of overwhelming proof he visits, but only briefly as a seeming formality. He wrote, "People feel like they have to take sides on this plant/animal divide, and I don't think we do. [*Mother Jones* interviewer, "There's no dilemma?"] "No dilemma."[209] Pollan advocates we get chickens out of cages, reduce the consumption of animal-sourced foods, especially those produced under industrial conditions, and increase access to healthy foods for the underserved poor in cities. These are a few of the many other unquestionably good changes he promotes. Pollan gives the industrial botanical agriculture and industrial animal agriculture a well-deserved kick in the pants but he fails to offer adequate justice for ecosystems, people who depend upon them, and the billions of sentient beings he approves of wasting.

He may still see past his self-imposed limits and come to a vegan conclusion. Pollan appreciates the power of our food choices to create the best, not insufficiently better, outcomes possible. We owe Michael Pollan our thanks for those awakenings. Perhaps he has been planting unwittingly the seeds for a vegan new human ecology while denying the need for it.

Relax

Michael Pollan comforts doubting carnists. Aside from an occasional comment about his queasiness when he kills chickens, he artfully sooths his readers, dulling concerns they may have about the omnivore's obvious penchant for killing sentient species. One supposition he employs is that the chickens he is killing are like zombies who are not experiencing anything as he kills them. Pollan chose to interpret what he saw in the eye of these chickens as the "seeming obliviousness" that is suspiciously like what he said about steer number 534. Grabbing the chicken, "[He] looked into the black eye of the chicken and, thankfully, saw nothing, not a flicker of fear."[210]

Can a chicken be in shock from being pulled from the known security and community of his portable roost, carted to an unknown place on the farm where chatting strangers moved quickly with their bodies, arms, and hands that grabbed him by the neck and turned him upside down? If chicken were a songbird knocked from the sky after flying into a reflective glass building or power line, perhaps Pollan would recognize shock. Pollan does not cite scientific papers written by ethologists describing animal behavior. We know that accurately severing neck arteries with a knife brings rapid unconsciousness, but that is not the same thing as knowing what is being experienced by the chicken before the lights go out. Pollan is preparing chickens for an economic order of value, not the natural order where individuals are living a life and have intrinsic value. What, I wonder, did the chicken see in Pollan's eye? Anything?

Despite his occasional misgivings about eating chicken after seeing their composting remains, Pollan moves on quickly. He gets over it. Repeatedly, he holds out ideas and reasons to turn away from the omnivore's carnism and briefly acknowledges the suffering and destruction we inflict. But he gets over it. When he writes a chapter about "The Ethics of Eating Animals," you can count on him to weaken all reasons that compel us to make wholesale vegan changes in our relationships with individuals from other species. In a few sentences, he tells us that we have reasons for being culturally confused about eating animals, that we seem eager to extend moral consideration to them especially in factory farms, and that science is revealing the complexity of their abilities in language, culture, tool-making, and even self-consciousness. But he gets over that, too.

As *Dilemma* does what it does throughout the book, we see the weight of those important factors immediately brushed aside, illogically: "And yet, most of the animals we eat lead lives organized very much in the spirit of [Rene] Descartes, who famously claimed that animals were mere machines, incapable of feeling or thought."[211] Assuming that Pollan is merely observing what his omnivores do to animals, omnivores who impose this organizing upon their lives, and does not mean they are indeed machines, why does he choose to ignore them as individuals from other species and the science revealing their abilities in the language, culture, and tool-making he mentions? He gets over that and moves on, not answering what science is revealing and how to respond to it fully as vegans do. What he has done is insert a sentence affirming the complex abilities and sentience of other species, then ignores the need for us to respond to those discoveries. We are not supposed to notice this shell game.

Ethologists study nonhuman species' behavior. They would not look a chicken in the eye and pronounce to the world, no fear here! It would be an unacceptable statement without proof in the ethologist's world of scientific methodology; it should be just as unacceptable in *Dilemma*. Pollan has acknowledged complex sentience as if obligated to check a box, but then abandons the trail of evidence that would bring him to an unavoidable conclusion far different from the killing he embraces. Carnism is the predominant pattern that runs throughout *Omnivore's Dilemma*. Its allegiance to the omnivore's carnist culture was never really in doubt.

Dismissing Philosophers

Dilemma continues its case against the vegan alternative worldview and tells us that animal advocates require sentience in animals, and without sentience, we believe there is no innate value. Therefore, without innate value, animal activists will not advocate for their protection. I have met some animal advocates who do seem to be concerned only or chiefly about individuals and species who are sentient. They seemed not to be overtly environmentalists. That is a problem. Requiring sentience before we care runs counter to biocentrism wherein all have innate value. This attitude is useless to any human ecology because all species, and their ecosystems, are required for all others to exist. Mountains have innate value because they are integrated and essential to the characteristics of ecosystems, if for no other reason. Fortunately, most species rights advocates I know do value ecosystems and the non-sentient species. Animal advocates are rising on the same tide of increasing awareness as all humanity awakens to global environmental issues.

Environmentalists, seeing at least the mechanical connections between species and their ecosystems, do not require sentience before respect, even reverence, is given to them. Their shortcoming is that sentience does not figure prominently in their advocacy. *Dilemma's* brush is too wide and misses the environmental work of many species rights NGOs. Perhaps Pollan is relying too narrowly on Peter Singer's work, *Animal Liberation*,[212] where sentience, the ability to feel pleasure and pain, to be conscious, is linked to intrinsic value.

Dilemma is overly dependent upon citing a few philosophers who have developed arguments about the value of individuals from other species. They do not agree on all points. Their arguments regarding the value of lives are momentary snapshots in an evolving deliberation, not its whole. Confined by the rules of logic required by philosophical debate, these arguments can give rise to conclusions and choices none of us would ever make. In *Practical Ethics*, Singer acknowledges this when he writes about the logic that would "approve" of killing an "unlimited" number of domesticated species if they had enjoyable lives, and after being killed, were replaced with others experiencing the same, equally enjoyable life. Singer writes, "As a piece of critical moral reasoning, this argument may be sound. Even at that level, it is important to realise how limited it is in its application..., at the practical level of moral principles, it would be better to reject altogether the killing of animals for food, unless one must do so to survive."[213]

We could have used Singer's admonition in *Dilemma* because it reveals a more comprehensive representation of what Singer wrote. Additionally, in "Does Helping the Planet Hurt the Poor?" Peter Singer does make the connections between sentient species, ecosystems, and human poverty even when he does not ascribe innate value to ecosystems.[214]

Dilemma's bias ensures the arguments of vegetarians and vegans will look weak and the omnivores' positions look strong. We should reject the book's inference that Peter Singer and Tom Regan represent all beliefs held by millions of practicing vegans whom Pollan attacks in his imagined "vegan utopia." Debate is healthy and ongoing in the vegan community.

For instance, philosopher Tom Regan cites in his book, *Empty Cages*,[215] many compelling examples about the rights of individual domesticated animals, but the closest he comes to including wildlife, and ecosystems not at all, is concern about trapping wildlife for their fur and its undeniable cruelty. Why this gap? Regan deems those species "our moral equality" when they are "subjects-of-a-life." As a result, there is a vacant sign on ecosystems. This is curious given "subjects-of-a-life" depend upon ecosystems and non-sentient species to live. He allowed "compensatory justice"[216] for endangered species, but that is as good as it got. It is simply painful to me that some philosophers associated with animal rights do not integrate the worth and rights of sentient species with ecosystems. Their moral reasoning must find a practical way to bridge this fault line.

Josephine Donovan, in *Feminism and the Treatment of Animals: From Care to Dialogue*, rings most true with me. I found this guiding light from her:

> It is not so much, I will argue, a matter of caring for animals as mothers (human and nonhuman) care for their infants as it is one of listening to animals, paying emotional attention, taking seriously— *caring about*—what they are telling us. As I stated at the conclusion of 'Animal Rights and Feminist Theory,' we should not kill, eat, torture, and exploit animals because they do not want to be so treated, and we know that.

She criticizes both Regan and Singer because "... both rights and utilitarianism dispense with sympathy, empathy, and compassion as relevant ethical and epistemological [the study of human knowledge, including its limits] sources for human treatment of nonhuman animals."[217]

Why does Pollan not consider deep ecology philosopher Arne

Naess?[218] He and his many advocates acknowledge the intrinsic, biocentric value of individuals from other species with absolutely no requirement for them to jump through the sentience hoop, as some philosophical arguments require. In Naess' biocentric world, nonhuman life is given intrinsic value, as are ecosystems. They are inseparable from the sacred whole.

I did not come by my own beliefs because philosophers convinced me of one argument or another. They did, however, challenge and help me develop my views. Philosophers never caused me to exclude any being from my orb of compassion even when their arguments would have allowed it had my allegiance been to them instead of nonhuman individuals. Using Peter Singer and Tom Regan as a shield to justify doing unnecessary harm to individuals from other species is something I do not understand about *Dilemma*.

Pollanist Destiny

Michael Pollan wants us to believe that our predation on individuals from other species should exist in the future because it existed in the past, and that our current predation upon domesticated and wild species is a *natural* (my word) human behavior. He attempts to equate the predatory relationships that evolved over millennia between wolves and deer to those between humans and chickens today. In this view, the evolutionary complexity of relationships between the wolves and deer where two species are free agents acting out their dramas in the context of ecosystems over a grand expanse of time is supposed to be the same as humans completely controlling domesticated species like chickens who are used as food but are not free agents. Instead of ecosystems, we have unnatural captivity. Instead of being shaped by all of the variables found in ecosystems, they are shaped by one species, us.

From that, we are supposed to conclude, "The surest way to achieve the extinction of the species [chickens] would be to grant chickens the right to life."[219] What I get from that is raising billions of short-lived, genetically mutilated chickens is a good thing; far fewer chickens who are life-long companions, his extinction theory, is a bad outcome. There is no ecological imperative to keep billions of domesticated chickens. Quite the opposite. Ecosystems do not want them.

There is one species (with sub-species) that we need to protect from extinction. The Red Junglefowl, the ancestor of all of today's domesticated chickens. Though threatened by gene pollution from domesticated chickens at forest edges, they are not endangered. They are stunningly beautiful and found in parts of India, China, Indonesia, Thailand, and adjacent countries.[220]

The mantra I hear in Pollan's writing is this: We are animals who are destined to eat other animals because we are animals. Then, after illustrating how American Indians shaped bison and the habitat both shared, he infers it is the model we can paste on top of the omnivore's ideology. By that reasoning, we should believe it good that African elephants now have shorter tusks and shattered, traumatized familial herds, while their elephant ecology and habitat is similarly disfigured, "shaped" by humans preying upon them. *Dilemma* rallies for the current human ecology as if nothing has changed, and does not apologize that Earth now serves our one species over all others. Extending a human ecology of the past into the present and future goes against all evolutionary precedent when it is no longer adaptive to ecosystems. Omnivores are maladaptive to ecosystems.

As long as omnivorism reigns, carnists will slit the throats of chickens at Polyface Farm. Millions of 534s will still die, if not near a feedlot, then at some other butcher's hands. *Dilemma* is not so much a discussion of the bewildering choices for which we have too little information as it is an extravagant self-justification for the continuation of carnism, even when the evidence of advanced sentience and ecological collapse is everywhere around us.

If he truly believes "that nature doesn't provide a very good guide for human social conduct," I hope he reconsiders. Nature does inform our behavior. She has always taught us to adapt to the grand unfolding of life. From the lives of other species, we see our own experience. Ethologists who study the social relationships and behaviors of other species know they transmit culture and norms from one generation to the next, including a sense of right and wrong, knowledge about their ecosystems, and how to survive. They possess these attributes and have no need for human validation. Reading the contemporary works of Marc Bekoff, Amy Hatkoff, Franz de Waal, Conrad Lorenz, Jeffrey Moussaieff Masson, Toni Frohoff, Brenda Peterson, and many other animal behaviorists, scientists, and writers on the subject would provide Pollan more ballast to his compassion.

A new era is unfolding. Our understanding of how the biosphere does and does not work should expand our awareness. I am vegan *because* of what I have seen and experienced with ecosystems and other species while doing both animal welfare and rights advocacy and environmental campaigns. Pollan goes out of his way to insult tens of millions of people when he writes,

> To contemplate such questions from the vantage of a farm, or even a garden, is to appreciate how parochial, and urban, an ideology animal rights really is. It could thrive only in a world where people have lost contact with the natural world, where animals no longer pose a threat to us ... and our mastery of nature seems unchallenged.[221]

He is being ridiculous. Like other conclusions found in *Dilemma*, he bases his beliefs on false premises. He believes if we choose a vegan response to what ails the Earth and humankind, we are disconnected urbanites who only need to wake up to the reality of his carnist worldviews. Pollan's dismissive attitudes and misrepresentation of vegetarians and vegans exposes his failing to explore adequately what a vegan human ecology offers. It is insulting and more than that, aggravating, because an important portion of the progressive community that really cares about issues is being misled.

I have been charged by a grizzly bear, watched a black bear at play in the wild, had sea otters mating within a few feet of my toes, walked among the poor of many cultures, had close calls with whiteouts in the wilderness, been swarmed by mosquitoes, covered in leaches, and suffered frostbite and heat stroke. Those experiences made me deeply committed, spiritually committed, to the vegan new human ecology and the ecosystems it relieves. By Pollan's accounting, I have never been to a farm or garden, left a city, or otherwise come to understand anything he experienced in researching his book. I have, and I refuse to be ever again, an omnivore.

The Omnivore's Disappointment

It is our experience with nature, our increasing awareness of ecosystems, the operational norms of animal agriculture, and the sentient and non-sentient individuals under the yoke of carnism that leads millions of people to campaign for what must come next, a deeper, new human ecology that reflects the intrinsic worth of it all. I did not need to buy, watch the mistreatment of, and have killed steer 534, shoot a pig, cut the throats of chickens, nor pretend that we possess unique genes that compel us to hunt other species to figure out what the Earth and the impoverished other half of all humans on Earth need. The intentional, premeditated purchase, transfer, and slaughter of 534 for the purposes of writing *Omnivore's Dilemma* is, in my mind, an act of inexcusable cruelty. Observing any one of the millions of steers who are in the industrial agriculture machine would have been sufficient. Pollan's self-indulgent thrill after he shot a feral pig is the same mistake.

I want to believe that the omnivore movement will wake up from its carefully crafted dream that is really the same old nightmare for ecosystems, individuals from other species, and us. The vegan new human ecology, though far from perfect, responds thoroughly to our collective environmental and moral responsibilities as no omnivore's human ecology can.

We can join hands and create a humane existence that is unbelievably wonderful. Who would disagree with the warmth and truth of what Buddhist monk Thich Nhat Hanh wrote in his book, *Going Home*:

> If we observe things deeply, we will discover that one thing contains all the other things. If you look deeply into a tree, you will discover that a tree is not only a tree. It is also a person. It is a cloud. It is the sunshine. It is the Earth. It is the animals and the minerals. The practice of looking deeply reveals to us that one thing is made up of all other things. One thing contains the whole cosmos.[222]

From the very base of the food chain to the very top, from bacteria to baboons, there are countless chemical and biological interactions, and dynamic trends and changes that alter the outcomes of ecosystems and our future. We must not abandon our awareness of the complexities swirling around us. We are biologically attached.

Writing in another one of his books, *In Defense of Food*, Michael Pollan does not take much time to dismiss directly the validity of vegetarians and vegans. He does continue his defense of cultural preferences and the epicurean's approach to "ethical" eating. He writes that he has not found compelling health reasons to exclude meat from the diet, but puts in parentheses, "That's not to say there aren't good ethical or environmental reasons to do so."[223] This is the same pattern that we found in *Dilemma* earlier; he gives a brief nod instead of an answer to the evidence that calls for a vegan human ecology. Then he moves on.

Bell-Ringers

Many writers are ruminating about food-related cultural shifts. Their stories are often personal and about their own navigation through carnist omnivore worldviews. Jonathan Safran Foer arrived at a vegetarian conclusion. His journey, described in *Eating Animals*, will be valuable to others struggling with dietary choices. Though critical of some of Michael Pollan's findings, he wavers about his own choice. For Foer and his family it was that "… my concerns about the reality of what meat is and has become are enough to make me give it up altogether."[224] Yet on the next page he writes, "I have placed my wager on a vegetarian diet *and* I have enough respect for people like Frank … to support their kind of [animal agriculture] farming." This sounds a lot like Pollan's "eat mostly plants" and his belief that slaughter is fine on some farms. Respecting people and opposing what they do is not a contradiction; Foer's vegetarianism and support for any animal agriculture is.

Foer did not concede that taste perceptions and preferences change over time. He still believed, "… I couldn't honestly argue, as many vegetarians try to, that it is as rich as a diet that includes meat." For some of us, experiencing this *memory taste for meat* is part of the vegan's transition, but it fades. I experienced it. We only have to look at the cultures of the world to see that taste preferences are learned, not innate. I found that I was craving the combination of salt and fat in my first vegetarian year or so. It helps to have peer support and access to the vegan and vegetarian community. Our perceptions change during this time of transformation. We begin to see what we did not notice before. Our knowledge and empathy deepen. The connections between the fates of individuals from other species, ecosystems, and our own become tangible.

Like other talented writers in this field, Foer rails against industrial factory farms, but leaves open the approval of other types of animal agriculture. That he seems to believe offering other individuals a "life at all" is missing the point. The intentional and artificial enabling of births for the express purpose of killing them to eat is a depraved act based on the carnists' belief system. We never gave these animals the ability to have a life; their ancestors did that quite well already.

My hope is assaulted when wizened and otherwise compassionate people limit the good they can do with their diet and human ecology. In *Dominion*, Matthew Scully does a superb job at excoriating Safari Club International, hunting, and some environmental aspects of carnism, yet he excludes dairy and wool-producing species from his protection, writing "it is perfectly acceptable provided they and their young are treated humanely, as they are on smaller family farms.... Indeed, such animals would never know life at all were it not for these small businesses." He is resurrecting the "volunteers for death" refrain and that our enabling the creation of millions more animals for slaughter is how we define a species' success as Pollan argues. Why not *create* as many lives as possible to kill if that is the greatest good? Preceding that fallacy, he tells readers that "I debated long and hard with myself about whether to include farm animals in this book."[225] Perhaps that explains why he did not examine the reality of dairy, the taking of calves' milk from the calf, and the calf from the mother.

Al Gore, former vice-president of the United States, is a justly celebrated bell-ringer and environmental activist. While he motivated millions of us to become personally responsible for climate change, he has yet to call for ending the 18 to 51 percent portion of greenhouse gasses[226] coming from animal agriculture. Whenever one of his new books comes out, I immediately go to the index and look for the words "vegan," "vegetarian," "food," and "meat." Finally, Gore spoke to animal agriculture and its contribution to climate change in *Our Choice: A Plan to Solve the Climate Crisis*.[227] He devoted just six pages out of 404 to the subject.

Gore's boyhood life was played out on a tobacco and Angus cattle farm. Perhaps that is why he minimizes his call for dietary reform when he writes, "Return animals to farms and use the manure as natural fertilizer" and "Eat less meat." In his documentary, *Inconvenient Truth*,[228] Gore tells the story about his father ceasing to grow tobacco after his daughter, Gore's sister, died of cancer. Given the links found between charbroiled meat, cholesterol, disease, and the searing of our planet, perhaps Gore will see his own "Inconvenient Truth," the terrible impacts of carnism on the health of people like his sister and the planet.

Economist Lester Brown reminds us that there are some 4 billion people wanting to follow the Western dietary standard of moving "up the food chain and consume more grain-intensive livestock products."[229] But Brown did not call for a response to all of what is needed. It appears this wonderful visionary and humanitarian cannot bring himself (and his cattle-ranching relatives) to do what is necessary: end the carnist plague on Earth. Brown offered a modest proposal in 2001 and noted the environmental and health benefits of consuming less meat.

That does not prevent Brown's biased reference to humanity's taste for meat. He tells us, "This long history as hunter-gatherers left us with an appetite for animal protein, one that continues to shape diets today." This worldview shapes his responses, including "... moving up the food chain also adds to the pressure. The challenge is to do so as efficiently as possible, minimizing additional demands on land and water."[230] For all the goodness and leadership he and his life work have given us, it is difficult to understand why he has refused to advocate for veganism. Instead he calls for efficiency in what we do to other species.

These bell-ringers advocate for a continuation of the current human ecology using animal agricultural models. We are living in increasing numbers where ecosystems cannot support us and an abundance of other species in the same place. It is time for a different response.

Adopt an organic whole-food, plant-based diet that replaces the slaughter of other species. Create humane and just economies beneficial for us and the greater good, everyone whom our actions and purchases affect. They must be considered in how we perceive our own self-interests. The omnivore models Pollan, Gore, Foer, Brown, and others propose are variations on carnism. This does not solve the moral and ecological crises we created. They are prolonging the time to when we start acting more honestly, honorably, and consistently toward ecosystems, individuals from other species, and biodiversity.

From ducks to kangaroos, goats to mice, beaked whales to coyotes, fish to monkeys, ground squirrels to mountain lions, scarlet macaws to the extinct Steller's sea cow, lobsters to corals, beaver to cassowaries, wolverines to bison, bees to pythons, proboscis monkeys to picas, Komodo dragons to Kermode bears, elephants to snow leopards, and dolphins to Quetzals, they and the ecosystems they once enjoyed are victims of our unceasing, unnecessary, cruel waste and violence that characterize the current human ecology under the reign of omnivores and their carnism.

Chickens and Eggs

The hens were barely two years old and prematurely exhausted from forced egg-laying. They were trucked from south of Seattle to Mt. Vernon to the north. They are some of the 340 million hens who lay more than 90 billion eggs in the United States every year. Commuters see chickens transported along our highways to slaughter somewhere every day.[231] Who stops to wonder at the meaning behind the sight? In this case, the chickens were taken to a newer metal industrial building that stands two blocks off Mt. Vernon's main thoroughfare. This is the killing factory. These particular Washington hens were taken from their cages in warehouses or *free-range* buildings. There, they lived in insanely crowded cages or were packed together in interior cage-free open areas.

Were chickens not intentionally birthed for killing in massive, industrial scale animal factories and on smaller owner-operator farms, they would live 7 to 15 years and more, similar to dogs and cats. Commercial factory egg-layers typically live for 12 to 23 months, while broilers, the chickens people buy hot off the rotisserie at grocery stores, live six weeks.[232]

The hens' non-domesticated ancestors would lay a clutch of a dozen or so eggs once or twice a year. That would be their rhythm in ancestral ecosystems and within the needs of their bodies. Now, they are manipulated to lay as many as 250 eggs annually. That is a grotesque change since, as chicken advocate Karen Davis writes in *Poisoned Chickens Poisoned Eggs*, "Egg-laying as an independent activity detached from the giving of life is not a natural phenomenon in birds."[233] Male chicks hatched from laying hens do not have value in the egg-layer industry. They are separated from the females at hatching. Egg hatching operations are well documented for throwing male chicks into plastic sacks, alive, where they slowly suffocate to death. In other instances, the chicks are thrown live into grinders. Whatever the method of killing, peeping for an hour or so is all these chicks get to do before they are destroyed as a waste product. The scale, like all of animal agriculture, is hard to comprehend.

Science Daily reports "... in 2006, Delaware farmers produced over 269 million broiler chickens—1.8 billion pounds of poultry.... Those chickens produced more than 280,000 tons of waste."[234] The annual U.S. slaughter of chicken broilers, not including egg-producing hens, rose from 1.53 billion birds in 1960 to 8.84 billion in 2006, while their average weight was induced to rise from 3.4 to 5.5 pounds.[235] Millions of them suffer terribly from Ascites because factory farming manipulates them to grow in a very short time. Ascites is a health condition where their cardiovascular system, heart and lungs, cannot keep up with that growth. As a result, tissues do not get enough oxygen, body fluids accumulate, and then heart failure and a host of other maladies kill them.[236, 237] Their artificially induced breast weight can exceed the chickens' legs strength. Walking can be difficult and painful.

Being animal agriculture is the largest consumer of soybeans, soybean farmers have a stake in the chicken market. As we saw in the dairy industry, partnerships are formed to increase business for both. These partnerships have included the "Eat Chicken Tonight" sign campaign and "Thankachicken.com" promotion.[238] One of the partnerships was with Delmarva Poultry Industry, Inc.

Cited regularly for water pollution in Chesapeake Bay, Delmarva feels the government intends to make them disproportionately responsible for paying to fix the pollution. They argue that competitors elsewhere, nationally and internationally, will gain a financial advantage if Delmarva is made to pay for the environmental costs not presently included in the price of chickens.[239] Meanwhile, the estimated "70 percent of the Nitrogen and 82 percent of the Phosphorus coming into the Bay from the Southern Part of the Delmarva Peninsula can be attributed to the poultry industry."[240] It comes from the "approximately 5,670 poultry houses, including slaughterhouses, hatcheries, feed mills, rendering plants, and a deboning plant."[241] The issue is well studied but not under control. Air and water pollution from this carnist industry is causing environmental harm and costs to Chesapeake Bay users and taxpayers.[242]

I have witnessed tens of thousands of chickens crammed into wire cages that filled immense warehouses in Maine. Their economic purpose and value was to lay eggs. Entering several of the warehouses that belonged to DeCoster Egg Company over two decades ago is an experience I will never forget. In the din and stink coming from the nightmare the birds were forced to endure, I watched in despair as I looked upon their sad, crazed, cramped lives; it was nothing less than a madhouse. That kind of depravity is a norm in the animal agriculture we have supported. On a hot day, the temperature was unbearably high in one particular, ammonia-filled chicken warehouse. I called the company. Not understanding I was there, I was told they did not have that kind of problem.

More recently, Wright County Egg and Quality Egg, owned by the same Austin "Jack" DeCoster, has been cited for violations time and again. DeCoster is an equal-species abuser: "Labor Secretary Robert B. Reich has publicly denounced DeCoster Egg Farms as 'an agricultural sweatshop,' where the workers are treated like 'animals,'" according to a 1996 *New York Times* article.[243] The prosecution of DeCoster was justice gained for workers but injustice continued for the chickens who were not seen as victims suffering infinitely worse. This one egg factory housed "… Five million hens producing 23 million brown and white eggs a week."

Typical of CAFOs (Concentrated Animal Feeding Operations), factory farming chickens can foul both waterways and our moral well-being. The ammonia it produces can burn the eyes and lungs of the chickens who cannot escape their cages. After Austin DeCoster expanded the family's business into Iowa and took over businesses supplying other egg producers, his enterprise was declared a habitual offender. An AP story run on the Huffington Post website in August 2010 described DeCoster's involvement in a recall of half a billion eggs for salmonella contamination that sickened 1,300 people. Fines and citations cling to his businesses like two-sided sticky tape for his treatment of workers, environmental pollution, and finally in 2010, animal cruelty.[244]

My own relationship with eggs changed early in my conversion to vegetarianism. One egg in particular had its own way of telling me a story. While trekking into the Himalayan foothills of Nepal in the early 1970s, I stopped into a hut that served sparsely provisioned food next to a river I had just crossed on a rope bridge. I cannot exaggerate the limited choice of food I had. I chose a hard-boiled egg, even though I struggled with my pledge(s) to not eat them.

Trekking across the expanse of cultures from Europe through Turkey and onward to India and Nepal was a magical and mystical time of my life, a personal spiritual journey as I sought self-awareness and an expanded consciousness. Our culture encouraged it at the time. Immersed in the sensate miracle of each moment, and astride the trekking path in the middle of a sunny day, I peeled off the brown shell of the hard-boiled egg I asked for; on the white of the egg inside were my initials, WA. They were clear, straight-lined, and proportional as if intentionally produced in a printing shop. The rest of the egg's white was white. The two letters were in dark blue. The inside and outside of the shell itself bore no color or mark of any kind. Just "WA" on the egg's white with the A slightly below and to the right of the W. The message could not be clearer to me. Absent egg surprises, we know enough about where they come from and the hens who are amazing individuals of another species. We know enough to stop eating eggs.

After noting that chickens crow before dawn because they can see ultraviolet light well before sunrise, and that roosters can recognize the calls of at least 30 other roosters, Karen Davis tells us, "She [Viva] was not 'just a chicken.' She was a chicken. She was a member of earth's community; a dignified being with a claim equal to everyone else's to justice, compassion, and a life worth living."[245] It is unfathomable how our species came to such an ugly denial of the value of individuals from other species. We, who talk about ourselves as being made in the image of God, seem to not care. We are disconnected from who we are and who we claim to be.

Carnists excuse their transgressions because, in their view, this is approved behavior. Their insensitivity to other species they call food is revealed in variations of "Oh, I could never give up meat—I like the taste too much." Carnists look the other way in denial of the horror and environmental damage they cause. They live within artificial constructs that put one nonhuman animal in a box labeled "food" and the next animal "companion, inspiration, wildlife too intelligent to eat." Carnists get away with this illogical reasoning because it hides within majority worldview norms. This is the "kind of willed ignorance" to which Jeffrey Moussaieff Masson was referring. [246, 247]

More or Less Different? Our Sense of Other

As a species, we seem to see differences better than similarities, differences we notice because of our personal norms and worldviews. We have a history of devaluing those who are different from us, those whom we deem *other*. Ecosystems can be treated like other as well. Our wonderful capacity called empathy enables us to feel what another being is or may be experiencing. This is not an ability unique to humans. This was demonstrated recently in rats who freed other rats in distress,

> ... even if there wasn't the payoff of a reunion with it. The successful release of the caged rat [by the other rat] led to what strongly

resembled a triumphal celebration between the two. ... if given access to a small hoard of chocolate chips, the free rat would usually save at least one treat for the captive ...[248]

Empathy can bridge the gulf between us and other species. Feeling empathy inspires the Golden Rule and similar societal guidelines of "Do unto others as you would have them do unto you." Applying the Golden Rule to all species, ecosystems, and the Earth is new to us. Love, a universal companion to our empathy, is essential to the new human ecology. In fact, it is one of the Seven Results.

It is his empathy and love, I believe, that created Norm Phelps' observation in his book *The Longest Struggle/Animal Advocacy from Pythagoras to PETA*:

Work is not a biological imperative of herbivorous animals; it is alien to their nature. They graze; they do not labor. When they are forced to work, it does violence to everything that they are. To break an animal to the yoke, the harness, or the saddle is to crush the animal's innermost self. What is broken is the animal's soul. It is true that most arrive as some sort of accommodation with their servitude, just as most human slaves reach an accommodation with theirs—it is a way of maintaining one's sanity—but they are broken nonetheless, and their lives—like the lives of all slaves—are drenched in the pain of living contrary to their nature.[249]

We have limited our empathy for them and deny that they experience lives much as we do. To make it easier, we stereotype entire species. It is the same dehumanizing, categorical stereotyping that feeds racism, religious hatred, disdain for "lower" economic, educational, and social classes, and genocide. That dehumanization of "other" still lurks in the social, economic, and gender caste systems of the world, including the arrogance of men demanding control of women. Given the horrific things humans do to each other because of how we prioritize our differences, it is no wonder that we accentuate our dissimilarity with other species. Despite that, "Vegetarian communities may have existed as long as 8,000 years ago ..." according to the editors of *The Animal Ethics*

Reader.[250] After all that time, vegetarian and vegan movements are still overwhelmed by carnism.

Toxic waste, air and water pollution, slaughterhouses, abuse of companion animals, spousal abuse, hunting for sport, leghold trapping, political persecution, denial of human and species rights, putting whales, dolphins, and elephants in aquaria and zoos, clear-cutting forests, and my favorite, the possession of and willingness to use nuclear weapons capable of incinerating everything, are all sponsored by the devaluing of *other*. Abuse of power, disrespectful power, runs through it all. These are places where we have killed empathy.

World Wildlife Fund reports that Riau Province, in Indonesia, "has lost 65 percent of its forests over the last 25 years ... In the same period there was an 84 percent decline in elephant populations, down to only 210 individuals, while tiger populations are estimated to have declined by 70 percent to perhaps just 192 individuals."[251] More disrespectful abuse of power. No empathy.

Peat mining and clearing the Indonesian forest is killing the few remaining Sumatran tigers and denies endangered Asian elephants their habitat. The traumatized, decimated elephants are being poisoned by villagers trying to defend their crops as the elephants try to survive the loss of their ecosystems. It is just as true that in doing this, the elephants are trying to defend themselves from the flood of villagers colonizing their homes. Humanity is becoming barely more than a criminal enterprise against nature. There is enough evidence.

Despite progress in human rights and increased awareness of environmental, human, and species suffering, our norms of behavior remain deeply entrenched. Access to shelter, food, the social company of one's own kind, freedom of movement, clean water, an environment unburdened by toxins, and psychological and material contentment are quality of life attributes shared by many species. As the rights of people and individuals from other species become more inclusive, they overlap. When ecosystems suffer, so do the individuals from other species living there. For at least the sentients, torment, loss of home and habitat, fear of the unknown, lack of food and water, social separation from others of their own kind, and being pushed onto another's territory cause pain, distress, and suffering across species. Our empathy opens our minds and hearts to this. They are more like us, not less.

We can do a better job of embracing our evolutionary relatives across species. Together we face an unprecedented combination of challenges that are in the process of ending life on Earth as we would prefer it. This may be the first time in human history that the vegan new human ecology relationship with Earth is a requirement, not an option.

My Youth

As a boy, I did a number of things I would not do today. I trapped fireflies in glass jars when the Chicago summer nights were warmest, put live insects into vials of alcohol to preserve them at camp, and from fear, directed a powerful jet of water at a bumble bee after which I grew sad and disappointed at what I had done. At a Boy's Club camp I attended when I was about 10 years old, I saw a frog who was pinned to a dissecting tray, cut open, and very much alive. He was displayed under a hot light bulb in a cubbyhole office tucked under some stairs. Over him or her stood a microscope where any happy camper could see the flow of circulating blood that visibly pulsed with each equally visible heartbeat. I was told the hapless frog was *pithed*, had his brain scrambled with a needle in a way he would not feel pain, at least not after the pithing was completed. I remember this clearly, though it was 50 years ago. Since then, I have had surgical procedures where pain was blocked, but other sensations drove me up the wall.

Pain or not, I knew even at that age, that subjecting this frog to scalpel, pins, pithing, and an incessant incandescent bulb that loomed inches away from his face was a callous act. My lesson gained was how the counselor cheapened life without a whisper of empathy. I remember seeing the blood flow and the heart beat, but learned nothing about the frog, frog life, or frogs in ecosystems. I saw his parts, but not his whole. Long a standard practice in high school biology classes, this practice remains demeaning and disrespectful. Frogs, the wholeness of frogs whose health and now disappearance are sentinels of their ecosystems' condition, are now suffering massive losses in their biodiversity. Is it any wonder why we do not consider them in our human ecology?

With the urging of a different counselor at the same summer camp, I aimed a .22 caliber rifle at a white bird perched in the top of a distant tree bordering a cornfield. I squeezed the trigger. High above me, he or she had a life. Her name was Target. She had capacities to suffer and enjoy and woke to purpose every day until I ended it one afternoon. All I and the other young boys understood was that something was defined as a small burst of white feathers that flew upon the impact of my ignorance. I recall immediate remorse as we searched in vain under the stand of trees for that poor bird. As creatures suffered for my ignorance then, they suffer today at our hands in ways we may not be thinking about. There is always something new to learn about how we can reduce our callousness and harm. That never ceases.

What do we require, to what extent will we continue to demand individuals from other species be just like us before we treat them the same as we would choose to be treated, acknowledge them as being more like us than not? When will they qualify, in our worldview, for inclusion under the Golden Rule? Humans and nonhuman species experience the satisfaction or dissatisfaction, the pleasure or the pain, the comfort or discomfort, the fear or security, the ecstasy or the agony of having physical and psychological needs met, or not. As to who is sentient and who is not, we are still learning. Our awakening to the lives of other species is just beginning.

Chapter 6:

Beyond Anthropomorphism

One hundred and fifty years ago Charles Darwin published his classic book, 'On the Origin of Species.'... There and elsewhere Darwin emphasized that differences among species are differences in degree rather than kind, and his ideas about evolutionary continuity revolutionized the ways in which we think about who 'we' (humans) are and who 'they' (other animals) are ... While there are obvious species and individual differences in behavior, in and of themselves they mean little for arguments about animal protection.
— Marc Bekoff, "Individual Animals Count:
Speciesism Doesn't Work"[252]

Anthropomorphism occurs when an observer from our species falsely attributes human characteristics, motives, and meaning to the behaviors and supposed emotions of other species. Claiming that individuals from other species might, or could, experience life and states of being similar, shared, exceeding, or equal to that of humans is risky business. It can be difficult to prove. We have used that difficulty of proving what we sense in other species as if it were permission for us to do harm to them. Does anthropomorphism in fact exist? Yes. But in our biased attempts to defend our own uniqueness as a species, and to meet scientific standards of proof, we erred not on the side of caution, but chose instead to be irresponsibly careless and inhumane toward individuals from other species. Adding to this mistake, the threat of being charged with anthropomorphism was enough to make scientists pause in stating their personal beliefs and experience about what they observed in other species. Their scientific credibility was at stake.

|Many of us still wrongly believe that humans are entirely separate and distinct from the rest of the animal kingdom. Some still deny that other species possess their own emotional, sensory, social, and behavioral complexities that require fulfillment.|Out of this ignorance arose

the dark ages we have been imposing on the nonhuman animal kingdom. But there is good news. Our intentional ignorance is dissolving. We are learning about the capacities of other species to experience life in many ways both similar and the same as our own. Yet we also continue to deny them their rightful place in our human ecology.

We do fairly well when we establish moral codes of conduct between ourselves but we lag in showing the same moral concerns for ecosystems and other species. From a biocentric perspective, the innate value ascribed to all individuals from other species and ecosystems means they have innate rights to existence as a minimum and protection from harm as the norm. We are compelled by that value to include them in the rights we once reserved for individuals in our personal tribe, village, town, city, culture, and species. Deep ecology and its biocentric standards must include this value and rights without requiring sentience. This will carry us a step further toward a humane sustainability. Here, we do not have to imagine or prove anything about other species before we care about them. Concerns that anthropocentrism will be used to create false value in other species is substantially muted. Their value and rights are already accepted as fact. We can build on this foundation of value and understand that we are abusing the rights of the species in *the wild* and those we have domesticated.

As cognitive ethologist, Marc Bekoff, wrote,

Anthropomorphism is a much more complex phenomenon than we would have expected.... the seemingly natural human urge to impart human emotions to animals ... may actually reflect a very accurate way of knowing. And the knowledge that is gained, supported by much solid scientific research, is essential for making ethical decisions on behalf of animals.[253]

This is a relatively recent development. An anthropocentric denial of innate value and species rights is what I inherited from my culture. It did not support what I thought I was seeing, rightly or wrongly, in sentient species when I was young. I saw myself in them. Only in my adult years would I read books about ethology, the study of animal behavior in natural habitats, that validated what I and just about everyone else suspected about the capacities of other species. We were just too afraid to go against norms of belief.

Early Imprinting

My earliest 1950s impressions of wildlife that I remember were from television shows. Reflecting our bias and lack of knowledge, we chose to assume that other species were one-dimensional *its*. Their lives consisted of the machine-like need to either kill or avoid being killed. It was all about *the law of the jungle*. Narrators with authoritative voices confidently described species long before today's more science-based wildlife documentaries. *Play* in other animals was a behavior that developed motor skills, established hierarchy, and prepared them for the coming brutal game of survival. There was lots of lurking, hiding, and desperation. They were relatively simple *animals*, not all that complex compared to humans. So I learned.

Though some of what was described was true, they left a lot of things out. They did not have emotional lives, species rights, and they did not suffer. Staged conflicts between members of the wildlife community produced violent drama for a TV audience and reinforced our beliefs about the base nature of other species. When savagery was not the theme, a countering view of other species was just as unbalanced, often along the lines of Walt Disney's Bambi.

In my early twenties, I got the first validation for what I saw wherever I looked. It came from Konrad Lorenz who went on to share the Nobel Prize with fellow ethologists Nikolaas Tinbergen and Karl von Frisch. They revolutionized the field of ethology by living with and observing individuals from other species in their more complex social and natural environments. Prior to Lorenz' era, ethology was often conducted by studying individuals from other species in barren captivity. Our understanding has come a long way.

Ethologist Jonathan Balcombe tells us in his book *Pleasurable Kingdom* that

There is now empirical evidence for a range of behaviors consistent with consciousness in animals from octopuses to orangutans, including concept formation, anticipation, audience effects— changing one's behavior depending on who's watching—deception, problem-solving, insight, having beliefs, and a sense of fairness.... they communicate requests, answer questions and express emotions.[254]

They also experience functionslust. The term *funktionslust* comes from the German language and refers to feeling great about doing what one does best. We observe it all the time in other species: A dog runs freely on a hard-sand beach, a bird flies gracefully on the wind, a fox nurtures her kits, lionesses run down their prey. Funktionslust is observable across species. We experience it when we run, play, see the effects of our communication, and the good feeling we have when we succeed in our efforts. But think of the frustration we feel when, no matter how hard we try, our efforts fail, or when we feel helpless, hopeless, and powerless to satisfy what our deepest drives and desires tell us to do. If we are locked in solitary confinement, we are denied functionslust. If we are crammed into a room full of strangers, given the same bland meal day after day, are restrained from moving freely, and not allowed to hear music, read a book, or converse with family, we are denied functionslust. When we are chronically deprived of our functionslust, life is not worth living. We become dispirited, depressed, lethargic, and eventually ill. It is perhaps the worst state of being that we and other species can feel.

Like sentience, we do not know where functionslust begins or ends. If it is anything like the ability to experience pain and fear, functionslust may exist in other species where we do not expect to find it. As reported on MSNBC's Discovery Channel, scientists are changing their beliefs about lobsters and crabs: "... crustaceans feel pain and stress ... The findings add to a growing body of evidence that virtually all animals, including fish, shellfish and insects, can suffer."[255] The newest information also tells us that individuals from other species, including fish, show all the signs of feeling pain and appear to demonstrate *fear of pain* as well.[256]

As the European Food Safety Authority has written,

"There is scientific evidence to support the assumption that some fish species have brain structures potentially capable of experiencing pain and fear.... there is some evidence for the neural components of sentience in some species of fish."[257]

Environmentalists do not talk much about suffering in wildlife communities. They should. There is no basis for artificially dividing wild from domestic sentience. In the wild, in the laboratory, in captivity, and when they are domestic companion animals, we must remember that individuals from other species are capable of complex physical and emotional capacities. Behind their eyes we find beings. What would they love doing, but cannot because of the way we treat them? What do they experience as their ecosystems collapse around them?

Flowing Empathy

When we live consciously aware of the lives of other species as consistently as we can, we have access to our empathy for them. When we see or think about them, we remember that they have individual lives that they experience in exquisite detail, moment by moment, through their endowed senses, physiology, and unique capacities to feel. When we do this by habit and without constant effort to remember, our empathy flows for them. They groan, they dance, they socialize, they mate, they sing, they court; they act, react, and make choices. They feel, have needs, and influence the lives of others, including us.

Like us, every one of them is unique. We share with them abilities and experiences in common, this is all we need to know to grow up and *grow out* of our abusive behaviors toward them. Here is a partial accounting of states of being I have seen in Orion, Serengeti, Ophelia, and Moo (he meows with his mouth closed), four domestic companion cats with whom I have had the pleasure of living over the years.

- Satisfaction
- Dissatisfaction
- A good day
- A bad day

- Hunger
- Fullness of food
- Sleepiness
- Patient
- Impatient
- Tired
- Wired
- Playful
- Lethargic
- Disappointed
- Exhausted
- Contented
- Mournful
- Frustrated
- Communicating want for a specific thing in varying degrees of emphasis (wanting it a lot or a little)
- Curious
- Attentive
- Not attentive
- Annoyed
- Angry
- Happy
- Feeling the need to yawn
- Sighing
- Hot
- Cold
- Itchy
- Fearful
- Confident
- Passive
- Aggressive
- Possessive
- Waking up groggy
- Startled
- Sneezing
- Gotta mate (ASAP)

- Coughing
- Puking
- Graceful
- Ungraceful and slipping off the edge
- Embarrassed
- Greets
- Investigates
- Looks/sees
- Smells
- Hears
- Feels/touches
- Constipated
- Gotta pee
- Feels pain
- Feels pleasure
- Feels a wound
- Good mood
- Bad mood
- Nervous
- Unsure
- Conflicted
- Jealous
- Friendly
- Not friendly
- Trusting
- Distrusting
- Confused
- Gotta move
- Anxious
- Just being
- Missing someone
- Lonely and socially unfulfilled
- Taking a victory lap around the house after every poop
- Unprepared for the 60-miles-per-hour bright headlights
- Touching and being touched
- Really does not like the plastic veterinary cone wrapped around

his head and the amplification of sound it pushes into his sensitive ears

Philosopher Tom Regan wrote something of his perception of how sentient species experience life: "Some nonhuman animals resemble normal humans in that, like us, they bring the mystery of a unified psychological presence to the world. Like us, they possess a variety of sensory, cognitive, and volitional capacities.... as is true in our case, what happens to them maters to them."[258]

Paying Attention and Knowing Empathy

Grazing livestock control the bottomlands where deer and elk once foraged. In those valleys, we build our homes and lay our roads along their rivers. We restrict wildlife's movements by fragmenting their habitat, deny them food by reducing or eliminating their prey, deny them access to water with our high-speed highways, and control their social relationships by shooting family members of elephants, coyotes, wolves, and prairie dogs. We stress them, destroy the resources they need to live well, and cause their extinctions. They feel this. We now understand that hunting and other harms to wildlife causes documented cases of post-traumatic stress disorder (PTSD). That PTSD exists in farmed animals should trouble all omnivores deeply. While organizations like The Kerulos Center are working to raise our awareness about this trauma,[259] why did it take so long for us to even consider it?

Cats half-asleep who walk into the kitchen appearing disappointed that this did not produce a snack; cats wanting to go out and wanting to come in; cats translating the countless messages revealed by sniffing the wind and tasting the air; cats scratching the telephone pole high up to signal their presence; cats being diabetic and feeling starved of life itself when there's not enough insulin flowing through their bodies; cats killing wildlife we are responsible for protecting; Orion the cat being hungry but not able to eat because cancer has made his tongue unable to initiate swallowing; Orion not seeming to understand why I, his human male mother, no longer feeds him well enough to stop his hunger; cats who "bark" at me in displeasure when I wait too long to make their beds or feed them; cats who take me away from writing here, then lead me to a sunny spot, roll over and invite me to rub their furred bellies; cats comfortable and secure, purring in contentment on the bed, snuggled next to warm possibilities of a good day; domestic cats. Bobcats. Lions. Panthers. Cheetahs. Tigers. Cougars. I would never support their domestication or the hunting that weighs so heavily upon them, but I have heard a mountain lion purr, and my domestic companions remind me of that experience.

How many of the millions of cat owner–guardians neglect seeing any sort of complexity in individual animals of other species even when they see it in their feline companions? How many of them pay someone every day to confine chickens, goats, camels, pigs, buffalo, ducks, cattle, sheep, and turtles in unnatural and socially and behaviorally impoverished environments? They suffer. Then come the killing teams and butchers hired by the cat owner–guardians who not long after eat these individuals who are as sentient as cats.

Billions of individuals from other species with complex lives and sentience are betrayed every year, dismissed as food by guardians of companion dogs, cats, rabbits, rats, and birds. They are disposable food but the others are members of the family. For instance, the Audubon Society is selectively concerned about birds. While working diligently to protect songbirds and their habitat, the society encourages the slaughter of chickens, turkeys, ducks, and geese. At Audubon's Aullwood Audubon Center and Farm in Dayton, Ohio, they raise and sell what they claim to be sustainably raised organic meat. Audubon teaches 60 thousand impressionable children every year on this farm that meat is good, and that raising animals for slaughter is a humane enterprise. Or as they advertise, "That means Aullwood will continue teaching children delicious life lessons through humanely raised fare."[260] We can imagine how many issues they never discuss—the chickens, turkeys, lambs, pigs, rabbits, and cattle they kill and the fact that such boutique farms falsely represent the global scale of meat production. They import their chicken chicks and turkey chicks called poults, and they kill the egg-laying hens when their productivity declines. A few pages before the Aullwood Audubon Center and Farm article in *Audubon Magazine* is a full-page ad for Organic Valley milk.

As I sit at my desk, I take a moment to be conscious of my surroundings. My experience at the moment is defined by what I see, hear, and feel physically and psychologically. My senses are, in the most important but not all ways, much like those of goats, cows, horses, chickens, and pigs we abuse as food. Together, we experience in vivid detail our lives: I, feeling secure at my desk, a white-tailed deer started by gunshot, and a cow in the abattoir with the smell of fear and blood everywhere.[261]

In our personal relationships with individuals from other species, we see how they, like us, respond to love and affection, as well as being denied it. Do you think your companion animal of another species would be the same being if he or she were bonded to a different person, perhaps one less affectionate? I have witnessed individuals from other species emotionally healed, restored, and completed by a constant flow of comforting, unconditional love, nurturing, and attention. Trans-species psychology is an emerging field that will soon tell us even more. It is easy to love another person when he or she loves us in return, but love has the greatest value when it is given to those who seem impossible to love. They need it the most. This applies to cranky people as well as other species.

In Hawaii, dive leader Jennifer Anderson cut away fishing lines that sliced deep into a manta ray. After being freed, the ray swam off, but then returned. "She approached me and stopped, her wing just touching my head. I looked into her round, dark eye, and she looked deeply into mine... Then, as silently as she came back, she lifted her wing over my head and was gone."[262] People around the world followed the accounts of Alex, a gray African parrot. Researcher Irene Pepperberg studied and reported his abilities for 30 years. Alex used 50 labels to describe, choose, and request what he wanted. He was able to modify learned labels into words that, apparently unknown to him, represented actual things. When Alex played with *gray* he inadvertently came up with the word *grain*. Alex was then provided with an actual grain, and it became part of his vocabulary. When other gray parrots did not do well in these skills, Alex would tell them, "Say better; pay attention; bad parrot."[263]

At the Intersection of Our Empathy and the World

Look at a bird fly. Try to sense what she is experiencing. The wind presses on her wings. What does that feel like during flight? What sounds rise from the land and sea below at that height? What is it like to fly at night? Imagine what a sudden fall and rise of flight feels like as gravity pulls on blood and body, then, at the point of arc at the top before dropping downward, what the lightness of weightlessness feels like. Anyone who has flown in an airplane has some idea of what she experiences. To that, we add what we have learned from research about their vision and hearing abilities. If, throughout the day and night, we make an honest effort to sense the wonder of other species' experiences, we will feel a flowing empathy and consistent mindfulness of *other*. It is a meditation on being in awe.

We can apply that same mindfulness to people. Reflect on their lives. Perhaps they live in remote tropical regions; imagine hearing heavy drops of rain falling on the corrugated tin roofs of their homes and on the broad, green leaves in the forest that surrounds them. We can sense a bit of their experience. Those sounds and smells marinate my memories. I have witnessed and remember the people who pedaled bicycles long distances to buy, barter, or stare at food they cannot grow or afford. Consider how they hope the lives of their children will be better, that they will not get sick from the water they drink. We may not see each other, but our lives, experiences, and fates are intertwined just the same. Think of the poor who do not have freedom of choice, comfort, and food security. They can be as homeless and full of anxiety and fear as individuals from other species fleeing the destruction of their rainforest, the plowing of their prairies, and the building of our homes and communities in theirs.

Imagine a polar bear and her cubs walking in silence save for the squeak of snow with every footfall; you can hear their breathing in the still Arctic air. Remember the monkeys, rats, mice, dogs, rabbits, and cats powerless in metal, barren cages. They are subjected to experimental procedures in labs where researchers seek treatments for diseases that we often create with our own gluttonous lifestyles. Remember that there are wild, other-world sounding symphonies of underwater sound made by ribbon, harp, spotted, bearded, and hooded seals, sounds muffled under the surface of the Arctic Ocean by ice.[264] Their world is as real as ours. Some are candidates for protection under the U.S. Endangered Species Act. We are melting their ice and by that, their lives.

Plastic Out/Plastic In

Marine birds live in a sea of ocean-borne plastics. One notorious area is the *garbage patch* of the Pacific gyre. Depending upon the study cited, these areas of concentrated plastic garbage are extensive, larger than Texas, or much smaller. In all cases, the water contains masses of plastic in pieces from large to miniscule. They are trapped in an ocean eddy, a monument to our lack of ecological sensibilities. Thinking it is food, seabirds mistakenly eat the floating plastic. Oceanic Society marine biologist Wayne Sentman tells us, "Between birds dying due to plastic or regurgitating it to their chicks, some five tons of the stuff are deposited on Midway [Island northwest of Hawaii] each year." He routinely found dead birds whose "stomachs were filled with bulbs, flashlights, small toys and syringes—complete with needles."[265] That plastic is deteriorating into particles so small that they are ingested and passed up the food chain. If that were not bad enough, the debris also entangles life unto death, and releases toxic chemicals.

Jose Derraik, in reviewing the scientific literature about plastic tossed into the ocean, found that it affects more than 267 species, including turtles, sea birds, fish, and marine mammals. It causes internal injury and poisoning from the tropics to Antarctica. The chicks of Laysan albatrosses in the Hawaiian Islands accumulate the plastic in their stomachs. It is a "significant source of mortality, as 90 percent of the chicks surveyed had some sort of plastic debris in their upper GI tract."[266] *The Vancouver Sun* reported on the findings of researchers in the Arctic: "Fulmars are strong flyers that skim the surface swallowing tasty tidbits, and 84 percent of the ones the researchers examined from two Arctic colonies had plastics in their guts."[267] Using your flowing empathy, what do you think these birds are experiencing?

Crossing Dexter Avenue

Near my home in Seattle, I caught a glimpse of a feral mother cat carrying a kitten by the scruff of her neck. She was heading toward busy Dexter Avenue. The road is wide and consists of a traffic lane in both directions, two lanes that are used for parking, and two for bicycles. Mother cat and her kitten are approaching four lanes of car habitat. My first reaction was to "help" mother cat, but I saw my approach caused her to look over her shoulder, which created a distraction that could get her run over. I sat down on the curb to anxiously watch her, unable to stop traffic because of her reactions to me making a commotion. Perhaps by accident if not curiosity, I stooped low until my head was nearer to the level of her eyes. My world was transformed in an instant.

The street seen at her level became a terrifying, barren expanse of asphalt. Everything on this vast plain moved faster than I could anticipate or run from were I to see and move like a cat. Cars became unpredictable and oblivious predators. At about a foot above the unforgiving pavement, I could not see very far ahead, to the left or right. My horizon was so low that cars appeared out of my near horizon without warning. There was very little time to react to the rolling tons of metal and power on wheels. It was overwhelming. Tires howled, and hissed a white noise; engines whined, rumbled, and roared. The noise from the cars and occasional busses and trucks was loud. It seemed to come from every direction.

Mother cat stopped on top of the curb that defined the frontier of Dexter Avenue. Until she reached the other side, this was wide-open space without cover and thick with traffic going 30 to 35 miles per hour. Occasionally, cars would emerge from three smaller side streets, adding to the sensory overload. I watched as she waited at the curb. She appeared anxious with uncertainty, moved hesitantly, partially crossed the avenue with her kitten still held firmly in her mouth, then turned back with a great deal of fidgeting and seeming nervousness born of conflict. We know what risk feels like and the difficulty of overcoming our fear of danger. She did this several times and finally succeeded. One by one, she moved her kittens from under the bushes on one side of the road to the shelter of more bushes on the other side.

With all of my experience as a human, knowing what I know about traffic, the use and behavior of cars, and the drivers behind the wheel, with all of that, if I were a human 10 inches tall, it's unlikely I could cross Dexter Avenue many times before being run over and killed. Yet, our roads are everywhere. They are, save for the humans cocooned in steel on wheels, sterile. For every nonhuman being landing on or trying to cross our roads, there is a high risk of death. Roads also provide access for us to wildlife habitat where some of us kill with guns, bows, traps, and poisons, while others develop it for human occupation and resource extraction. As mother cat's tense drama played out, I could empathize enough about her experience to expand and rekindle my own awareness of wildlife killed by cars, busses, trains, and trucks.

Take a moment to do the following exercise: Put down this book and go to the nearest busy street, similar to Dexter Avenue, in the daytime. Take precautions to avoid causing an accident or being run over. Then sit on the sidewalk near the curb and lower your head as far as your body will allow, to nearly the head height of dogs, cats, raccoons, possums, low-flying birds, and squirrels who sit up just before they run into traffic. Now, imagine them trying to get to the other side of the busy street. Take your time and let it sink in. That is empathy.

Next, picture yourself as an individual of another species who needs to get to the other side of a highway. At three feet you can be a bear, and at four to six feet be a white-tail or mule deer. Do not forget the rattlesnakes and otters. In your imagination only, stand on four legs beside an interstate highway. The traffic is going 65 miles per hour in one direction and in the next two lanes it goes in the opposite direction. There are caravans of trucks, more cars, view-blocking hilltops and curves, and an increase in noise hissing from the tires. Diesel truck compression brakes are blatt-blatt-blatting as they speed down the hill. At night, blinding headlights keep you from seeing the ground in front of you. There is little time to react, and more likelihood of death than life but that is not an idea in your brain; instead you feel fear, anxiety, uncertainty, and need to get to where you want. This is the experience of countless individuals from wildlife and domestic species. That experience waits for them 24 hours every day and night. Our experience is different.

When we are inside our car or truck on a street or highway, we are insulated from the struggle and fear we have created for the individual animals outside. We roar over pavement through their ecosystems. Cars, trucks, and trains are the teeth in a buzz saw through which wildlife must pass to fulfill their needs. The faster we go, the less we are able to see and feel their ecosystems. The bigger and more luxurious the car and truck, the softer the ride, the less we pay attention to the surface of the Earth. Our vehicles erase a part of our empathy.

Nearly 5 percent of all auto collisions in the United States involve wildlife.[268] According to the U.S. Department of Transportation, there are 1 to 2 million collisions between cars and individuals of large species of wildlife. The 26 thousand reported human injuries come with the loss of $8.388 billion dollars in damages. In 2003, 210 people were killed this way. Some of them would have survived had they been wearing seatbelts.[269] The number of wildlife-vehicle accidents as a percentage of all auto accidents is increasing, perhaps because we are encroaching on wildlife habitat more than ever before. There are no winners in these collisions that are spread over 3.9 million miles of U.S. roads and highways.[270] There are many more than 1 to 2 million of these accidents since most are not reported. In addition, this figure does not include the toll on the smaller individuals from other species who are injured or killed every year. Road mortality is a major threat to the survival of "21 federally listed threatened or endangered animal species in the United States."[271]

I dislike driving at night because of the increased likelihood that I will run over wildlife. I remember those I have killed with a car: the Jefferson ground squirrel I saw in my rearview mirror who literally did somersaults from the pain he experienced before death. There are several birds whose species I do not recall. I remember the raccoon I struck one night. He died.

Killing Whales

With empathy, pause and think about what it must be like to be a whale fleeing a whale- killing ship. Whales are made of lungs, a brain full of evolutionary experience that carried them through millennia, consciousness that enables them to create flourishing cultures, and a wonderfully adapted body. They will try to avoid ships that approach aggressively. But in whaling, when the vessel starts its deadly, relentless pursuit, whales have little chance of escape.

Every turn the whale makes, with every evasive maneuver she knows, the steel ship follows loudly in the water. She hears the engine vibrating through the hull, the propellers cavitating and slashing the sea. During every dive the whale takes to hide underwater, she depletes her muscles of oxygen and strength. She tires but fear drives her to keep trying. She tires but the ship does not. The whale-killing vessel is fueled with reserves of diesel, has the entire atmosphere for its metal lungs, and the technology to make the pursuit endless. The vessel does not know exhaustion, and the vessel does not know feeling. It is eternally uncaring, like the men who operate the factory of winches, compressors, knives, and generators.

This whale has nothing in her species' knowledge, or in her personal experience, to shake this terrible, relentless metal predator. The unknown, the mystery of this noisy, ominous, mechanical threat that keeps bearing down fills her with increasing fear. She cannot escape ... Wherever she surfaces for a desperate breath, there it is again, the ship without mercy or empathy, ready to kill for carnism.

She is unprepared for what comes next. A harpoon is fired from a cannon on the ship's bow and speeds toward her as a missile. The harpoon rips through her skin, breaks her bones, punctures her organs, and rips apart her muscles while nearly instantaneously the penthrite grenade on its tip explodes within her and along the pathway of the harpoon's ravaging entry. So beautiful and so large, she cannot die quickly. Sometimes another missile is fired into her. Whale, after whale, after whale is hauled from the ocean, reflecting the carnist's inability to discern balance between taking and need. The cannons of war fire into family members of her pod, propelling the explosive packages into their quivering, pain-twisted bodies. The detonations inside of them replace mammal warmth with violent fire; each whale is shred from within, not unlike putting your hand into a whirling blender.

Scientists Phil Clapham and Yulia Ivashchenko tally the toll in "A Whale of a Deception":

> During the 20th century, the other whaling nations together killed more than two million whales in the Southern Hemisphere alone. More than half of this total was made up of catches of the two largest species: 350,000 blue whales and a staggering three quarters of a million fin whales were slaughtered for meat, oil, margarine, pharmaceuticals, and a host of other commercial products. So were 160,000 humpbacks, 380,000 sperm whales, 180,000 sei whales, and around 160,000 others. Add to this the innumerable whales killed in the Northern Hemisphere and you have a slaughter which, in terms of sheer biomass, is greater than anything in the history of human hunting.[272]

Other whales face an even more agonizing fate because some whale hunters, including aboriginal people, use guns and handheld harpoons instead of the more powerful cannons. Unlike the commercial whalers who seek the largest whales to produce the most money, aboriginal whalers often target the smaller juveniles who are two or three years old because they are more likely to be naïve about hunter-humans and less likely to respond with adult strength to being attacked.

After an 80-year lapse of whaling, the Makah tribe in Neah Bay, Washington State, insisted on killing gray whales with handheld harpoons and an anti-tank weapon. It was on May 5, 1995, that the Makah Tribal Chair, Hubert Markishtum, wrote to the U.S. government asking it to represent them and argue their case before the International Whaling Commission (IWC). Except for aboriginal whaling in Russia, gray whales had been protected internationally since 1947. The young, two-year-old female gray whale who the Makah harpooned and shot in 1999 took about eight minutes to die. The National Marine Fisheries Service monitoring this hunt was satisfied that it was a good killing, even with her painful, fearful death.

In 2007, several Makah illegally attempted to kill another whale. This gray whale took over nine hours to find relief in death before sinking into the depths of the Strait of Juan de Fuca on the U.S.–Canadian border. After wounding "CRC-175"—as researchers referred to this whale—with several harpoons, the Makah shot him (sex was not determined) at least 16 times with rifles before being stopped by the Coast Guard. A slow federal bureaucracy contributed to the prolonged suffering, and prevented euthanasia and relief for her bullet-riddled body. Though tribal officials denied sanctioning the killing, these thugs had gone to several top official tribal members to get the needed whaling gear beforehand. After months of saying there would be tribal justice, Makah tribal officials instead defended the accused who were later sentenced in federal court, two to short prison terms.[273]

CRC-175 was well known to researchers, with 143 sightings logged between 1995 and 2007. For seven years, CRC-175 was seen near Neah Bay, living, presumably, peacefully as his ancestors had.[274] The eastern North Pacific gray whales are unsuspecting since they have not been commercially hunted off the West Coast of the United States since 1936 when they were protected in territorial waters. The main population of this species migrates to the Bering and Chukchi Seas as well as other locations in the far North Pacific. While in the northern part of their range, some unfortunate gray whales are shot dozens to over a hundred times by economically distressed aboriginals using rifles. They live on the Chukotka Peninsula of Siberia. The 2011 season averaged 90 cartridges per kill.[275] However, CRC-175 was a member of a genetically distinct population of approximately 200 gray whales.

This population generally does not migrate north of Vancouver Island, Canada; instead they remain along the West Coast of North America where all they know is friendly humans. They know us from our whale watching, our recreational boating, and as whale-loving tourists at their Mexican calving lagoons. Gray whale mothers bring their calves up to tourist boats and allow—some believe encourage—touching between our two species. They are easily approached if done correctly, but their trust and open behavior is betrayed by Makah hunters who assert that killing gray whales is a courageous expression of masculinity, culture, and pride.

Many NGOs steered clear of the Makah kills because of the tricky issues of tribal sovereignty, cultural traditions, and the multitude of historic wrongs visited upon indigenous peoples in general. Despite the severe impacts the Makah actions have had on weakening the U.S. delegation and their whale protection efforts at the IWC, only a subset of organizations who described themselves as environmentalist whale-protectors risk the downsides of being called anti-tribal or even worse, racists. Since the Makah could not demonstrate a subsistence dependency on whale flesh as required by the IWC, they relied on their argument of a right to cultural whaling. That is the same strategy that Japan and other industrial pro-whaling cultures have used.

In the Makah campaign, I worked with anti-whaling tribal elders. Tribal elders belong to families who compete for political control of the tribe; they were split on the issue. The Makah pro-whaling faction reminded everyone that their culture is alive, and not in a museum. The gulf of understanding we cannot seem to bridge with the tribe's pro-whalers is that their external world, like mine and yours, has changed. Carnist human ecology everywhere is no longer adaptive to the ecosystems we have altered. I expect them to discount this idea. In its stead, they rely on their ancestral history of past relationships with ecosystems despite that fact they no longer exist. The Makah have wounded it as have I. Our relationships to the physical and biological Earth have changed.

I have logged a few hundred hours' kayak time in the presence of gray whales, mostly within their calving lagoons. For weeks on end, I drifted in the currents near Puerto Lopes Mateos, upper Magdalena Bay, in Baja, Mexico. There were special moments when they would swim within six feet of my kayak, roll to one side, and look up at me while folding their large pectoral fins to avoid hitting my kayak. On one occasion, near the entrance to the calving lagoon at Boca de Soledad, a gray whale surfaced under me.

My kayak and I were lifted smoothly a few inches above the water. I held my breath. Just as the whale was submerging slowly, and as my kayak settled back into the sea, I stuck my paddle into the water, too soon. I was propelled like a bolt of lightning into the air and at the same time ejected from my airborne kayak. I hit the water and was pulled under by the turbulence of 10- to 12-foot flukes propelling a presumably startled whale. My eyes were open to see the champagne-like bubbles all around me and a perfect blue glow of sunlight flowing through water, but there were no other traces of him or her. If gray whales were aggressive and dangerous by nature, I would not be here.

Commercial whalers entered gray whale calving lagoons in the 1800s. In this nursery, the calves were the first to be struck with harpoons. Whalers knew the mothers would come to protect their calves. That is when they killed her as well. Gray whales who fought back were given the name *devilfish* by the very devils who perpetrated their slaughter.

Efforts to reestablish or continue cultural traditions include the worst examples of wanton cruelty: Fishers in Newfoundland and other spots in Maritime Canada club young harp seals as a tradition and for off-season income; in Denmark's Faeroe Islands, the westerners bludgeon, stab, and slash pilot whales; and at Taiji, Japan, the fishers bludgeon, stab, and slash dolphins. Stay away from St. Vincent and the Grenadines, where recent history includes their wounding humpback whale calves to draw in the defending mothers. Inupiat aboriginal peoples in the U.S. Arctic use harpoons and shoulder guns that fire explosive projectiles to kill endangered bowhead whales. They have been unwilling in some years to stop their hunt even when they know sea ice conditions will make recovery of the dead or wounded whales difficult if not impossible.

Empathy and yes, love, are essential to our human ecology. If we are to keep flowing empathy alive within ourselves, we have to be open to the experiences of other beings as best we can, and err on the side of caution. The way we use language can help. In continuing a tradition started by others, we must call individuals from other species who have identifiable sexes *he* or *she*, not *it*. They are not rocks we kick down the hill. Calling them "it" diminishes our empathy.

The new human ecology creates a more objectively sustainable, consistent, and humane relationship with Earth. It is inconceivable that we do not yet practice a universal standard of compassion for ecosystems, humans, and nonhuman species alike. There is more to understand about why we must turn away from the old and embrace the new human ecology. We must look at how our ecological niche has changed and why we seem unable to understand how that change happened.

Part II:

We are Neo-Predators

Chapter 7:

Meet Mega Predator

Sylvia Earle: In my lifetime, ninety percent of the big fish have been extracted from the sea. That means the tunas, swordfish, the sharks, the halibut, the cod, the things we like to eat, and a lot of other things as well. At the same time, we've been putting just millions of tons of things into the sea that are altering the nature of nature.

Steven Colbert: I don't have to stop eating fish, do I?

Sylvia Earle: Well, I have.

Steven Colbert: You've stopped eating fish?

Sylvia Earle: I have.[276]

Earle is a celebrated oceanographer, served as the chief scientist at the U.S. National Oceanic and Atmospheric Administration (NOAA), and recipient of more than 100 national and international honors.

Mega Predator + Presence Predator + Economic Predator =Neo-Predation

In chapter 1, I described the three new and important developments in our predatory behavior. They are mega, presence, and economic predation. Bundled together, we can refer to them as our neo-predation. In the next three chapters, I will describe what they are and how they produce a predation against the Earth that is far different than our past models of hunter, fisher, and animal agriculture. I will start with mega predation.

There are two things that make us mega predators: The first is our relentless increase in human population; the second is our rising per capita level of consumption. Our per capita level of consumption has the added characteristic of being morally indefensible because it is inequitably distributed. When we multiply this rising net consumption by our human population explosion we get mega neo-predation. Never before have we affected Earth so much with so many people.

Diverse populations of early humans were direct subsistence hunters, fishers, and gatherers who had to follow their food sources. Only more recently did humans become engaged in agriculture and pastoralism some 10,000 years ago. There were perhaps 5 million people on Earth then.[277] The domestication of sheep, camels, cattle, goats, horses, dogs, cats, and pigs varied by time and location. This was a revolutionary step in human adaptation that allowed food to be produced consistently enough for people to stay in one place, where the food was grown, not followed, gathered, and hunted by season. We continued to threaten the viability of species through hunting, but we also began destroying wildlife habitat permanently wherever we created croplands and raised domesticated species.

Eventually villages and towns grew. With this stability, skills specialization, social organization, and accumulation of knowledge and wealth were enhanced. Our technologies and knowledge advanced. We created tools capable of extracting even more resources from ecosystems. Our population centers grew even more. Social, political, technical, and economic complexity increased, as did our skills in harnessing energy. If our population size and not sustainability was the only measure of the choices our ancestors made, then our 7 billion fellow humans prove that this was a great evolution for our species. Of course, there is more to the measure of success than that, including the fact we know the majority of people continue, 10,000 years later, to be deprived of a decent share of resources while a minority floats in excess.

The environmental costs of our hard-won success are evident: the ruined streams; forests lost; countless extinctions of species; bleached, dead coral reefs; mangrove forests destroyed for firewood and shrimp farms; erosion and loss of soil fertility; encroaching deserts; the salinization of fresh groundwater; and the poisoning of marine mammals with PBDEs (fire retardants), PCBs (insulating properties for electrical transmission and other applications), and PAHs (component of petroleum byproducts). Palm oil is now the most consumed vegetable oil in the world. That makes it our mega vegetable oil that is responsible for the mega destruction of ecosystems and species. That is our mega neo-predatorship at work. Given its ubiquitous presence in processed foods, we pay for the destruction of those forests and eat those orangutans out of their homes several times a day.

During my quest to reach a remote orangutan rescue center in Kalimantan (aka Borneo) several years ago, I tired from fighting a losing struggle with the Sekonyer River's current. While paddling a dugout canoe upstream, I accepted a ride from a small boat towing a raft of rainforest logs. I was blessed being in this beautiful, wild place, but I fell short of my destination as heavy rain and darkness fell. The first visible piece of dry land I had seen for some time came into view. I paddled toward it and found university students from Jakarta doing field research. They graciously offered me a place on the floor, where they slept, for the night. I paddled the remaining distance to the rescue and rehabilitation center the next day. It was founded by Dr. Birute Galdikas. It was there that the dedicated Indonesian staff worked to rehabilitate young, orphaned orangutans. As a sad irony, while billions of dollars of palm oil wealth were being extracted from the orangutans' forested home, the center struggled for resources. Getting the orphans fresh food and drugs to combat parasites and disease was sometimes impossible. Days later, I arrived a second time by chartered boat. It was not long after that it was needed to transport a young orangutan to take him to a clinic hours away. The infant died and then lay ashen and lifeless on my brightly painted boat. The natural order and value of those orangutans in their forest home was crushed by the economic order that values palm oil more.

Carnist Vampires

Carnism is only part of our mega neo- predation. Our ancestors' behaviors were like hoeing a garden plot compared to what we do now: We bulldoze entire ecosystems, build on top of the meadow, clear-cut the forest, and pollute the planet with uniquely human creations of toxins. Every human generation adds to these cumulative burdens on the biosphere. Much of what we do affects not only our immediate environments, but also those far from our homes.

We are linked to global economic systems that affect distant ecosystems and people. What I do in Miami, Florida, or Jakarta,

Indonesia, impacts the ecosystem where the resources were extracted to create my purchase and support my lifestyle. I do not have to live in those ecosystems to impact them; I just have to consume their exports. If the subsistence-farming people in Foria, Sierra Leone, are using imported nitrogen fertilizer while turning tropical forest wetlands into rice patties to survive, they alter both their ecosystem and the chain of supply connected to that fertilizer. No matter where we are, who we are, rich or poor, each product we consume has a unique genealogy of ecosystem impact. It starts before resource extraction—building the power and transportation infrastructure, for instance—and continues on through human labor that grows, mines, refines, manufactures, assembles, packages, and ships everything we buy and sell.

The cotton clothing I wear requires land, highways, trucks, fossil fuels, chemicals, machines, and human labor. The labor in my shirt is powered by energy and resource-intensive food that was planted, tended, and harvested. My shirt required refining the cotton, weaving the material for the shirt, making the shirt, packaging, and transporting that shirt to a store. When I bought the shirt, I paid for every one of those things to happen. However, I was not held accountable in the purchase of the shirt for my impacts on ecosystems, other species, and other people. The fact that some of my shirts are made of organic cotton under fair labor practices helps but it is not enough. The best practices possible in the making of my shirt are not sustainable when 7 billion people need shirts. We would still be mega-scale monsters, predators of ecosystems and people. Only a reduction in our populations will change that.

At any given moment, I own enough clothing to create a meaningful social and environmental impact, and I do not own a lot. This, our mega neo-predation, is unsustainable in itself, without insisting we hold on to our current human ecology identities as hunters, fishers, and animal agriculturalists.

We have entered the forests and scraped the land clear for the roads that will take away their natural order of wealth. The Kermode, polar, sun, giant panda, grizzly, spectacled, Blue Himalayan, Argentine short-faced, Gobi, Syrian Brown, and other bears have lost their habitats around the world to our mega neo-predation. At the same time, most of them struggle to escape our guns and poachers' snares. Logging roads in their forest homes bleed trees out and draw in human settlement. We are destroying the habitats of endangered Asian elephants, hippopotamus, and pythons. Humans live and work there now.

With less than 5 percent of their Brazilian forest habitat remaining, golden lion tamarins are endangered by cattle grazing, the making of charcoal, the tropical hardwood trade, and a growing human population. In Africa, poachers and dreadful political and tribal wars kill gorillas and people alike. A sampling of cases in revered parts of the world can give us perspective of just how mega we have become.

Killing Elephants

Maasai[278] and non-Maasai pastoralists use ecosystems in Kenya intensively. Human populations are soaring. Impoverished job-seekers set up camp near national parks. Operating in the background is a history of social and economic injustice imposed upon indigenous peoples, including the Maasai. In Kenya and surrounding countries, this results in a tragic and unsustainable human ecology.

Numbering between 500,000 and 900,000,[279] the Maasai people straddle the political borders of Kenya and Tanzania.[280] Mia MacDonald writes in *The Dilemma of Development* that, in 1999, the Maasai Mara National Reserve covered nearly 1,363 square miles. The reserve's fences, and the fences used to partition the inequitably distributed 5,000 square miles of Maasai holdings that surround the reserve severely restrict the 80,000 Maasai pastoralists and block migrating wildlife such as wildebeest. The population growth rate of the Maasai, noted MacDonald at the time, was between 6.5 and 7 percent.[281] It is in this region that the convergence of many factors has created poverty and conflict between people, ecosystems, and wildlife. Drought, poaching, livestock incursions, and human settlement are examples of the complexity of human ecologies. Human settlement alone is associated in the Mara-Serengeti ecosystem with steep declines in several large species.[282] This includes "... losses [that] were as high as 95 percent for giraffes, 80 percent for warthogs, 76 percent for hartebeest, and 67 percent for impala." There are also "... dramatic drops in the reserve of once abundant wildebeest, gazelles and zebras...."[283]

Alan Weisman, author of *The World Without Us*, has a number of things to say about the social, economic, cultural, and environmental drama that continues to unfold in and near Kenya. External forces are pressing the Maasai to settle down into an increasingly agriculturalist lifestyle. It is supposed to replace their nomadic culture that revolved around livestock. Weisman describes how cattle replaced wildebeest whose grazing once shaped the abundance of grasses and woody species favored by elephants. When elephants knocked down trees, they created openings for grasses to flourish. As cattle increasingly ate the grasses, wildebeest declined. What it would be like without the Maasai cattle? Weisman writes,

> Cattle now account for more than half the live weight of African savanna ecosystems.... Once cows were gone, there would be more than double the feed for anything else.... [zoologist David] Western ... calculates ... 'A million and a half wildebeest can take out grass just as effectively as cattle. You'd see a much tighter interaction between them and elephants.'[284]

Maintaining those cattle is increasingly difficult in the midst of competing demands from all people upon the land. When wildlife reserves and national parks were established, they pushed out Maasai who grazed their cattle there. When herders drive their cattle to watering holes and grazing areas used by elephants, close encounters can result in elephants occasionally killing cattle. This appears at times to be unintentional. When cattle are killed within Amboseli National Park, the herders are not compensated by wildlife officials. After one such incident, angry Maasai herders attacked the first elephant they met — Odile.

Habitat is being fragmented, impacted, and usurped by people of all ethnicities in all cultures. The hostility, violence, and conflict against wildlife in Kenya are no different than what wolves and cougars face in the United States. The constant factor underlying this sorrowful event and those like it everywhere else in the world is an inappropriate human ecology practiced by too many of us making too many unsustainable demands upon ecosystems.

Ultimately, it does not matter that they were Maasai spears. People in Nairobi create demands on elephant ecosystems as do the tourists who arrive to see wildlife in national parks as do those of us who are creating global warming's droughts that make for fewer and fewer watering holes. Therefore, there is a direct link to your and my spewing greenhouse gasses into the atmosphere and the spears in Odile's face. We all are squeezing the existence out of elephants. What matters is that the spears in her face represent how we are conducting ourselves as a species. And that conduct is what our unsustainable and inhumane human ecologies are all about.

The African elephant population in Kenya has fallen from 167,000 in 1973 to 32,000 as of 2009.[285] According to African Conservancy, for *all* of Africa, "5–10 million African elephants existed in 1930."[286] It appears there are fewer than 500,000 today.[287] Because of the difficulty of counting elephants and the variety of ecosystems they inhabit, counts are often in dispute, including these. Counts also can fail to represent what is happening from one region to the next. For East Africa overall, of which Kenya is part, according to the IUCN, "While there are signs of recovery in some of the most important elephant populations, the growth of human populations in the interim has been considerable. If these human growth trends continue, it is it unlikely that elephant numbers will reach the peaks of the 1970s."[288]

Morans are an age-class of young Maasai warriors. Their dress typically includes a machete, spear, and club. According to this 2012 news report, "Three villagers have been left needing medical attention after they were attacked by a pride of lions in Loitoktok…the Maasai morans are said to have mobilized to pursue a pride of lions that had killed a cow at the Elangata Ngima area of kuku group ranch—but the lions turned against them…."[289] Seldom are lions and other wildlife winners. The brutality against wildlife needs no more reason than resentment against national parks, foraging elephants, and lions. Lions are chased down and then speared and hacked to death.[290] Kurgat Marindany reported in *The Star* newspaper of Nairobi in 2012 that, "More than 10 morans were yesterday afternoon injured when they were ambushed by Kenya Wildlife Services rangers in Loitoktok. The 10

After Maasai herders led their cattle to a watering hole used by elephants inside Amboseli National Park in Kenya, a close encounter between elephants and cattle ensued. Because the elephants killed two cattle *inside* the park, the Maasai herders were not compensated for their losses. The herders then vented their anger against Odile, who happened to be the first elephant they met. Odile was saved by human intervention and bore a calf the following year. Photo credit: © Harvey Croze, Amboseli Trust for Elephants (ATE). http://elephanttrust.org/

were among morans who had killed an elephant at the Olkulului Group Ranch farm on Wednesday night. Senior warden in-charge of Amboseli National Park, Richard Cheruiyot, said the morans were arrested as they escaped. "'I can only confirm that there was a clash between the rangers and the morans who wanted to kill more elephants.'"[291]

While researchers and organizations try to keep up with rampant poaching and habitat loss, we can be thankful for forensics tools now available. Illicitly taken ivory can be traced to its geographic origins through DNA analysis.[292] Still, an underfunded protection of elephants and DNA fingerprinting of ivory from poached elephants cannot hope to stop what the current human ecology in Africa, as elsewhere, is doing to wildlife and ecosystems. Most wild elephants live in protected areas that are not large enough to allow them to return to their species' former glory as the largest land mammal on Earth.

The fate of elephants changes radically every few years in most of its range. Droughts, climate change, and poaching take their toll. The genetic stronghold of elephants has been broken into and damaged by trophy hunters who lust after souvenir elephant ears and ivory. The public purchases ivory jewelry, which encourages poaching. Elephant populations and human populations with their agricultural activities are generally incompatible.

Killing Lions

When a lion preys on their cattle, goats, or sheep, the Maasai, like other ranchers and pastoralists, kill the offender. Unlike them, the Maasai use spears.[293] They and many others kill lions with poison as well. The preferred prey of lions in Maasailand are wildebeest, but they have declined 70 percent because ranchers-pastoralists have erected fences, taken control of grazing habitat, and fragmented ecosystems. Now, cattle have become the lion's most abundant prey and the easiest to catch.[294] The doubling of the Maasai population in a decade within the lion's former stronghold of Mara Maasai, and hoards of eco-tourists who are encouraging the construction of more eco-lodges, are, again, having their impact. In search of jobs, Maasai bring their cattle to these tourist sites near protected areas. During the four decades following 1960, the overall human population throughout Africa nearly tripled, so the fences, habitat fragmentation, and loss of grazing for wildlife to domesticated animals are continent-wide threats to ecosystems.[295]

It is helpful to look at the history and trends of people and their ecosystems. "Kenyan Maasai warriors have killed 10 lions from the Nairobi national park in revenge for killing their livestock," reads a 2003 BBC news report, accurately adding that the park covers traditional Maasai lands.[296] But there also is the Maasai tradition of killing lions with spears as a rite of passage for young men. Maasai advocates of this tradition have a website that defends the spearing.[297] Drawing on the same cultural traditions, other Maasai and non-Maasai have founded the Lion Guardians. They seek ways to reduce pastoralist revenge killings and ritual killing.[298]

The complexity of the human ecology interacting with local ecosystems is complicated further by social and economic factors. In diverse communities surrounding Serengeti National Park in Tanzania, there are as many as 52,000 to 60,000 people who hunt illegally within protected areas. Approximately 5,200 young men derive their income from hunting. One study noted that three-quarters of the illegal hunters who were arrested were hunting to generate income, the others for food. Those arrested were often young and had low income or very few cattle. The more cattle a person owned the less prone they were to hunt illegally because cattle are sources of protein and a measure of wealth and status.[299]

Lion populations are falling precipitously throughout much of their range. In October of 2007, I accessed the Wildlife Conservation Society's "Saving Wildlife" page where their work in Kenya's Laikipia District was described. It is an area where private land ownership is parceled off into large ranches owned by descendants of British colonists, in addition to Maasai holdings, some of which are cooperative efforts of considerable size. Properties typically covered 5,000 to 100,000 acres. The Saving Wildlife project's efforts included innovative research hoping to identify the specifics of conflicts between lions, ranchers, and traditional pastoralists. There were several encouraging developments. Traditional pastoralists set aside areas for wildlife. Ranchers' tolerance for predation increased as they learned about the specific individual predators living on "their" properties. At the time, researchers said, "It is the only unprotected area in Kenya where wildlife populations are actually increasing."[300] That soon changed.

In October 2009, Public Radio International reported on a proposal to save lions in Kenya by having trophy hunters pay landowners the right to kill them. Andrea Crossan interviewed Dr. Lawrence Frank, the scientist who headed up the Wildlife Conservation Society's hopeful project in the Laikipia district. She reports,

> Lawrence Frank ... is working to save Kenya's remaining wild lions and other predators living outside national parks. It is an increasingly difficult job. Here in the Northern Kenyan district of Laikipia, more and more land is being converted from wildlife habitat to farms and that is bad for lions. Frank: 'When the young lions move out of their prides into the community areas there is so little wildlife there, and so much livestock, that they start taking livestock [and] they're promptly poisoned. ... We like to sit in our New York apartments or our San Francisco houses and think about all the wonderful wildlife in Africa and watch them on the Disney Channel. And yet, we wouldn't dream of tolerating grizzly bears and wolves and mountain lions where we live.'

In Laikipia, protection efforts faced varying levels of opposition. The Laikipia Wildlife Forum was established[301] and scored some success in mitigating human–wildlife conflicts. Gains were followed by losses.

Poisoned

Pastoralists poison lions by lacing dead livestock with the insecticide carbofuran (aka Furadan). They leave the toxic corpse in the wild hoping lions will be among the carnivores killed. Whether or not lions are killed, the poison continues its legacy as it spreads through the food web. Wildlife Direct, a Kenyan-based nonprofit founded by Richard Leakey, reported in 2009,

> Three more lions have been killed in just four days ... bringing the total to ten in less than eight months. ... two lions were speared ... on a Maasai group ranch adjacent to world famous Amboseli National Park.... 'Spearing appears to be the main way of killing lions in

Maasailand, but elsewhere poison is by far the most urgent threat to lions and all other carnivores and scavengers. On one small group ranch in Laikipia, 9 hyenas were poisoned in 7 months, and no lions survive on those areas.... Even vultures and scavenging eagles are now rare in most parts of Kenya,' states Berkeley, California–based based lion specialist Dr. Laurence Frank.[302]

In March, 2011, a *60 Minutes* television airing of the issue resulted in a ban on carbofuran and a buyback program by its U.S. manufacturer. Reports are mixed on the results but many agricultural poisons remain available. Lasting damage to many species is already complete.

Good and bad political decisions, scientific research, Kenyan and international conservation work, and human development agency projects have been unable to stem this warped human ecology. Maasai pastoralists, colonialist ranchers, and Kenya's fractured-to-failed social and economic justice have contributed to the complex conflicts between people and Kenyan ecosystems. The current human ecology of Kenya has undermined all of these efforts and will eventually defeat them. Biodiversity is still crashing.

With our own guilty fingers, do any of us want to blame the Maasai and other cultural groups living there? Or blame the Kenyan government that, with the urging of environmental groups, created a national park on traditional Maasai grazing land? And what about the water pipeline constructed by the government through Maasai land without sharing it with them? The economy relies on tourism but how can this be reconciled with the multiple impacts of the tourist industry?

The Maasai had coexisted with lions before European contact and when human populations were far lower.[303] The Maasai are an admired culture. That is one reason I chose to write about their struggles. Why not cite the Kikuyu, or Samburu, or colonial descendants in Kenya? Certainly, colonists brought attitudes and practices that overran indigenous cultural traditions. But there is not much value in talking about any one culture because this is about all of us. We are living unsustainably to greater and lesser degrees everywhere. There are no cultures off-limits to examination and self-reflection. Curing our various human ecologies is the responsibility of the people practicing them. To move forward, we must first acknowledge that we have been living unsustainably across the span of cultures for a long time.

The organization Lion Alert reminds everyone, "In Africa, the last wild Cape lion of South Africa was shot in 1865; the last Barbary lion of Northern Africa was shot in 1922."[304] Once widespread, there were more than a million African lions before the colonialist powers invaded. There are now an estimated "39,000 lions in Africa, with a range of 29,000–47,000" and decreasing.[305] Research indicates that there are several genetically distinct lion gene pools within those 39,000 that represent millennia of evolution.[306] This creates an even greater urgency to save those unique populations under the greatest threat of extinction, a threat that comes from every one of us.

Because we are current human ecology carnists *and* mega neo-predators, there are about 2,000 lions left in Kenya, so far. Kenya has been losing 100 lions for each of the past seven years.[307] Lions are extinct in 26 countries.[308] Despite some success in local communities where attitudes improve if wildlife brings income, it is easier to kill a lion than change government and social policy or attract enough investment to support lion survival.

Lawrence Frank pushes for the default response that wildlife must die to pay for their species' existence. In 2009, he was quoted in *New Scientist* as stating,

'Under current policy, there is no way for rural people to benefit from wildlife,' says Frank. 'They get essentially no income from tourism, and the only other potential source of wildlife income—carefully regulated, high-paying trophy hunting—is prevented by the financial influence of American and British animal-rights lobbies.'[309]

In the same article we learn that individual lions consume an average of $270 per year in livestock value while providing "upwards of $17,000 per year in tourist revenues." In the midst of social and economic injustice, failures in political and social policy, and too many people in ecosystems, what is our answer? Will we expand our efforts to turn the natural order of value into an economic one? Will we continue to deny that we have exceeded the carrying capacities of ecosystems already and that is the cause of the decline of biodiversity? Do we want to shoot elephants and lions, or change human ecologies?

Eating Elephants: Trophies and Ivory Accessories

By presence or influence, we occupy every place on Earth. We believe we have a right to live anywhere we wish. Once established, we require species who also live there to prove their value by competing for a place in our economies. All over the world, we require them, literally, to pay their own way for a right to exist in *our* world. This anthropocentrism in which creation is supposed to orbit around *us* is the opposite of biocentrism, where we are part of a much greater whole. Once again, we convert the natural order of value into an economic order of value. Here are examples of how we do it.

As anthropocentrism exists in Africa, tourism and trophy hunting are two ways governments and impoverished people raise money to live. While tourism can put species at risk, trophy hunting is a disturbing category of its own. Trophy hunters insist that wildlife and something of the remaining ecosystems can be saved by putting prices on the lives of exceptional individuals of charismatic species. Their deadly hobby is abetted by a frequent lack of indigenous support for wildlife. The idea behind both tourism and trophy hunting is that local people will protect species, not individuals from other species, if it brings them relief from poverty.

This *fundraising by death* is supposed to provide funding for wildlife agencies and their rangers who are often underequipped, poorly paid, and outgunned by poachers. If we take time to think about proposals like this, trophy hunting and tourist revenues will never be able to counter our exploding human population and our increasing demands for ever more resources from the ecosystems that wild species need to survive. For instance, an increase in human populations increases the market demand for land. That demand drives up land prices in ecosystems. Wildlife habitat that was the natural order of value becomes the economic order of value: It is now worth more to people for farming, building homes, industry, logging, transportation, and grazing than wildlife habitat. The two values compete. Only one wins because it is about us (anthropocentrism) instead of ecosystems needed by all other species (biocentrism).

As land and other resource prices go up, so do the fundraising goals individuals from other species are required to meet by being killed. If an area of land doubles in value to the local human population, then wildlife, through tourism or trophy hunting, is expected to match it. Inexorably, this will exceed what killing and viewing wildlife will be able to pay out.

It is morally indefensible for us to consume ecosystems without restraint. To require other species like lions and elephants to be shot in order for us to protect them, from us, is obscene. What this says about us is that we are not willing to invest in their protection or assure their ecosystems will last much longer. Africa's estimated human population was 967 million in mid-2008. By year 2050, it is expected to rise to 1.9 billion.[310] The conditions contributing to unsustainability, poverty, and overpopulation in Africa are no different from the rest of the planet. The arrogance of human overpopulation is a cross-cultural crime. This *killing to save them* mantra is not going to stop human overpopulation, nor quell the upward spiral of our demands. What are we if we are unwilling to make room for abundant biodiversity and let individuals from other species live in relative peace?

It is unfair to ask poor people living in diverse parts of the world to protect ecosystems and wildlife. Even for the wealthy, there is not enough money in the world to pay for what ecosystem services are worth. Yet, we do owe people our compassion and support by investing in their future if it promises to be sustainable. And if we are not to be hypocrites, we must be well on our own way to sustainability in short order. As long as political, professional, and NGO sectors demand that other species must justify themselves to be worth something in our human economies, then trophy killers will continue to exploit, traumatize, and kill elephants, water buffalo, giraffes, elk, ibex, hippopotamus, zebra, lions, and others. This legal killing also provides cover for trade in illicit wildlife parts. Valued at $5 billion to more than $20 billion dollars each year, the wildlife trade industry stretches from poor villagers to the markets of Japan, China, and the United States.[311]

The illegal trade is often run by organized crime syndicates.

Trophy hunters, like poachers, look for *tuskers*. These older elephant matriarchs who lead their herd will yield the largest haul of ivory. Hunting safari outfitters specifically offer opportunities to kill tuskers for higher fees. These hunters are wealthy, privileged people. And irreverent. In addition to the tusks they cut off the ears for souvenirs. Once back in the United States, the ears are painted with a map of Africa or the images of other individuals the trophy hunter has killed.

The legal ivory trade provides cover for illegal traffic. Dr. Samuel Wasser developed a technique that creates genetic fingerprints. Each unique genetic signature fits a profile of elephants living in diverse regions of Africa. After collecting samples from confiscated illegal ivory, he calculated that "... in the 2 cases we investigated, the 25,000 kg of ivory seized by authorities between August 2005 and August 2006 actually corresponds to approximately 250,000 kg of smuggled ivory or 38,000 poached elephants."[312]

An article in *Scientific American* magazine describes how poachers kill:

> ... on the edge of the Selous Game Reserve in Tanzania, one of us (Wasser) came across two elephant skulls lying side by side. One, from a female, was big, and the other was small... The poachers had first shot the young elephant, a ranger explained, so that they could draw its grieving mother close enough to kill her for her enormous tusks.... between 1979 and 1989 ... At least 700,000 elephants were killed ... 70,000 in the Selous alone. Then, in 1989 ... a major anti-poaching initiative called Operation Uhai ... brought an end to most poaching in the country.[313]

The same article explains, "... the lull was short-lived." Why? People with increasing wealth in nations like China, Japan, and the United States put their mega neo-predation to work: They kill elephants every time they buy ivory. Their predatory purchases drove up the price of ivory from $200 per kilogram in 2004 to $6,500 per kilogram in 2008. Just one operation in Malawi trafficked illegal ivory from an estimated 17,000 dead elephants. Corrupt officials are believed to be using wildlife products as *barter currency* to purchase weapons and ammunition to suppress political opponents and intimidate their citizens. As a result of ivory being fashionable, "… 38,000 African elephants are being killed every year—8 percent of the entire African elephant population …" As for Tanzania, the Environmental Investigative Agency found that "Tanzania's elephant population declined by more than 30,000 elephants between 2006 and 2009, primarily from poaching to supply black-market ivory to Asia."[314] Forty percent came from The Selous Game Reserve.

The Trophy Business

What does the trophy hunting business look like? The hunter's magazine, *Outdoor Life*, published this story about the first woman to kill an elephant with a bow and arrow.

After several days of stalking, she shot an arrow into a male elephant. Her victim struggled for a reported 500 yards before appearing to bleed to death. Orion Multimedia[315] filmed the death of this elephant for the television show *Dangerous Game* on the Versus cable network (now NBC Sports Network as of 2012).[316] Trophy hunters fabricate and then market their self-delusion that their hobby is dangerous. Catered in luxury, they fly thousands of miles with their exotic and expensive gear to what one advertisement called "Africa Hunting, Bow Hunting and 5 Star Accommodation." Located in South Africa, their menu list includes 45 species available for killing.[317]

Despicable trophy thrill-seekers from organizations like Safari Club International (SCI) and the Boone and Crockett Club attack the genetic viability of species. They kill the largest and most spectacular appearing individuals. Like drug cartels, they dole out bits of money for research and some humanitarian aid, but this is really a ransom note attached to their lethal hobby. Author Matthew Scully interviewed SCI members while researching their claims of altruistic behavior. In *Dominion*, he writes, "The average Safari Club member owns eleven rifles, six shotguns, five handguns, and a bow. He spends $14,000 a year on hunting.... By the time you have attained all of Safari Club's awards … you will have extinguished the minimum-required 322 animals."[318]

Trophy killing is a cultural aberration that must be stopped.

We have failed to address adequately the poverty of billions of people. As a result, they are desperate to gain any chance of making money from the land and life around them. Their poverty is everyone's ecosystem loss. Overshadowing this injustice is that we in the developed economies do not care enough about the individuals from other species and their ecosystems to support them.

Developed economies could reduce the poverty that insists wildlife must pay up. In an Earth Policy Institute letter announcing the publication of *World on the Edge: How to Prevent Environmental and Economic Collapse*, Lester R. Brown calculated, "It will take about $200 billion per year ... to finance the various environmental and social components of Plan B, including reforestation, soil conservation, fishery restoration, universal primary school education, and reproductive health care and family planning services for women everywhere."[319] While more than half of Africans are living on two dollars or less per day,[320] trophy hunters pay $50,000 to kill a single individual of another species. What is an alternative?

In his paper, "Modeling species extinction: the case for non-consumptive values," Robert Alexander proposes that existence values, the value the global community places on other species' existence, must result in monies being collected and institutions created to get investment to those areas and people best positioned to protect species from extinctions. According to his calculations, consumptive and non-consumptive values will not be enough to raise sufficient funds. Referring to the demand a rising human population creates on land where elephants live, he writes,

"... tourism values alone are insufficient to offset the opportunity cost of land resources, and this leaves only one option for preserving the African elephant: the appropriation of existence values. Extinction is inevitable if some means for such appropriation to occur is not found. This conclusion may be generalised to many other endangered species as well."[321]

This is a solvable problem. The Earth is so saturated with us that demanding ecosystems and individuals from other species pay us for their existence fails to address the far larger crisis of our human ecology and our character.

The Fishers

We can understand the immense scale of botanical (plant) and animal agriculture because we easily see it on land. It is far more difficult, I think, for us to comprehend the size of the fishing industry. Primarily done underwater and out of our sight, the industry has devastated marine ecosystems. Ocean ecosystems suffer from our lack of being able to understand this. We believe oceans are so *vast* that we could never deplete an expanse of water stretching beyond our horizons. We need to comprehend what we have done. As fishers and consumers, we have altered marine ecosystems, their species composition, ratios of prey to predator, food webs, and nutrient flows. They are as vital to the ocean as are blood, tissues, and organs are to the inner workings of our bodies. The fishing industry is a huge player in our human ecology. Complicating matters is how the greenhouse gasses (GHGs) we produce are increasing the acidity of oceanic waters more than many species can tolerate.

Earth's oceans are absorbing 22 million tons of carbon dioxide (CO_2), every day. They have absorbed about 525 billion tons over the past 200 years. That is about half of the carbon we have spewed into the atmosphere from our burning of fossil fuels.[322] The absorption rate is increasing by 2 billion tons every year.[323] This absorption has been helpful for reducing the CO_2 in our atmosphere. However, as the oceans' acidity increases and warms, they are less capable of absorbing it. This will drive CO_2 to rise more rapidly in the atmosphere.

"Intensive fossil-fuel burning and deforestation over the last two centuries have increased atmospheric CO_2 by almost 40 percent above preindustrial values to levels higher than at any time over the past 800,000 years or longer," writes Sarah Cooley in "Anticipating ocean acidification's economic consequences for commercial fisheries."[324] For fishers and biocentrists who treasure marine ecosystems, this is frightening. It should scare us all. As the acidification of the ocean increases, species' ability to form shells of calcium carbonate decreases. Species at the base of the food chain (i.e., pteropods) are affected. Shelled organisms are a vital part of food webs. Coral reefs that provide habitat and protect shorelines from storms are in danger.

These changes in ocean ecosystems will impact the poor and subsistence fishers the most.

- According to the FAO, fish are important food sources for 2.9 billion people.
- Seafood provides at least 20 percent of the global animal protein intake.
- In FAO's 2008 estimate, 44.9 million people fished.
- Of the total catch remaining after bycatch was tossed back into the sea, 80 percent of world fish production was used for direct human consumption, while the remainder was processed into fishmeal and fish oil with much of that used for fish farming.
- FAO believes that "Some 53 percent of the world's marine fishery resources are fully fished, or fished to the maximum sustainable level. Another 32 percent is overfished, depleted, or recovering."[325]
- In many parts of the world, inland fisheries "remain lightly exploited."[326]
- According to a survey of the top 53 fishing countries, 30 failed "the FAO Code of Conduct for Responsible Fisheries." Again, these were the *top* 53 fishing countries. The survey did not include the rampant illegal and unreported fisheries.
- Impoverished governments do not have the resources to manage fishers. They are unable to or ineffective in preventing the illegal catch estimated to be between 11 and 26 million tons.[327]

The expected loss of 15 to 20 percent of the world's future fishery protein will affect the poor more than the rich. Ninety-nine percent of the world's 51 million fishers (several millions more than estimated in the previous source) are small-scale operators who live in developing countries. Any downward change in ocean productivity threatens them more than those of us who have alternative food choices.[328]

The resource-inefficient fish farming industry produces over half of the world's fish. On these *farms*, carnivorous shrimp and salmon are fed fishmeal and fish oil made from wild-caught fish. According to the Worldwatch Institute, 37 percent of wild fish caught are fed to farmed fish. It can take five pounds of wild-sourced fish food to produce one pound of farmed salmon.[329]

Scraping for a Living

Bottom trawling is an appalling way to fish. In "Scorched Earth Fishing," Carl Safina writes, "Bottom trawls—large bag-shaped nets towed over the sea floor—account for more of the world's catch of fish, shrimp, squid, and other marine animals than any other fishing method. But trawling also disturbs the sea floor more than any other human activity." It destroys the physical and biological structure of living communities over large areas of the ocean floor.

Safina explains that many seafloors are "raked by nets" once to eight times per year.

> A single pass kills 5 to 20 percent of the seafloor animals, so a year's shrimping can wholly deplete the bottom communities," he writes. "Much of the world's seabed is encrusted and honeycombed with structures built by living things. Trawls crush, kill, expose to enemies, and remove these sources of nourishment and hiding places, making life difficult and dangerous for young fish and lowering the quality of the habitat and its ability to produce abundant fish populations.[330]

Bottom trawlers are responsible for destroying deep-sea corals and sponges. In Alaskan waters alone, one million pounds of these biological wonders were scraped away in just two years.[331]

Longlining is another defective method of fishing. Here, baited hooks are strung on lines that drape for miles behind fishing vessels. Like bottom trawling, it is nonselective for the species it kills. Birds like the black-footed albatross, endangered turtles, and other wildlife are attracted by the bait. They take it, get hooked by their mouths, and after trying to swallow the bait, endure the agony of being towed behind the boat while the hooks tear at their throats. They eventually drown. When longliners *do* catch what they are looking for, they are nonselective for the age and sex of their catch. That reduces the reproductive potential of the targeted species. Imagine the carnage that 5,000,000 hooks strung on 100,000 miles of fishing line creates *every day*. A new longliner vessel under construction in 2012 has the capacity to set 76,800 hooks per day.[332] A draft report to the PEW Charitable Trusts called longlining the most widespread human hunting activity in the world.[333]

Up close and personal, seafood consumers purchase this mega neopredation when they buy seafood; these consumers pay for the drowning of millions of birds and turtles every year. For example, Patagonian toothfish longliners alone killed an estimated 265,000 birds in1996 and 1999, "mainly mollymawk albatrosses and white-chinned petrels ... with lesser numbers of wandering albatrosses ... and giant petrels...."[334]

The list of bird species decimated by fishers is painfully long. They are under attack everywhere. Gillnets set on fish also drown diving birds as the nets are dragged through the birds' feeding areas, or as birds are attracted to the fishing operation itself. Historically, fishers went to seabird colonies and killed the nesting birds for bait. Though outlawed in many parts of the world today, people in places like Brazil still kill birds, boobies in this case, for their lobster traps. If that were not enough, there are predator control programs against birds implausibly meant to increase fish populations. According to "The impacts of fishing on marine birds," there is no evidence that the birds being targeted have a significant impact on fish populations of concern. The Great Cormorant is targeted in Europe, the Double-crested Cormorant in North America.[335]

Bycatch

Bycatch in fisher operations refers to those species that are caught unintentionally along with the targeted species. When this bycatch is of no commercial value, illegal to keep because they are protected, or less valuable than the species sought and would take up room in the vessel's storage hold, they are thrown overboard back into the sea where they often die from trauma. Approximately "one million tonnes of biota is discarded every year by commercial fisheries in the North Sea" alone.

The good news is that bycatch is decreasing because of advances in fishing gear, an emerging market for *trash* fish, and changes in regulatory management. Even with reductions, bycatch was estimated in 2001 to be 7.3 million *tons* per year, or 8 percent of the world's catch. Tropical shrimp trawling has the highest discard rate at over 27 percent.[336] Those numbers are open for debate given the lack of uniform reporting, especially from remote locations, and varying defin-itions of bycatch. For the United States, the National Marine Fisheries Service reports bycatch at 2.1 billion *pounds* per year, or 17 percent of all fish caught. That does not include an estimated 11,772 sea turtles, birds, and marine mammals.[337] Globally, the "discard" rate of fish is between 17.9 and 39.5 (mean 27.0) million metric tons.[338]

In 2009, an FAO report redefined bycatch in a way that may be more biologically useful. The new definition attempts to cover the gaps in reporting and regulation. If "bycatch is catch that is either unused or unmanaged," the report "conservatively indicates that bycatch repre-sents 40.4 percent of global marine catches, exposing systemic gaps in fisheries policy and management."[339] But again, marine mammals, seabirds, and sea turtles drowned by fishers every year are not included in these statistics.

Bycatch is mega neo-predation. We do not eat bycatch but we kill it as a byproduct of our predation on fish. Fishers and their customers create additional layers of mega neo-predation because they reduce the food available for other fish, marine turtles, marine birds, and marine mammals. If we choose to support the fishing industry, then we are paying for the fish eaten plus the collateral damage in getting the seafood, the widespread destruction of ecosystems, and the killing of unintended individuals of mostly other species—bycatch.

The "Next One Hundred Years"

The paper "Predation and Competition: The Impact of Fisheries on

Marine-Mammal Populations Over the Next One Hundred Years" is a chilling assessment of the impacts of fishing upon marine mammals. The paper's authors predict these future outcomes based on existing trends: There will be a reduction in fish and shellfish available for human consumption; the number of marine mammal species and the populations of remaining species "will be reduced by the end of the 21st century;" we will continue to take much of the food other species need; and we will expand predator programs against marine mammals in order to take more fish. While the authors, highly respected marine mammal scientists, believe we will also be eating marine mammals, they wrote that "virtually all of the predictions regarding species composition and energy flow within a marine community ... will prove wrong on a decadal or longer time scale."[340] We are fulfilling their forecast.

Sinking Sharks

We are annihilating sharks. Of the pelagic (open ocean) sharks and rays who are killed intentionally and as bycatch, three-quarters of the 21 species reviewed are classified as threatened or near threatened with one being endangered. Another 11 are "threatened with higher risk of extinction," according to a 2008 paper titled, "You can swim but you can't hide: the global status and conservation of oceanic pelagic sharks and rays."[341] In the same year, FAO reported 750,000 tons of sharks were taken from ocean ecosystems.[342] This may be a gross underestimate because this fishery is notoriously underreported. The real biomass being killed and removed may be much higher: 38 million sharks with a total biomass of 1.7 million metric tons, according to other research[343]. In "Shark fishing in fin soup," A.R. Hoelzel estimates the kill may total 100 million sharks per year.[344]

A large number of shark species are *finned*. In finning, fishers cut off the fins while the sharks are still alive. Then they throw them back into the ocean. Finless, they struggle to swim only to sink into the depths in exhaustion as they suffocate to death. The buyers of shark fin soup are responsible for this indefensible fishery. Over 50 percent of the shark fin trade occurs in Hong Kong.[345] Similar transculturally careless, cruel, and ignorant attitudes are found in shark fishing contests such as the Downeast Shark Tournament in Maine. Despite protests from environmentalists and animal rights advocates, similar contests continue worldwide.[346]

Complicating the abilities of sharks to survive these intense killing fields is the fact that many of their species are slow growing and they do not reproduce in great numbers. Spiny dogfish, sharks despite their name, live for over 100 years. They do not become sexually mature until about 34 years old. Even then, they produce only nine pups on average after a gestation of 20 to 22 months. Spiny dogfish, you may be interested to know, give birth to live young after being nourished in utero through a yolk sac.[347]

Fish and sharks feel pain. Fish, not sharks, have swim bladders they fill and empty with air as needed to control buoyancy and balance. When fish are brought from great depth where water pressure is higher, to the surface where air pressure is much lower, the air in the fish's bladder expands beyond the air bladder's capacity; this distorts their bodies and blows them up like an overfilled balloon, only they are living fish who are sensate to pain, not balloons. The air bladder expands so much it kills the fish. As accurately described in a PETA brochure, the "… fish undergo excruciating decompression—often the intense internal pressure ruptures their swim bladders, pops out their eyes, and pushes their stomachs through their mouths. Then they're tossed on board, where many slowly suffocate …"[348] Fish, including sharks, are not covered by any law that would protect them from inhumane treatment. Carnists act like they do not care. Vegetarians who eat fish should not sleep well at night.

Ignorance should not be our bliss and their demise. Giant grenadiers are fish who live at depths ranging between 140 to 1,000 meters in Alaskan waters. The mortality rate from decompression is 100 percent. Pulled from the depths, they suffer every inch on the way up to the surface. In Alaska alone, an estimated 16,000 metric tons of harmed grenadier are thrown back into the ocean annually.[349] They are a *trash fish* because the high water content of their soft flesh makes them commercially unsalable.[350] Though some people are trying to solve the material waste of these fish, no fisher is thinking about ending their

suffering as they are pulled from the depths. Vegans refuse to participate in this mega neo-predator disaster.

There are many methods of catching seafood and creating bycatch
besides longlining, purse seining, and trawling. If they ever thought
about it, I like to believe that fishers would be happy if bycatch and the
pain of decompression could be avoided. But the fact is, it continues.
We can stop it and the hooking and drowning of birds, marine
mammals, and turtles right now. Step away from seafood forever.

No Middle Ground

It is our choice. We will continue propping up the short-term and
unsustainable economic order of value by buying ivory, trophies, meat,
dairy, and fish, or we will restore a semblance of a natural order of
value. Ecosystems and individuals from other species either have rights
to existence or they do not. Choice by choice, we create the conditions
that nurture and preserve the integrity of ecosystems and biodiversity
or we cause their collapse. There is no middle ground.

We are the billions of people from the North, Central, and South
Americas, Kenyans, Chinese, Europeans, East Europeans, Asians,
Australians, and the citizens of India who trample the biological and
physical integrity of the Earth. Together we generate mega neo-
predation, one of three components of neo-predation. Presence
predation is next.

Chapter 8:

Meet Presence Predator

Presence predation is one of three distinct components of our neo-predation. Presence predation and mega predation are both related to the number of people living on the planet. The presence of 7 billion humans is an intense form of predation.

Presence predation is the impact we create just from our occupying space. We occupy space and fill it with our activities and commotions when we walk, square dance, and move at high speeds in trucks, trains, airplanes, and recreational boats. Our activities in the space we occupy control the availability of physical space that is the habitat of other species. There also is a bubble of space we control that extends outward from us and our activities. If we are really noisy, for instance, we scare away individuals from other species and displace them. So, it is not just the space where we act out our lives, it is the type of our activity that determines how much and how far our presence extends.

Our predation by presence would not be a concern by itself if it were not for the fact there are so many of us displacing other species. We are mega in our presence, so we displace entire communities of species from spaces they need to survive, such as valley bottomlands and river courses where food, shelter, and water are available whenever needed.

We are noisy on land and sea. With our noise-generating activities, we impinge on the abilities of other species to find food, hear, navigate, live with less stress, travel, and locate one another. This is aggression. And it is predation that kills and limits populations of species. The mere presence of predators like us is a threat that changes the behaviors of other species. Research demonstrates that foraging and mating is measurably suppressed as the prey species acts to escape detection by their predators in the wild.[351] Because of our omnipresence, we cause this suppressing effect on a large scale. We also have the unique tendency of moving our presence from one place to another so quickly that we kill other species as we run into them at high speeds. Moose, birds, deer, manatees, insects, whales, turtles, snakes, ground squirrels, and field mice have died, not because we shot them, but because we collided with them.

On the other hand, glass-clad, reflective buildings stand still. Their presence in the space they occupy kills as well. Buildings are deadly, motionless space-fillers to the birds who fly into them. Fooled by the exterior windows that make glass walls look like open sky, they try to fly through the windowpane. The American Bird Conservancy (ABC) estimates between 300 million to a billion birds are killed each year by buildings, wind turbines, communication towers, and other human-made structures that are presence predators.[352] From our homes to skyscrapers, our presence predation is something new, and part of our neo-predation.

Soundscape Ecology

Loud people, things we do that make noise, and roads that bring our fast-moving car that are in the end occupied space drive other species away. In our frenzied motion and clatter, we drive individuals from other species to seek safety and a seclusion that is increasingly hard to find. The term *soundscape* has been around for decades but its value in understanding our human ecology is newly emerging. "'We're trying to understand how sounds can be used as measures of ecosystem health,' says [researcher Bryan] Pijanowski ... Some silent newts ... follow frog sounds to find the best breeding ponds. But one of the biggest questions confronting this field is figuring out how human beings affect the soundscape." In the presence of human generated noise, birds have fewer offspring, species richness is demonstrably reduced, bats are hindered in finding insect prey, and "some other bird species do poorly when nesting near the thrum of tires."[353]

Our sphere of presence predation is so powerful that we can control or influence the entire food-bearing habitat of other species.[354] Drop a pebble into still water. Our presence predation looks like the concentric rings you see rolling outward. A flock of birds will scatter when we walk quickly into their midst, and deer, elk, and wolves run from the movement and noise of snowmobiles. This costs them dearly in winter calories. When we lay pavement so cars can speed through surface space more quickly than any animal's reflexes, and when we encircle whales with too many whale-watching vessels, we are filling the environment with our presence predation.

Our presence is not inherently evil and undesirable; it just has to be at the right scale, speed, and design. We can be an expression of biodiversity as worthy as any other species with whom we have co-evolved; we have a place and a vibrant role to play in ecosystems. It is our wild excess of procreation, ill-considered consumption priorities, and unbridled frenzy of activity that drowns the possibilities and existence of individuals from other species. That is where we have gone wrong.

Our Presence in the Congo Basin

Our presence predation is real and it kills directly. After studying forest elephants in the Congo Basin, researchers concluded that they were witnessing a *siege* strategy. In an unprotected area, only one elephant would cross the road, and then at 14 times normal speed. Researchers attributed this to their trauma from being preyed upon by poachers. Even in the depths of the Congo forest the ranging behavior of the largest terrestrial mammal is driven by fear.

In the study area, the presence of people arriving to former wild areas by new roads has severely reduced the sizes of roadless areas, a 56 to 100 percent loss. The Belinga Iron Mining Project required roads, some 2,000 construction workers, logging towns, and "... a hydroelectric power station [that] will likely be built in the heart of Ivindo NP [National Park] ... These are not isolated cases. The strategy of both the private sector and the international aid community in Africa is focused on heavy investment in infrastructure, particularly roads,"[355] reported the researchers.

They describe the fear strategy of survival these elephants have chosen. But as these elephants crowd into temporary safe areas, competition for food availability and quality is expected to decay the elephants' social cohesion. Increasingly isolated in shrinking habitats, each elephant herd loses genetic diversity. The paper's authors concluded that if the current rate of road building continues, "this forest wilderness and the forest elephants they contain will collapse." This is not happening near a large city, it is happening in "the second largest rainforest block on earth ...."[356]

Roads take space from habitat. Then they give access to us, the space-takers. When 2,000 people at the Belinga Iron Mining Project live as noisily as we all do, they and we are not sharing space with most other species. The presence of people fills the wilderness to the exclusion of other species. No matter what we do, increasing human presence, mega predation predicts the forest's biological decline and the frightened death of elephants. People did not have to shoot elephants to terrorize and kill them. Our presence predation is just as effective.

Turn Down the Volume

Navies of many countries use active sonar that ensonifies (fills with human-made sound) entire ocean basins. Sonar is valuable for detecting potential enemy threats but it is also presence predation. Additional sources of noise having the potential to affect marine species include dredging, drilling, construction, seismic testing for oil and gas, pile driving, jet skis, and underwater weapons testing.

Mid-frequency military sonar has been linked to multi-species strandings of cetaceans. Physiological damage and mortalities were documented in the strandings of beaked whales in the Bahamas and correlated with the Navy's use of sonar. A hypothesis is that the intensity of the sonar upon deep diving whales and dolphins causes nitrogen to dissolve out of their tissues. This causes bleeding and organ destruction. Prey is also affected. "Fish show permanent and temporary hearing loss, reduced catch rates, stress, and behavioral reactions to noise," according to a paper titled, "The impacts of anthropogenic ocean noise on cetaceans and implications for management."[357] Research has revealed that even at several hundred feet distant, orca whale behavior is affected by smaller vessels.[358] In 2003, the U.S. Navy's USS *Shoupe* was using its mid-frequency sonar near the San Juan Islands in Washington State when researchers reported dramatic behavioral changes in members of the endangered Southern Resident killer whales belonging to J pod.[359] Those acute incidents were in the news, but the problems posed by chronic noise pollution in the world's oceans is underappreciated by the public and policy makers. We speed through the marine ecosystems with our boats and jet skis, and we support the oil and gas industry's seismic testing when buying fuel.

Vessels produce noise. The type and level of their noise is specific to their engine type, the vessel size, hull design, and propeller turning rate. The design of the vessel's propeller plays heavily in how much noise is produced. The vessel operator's course and speed produces the *behavior* of the ship and elicits the responses from other species. The composition and topography of the sea floor can increase, focus, or disperse these sounds depending on whether it is silty sediment or more solid rock, flat or sloping. Some regulatory guidelines are emerging in the United States that address the relationship between ship design and the noise it produces. Globally, little is being done to reduce vessel noise relative to how much is produced.[360]

This boat and ship noise creates many impacts. It can mask marine species' communication to one another, displace them from habitat, interrupt their foraging and mating opportunities, and disrupt the cooperative behaviors of socially dependent species like orca whales. We are presence predators because we deny other species the habitable space they need to survive. We displace them with noise and force them to move away at sea as we do on land and in the air.

Alien Invasion

We are presence predators when we introduce invasive species to ecosystems. It does not matter if it is intentional or unintentional, the results are the same. Invasive species are second only to habitat destruction in the annihilation of biodiversity.[361] Once established, invasives can out-compete native species and replace them physically, but they are unlikely to supply the same functionality of relationships to other species. A defeated native species was food; the invasive species may be inedible or less nutritious. Oceans, mountains, and wind currents once shielded ecosystems from sudden arrivals of multiple new species. When we changed the location of our presence, we brought the alien species with us. As more of us travel and our commerce expands, more invasives get free rides as we move about and expand their range unwittingly. Through us, they extend their own predation.

Our concoction of non-native species has striking results: Today, Arizona and Montana share 33 fish species; before our arrival there were none in common.[362] Between 1850 and 1970, there was one known successful invasion in San Francisco Bay; by the 1990s, there was one species attempting to establish itself every 14 weeks. Thankfully, most introduced species do not survive their new habitat for long. But when one does succeed, it can change everything.

"Alien" is how *Mother Jones* magazine describes one particular invasive: "The lionfish invasion of the Atlantic is like War of the Worlds: aliens with superior technology knocking over the hapless natives and feasting on their remains."[363] We may forget that our food crops, livestock, and companion species comprise a sizeable percentage, in population and habitat covered, of the invasive species' impacts to ecosystems. They are in addition to the estimated 50,000 other non-native species we have introduced into the United States. Invasives are involved in 42 percent of native species being listed as threatened or endangered in the United States, with rates as high as 80 percent in other countries.[364]

As mega, presence predators, we shape habitats and species to conform to our own biases. Our biases for species are untested by time, natural selection, ecosystem compatibility, and sustainability. They rework ecosystems and diminish their biodiversity. Our invasive livestock are, according to the FAO,

...by far the single largest anthropogenic user of land. Grazing occupies 26 percent of the Earth's terrestrial surface, while feed crop production requires about a third of all arable land. Expansion of grazing land for livestock is a key factor in deforestation, especially in Latin America: some 70 percent of previously forested land in the Amazon is used as pasture, and feed crops cover a large part of the remainder. About 70 percent of all grazing land in dry areas is considered degraded, mostly because of overgrazing, compaction and erosion attributable to livestock activity.[365]

There are about 155 ruminant species on the planet with six of them being domesticated. They are cattle and sheep, the most numerous, yak, reindeer, goat, and buffalo. According to researcher Peter J. Van Soest in *Nutritional Ecology of the Ruminant*, there are many more billions of domesticated ruminants than wild ones.[366] They all displace native species with their presence predation through us. Elk and mule deer will move to higher elevations when our cattle are present. Over millennia, elk and mule deer co-evolved in the absence of our cattle to occupy specific ecosystem niches. Cattle, on the other hand, are generalists, and overlap niches of both elk and mule deer.[367]

Our botanical agriculture employs invasive plants. Though necessary for our survival, our plant crops occupy space that was once the domain of native species. It is important we remember the extent that our invasive food crops play in our mega, presence predation.

Environment Canada commented on the idea of grizzly bears regaining their Prairie home in Alberta province: "It is unlikely that sufficient habitat could be managed or restored at a scale required to support a viable Prairie population of grizzly bears given past, current and foreseen human population growth and activities, and the extent of agricultural land use."[368] Botanical agriculture would exist on a much smaller scale in a vegan new human ecology that does not feed crops to livestock. The new human ecology supports the return of grizzly bears to the prairies.

Advocates for invasive animal agriculture often stress that plant communities thrive better if grazed by cattle under skilled management. In fact, the survival and robustness of grazed plants *is* partially dependent upon grazing animals, but the premise misleads us to a conclusion we should not accept at face value; it is far more complex. The idealized plant communities that cattle grazing advocates described as *productive* are intended to maximize animal agriculture yields; those maximum states are not necessarily the preferred conditions found in ecosystems that existed prior to animal agriculture. For both domestic and wild animal grazing models, diversity of grazers is important.[369] Restoring prairie ecosystems does not require livestock;

conservation biologists can and should employ native species instead.

One of the progressive rancher tenets is that the movements of livestock should be scheduled to mimic the variety of native species who originally grazed the land. In this scheme, livestock are herded over large tracts of terrain, allowed to intensively graze an area, and then are moved on to the next area. In this way, the grazed community of plants will be given time, ideally, to recover before the livestock grazers return.

This tweaking of grazing practices is unnecessary. Ecosystems do not need billions of domesticated livestock from invasive species to achieve *stimulated* plant communities; we can accomplish magnitudes of recovery more if conservation biologists introduce native species in tandem with the end of animal agriculture. As it dies, ecosystems will thrive. Conservation biologists will need generations before plant and animal communities regain at least some relationships that are essential to the ecosystems. Grazing cattle will be replaced by the original inhabitants, the bison, antelope, deer, tallgrass and shortgrass, prairie chickens, and ground squirrels. Highlands and lowlands, forests and plains, all should be rid of the pox that livestock represent.

Animal agriculturalists would have us believe that grazing by our domesticated invasive species is a good thing. It can be difficult to winnow balanced perspectives about animal agriculture from the scientific community that clings to carnist biases that domineer their culture. With their dominionist worldview in place, they work to convince us that our introduced invasive species should stay when, from biodiversity's perspective, it was a mistake from the start. Biocentric perspective recognizes that prairie plant communities co-evolved with the native wildlife grazers. Species, and undoubtedly individuals within grazing species, eat selectively. They have favorite plants, inedible plants, and plants in-between. Livestock were never needed as replacements to benefit ecosystems; maximum ecosystem restoration to the extent possible is best done with native species.

At first, we may be inclined to congratulate and support progressive ranchers for what they are willing to do. Sometimes, at great cost to themselves, they work for ecosystem restoration and protection of endangered and threatened species for its own sake. But their insistence on remaining animal agriculturalists reflects anthropocentric values that are futile starting points for measuring what needs to be done for ecosystems on a larger scale. As a result, in this human calculation of ecosystem manipulation, there is less love for restored ecosystems than the want to maintain the supply of meat and milk's cash flowing. The best that animal agriculture can propose is mimicry and conservation on the margins.

Instead, we must return large landscapes to the once-dominant species and their ecosystems. Bears, martins, snakes, coyotes, mice, birds of prey, songbirds, wolves, panther, and cougar are living and dying from the conflicts we have created by our inserting invasive domesticated species into ecosystems. Animal agriculture insists on it. Invasive livestock are agents of our presence predation.

Organic farming and land use changes can improve the health of some studied species,[370] especially when land is taken out of production and restored or allowed to recover as native habitat.[371, 372] But I have not found research that concludes appropriately restored ecosystems have less biodiversity than livestock-grazed or cropped land. A vegan human ecology spares the land and its species as carnist human ecology cannot. When restored to the extent possible, a non-grazed/farmed state will have more biodiversity and resilience than any option the animal agricultural industry can offer, including the small family-run animal agriculture businesses. Animal agriculture would have us forget that fact.

The Presence of Cars, Roads, and Barriers

To accommodate our burgeoning population, an ever-increasing number of trucks and cars require safe and efficient roads and highways. To greater and lesser degrees, all vehicles create noise, toxins, and the rapidly moving space we occupy while in them. Nothing lives permanently on roads and highways except pencil-thin lines of plant life sheltered in the cracks of pavement. We are the occupants inside vehicles who bring our presence predatorship wherever we go. Where roads are located and how they are designed determine which ecosystems, species, and individuals (roadkill) will become our prey.

We do not just run them over; our cars and trucks control this space and pass through it solidly at high speeds.

Mega, presence predatorship is an anthropogenic selection pressure directed at other species. In this case, we require them to adapt to our transportation systems or die. Their former genetic expressions evolved in environments nothing like the surface of a road, the speed of a car, or the noise and pollution our vehicles create. In some species of frogs, females favor the deeper-toned calls from males because they indicate larger size and experience. This genetic selection should tend to produce a more robust species. In the presence of traffic, however, these larger, experienced male frogs have to shift to higher-toned calls in order to rise above our noisy vehicles, even though it puts them at a disadvantage in attracting mates; they then sound like the smaller males.[373] Eventually, smaller, higher-voiced males may gain an equal mating advantage and result in their becoming a smaller-sized species. That traffic noise would create a smaller species is sobering, but there is much more to consider. Here are ways we create presence predatorship every time we get into a vehicle, even if it is an electric car.

What Road Barriers Do

Median barriers, those concrete walls installed down the middle of our highways, create mega, presence predatorship. The barriers are placed end-to-end to create walls that separate opposing directions of road traffic. We appreciate this as a life-saving necessity where needed. However, if, for example, the length of the median wall extends for more than a mile, how are individuals from other species supposed to get to where they need to be? Those lucky enough to make it halfway across the road will be stuck facing the barrier with the frightening traffic screaming close to their backsides. This is a new development in their evolution. They face a drastic, sudden change in their natural history and are ill-prepared to confront it.

Road barriers as manufactured environmental threats began appearing in the United States about 60 years ago. They come in several designs and typically rise to a height between 32 and 57 inches. They have gotten higher over time, with the taller Texas variety replacing the shorter Jersey barriers.[374] I have seen these barrier walls run 15 and 30 miles in unbroken lines, standing solidly down the middle of Interstate 5 in Oregon. Barriers, the roads they rest on, and the vehicles rolling over the pavement each contribute to our mega, presence predation, but they are more deadly together than apart.

The combination of barriers, roads, and vehicles kill and maim, fragment habitat, isolate populations of species, create corridors of noise and activity that exclude species beyond the roadway, and pollute the surrounding air and watershed with toxins. Wildlife require access to sometimes-seasonal food, a reliable source of water, potential mates who are genetically distant, shelter, cover from predators as they travel, and the freedom to disperse in response to population pressures. Barrier-free travel is essential to wildlife. Their survival requires unobstructed mobility.

In 2009, there were 254 million cars in the United States[375] speeding down nearly 4 million miles of roads. The U.S. Department of Transportation estimates that "Millions of vertebrates—birds, reptiles, mammals, and amphibians—are killed every year by vehicles traveling on America's roads."[376] Recordkeeping is inadequate, so we are unable to quantify more precisely how many multi-millions of wild and domestic animals we kill with our presence-predating vehicles. There are an estimated 750,000 to 1,500,000 collisions with deer alone. Perhaps newer, on-board computers like OnStar installed in cars to report accidents, emergencies, and location will someday feature a system for drivers and passengers to report every bird and individual of other species struck along the way.

Despite what seems like a common-sense conclusion that long walls of median barriers will expose wildlife to injuries and death, I have found little scientific evidence to support my assumption conclusively. In their paper "Highway Median Impacts On Wildlife Movement and Mortality," researchers Anthony P. Clevenger and Angela V. Kociolek found that standards for highway design do "... not address the effects of highway median barriers on wildlife habitat fragmentation." But "Local wildlife biologists believe these structures present formidable barriers for almost all species of wildlife, large and small." After reviewing the scientific literature, Clevenger and Kociolek find there may not be correlations between the barriers and collision mortalities.[377] More study is needed.

The Washington State Department of Transportation (WSDOT) has published a decision matrix that guides state agencies when to seek input from biologists when constructing roadways. They believe that wildlife, when meeting these barriers, will travel parallel to them and remain on the road doing so.[378] Given the number and length of barriers on interstate highways, common sense insists we need more studies. Certainly, barriers or not, our highways and vehicles continue raging at a mega scale of presence predation.

New York Times' Jim Robbins describes what an endangered grizzly bear has to overcome while crossing Interstate 90 in Montana near Glacier National Park: "To arrive from the north, a bear would have to climb over a nearly three-foot-high concrete Jersey barrier, cross two lanes of road, braving 75 to 80-mile-an-hour traffic, climb a higher Jersey barrier, cross two more lanes of traffic and climb yet another barrier."[379] If that were not bad enough, grass is intentionally grown on the shoulders of roads, which attracts wildlife. Reengineering roads is a costly undertaking

Going Over and Under

In heavily traveled wildlife corridors, we are building culverts under highways and lids over highways to provide safe passage. These efforts are the exceptions rather than the rule. A combination of culverts and lids is being built along Interstate 90 in Washington State. Another project is in Montana, with 43 under crossings planned on one stretch of road alone.[380] They can dramatically reduce wildlife-vehicle collisions in those areas, but do not address the problem everywhere else.

In "Ecological Effects of Roads on Terrestrial and Aquatic Communities," the authors reviewed the scientific literature and concluded that roads are associated with "negative effects on biotic diversity" in seven ways:

- "increased mortality from road construction;
- increased mortality from collision with vehicles;

- modification of animal behavior;
- alteration of the physical environment;
- alteration of the chemical environment;
- spread of exotic species;
- and, increased alteration and use of habitats by humans."
  (Remember the devastating impacts roads had on elephants in
  the Congo Basin.)

They calculated that "road lanes of all types … in the conterminous United States … have destroyed more than [11.8 million acres] of land and water bodies that formerly supported plants, animals, and other organisms." Every square inch of that destruction came from our mega, presence predation.

Presence predation extends far beyond roads and their traffic. Sandhill Cranes avoid nesting near paved and gravel roads; bald eagles in Oregon are less likely to be successful reproducing near them; and cotton rats, prairie voles, and other rodents avoid even narrow secondary roads. Toxic contamination from gasoline combustion and de-icing salts travels 200 meters and more washed off the road surface, tainting water, animals, and plants.[381]

In his statement touting Ford Motor Company's foresight about emphasizing cars with greater fuel efficiency, William Clay Ford Jr. said, "Well, just to put it in perspective, there are about 800 million vehicles on the road today worldwide. And within our lifetime, that will be 3 to 4 billion. And where are they going to go? And how are they going to drive?"[382] He might have added, "And how will ecosystems survive?"

Speedboats disrupt and run over wildlife. They are the speeding presence predators in lakes, rivers, estuaries, and oceans. Feeding, preening, traveling, procuring food, socializing, caring for young, communicating, and resting across many species are all affected. The endangered, propeller-scarred Florida manatees are an example. An estimated 20 to 40 percent of manatee deaths are caused by humans, often by collisions with fast boats. Large ships can kill the largest individuals on Earth at slower speeds: Whales are injured and slain by ships traveling the equivalent of 16 miles per hour. The injuries and death of a young female humpback whale who was struck by a large ship are described by researchers who examined her remains: "There were at least five significant injuries on the whale ... The most serious was ... not only deep but had sheared off the top portion of at least two vertebra.... this injury appeared to be the likely cause of death ... close examination confirmed ... that this injury had occurred many weeks or months previously."[383]

Four blue whales were killed within three months' time in the Santa Barbara Channel, in California, in 2007. They are the largest species on Earth. Although restrictions on speed and route are being considered, those considerations are being weighed against the costs to the shipping companies.[384] Speed and course reductions are being considered also for endangered right whales on the eastern U.S. coast. Speedboats are supposed to slow down for manatees in Florida and cars are supposed to slow down for elk coming out of Olympic National Park in Washington State. But like the lids and culverts built on highways to protect wildlife, these changes are good, but ineffective in producing reductions sufficient to offset our net mega, presence predations.

We are nowhere near to responding to William Clay Ford Jr.'s predicted three to four billion vehicles nor the expected massive increases in highway construction. This will triple to quadruple their presence predation. The more we move our *presence* around in increasing numbers, the more we kill. Why did the chicken try to cross the road? To find other chickens; he tried—but never made it to his destination.

Several years ago, near dusk, I witnessed a toy collie dog trapped in the middle of Interstate 5 at Rice Hill in southern Oregon. She could not get over the median barrier and cowered against it, trapped by cars and trucks going 65 miles per hour. She appeared uninjured but cringed and pressed herself against the concrete barrier wall. Suddenly, she tried to get from the middle of the road and back to the grassy shoulder. Midway, a truck struck her a glancing but powerful blow. I had pulled over just before this happened and tried to stand in the freeway in the fading twilight to signal the traffic to stop. It took but a few seconds before I yielded to my fear of causing an even larger accident. She tried one last time to get back to safety. Again, she was hit by another truck. She rolled again, this time toward the green coolness of the shoulder where she died a short time later.

Years passed before I drove that stretch of mountain freeway again. It was in the spring. The change of seasons had thawed the winter's accumulation of deep snow. Revealed in the melt were an astounding number of the furred remains of many, many wild lives. Silent and lifeless, they were strewn where there were, and were not, walls of Jersey and Texas-sized median barriers. Whether other drivers noticed and reflected on the dead, I do not know.

As my partner, Hal, said, "There's no reason why those barriers can't be designed to support wildlife with ways to get through." It was the same year he thought aloud, "It's a sad world for cows." Those are the kinds of connections we need to make; our thoughtlessness and self-centered worldviews needlessly harm both the wild and domesticated individuals from other species. North to south, east to west, and at all degrees of the compass, wildlife is effectively blocked by the "Great Walls of Median Barriers." Wildlife are hampered and prevented from moving toward the coast, inland, to higher and lower elevations, prevented from moving in all the directions they need to survive and thrive. Millions of individuals from other species die trying to travel, paying the ultimate road toll: our mega, presence predation. Four million miles of road stops them cold while we go where we wish.

Presence Predation at Fur Rendezvous

The annual Fur Rendezvous, in Anchorage, Alaska, I attended in the 1970s was held in an indoor area for merchants who displayed the furred remains of their worldviews. In that context, I encountered a giant of a man and his friends. Somehow we quickly came to know each other's view about killing wolves. Neither of us was going to change the mind of the other. Aside from the fact that I felt intimidated by his, well, biomass, I came away understanding at least part of his anger and hatred for wolves.

He built his house in a wild area, wolf habitat near Denali National Park. His homestead included a number of dearly loved dogs. Wolves can react to domestic dogs as they would to wolves from other packs intruding on their territory. *Protecting* in this man's case meant that wolves killed his unprotected dogs. In his insistence of dominion with an assumed right to build his home anywhere he chose, the large man created conflict. In his hurt and anger about wolves killing his dogs, he blamed the wolves.

That was over three decades ago. I do not know if he sees things differently now. Our new human ecology requires a different, non-anthropocentric perspective. We are biocentric and do not believe that we are above all creation; we are within it, not astride and on top of it. In the new human ecology, we do not have a right to live wherever we choose; damn the environmental consequences of our mega, presence predation.

Chapter 9:

Meet Economic Predator

Economic Predation

We understand why anything 7 billion people do is inescapably *mega*, and we understand how our *presence* in so many places preys upon ecosystems and other species. Now, the third component of neo-predation we will look at is *economic predation*. We create economic predation through our consumption of material goods and services. Instead of killing other species and consuming the landscape directly with weapons and tools in our hands, we replicate our former ecological niche as hunter, fisher, and animal agriculturalists with the impacts we cause by our consumption.

Every one of our economic transactions in cash and non-cash economies creates an outcome for ecosystems, individuals from other species, and other people. From an ecosystem perspective, when we buy and consume goods and services, we create or contribute to the impacts that kill, degrade, alter, deplete, and only sometimes restore the physical and biological integrity of species-filled ecosystems.

A natural order of relationships between individuals of all species once ruled Earth. The intrinsic value of each individual and their species was about those relationships and the roles they played in ecosystems. They fulfilled the needs of other individuals and their species living within the interdependent ecosystems of the biosphere. The natural order of relationships and intrinsic value served the big picture of life evolving on our planet. We changed that order and value system.

We imposed economic systems that acted as if they were independent of ecosystems and the natural order of value. With the natural order in disarray as a result, species and ecosystems are imprisoned in our economic order of value that is nothing like the natural one.

The value we assign them in our economic systems is artificially human. If orangutans value Indonesian rainforests for food and shelter under a natural order of value, human demands for palm oil, peat, and wood create a competing economic order of value. This will be to the detriment of orangutans, all the species living in that rainforest, and the rainforest ecosystem itself. Since the value of other species is now measured in economic terms, we have reduced, even eliminated, their intrinsic values that are needed by other species and ecosystems. The natural order of value that is based on life-sustaining relationships has been replaced and exceeded by a human economic order.[385]

That is how we decide who to kill, what to take, and how much. Who lives and who dies is less about the functioning of intact ecosystems and the innate value of individuals from other species and more about us and our economic demands. This *economic ecology* distorts, and worse yet, ignores, the value of species and ecosystems we are buying and selling. If we let our moral conduct revolve around only the needs of humans, we will seize a cow to produce milk and take away her calf each time. The natural order gives the highest value to milk because it was intended for her calf; our economic order ignores it. When a dairy cow stops producing enough milk to justify the economic costs of keeping her alive, she is sent to slaughter. She, like her calf, was denied her intrinsic value.

It should not be a surprise that our consumption is inaccurately measured as economic costs and benefits. Just as the cow and her calf were discounted, so are ecosystems. I may have missed it, but I have yet to see an economic report or forecast in animal agriculture described as the use, depletion, or restoration of ecosystem services, or the intrinsic value of both cow and calf.

Our mega, presence, and economic predatorship by consumption is so full of wanton destruction that it cannot be called an ecosystem niche. It is, instead, our ecosystem abyss. Our consumption has exceeded Earth's capacity to meet our gluttonous demands and by doing so, we have dug a hole through the center of the Earth into which biodiversity is sliding. Agriculture of all kinds and where we choose to be in the food chain (trophic level) are important factors, but there is much more to think about.

Consider that "...cotton consumers in the EU25 countries are calculated to be indirectly responsible for about 20 percent of the desiccation of the Aral Sea."[386] Those "... massive irrigated agricultural projects triggered the collapse of the Aral Sea and its fishing industry, with feedbacks that include wind-dispersed deposition of surface salts from the dry sea bed on adjacent agricultural lands and even on the glacial sources of rivers feeding the sea."[387] The salts damaged croplands. The sheer size of our human population magnified this economic predation by cotton consumers. No one *intentionally* wanted to kill the Aral Sea and damage its surrounding ecosystems, but we did when we bought the cotton.

It works the same way when carnists *and* non-carnists create economic predation; we create the environmental destruction and suffering. Still, carnism is uniquely damaging when consumers demand the crops and grazing to produce their meat. Soybean exports that go to "livestock" consume 20 percent of Brazil's land area[388] while "70 percent of previous forested land in the Amazon is covered by pastures ..."[389] Rather than stopping the annihilation of the Amazon Basin, economic predatorship, via our demands for livestock, increased nearly "six-fold in volume between 1998 and 2008." In the new economic order, we traded the Amazon Basin's natural order of value for beef and veal.[390] This is a global phenomenon. "At the turn of the twenty-first century, 72 percent of poultry and 55 percent of pigs were raised in global industrialized animal-production systems sustained by feed from other regions and often consumed far from the point of production," according to the paper "International Trade in Meat: The Tip of the Pork Chop."[391]

We are mega economic neo-predators. Though animal agriculture causes between 26 and 51 percent of GHGs,[392] it is not just CO_2 that endangers us. Agriculture contributes other powerful GHGs: Its methane is 23 times more powerful and nitrous oxide is 296 times more powerful per part than CO_2; ammonia emissions "contribute significantly to acid rain and the acidification of ecosystems."[393] We paid for these when we made decisions as consumers. This, our economic predation, destroys entire species who cannot adapt to the ecosystems we have altered and destroyed.

Eating Salmon like an Economic Neo-Predator

Economic predation kills salmon throughout the western United States. The causes behind declining wild salmon populations vary; fishing, dams, fish hatcheries, and habitat destruction top the list. Salmon returning to the rivers of Washington, Oregon, Idaho, and California once had an estimated biomass of 160–226 million kilograms (kg). Today, their biomass is estimated at 11.8–13.7 million kg. This over-the-cliff decline impacted the species who preyed upon salmon as much as the salmon themselves. Coastal and inland ecosystems suffered as well.

As I wrote about earlier, after swimming far upstream into the mountains where they were born, their spawned-out salmon bodies decompose and release nitrogen, phosphorous, carbon, and other nutrients. They have transported those nutrients gained from the food they ate in their ocean home to the rivers and streams where they began life. Inland ecosystems benefit from these nutrients as do species feeding directly off the carcasses. Because we have diminished their numbers, salmon now contribute a mere 6 percent to 7 percent of the nutrients to land-based ecosystems today as they did 140 years ago. The fishing industry's peak of salmon removals ran from 1882 to1915. After that, overall salmon populations steadily declined south of the Fraser River in British Columbia, Canada.[394] The direct takes of salmon by fishers was the first cause of salmon decline, the first predation as fishers. True to the definition of economic predation is what our dams do to salmon.

We create economic predation with our hydroelectric and reservoir dams. Those dams play a decisive role in salmon mortality: They block access to upstream spawning habitat, they kill when out-migrating smolt pass through turbines, and they cause the water retained behind the dams to get so warm that salmon perish or are blocked by the thermal barrier. When we consume hydropower electricity for heating and industry, and the water impounded behind those same dams for irrigation, we have imposed our economic predation on salmon and other species affected by the dams. In effect, when we use the benefits of dams for our needs, the dams *neo-eat* salmon through our economic predation. Here is how it works.

Most of us likely are not making the connections between the products we consume and the salmon-killing, ecosystem-starving hydroelectric power that goes into creating them. We do not make mental connections between salmon, ecosystem nutrients, and the aluminum construction of aircraft when we purchase airline tickets. Aluminum smelting requires lots of electrical power to transform bauxite, the ore, into first aluminum and then airplanes.

Depleted salmon populations and nutrient-deprived ecosystems are directly connected to the dams, the dams to aluminum's electrical consumption, and all of it to our airline tickets. The same model extends from reservoirs behind dams and the irrigated food we buy. It does not stop there.

Our airplane tickets and products created with hydropower prey on orcas as well. Endangered Southern Resident orca killer whales (aka SROs or SRKWs) depend upon salmon, especially the large, high-fat content Chinook. A number of Chinook salmon runs are on the U.S. endangered species list. They are impacted by dams as are other salmon species. So when we buy a plane ticket, power our homes, or buy consumables made with hydropower, we kill salmon and harm orcas, every day without eating a single one.

At the same time we are killing salmon as economic predators, people insist on eating them. They want to continue the current human ecology model of hunter, fisher, and animal agriculturalist predation alongside mega, economic predation. This creates more demand for salmon than ecosystems are able to provide. Responding to our excesses, fish and wildlife agencies as well as tribes got into the business of fish hatcheries. That was, and remains, a mistake.

It can be argued that temporary exceptions should be made for critically endangered salmon runs and species. Unfortunately, state, tribal, and federal fishery agencies have a bad habit of using the ecosystems under their care to propagate fish for fishers, meet outdated carnist consumer demand, create jobs that feed off of a non-adaptive current human ecology, and raise revenue. The agencies appease the demand for salmon with hatcheries even though they harm wild fish.

Hatchery fish are inferior to the wild population but still compete for prey and habitat. Wild young fry are more robust than their competing hatchery transplants. In some instances, too many returning hatchery fish crowd out the natural runs during spawning. Once in the gravel, these spawning nests, called redds, are indistinguishable from those created by wild salmon. In an effort to reduce competition over streambed habitat, agencies urge recreational fishers to step up efforts to kill returning hatchery spawners. The Washington Department of Fish and Wildlife recently sent this advisory:

> Anglers ... are required to retain any hatchery-origin ... steelhead they catch ... [this] will reduce the number of excess hatchery-origin steelhead and consequently increase the proportion of natural-origin steelhead on the spawning grounds. Higher proportions of naturally produced spawners are expected to improve genetic integrity and stock recruitment of ... steelhead through perpetuation of steelhead stocks with the greatest natural-origin lineage. Hatchery fish often outnumber the wild-originated salmonids.[395]

We have tried to outsmart natural salmon genetic viability that is adaptive to ecosystems instead of us. Hatcheries were meant to supplement declining natural salmon runs and provide more salmon for fishers. That included hatchery releases that are timed to create fishing seasons where there were none historically. This gives commercial and recreational fishers more seasons but at a cost to wild runs, and it still does not meet our insatiable consumption.

More than 5 billion hatchery-raised Pacific salmon and steelhead trout are released into the North Pacific every year. They do this despite the fact that researchers have documented a decline in reproductive abilities of nearly 40 percent for every generation salmon are captive-reared.[396] Captive rearing also creates genetic changes that are harmful to wild runs when they interbreed. Say what we will about the natural order of gasping, dying, spawned-out salmon, but there is a different event created when hatchery staff imposes the economic order as they forcibly squeeze sperm (milt) out of the males and slit open females for their eggs, while they are alive. This gross manipulation and gambling of ecosystems exists because our economic predation exceeds the productivity of ravaged, dammed ecosystems. Fishers and our mega, economic predation caused the decline of wild salmon runs. It is the ghost in all of this.

Fish and wildlife agency wisdom is questionable in other respects. They introduce non-native fish species into ecosystems to appease fishers. Chinook salmon and other non-native species are introduced from Wisconsin and Michigan to North Dakota and beyond. Ecosystems are undoubtedly reshaped. From a biocentric, ecosystem perspective, this is corruption.

The Great Human Divorce: Separating Ourselves from Cause and Effect

Our economic predation rides on our spending decisions. Purchase an item or service, and we create our presence in places near and far, wherever the item was made. The Dollar, Bhat, Peso, Ruble, Yuan, Euro, Rupee, Rand, Rial, Shekel, Naira, Guilder, Rupiah, Dinar, and Yen transport us everywhere through cause and effect. Spending money causes things to happen elsewhere; money is at the center of economic predation. It is where we transform the natural order into an economic order. When we purchase a product, we pay for an impact that has already happened somewhere else. We also buy the condition of the ecosystems from which the raw materials were drawn and we buy the living conditions of the people where the product was made, extracted, taken, or grown. To the extent that we keep making the same purchases tomorrow and beyond, we will purchase and predict the future health or disease of those ecosystems and people, and either support or diminish individual people and their families.

It would help if we lived where the raw materials, labor, and products we consume are made. Instead, we are usually separated by time and place. The severance, the great human divorce from cause and effect, lies in the fact that we do not see what our purchases do to ecosystems, other species, and people. In these matters, we have literally lost our senses. We become nearly blind, deaf, and intellectually and emotionally disabled because we do not see the chain of events between our initial causation through a purchase and its effects upon people and ecosystems. Our consumer behaviors need reliable information about what we buy. "When Anne Croft fertilizes her tiny lawn in Washington, D.C.'s Capitol Hill neighborhood, she has no idea that she is contributing to the pollution that still vexes the Chesapeake Bay after 25 years of cleanup.... a stretch of it dozens of miles long is unsuitable for fish or most other creatures," said Elizabeth Shoran, reporter for National Public Radio.[397] Chesapeake Bay is on the receiving end of 17 million people living in Anne Croft's watershed. Most residents do not feel, smell, and understand the impacts they create.

This great human divorce from cause and effect also can be the result of not knowing what we are seeing. Here, our senses can be fooled, where seeing will not reflect what is happening. The scenery may look beautiful but it does not mean the ecosystem is healthy. The surface of an azure sea can hide how barren of fish it is and how only dead coral remains; the canopy of tropical rainforests seen from above can hide the loss of many species below, the "empty forest syndrome," and the pastel vistas of a desert do not tell us about the lack of native plants and the presence of invasive species.

I have trekked in those deserts and walked on their brittle soils. I did not understand that the crunch under my feet was signaling the demolition of a thin, crispy layer, a community of moss, fungus, bacteria, and algae that protected the soil below. It took centuries to build. As KUOW's Northwest News Reporter Anna King wrote, this "crust is the living skin of the desert. It holds down the soil. It absorbs carbon from the atmosphere. It holds water. It puts nutrients back into the ground. It wards off invasive seeds like cheat grass and Russian thistle." Our livestock and we have been busy destroying this protective crust. Since I had walked upon it unaware for many miles, I have contributed to dust storms that blow from continent to continent. That dust speeds global warming because it coats glaciers. Coated glaciers reflect less light and absorb more heat from the sun. I melted glaciers and still, at the time, felt nothing. My senses failed me.[398]

Whether it is the brutalized life experience of a Brazilian steer, or a sweatshop laborer, any intentions we may have to practice good Earth citizenship on their behalf can be transformed into bad because we lack the sensory clues to avoid harming them. It takes extra effort from us to create a just and sustainable economic system. We can reform the place where economic predation lives.

Reconnecting

The good news is that we can buy goods and services that are being created more sustainably than before. Fair trade, shade-grown coffee is an example. Fair trade means the people who owned the coffee beans are paid more fairly for their work while shade-grown encourages the retention of forests needed by other species, including migratory songbirds. What we purchase and how much we reduce our consumption sets the speed of ecosystem decline. We can slow it.

Stopping it is another matter. It is critical to remember that 7 billion people are not going to do anything with a net sustainably. There are too many of us. Without changing our human ecology, we are set to lose ground if we passively accept 9.3 billion people populating Earth in 38 years.

This is why the new human ecology stresses natural population reduction. Our ideas about our population and procreation have to reconnect to the needs of biodiversity. Imagine fewer people with more access to resources and improved standards of living for poor humans and other species at the same time. We can behave like our consumption has consequences for individual people and individuals from other species; our economic systems can reflect a natural order of value. The lives of all species and our sustainability depend on the morality of our purchasing behavior.

We are not sensing and feeling enough about what is already lost. If we never experience wilderness, native trees, or wildlife freely migrating long distances in thundering numbers, would we miss them if they disappeared? How would we understand the innate value of a large, socially tight-knit flock of wild scarlet macaws if the only standard we could reference is a bird in a cage? If captive populations of rare species languishing in zoos have no habitat to return to, how many generations of humans will it take to forget what was? We must memorialize the species and ecosystems we have already destroyed. We have discovered only a tiny fraction of species that inhabit Earth and will never know about those we have erased with an unforgiveable finality. We have no idea of who would still be were it not for our behavior. They are gone, already forgotten, forever.

Today, we affect all species and ecosystems at all times. Geography no longer insulates us from the actions of other people either. We are in the same room, so our worldviews and norms matter; you will affect me and I will affect you, even though we are unlikely ever to meet in person. The changes we need lie partially in the models provided by the social and economic justice, fair trade, sustainable forestry, certified organic, and sustainable practices movements. By default, they are part of the new human ecology. Being a more ethical consumer is made easier when we consume less. But we will struggle with short-term inconvenience and the extra effort it can take in the beginning of change to do the right things. Researching every one of our consumer decisions is impractical. We need transparency and honesty in our economic, corporate, political, and regulatory institutions. They must give us an honest accounting of the good and harm contained in the goods and services they provide and regulate.

Money can buy access to humane and environmentally sane alternatives to what we are doing now. That same wealth can do just the opposite; it can insulate us so much that we are entirely divorced from the natural world. Improper use of wealth can make the divorce complete. Buying a large, hybrid SUV is not sustainability. In its cushioned ride we feel less, hear, smell, and see less of our living world. Even electric vehicles require highways and the hydroelectric, gas, or nuclear-sourced electricity to charge their batteries. Gas or electric, we seldom feel the bumps signaling that lives of smaller species are being crushed under our tires.

Every individual from other species who we kill with our mega, presence, economic neo-predation is also being attacked by the still existing hunter, fisher, and animal agriculturalist predatorship we have refused to stop. In buying this or that piece of furniture, or candy bar with palm oil as an ingredient, we felled the forests and the individuals living in them. They were places where orangutans lived, sloths climbed, snakes hung, air-dwelling plants grew, and insects thrived. Every wood product and piece of metal, every particle of plastic, every apple, piece of fried chicken, and computer has a history. Each one has an ecological genealogy traceable in our global market economy. At every step, we moved further away from the natural order of value toward the economic order. This system allows us to act impersonally, without acknowledging that pigs, old-growth forests, powerless people, fish, antelope, chickens, cows, arctic tundra, ducks, clean water and air, and sheep are important. Our current human ecology needs a reformation.

Our development of agriculture and the domestication of other species was a watershed turning point in our evolution. It transformed our relationships to all other life on Earth. Today our mega, presence, and economic neo-predations equal or exceed that event. It drives our relationships with other species. Controlling it is essential to our survival.

We inherited the current human ecology. It knows how to adapt to ecosystems by destroying them. Hunter, fisher, and animal agriculturalist models of predatory behavior are at their end. Now we get to choose how we play our new identities as mega, presence, and economic neo-predators.

Part III:

Destinations

Chapter 10:

The Incomplete Environmentalist

After having laid down such a strong rhetoric, however, the movers and shakers of conservation and environmentalism, with rare exceptions, stop dead in their tracks when they approach the Animal Question—the whole sticky mess of human views toward, relations with, and uses of animals. This part of the Nature Question [what is our relationship to nature going to be?] is oddly off limits.... Those who address it are regarded as emotional, sentimental, neurotic, misguided, and missing the bigger picture of human relations with the living world. One's bigness and seriousness as a thinker on the Nature Question is measured, in part, by how well one steers clear of the Animal Question... On the contrary, the Animal Question is the very heart of the Nature Question.

—Jim Mason, *An Unnatural Order: The Roots of Our Destruction of Nature*[399]

The humane cause is about preventing suffering. A species does not suffer; individual animals suffer. Organizations which favor causing individual animals to suffer in the name of conservation should accordingly receive no support from any humane donor.

—Merritt Clifton, Editor in Chief, *Animal People*[400]

Our guide is the biocentric deep ecology declaration that individuals from other species, all species, and ecosystems have intrinsic value. Intrinsic value and rights for other species and ecosystems are our reference points. It is here where justice for us and other species begins. Environmentalism is incomplete without these biocentric standards.

We are not environmentalists if our vision and effort allow continued ecosystem collapses, extinctions, untold suffering, and unsustainability to continue. Each of these is the inevitable outcome of the anthropocentric current human ecology. If we want to stop the loss of biodiversity, create social and economic justice, and survive, we, our cultures, and our institutions, must abide by a morally defensible human ecology. That is the way we can protect the innate value of ecosystems, species, and inseparably, individuals from other species.

The environmental community has not addressed the problem of our two incompatible predations. Both are narrowly focused on short-sighted outcomes for us and are decidedly non-biocentric. We live as:

- hunter, fisher, and animal agriculturalist predators, and at the same time, as
- mega, presence, and economic neo-predators.

Human sustainability is impossible as long as the former exists and the latter remains unchecked. Environmentalists are reluctant to challenge our worldviews, cultural beliefs, and deeply embedded personal behaviors that lie behind the decline of ecosystems. It is no wonder that we do not understand the depth and seriousness of what ecocidal agents we have become compared to how much Earth needs us to be a biocentric species.

We face an additional challenge. There is no certainty that a person's passion for social justice, for instance, will automatically transfer to supporting ecosystem health for the benefit of the poor or any of the other Seven Results. In a review of studies about relationships between people, our histories, individual animals, and ecosystems, Joanne Vining wrote, "We do not know whether caring for individual animals translates to caring about species, any more than we know that caring for an individual human leads to caring for humanity. We cannot assume that caring for species leads to caring for ecosystems."[401]

Poverty, ecosystem destruction, overpopulation, the education and social emancipation of women, corporate dominion, who we eat, social and economic justice, the loss of biodiversity, our compassion, the rights of species, and the health of ecosystems are related issues. Each problem flows to and from all the others. What is the common denominator to all NGO missions, environmentalists included, and the challenges we face if not our human ecology? We are dealing with an ecosystem of related issues; our human ecology is the cause and the cure.

Sounding the Depths

The Puget Sound Partnership[402] provides us with an example. The Partnership was created to represent the interests of state and federal agencies, tribes, NGOs, and the public. It is tasked with creating a vision and a plan to stop the deterioration of the Puget Sound ecosystem in Washington State. The Partnership created an evolving Action Plan to restore the Sound. While their resources and expertise are not in question, from a new human ecology perspective, the Action Plan was predestined to fail. Reflecting the Partnership membership, the Action Plan relied on the current human ecology that was unable to confront human population growth, our dietary choices, and our overzealous consumerism. This is how the Partnership tiptoed around the population issue.

After 18 months of hard work, the resulting Action Agenda was careful to state that the expected increase in human population was a serious threat to our beloved Puget Sound and efforts to restore her.

> In a scant 150 years, the human population of Puget Sound has grown from 50,000 to 4 million people.... In creating our productive society and economy we: eliminated three-quarters of the saltwater marsh habitat through dikes and drainage; lost 90 percent of estuarine and riverine wetlands; and armored one third of the Puget Sound shoreline. We removed 66 percent to 84 percent of the old-growth forest in the basin in the past 50 years. We spilled at least 230,000 gallons of oil and hazardous waste (just since 1985), constructed 10 major dams and thousands of small diversions and stream blockages, re-plumbed the Cedar River system, straightened and diked hundreds of small and large rivers, filled wetlands, and introduced almost 100 invasive marine plant and animal species [does not include terrestrial invasives]—sometimes intentionally. ... the entire region faces challenges from a growing human population.[403]

The Partnership repeatedly acknowledged the relationships between human population and the decline of the Puget Sound ecosystem but never addressed our personal responsibility to stop it. The Partnership experts proposed "a conversation" about our overpopulation while knowing that this inaction dooms the recovery effort. The realistic level of support we can expect for restoration—the funding, new regulatory initiatives, and citizen consensus—will not save Puget Sound. Overpopulation is the stronger force.[404] The Puget Sound region is expected to support an additional 1.4 million more people by 2025.[405]

The Action Agenda was written by a committee of representatives, the Partnership, that had to include something for everyone. After stating "... the entire region faces challenges from a growing human population," they relieved us from being responsible about our procreation: "We can help accommodate this growth through: projects, regulations, and incentives to better protect intact areas; focusing growth in urban areas; conserving freshwater resources; and protecting working farms and forests."[406] There is not a population policy here. We are told how destructive population growth is and then implausibly how we can accommodate population growth. This is as good as it gets during Puget Sound's ecosystem emergency.

In the present social climate, there would have been a social and political firestorm if the Puget Sound Partnership told us to sharply curtail conception as part of the recovery plan. Yet, had they been willing to stand the heat, the Partnership would have elevated the population issue to its rightful place: front and center. Social and political fireworks are a necessary part of gaining restoration and moving toward sustainability.

Agencies and organizations charged with protecting our ecosystems are not willing to grab the "third rail" to challenge our population excesses. They have been just as unwilling to call for the transformation of economic systems addicted to endless growth and a *vegan human ecology.* Yet all of them are doable, powerful, and effective solutions.

This problem is not unique to Puget Sound restoration efforts. Bill Devall and George Sessions observed in their 1985 book *Deep Ecology* the following:

[Environmental] Reformist activists often feel trapped in the very political system they criticize. If they don't use the language of resource economists—language which converts ecology into 'input-output models,' forests into 'commodity production systems,' and which uses the metaphor of human economy in referring to Nature—then they are labeled as sentimental, irrational, or unrealistic.[407]

As a result, the people and organizations we look to for guidance and leadership about what we need to do to heal the Earth and live sustainably are not telling us the truth. We get part of the story, an incomplete understanding, and a plan that will not succeed. In that communicated ignorance, we lack the urgency to do what is required for our future on this planet.

Incomplete Environmentalists and Other Advocates

The incompleteness problem applies to environmentalists, but also to those of us who campaign for species rights, social and economic justice, human rights, and the end of hunger and poverty. We are missing an opportunity to fuse all of those issues into one context, our human ecology. Fusing them together is what makes solutions synergistically complete and our work more efficient. Again: What is the largest context for NGO goals, objectives, and campaigns if not our human ecology? What is the overarching system of belief we need and how is it all connected?

We certainly know how to make it disconnected. Mainstream sustainability advocates give little time and weight to the suffering of individuals from wild and domestic species as people abuse and kill them for recreation and food. Though some NGOs are finally getting serious about the ecosystem consequences of animal agriculture, they have not confronted the damage that ecosystems and gene pools suffer when manipulated for hunters and animal agriculture. As Devall and Sessions just noted, environmentalists are discouraged from challenging the status quo more effectively because they can be "labeled as sentimental, irrational, or unrealistic." It is not enough to explain why pain and suffering are ignored by the environmental community, absent, and banished to a tomb of silence. That makes innate value a nonstarter.

In fact, the environmental community *actively* supports unnecessary suffering of wildlife and ecosystem disfigurement at the hands of humans hunting, fishing, animal agriculturaling, and overpopulating. Most of the environmental NGOs I have had the pleasure of meeting and working with care about species, but not so much individuals. Individuals from other species are left out, not allowed intrinsic value unless they are a totemic, charismatic species like harp seals, sea otters, orca whales, and songbirds. Bowhunting, trapping, gun hunting, fishing, and animal agriculture are examples of suffering that are not opposed by mainstream environmentalists and their NGOs.

Environmentalists look away in willed ignorance from the place where ecosystem suffering, degradation, and death occur—at the individual level. Ignore suffering, and our definition of healthy, intact ecosystems will be full of holes. Quality of life for other species and their individuals counts. If we fail to care about them, we enable the destruction of ecosystems with our intentional emotional distance. When we ignore the experiences of individuals and see only their species, how does that affect our urgency for effective change? Our empathy for an individual from our own or another species will be intense if he or she is within a few feet of our ears, eyes, and nose. We care about individuals as soon as we pay attention to them, as soon as we allow the chance to experience empathy with them. Hypocritically, environmental NGOs will use images of individuals to gain our empathy and support for their campaigns to save species, even though their policies ignore the suffering that is experienced at the individual level.

Conservationists and mainstream environmental organizations, forever believing that wildlife management policies will bring a just and sustainable future for us and other species, are a huge part of this problem. Biocentrism, the only pathway I would ever hope for, cannot be achieved without solving Jim Mason's "Animal Question"—"... the whole sticky mess of human views toward, relations with, and uses of animals."

Mainstream environmentalist NGOs and fish and wildlife management agencies approach the "animal question" similarly. They both undervalue the harm done to individuals because they are more interested in the condition of species, communities of species, and ecosystems. When this involves sentient species, as one sentient species to another, how can we do that? This *speciesism*, combined with our tendency to accept manipulations of ecosystems for human ends, ensures that pain and suffering will be neglected as issues worthy of environmentalist consideration. Our cultural bias diminishes the intrinsic value and sentience of wildlife species, so it is not a surprise we find it in environmental organizations and wildlife management agencies. For them, ignoring the animal question thickens the walls of their fortress that protects the current human ecology of carnism. It makes their jobs easier.

Author Jeremy Rifkin writes in *The Empathic Civilization*, "The divide between the environmentalists and animal-rights people is illustrative of the difference between an older ideological consciousness, with its emphasis on rationality, utility, and efficiency, and an emerging biosphere consciousness grounded in personal participation, emotional identification, and empathic extension."[408] He is comparing the anthropocentric current human ecology where mainstream environmentalism lives and the biocentric new human ecology that includes species' rights. The future of environmentalism has to be a biocentric, deep new human ecology.

Those who identify themselves as conservationists, and the conventional kind of wildlife management that entertains them, are not shy about causing pain, fear, and suffering in wildlife. Like these non-compassionate conservationists, mainstream environmental NGOs and wildlife management agencies practice an unsavory splitting of values—compassion and conservation. Non-compassionate conservationists narrowly interpret what it means to love nature, aka biophilia. They accept the dreadful experiences of individuals from other species as collateral damage for gaining the health of favored species they hunt, fish, trap, and also eat from the animal agriculture sector.

Wildlife management agencies use recreational hunters to achieve their social and biological management objectives and revenue streams. Their tools include bowhunting, *varmint* hunting, gun hunting, and snaring and trapping to maintain unnatural ratios between different species who are often predator and prey. Managers also manipulate the composition of sex and age classes within species to produce more product from their wildlife management business for hunters and fishers. These management practices are a waste of resources at a time when the loss of biodiversity under their regime should be enough to call for deep reforms in wildlife management. Environmental organizations should demand a change in our human ecology and a concurrent wildlife management reformation. But environmentalists will not because they accept the current human ecology. That is, as long as environmental NGOs condone carnism they are supporting both the massive grazing of ecosystems by livestock and the continued practice of using ecosystems to grow endless acres of grain to feed livestock.

Wildlife management is intent on protecting carnism. This does not support ecosystems. It is not biocentrism. The harm this causes is the reason why fish and wildlife management agencies employ hunters and trappers to "fix" the problems their support for carnism creates. I refuse to ignore that.

Without question, NGOs give it their all. I have seen and been part of their underappreciated self-sacrifice, dedication to work, skills, and successes that took long hours and often low pay. It is not enough. Earth is not getting the changes in our behavior she needs. No combination of institutions, governments, and nonprofit organizations can end poverty, environmental destruction, and suffering without all of us changing the way we live. They lack the resources and power to overcome the overwhelming inertia of the current human ecology that drives the decline of ecosystems. Institutions, agencies, and NGOs are limited in what they can accomplish because they are forced to work within the political, economic, and consumer disasters we create with our behavior.

By choice and belief, we do both so much evil and so much good. If we believe in the importance of being inherently good, as individuals and as a species, then we must take responsibility for our human ecology. Aside from having good hearts, we need to question who we really are by looking at how we behave.

NGOs Giving Comfort

Environmentalists and other advocates should lead and inspire our journey out of the current human ecology and into the humane and sustainable new human ecology. Instead, they are not telling us the entire story about what is required for our biological and moral survival. I fear that incompleteness. It scares the hell out of me. And I ache when I see the false hope and comfort the environmental community continues to give the world community. Without a new human ecology, we will get incomplete environmentalists, incomplete humanitarians, incomplete conservation biologists, incomplete economic justice advocates, incomplete aid programs for destitute people, and incomplete species rights platforms.

Part of the reason NGOs of all types are not asking what is required of us is because they run into this reality: We have not agreed on shared elements of a transcultural worldview and value system. We need this to underwrite a universal and cooperative response to global issues. To make matters worse, this is a cultural minefield. The process of agreeing to a viable human ecology for our species requires some uncomfortable confrontations between deeply held cultural beliefs. Then there are the dominionists, the anthropocentric people who believe Earth is here for our pleasure and limitless demands that masquerade as needs. They are a stark contrast to the biocentrists who believe we are part of the whole, not its center and the sole reason for the existence of the Universe.

NGOs have to struggle with their members and financial supporters as well. They can hinder organizational success because they lag behind their NGO in information and vision. NGOs can lose their members and donors if their policies and vision get too far ahead of them. Progressive goals, policies, strategies, and campaigns are not something all of their supporters will accept. What would happen to organizations that coerce their members, donors, and the public to reduce carbon footprints, procreation, and personal consumption immediately and drastically? Or tell their support base they should not own an ecologically smart, much less a dumb, home larger than say 1,400 square feet because heating, cooling, building, maintaining, land occupation, and furnishing consumes an unsupportable amount of ecosystem services?

What would happen if mainstream nonprofits made their members and supporters uncomfortable despite Herculean efforts to use effective messaging and education?

As John Feeney points out in *Earth Needs Our Renewed Attention to Human Population Growth*,[409] population has become a taboo subject since getting a lot of public press coverage in the 1960s and '70s. Environmental and other advocates have shied from the issue even though it drives massive social and environmental harm. What would the United States look like today if we had increased the tax deduction 20 years ago for the first child by 150 percent but gave none for any child born thereafter? What is more radical from a biocentric and practical perspective: sharply curtailing procreation or letting Earth die under our weight? We have foolishly chosen to affect every species and change every ecosystem. Now is the time for environmentalists to speak out on population and every aspect of our human ecology that will destroy the living systems of Earth. Being incomplete is not a survivable option.

Psychologist and author Albert Bandura wrote, "Greenpeace announced that population 'is not an issue for us.' Friends of the Earth declared that 'it is unhelpful to enter into a debate about numbers.' [But]... David Brower ... put it well when he once said, 'You don't have a conservation policy unless you have a population policy'"[410] Brower founded Earth Island Institute. It is one of the most capable NGOs whose campaigns demonstrate the interconnectedness of issues. Their award-winning *Earth Island Journal* reflects consistency in their responses to issues. The *Journal* describes how palm oil consumption causes not only the clearing of rainforests in Asia, the decimation of wildlife, and the release of greenhouse gases, but also how it creates social injustice for the people living there.[411] In the same issue, we read about the suffering of domesticated elephants, human population problems, the slaughter of dolphins at Taiji, Japan, and calls for "putting food near the center of the environmental movement."[412, 413]

Crawling, Not Walking

When I think of the decades-long fight by NGOs to save Earth's life-sustaining wholeness, I cannot believe how many of the same original issues from the 1960s still plague the planet. Year after year, campaigns emblematic of our challenges remain on a treadmill. They include fossil fuel consumption and pollution; whaling; loss of soil and soil fertility; diminishing freshwater resources; barbaric leghold traps and the associated fur industry; our loss of biodiversity; the inhumane practices, habitat losses, and resource-guzzling by animal agriculture; public transportation; human poverty and disease; human overpopulation; social inequality between men and women; resource depletion; the despots who sell off tropical forests for their own profit while denying democracy to their citizens; denial of rights and access to land; the spread of toxins; and the self-destructive ignorance of our economic systems. Important victories and progress has been won, but all of these issues originate from our current human ecology.

All of the terrible things we do to Earth spring forth from our practices, beliefs, and worldviews that make it okay, that make it the norm, that make it just fine to put humankind in the center of all that is most important. In our arrogance, we will find our pain and our doom and cast that sad misfortune upon all the creatures of the Earth. We can do better.

Our approaches must be as comprehensive as the problems we face. Piecemeal NGO solutions do not work any better than fragmented ecosystems. In 1992, at the United Nations Conference on Environment and Development held in Rio de Janeiro, better known as the Earth Summit, a goal was established to reduce the loss of biodiversity by 2010. Twenty years later in 2012, the opposite has happened. Biodiversity loss has accelerated.[414]

I have long admired this explanation about our illogical behavior in Daniel Quinn's, *Ishmael*. [415] We are like the pilots of gliders. We get a running start and then leap off of a cliff and mistake gliding for flying. We become self-absorbed and intoxicated with the false belief that we have acquired the power of flight. We ignore the fact that we are forever losing altitude as we glide downward. Even as the ground nears and promises a crash, we continue believing that we are in control because we are *flying*. We are not flying as much as we are gliding on what is left of ecosystems. We are not taking seriously that the ground is always coming closer at an increasing speed. In the foolish complacency and comfort of our flight, we do not fight the illusion. We are not moved to act in this emergency. We think we will avoid the deadly crash at the last minute. We never think it is too late. We cannot even imagine it. Our end.

Species and Ecosystem Rights, and Species versus Individuals

There are significant differences between the perspectives of environmentalists, animal welfare advocates, and species rights campaigners. I believe those differences are waning and that we are in a transition that will find biocentrism at its end. But we will have to fight for biocentric responses before the collapse of ecosystems imposes it upon us. Though we all are motivated by the relationships, values, understanding, and perceptions we have with and of the world, our responses differ. Anything we can do to bridge those differences, to move our human ecology forward, increases our collective strength.

For expediency and the sake of discussion, for the first camp, I am combining mainstream environmentalism with the more socially conservative conservationism. Their advocates believe that wildlife management allows us to continue our current human ecology lifestyle; we can be hunters, fishers, and animal agriculturalists, and mega, presence, and economic neo-predators at the same time. They do not generally question the humaneness of hunting, fishing, and trapping as these are ways of getting resources for humans and maintaining control over ecosystems. Those who view themselves as ethical *sportsmen* take pride if they make a quick kill, in part to reduce suffering. And there are those who intentionally make it more probable that suffering will increase when they chose muskets and arrows to kill others.

In the second camp, we find the animal welfare advocates (welfarists) who are concerned with the humane standards for the treatment of other species. They do not necessarily oppose our use of and killing them. That is their public face. But unlike past generations of animal welfarists, they increasingly support the rights of individuals from other species, including the right to live non-exploited lives. They share space with other tents in this camp, the animal/species rights campaigners (rightists). The rightists are opposed to the assumption that we have a right to harm, kill, or use sentient species for food, medical experiments, clothing, and entertainment.

There are conservative and progressive, *old school* and *cutting edge* organizations and supporters in the environmentalist/ conservationist and welfarist/rightist camps. They all interact with one another in the public arena and can take both similar and different positions on issues.

Deep ecology and conservation biology are unique unto themselves in the third camp. They influence the way *everyone* in the other camps thinks about our relationships to other species and how we should go about restoring ecosystems. Deep ecologists are, as you have already heard, biocentric and act from the belief that all individuals of species and ecosystems have innate value. Conservation biology is an academic discipline that has been steering wildlife and ecosystem management agencies to focus on ecosystems and communities of other species instead of a few specific species important to fishers, trappers, hunters, and animal agriculturalists. They look for the causes of extinctions and work to correct them.

Mixed Experiences

Vegetarians and vegans value individuals from other species. That does not mean they are deep ecology environmentalists rallying for species and ecosystems. The motive for *going vegetarian* is often for personal (anthropocentric) health reasons. On the other hand, polls indicate that vegans are motivated by several considerations, including environmental concerns. [416] Single-issue (health) vegetarians stand on a weak platform. Dietary fads come and go. I am still surprised when I am told, "I was a vegetarian once." Many of us have gone on diets to lose weight and paid for gym memberships that were equally brief. These single-issue vegetarians have too few inspirations to make their vegetarianism more than transitory. For vegans I know, their motivations are numerous and focus on the experiences of other species with thought and empathy. By default if not intent, biocentrism grows with the addition of every new vegan.

From my experience with their policies and public posturing, I find that mainstream environmentalists and their organizations are still comfortable with manipulating ecosystems for carnist pleasures. Whether it is for eating grazed species from animal agriculture, or shooting wildlife, mainstream environmentalists try to avoid alienating the 5.5 percent of the U.S. population that hunts and dominates wildlife agency policies. The hunting lobby is a powerful ally when their interests coincide with environmental campaigns. They do not seek vegan support. In fact, they do not want to be associated with veganism out of fear of looking unreasonable.

I have known many environmentalists who hide their compassion for the individuals of species when campaigning in public. The maxim of "species count but not so much the interests of individuals from other species" helps environmentalists work with resource managers who try their best at being objective science-based mechanics, utilitarians responsible for getting resources, including lethal recreation, supplied to people. Though mainstream environmentalists will take exception in some cases, their general allegiance to wildlife management agencies predominates. This protects and perpetuates animal agriculture and as much hunting, trapping, and fishing as the agencies can produce. This gives species welfare advocates and rightist campaigners heartache and a sense of hopelessness.

For perspective, consider that the justification for today's extreme wildlife management starts with animal agriculture. If we accept animal agriculture's pervasive grazing of ecosystems and the bastardization of ecosystems to grow food for livestock, then the kind of wildlife and ecosystem management we have is inevitable. When we change our dietary choices, wildlife managers will not so easily claim they need hunters and trappers to protect the animal agriculture and its food industries. When we wrest control of wildlife management from the hunters, which we will at some point, wildlife management will change.

Animal welfarists and rightists believe that sentient individuals from other species are most important and given a hierarchy of value over the non-sentient. The difficulty of this proposal is visible when the rights of sentient invasive species who were introduced by humans are pitted against the survival of endangered species, non-sentient species like endangered plants, and ecosystems. The work of killing tens of thousands of introduced rats, multitudes of feral pigs and cats, or hundreds of fox to help recover native marine bird species on islands is deeply painful to species welfare advocates and rights campaigners. This is true even when they understand the violence done by the invasives to the ecosystems and the indigenous species who cling to existence. Animal welfarists and rightists often have no prescriptions for stopping the suffering and death of individuals from other species and ecosystems where invasive species are doing the harm. It is an impossible situation created by human ignorance. The pain and suffering will fall on one species or another. But it is our original fault, not that of the invasive species. So, humane and nonlethal control of invasive species is what welfarists and rightists want. Birth control, making habitat non-friendly, and reigning in human encroachment on wildlife habitat are approaches they want to see.

We are sometimes able to airlift burrows out of ecosystems or reduce wild horse populations even though it is the cattle who are doing far more chewing on the landscape. But when a need to eliminate invasive species is proposed, we seem to have nothing as effective, as crude, and as cruel as rodenticides that kill rats and mice who prey on the eggs of native birds. Species welfare advocates and rights campaigners are a pain to wildlife management agencies trying to restore habitat and biodiversity. Mainstream environmentalists are offended by this lack of concern for species and ecosystems.

Deep Ecology

The deep ecology philosophy pushes environmentalists, vegans, advocates for species rights, everyone, to go much deeper into our human ecology. In their book *Deep Ecology*, Bill Devall and George Sessions criticized the animal rights efforts of that 1985 era. They saw correctly at the time that animal rights advocates believed in a false hierarchy of species; sentient beings were of utmost importance while non-sentient individuals and ecosystems were valued less or not considered at all. Devall and Sessions saw in this hierarchy yet another version of anthropocentric worldviews.

In deep ecology, all individuals of all species and their ecosystems have intrinsic value independent of any benefit for humans. Bacteria and fungi, so essential to ecosystems and life, have the same *biocentric equality* as all other species. In the years since *Deep Ecology* was published, animal welfarist and rightist organizations have sunk their teeth into environmental issues; they are often led by their concerns for sentient individuals from other species, those capable of being aware of the experience of life. I do not know the extent to which vegans do or do not still cling to such a hierarchy where the perceived non-sentient are given little or no thought. The vegans I know, have worked with, and had the pleasure of meeting both fit and do not fit Devall's and Sessions' criticism.

If vegan views on environmental issues are not founded on deep ecology, they will lose the sentient species they cherish. Those who are vegan environmentalists may already realize that a vegan human ecology alone is not enough to make one wholly biocentric. Still, deep ecology's creed of biocentrism requires a vegan human ecology. Arne Naess, philosophical founder of deep ecology, had this to say about individuals from other species during an interview conducted at the Zen Center in Los Angeles,

> There is a basic intuition in deep ecology that we have no right to destroy other living beings without sufficient reason. ... human beings will experience joy when other life forms experience joy and sorrow when other life forms experience sorrow. Not only will we feel sad when our brother or a dog or a cat feels sad, but we will grieve when living beings, including landscapes, are destroyed.[417]

This is where today's environmental movement and species rightists must meet. Individuals, communities of individuals, their species, and ecosystems are not separable considerations in the new human ecology or deep ecology. Though the new human ecology includes many other subjects like human overpopulation, much of the incompleteness of environmentalism comes from its not caring about individuals from other species, sentient and non-sentient alike.

When Naess wrote "Lifestyle Trends within the Deep Ecology Movement," he listed 25 "ways that supporters of the deep ecology movement can joyfully adapt their lifestyle to the movement." His list includes vegetarianism and the end of excessive material consumption. He asked for "lifestyles that can be maintained universally—lifestyles that are not blatantly impossible to sustain without injustice toward fellow humans or other species." In other writings, he stressed Gandhi-style nonviolence and a limit to human population.[418]

Since the time of his writings, our global population and consumption have grown wildly out of control. There is little left of what Arne Naess inferred was *reasonable* human use of ecosystems and "living beings." Our species has overwhelmed Earth. What seemed reasonable in Naess' lifetime no longer is; we are so absorbed in ourselves that what we take as being *reasonable* pits the survival of ecosystems, species, and individuals from other species against our insatiable demands. That, to understate it, is a problem. Incomplete environmentalists need to understand that there is a more fundamental issue they need to ask. Is our human ecology appropriate or not? Does it constantly violate the decencies of deep ecology?

Research is finding sentience in more species, not fewer. Our knowing that honeybees exhibit pessimism and "a vertebrate-like emotional state"[419] reinforces deep ecology, biocentrism, species rights, and a new human ecology that incorporates our responses to a biodiversity that we still know little about. Jellyfish, the most ancient multi-organ animals on Earth, existed 600 to 700 million years ago.[420] They were once thought of as passive, unintelligent creatures. Not anymore. Box jellyfish have 24 eyes of four different types. They use them to get bearings of landmarks on the shoreline and peer upward to the sky to navigate actively to where they want to be. Then they rise or sink into the currents that will take them to where they want to go.[421] Deep ecology and the new human ecology assume their innate value; other species do not have to thread their way through the artifice of human bias and exclusion.

Studies also reveal that nonhuman species have culture. In "Culture and Conservation of Non-Humans with Reference to Whales and

Dolphins: Review and New Directions," the authors define culture as "information or behavior—shared by a population or subpopulation—which is acquired from conspecifics [two or more individuals from the same species] through some form of social learning." The authors ask, should identifiable culture that varies from place to place in the same species be considered for specific protections, cultural protection? "Conservation is often believed to be promoted through considering the status of populations below the sub-species level, sometimes called 'evolutionarily significant units (ESUs).' ... should culture be considered in the determination of ESUs?"[422]

This is no small matter. Great expense, agency resources, and environmentalists' efforts are invested to protect threatened and endangered species. It makes sense that we should save other species' cultures for the same reasons we would human cultures. Going appropriately further, we should protect them from all harm of our doing. All cultures contain local knowledge; this gives evolutionary advantages for adapting to specific ecosystems. It is reasonable to believe that many cultures exist within each species capable of them. If that is the case, we have another reason to stop being carnists. Lost cultural diversity in other species hastens the loss of biodiversity.

Suffering Ecosystems

Within ecosystem decline and destruction lies immense, unfathomable suffering. Ecosystems are full of sentient life able to suffer pain, fear, discomfort, thirst, starvation, and distress, all very real issues caused by habitat loss. The life pulsing within ecosystems enjoys dependable shelter, species culture, social communities, abundant food, clean water, a lack of stress, and comfort. Since sentient individuals depend upon the non-sentient life within the ecosystem as well as the ecosystem's physical geography and biological processes, the destruction of any aspect of an ecosystem promises to cause suffering to those who are sentient. Oddly, environmentalists shy away from acknowledging this physical and psychological environmental suffering when it should be one of the mainstays of their campaigns and in their hearts.

Environmentalists will use an image of a polar bear seemingly stranded by global warming on an ice floe and a mountain gorilla who faces poaching and habitat loss. But they neglect to message how constant and deep the suffering in environmental destruction really is. The environmentalist communities are missing both the depth of ecosystem suffering and its powerful message.

Given the extent of the torment, it does not make sense for environmentalists to distance themselves from species' welfarist and rightist organizations. Environmentalists already practice species welfare and rights as a de-facto outcome of environmental campaigns. When they work to protect fauna and flora from starvation due to habitat loss, disease, invasive species, and displacement by humans, they are practicing a limited version of species rights. Why is it not just as important to them to oppose the hunters, fishers, and animal agriculturalists who destroy ecosystems, cause disease outbreaks, wounds, death, dehydration, fear, and stress? And what does the futility of a cow wanting her calf returned or the pain of wolves seeing their pack mates killed by aerial gunners mean to environmentalists? Displaced, chased, and hunted wildlife are homeless refugees. Pigs and chickens crammed into barren cages and denied anything socially normal in life should elicit the same response in environmentalists. The sick, the dying, the hungry, thirsty, and impoverished, all are characteristics of ecosystem decline, characteristics that should sound familiar since we readily acknowledge these conditions in human suffering.

Species and the individuals comprising them have a right to exist and play out their personal evolutionary drama. What happens to an individual of a species also happens to the ecosystem. If we care for one, we are required to care for the other. Environmentalist campaigns are operationally and ethically deficient when they do not acknowledge this dynamic. Advocates for other issues are bound in the same way, since the state of ecosystems determines the outcomes for social and economic justice and our economies.

In a positive trend, the environmental community is slowly recognizing that the production and consumption of food is at the heart of environmentalism. How food is grown, processed, transported, who owns what, what kind of values are applied, how inequitably the producers are paid, and who is doing what to which part of Earth in the agricultural economies of the world determine our relationships with Earth. The fate of ecosystems, the poverty and prosperity of people, and the morality of our consumer choices are linked.

The Gobi bear and snow leopard are in conflict with invasive camels, goats, sheep, and donkeys brought by nomadic peoples. They create desertification.[423] And it does not matter whether we are urbanites or nomadic tribes. Domesticated individuals from other species killed for human consumption, and the grazing and plant crops that feed them, are the new fauna and flora that overrun and grossly distort the ecosystems that environmentalists are pledging to save. If they do not oppose animal agriculture, they support it.

Evolution and natural selection, in their cold and unflinching creation of life and death, delivered singular and wholesale disasters that befell the living. But these also serve a higher purpose that have produced all of the glory and grandeur of nature and the ecosystems that nurture us. Our current human ecology does not have such a grand design and purpose and no sense of geological scale. Human selection pressures are not producing an ecologically stable, diverse, or beautiful outcome.

Our human existence and human ecology are not so much planned things as they are a haphazard, self-indulgent, and limitless power grab. We have had the chance to prosper in a planned way, to find consensus on what a reasonable presence of humanity would look like, and move toward greater sustainably. Instead, we chose to be irresponsible in the center of our lives and responsible here and there a bit on the edges. We recycle but ransack ecosystems.

We stumble in our feeble attempts to correct our destructive relationships with nature. Relatively few people do most of the work of saving us from ourselves. If not for the leadership, good works, personal examples, and validation of our personal beliefs coming from environmental and other NGOs, the world would be a far sadder and tattered place. These NGOs, their staff, and volunteers are the authors of the changes already begun, the hopeful starts for transforming human ecologies. They have assumed a noble role: We are to be mindful about how we choose to live. I thank them for that and so should you. Support their work. But their biggest bottleneck to moving forward is their support for the current human ecology and their unwillingness to confront the sentience and rights of individuals from other species. That is where the environmental community's incompleteness originates, but does not end.

An Inconsistent Relationship with Earth

The environmental community should be panicking over their support of the current human ecology, the culture of carnism, and the institutions of wildlife management. Those agencies not only lack the ability to prevent the loss of ecosystems and biodiversity, they are ensuring it will happen. I will explain why in a later chapter.

Environmentalists may not think of themselves as being in the animal/species rights camp, but they have at least one foot in the tent. They feel anguish when polar bears and seals starve, or have no place to bear their young, because global warming melted their ice. Equally telling, would meat-eating environmentalists approve the commercial raising of elephants, rhinos, bears, orangutans, mountain gorillas, dolphins, and lions for food if their numbers were plentiful on the ranch and in the wild? Yes or no to which species? Where would they draw the line, if any, and what does our response say about our worldviews, our moral guidelines, and the kinds of conservationism and environmentalism we support?

What about companion dogs, cats, rabbits, mice, rats, and birds? We know them as fascinating, complex individuals who possess unique personalities within the overall attributes of their species. Should we raise any sentient being to a tender weight for six weeks to three years then slit her unsuspecting throat or hit him in the head with a pneumatic hammer? Can we kill, butcher, and eat a companion cat or dog who we raised, played with, grew in character with as companions, sat with together looking out the window, intimately touching, smelling, and watching each other in endless fascination and trust? Should environmentalists dismiss her value because we are only concerned with the survival of her species? Yet, that is what we accomplish as environmentalists if we accept carnism and all the activities associated with it.

When we arrive at a place full of empathetic appreciation for their individual complexity, when we see this individual of another species who is not us but similar to us in many more ways than not, when we appreciate her for the miracle she is, do we then abandon our compassion, kill her without need and in betrayal because she fits our learned idea of *tastes good*? Cultural traditions and practices are not the most important issues; the sentient beings' abilities to suffer are, the rights to existence are, and the innate value of all species and ecosystems are.

Long ago, I read a letter to the editor in *Alaska Magazine*.[424] It concerned a grizzly bear on Kodiak Island. The letter described how this grizzly bear was on her back playing with a log balanced in the air between her four massive paws amidst the autumn colors. The writer watched this bear playing in her unguarded moment of bear enjoyment, and then killed her. That mental image remains stuck in my gut as the norm-driven injustice and ecological depravity I am writing about. A beautiful life so violently and arrogantly taken without need is an irreverent and repulsive human behavior.

With overwhelming technology, firepower, and no risk, hunters and fishers brag and pose in photos with the individuals they have chased and slain. They kill and wound as if wildlife are unfeeling commodities, individuals who do not count, who do not have intrinsic value. Then there are the fur trappers who make underwater drowning sets.

By following the U.S. Department of Interior's Minerals Management Service[425] manual of instruction, trappers ensure beavers are held underwater by a trap and then forced to struggle for up to 15 minutes of panicked and gasping attempts to swim upwards to the surface to breathe. The beaver fights for his life, terrified. Mink, muskrat, otter, and nutria are trap-drowned this way, too. How many in the environmental community campaign against trapping or instill in children how wrong is this cruel disregard for the trapped individuals' suffering? Wildlife management agencies accept this barbaric behavior as well.

Part of the Wisconsin Department of Resources mission is to recruit young people into the trapping culture. On the cover of their trapping regulations brochure is the photo of an 11-year-old boy with a dead otter in his arms. Under it, the caption reads, "The content of this pamphlet was prepared by the Department of Natural Resources. Part of the printing costs was paid for by the Wisconsin Trappers Association."[426]

According to the summary Karen Dawn provides us in *Thanking the Monkey*, "To make a forty-inch fur coat it takes between thirty and two hundred chinchilla, or sixty mink, fifty sables, fifty muskrats, forty-five possums, forty raccoons, thirty-five rabbits, twenty foxes, twenty otters, eighteen lynx, sixteen coyotes, fifteen beavers, or eight seals."[427] Some were taken from their families and communities in the wild; others were raised on fur *ranches*. Some were drowned, some taken by leghold traps and snares on land, some were crushed in the wild by Conibear traps, and on the ranch, many had an electrode forced up their anus and were electrocuted to death. I have yet to hear environmental organizations express moral outrage or conduct campaigns opposing this. Is it what they want that 11-year-old boy to believe in? This is how ecosystem decline is nurtured.

Beaver and their dams, now eliminated over much of their range by burgeoning human encroachment, were important ecosystem players when beaver numbers were much higher than today. The pre-European contact beaver population in the United States is estimated to be between 60 and 400 million. We have reduced them to a population of six to 12 million.[428]

Beaver dams create wetland and meadow habitat, refresh aquifers, and as silt settles in the ponds behind them, clarify the water that moves downstream.[429] Trappers who drown beavers and agencies that endorse drowning wildlife are examples of the current human ecology that environmentalists passively accept. Remember that these agencies use trappers and hunters to do their bidding so that the current human ecology of human excess can continue. As long as environmental organizations are unwilling to reform the goals and philosophies of fish and wildlife management, they will be inconsistent with biocentric principles and support a dead-end human ecology.

What Revolution? Still Grazing the Prairies and Forests

The issue of grazing belongs in this section about environmentalism. It ties into the ready willingness of many environmentalists to support small-scale animal agriculture, regulated grazing, and the neo-omnivore movement I described in the section about *The Omnivore's Dilemma*. Many environmental NGOs have campaigned against the most egregious practices of livestock grazing. A few of those organizations work with livestock-raising businesses that are deemed progressive. Progressive animal agriculturalists do preserve landscapes, oppose mining, set aside habitat for endangered species, and forgo money in their pocket to preserve some of the integrity of biodiversity. The scale of these selective protections can be large.[430]

Though I disagree with many assumptions Courtney White makes in his book *Revolution on the Range*, he does a good job in describing the evolution of attitudes between some ranchers and some environmentalists. I use the term *rancher* generically and do not accept its romanticized culture and business to hide a horrific industry. Ranchers and environmentalists can cooperate to reduce harm to ecosystems, but the slaughter of cattle and sheep continues and the ecosystems remain subservient to invasive livestock.

In the book's prologue, White defines his vision: "The New Ranch describes an emerging progressive ranching movement that operates on the principle that the natural processes that sustain wildlife habitat, biological diversity, and functioning watersheds are the same processes that make land productive for livestock."[431] Done correctly, he asserts, new ranches can increase the diversity of grasses, restore dried-up streams, and increase wildlife abundance.

White advocates that livestock be tended to mimic what wild herds of bison and other grazers did before livestock grazing took control. He emphasizes that grazing, whether by wild or domestic individuals, creates a plant community that would not otherwise exist. White then compares "new ranch" livestock grazing to historic grazing's worst possible abuses to the land. However, he and those environmentalists who remain omnivorous carnists miss an important point: This is a program about replacing native species with invasive species in order to promote an animal agriculture we do not need. Biocentric, non-carnists recognize this. Incomplete environmentalists do not.

Grazers, wild and domestic, do shape plant communities. They account for much of natural selection pressures on the plant community, but not all. Soil, weather, and the relationships with other herbivore species like prairie dogs are also critically important. And when environmentalists support commercial grazing, the terrain must be *anthropocentrically* productive, not *biocentrically* productive, for its natural order of value. The ebbs and flows in ecosystem productivity, the natural ups and downs of indigenous species, the variability in nutrient recycling, and the unevenness of land use by native species over time are from a different, biocentric norm than what White's "new ranches" seek.

Like any business, the ideal state of all ranching is one of predictably consistent productivity. We are asked to believe that grazed landscapes should be manipulated to produce as maximally and consistently as possible; they must produce an optimum biomass for our domesticated invasives. Consistent ecosystem productivity is required by animal agriculture. This is not necessarily the same as what the ecosystem would produce under natural, noninvasive, conditions. If the goal of commercial grazing is a maximized root system and the scheduled productivity of plant communities, then that is the standard they impose on the ecosystem.

Livestock grazing advocates begin by assuming animal agriculture is necessary when it is not. There is enough botanical agricultural bounty in the United States to feed all of us using a fraction of ecosystems, water, fossil fuels, killed wildlife, and lost soil. Progressive ranching feeds an economic order, not a natural, biocentric, deep human ecology one. Biocentrically, ranching is not an ecosystem's purpose.

Livestock ranching occurs in a variety of habitats, including short-grass prairies, tallgrass prairies, forested areas, and the transition zones between them. For much of the landscape, where these prairies once thrived and had evolved with hoofed wildlife, there are now immense and unrelenting fields of corn and soybeans. As we have visited earlier, most of it goes to feed livestock. Livestock invasives are grazing what land is left. New ranching drives cattle from place to place in large numbers in an effort to replicate what bison used to do. This does appear in some important ways to interact with some ecosystems similarly to bison.[432] Yet, there is much debate about the matter.

Researchers are faced with the scope of the grazing industry, the multitude of different micro-habitats, human history, the variety of grazing practices and regulations, and the highly variable responses that occur between grazing species, plant communities, soils, fire, and climate. This contributes to researchers coming to inconsistent conclusions about livestock grazing and the biotic communities where they are placed.

Some recent studies appear to indicate that cattle, under the right schemes, can reproduce nearly the same results as bison in plant communities. One paper notes, "Although bison and cattle differentially altered some vegetation components, the plant communities in bison and cattle pastures were 85 percent similar after 10 years of grazing."[433] Other papers, but not all, came to the same conclusion that grazing by keystone herbivores like bison, or their surrogates, cattle, under certain conditions, supported biodiversity.[434, 435] Researcher Richard Hart writes in "Plant biodiversity on shortgrass steppe after 55 years of zero, light, moderate, or heavy cattle grazing," ... "Although behavior of the two species differs somewhat ... rangelands appear to be sustainable under optimum management for each species."[436] But, in addition to the biocentric versus anthropocentric objections I raised, there appear to be problems with the way some studies are conducted.

Law professor Debra Donahue meticulously researched the history and circumstances of grazing on public lands. Grazing takes place in national parks, wildlife refuges, and in national forests. She found that "The first domestic livestock (500 cattle, 5,000 sheep, and 1,000 horses) were introduced to what is now the American Southwest in 1540. An estimated 50,000 sheep and 20,000 cattle were brought from Mexico to missions in Texas and the Southwest in the 1700s."[437] While much of today's debate concerns cattle grazing, sheep grazing was responsible for the original degradation of our western ecosystems.

As Donahue reminds readers throughout her book *The Western Range Revisited*, studies are often very site-specific, are often not applicable to large landscapes, and there can be a lack of discernment whether the resulting plant communities are being given appropriate weight. Not all plant species are equal in importance to the ecosystem. A 15 percent change in one or more species existence may be disproportionately more, or less, important than others. Researchers may be ignoring other factors, she notes. Were the studied ecosystems ever grazed pre-settlement by large, native herbivores? Were there other factors besides grazing, such as climate change and the accompanying differences in atmospheric gasses that biased the data produced by researchers?

Donahue is perhaps the leading advocate for removal of livestock from all *arid* lands leased by ranchers from the Bureau of Land Management (BLM). Arid lands are the most fragile, more so than landscapes with more rain and snow. Including the arid ecosystems, Donahue reports that 285 million acres of public lands are grazed under BLM management.[438] This figure does not account for the additional grazing leases in national forests and wildlife refuges.

Allison Jones' paper titled, "Effects of Cattle Grazing on North American Arid Ecosystems: A Quantitative Review," analyzed 54 papers on grazing in xeric [arid] ecosystems. It found that "[69 percent] revealed significant detrimental effects of cattle grazing, suggesting that cattle can have a negative impact on North American xeric ecosystems. Soil-related variables were most negatively impacted by grazing ... followed by litter cover and biomass ... and rodent diversity and richness."[439] She did note that there were many variables that could affect her findings. Succinctly summing up relevant studies, Charles Curtin wrote in "Livestock Grazing, Rest, and Restoration in Arid Landscapes," "The inadvertent consequences of not controlling for key driving variables (e.g., climate, fire, native herbivores, human activities) and only removing cattle is that studies limited to contrasting grazed and ungrazed areas cannot accurately reveal the ecological implications of grazing."[440]

There are impacts from grazing by cattle invasives that we are still discovering. In the Blue Mountains of Asotin County, Washington State, researchers studied the effects of cattle grazing on mule deer and elk. As reported in the *Seattle Times*, the plant community responded by producing forage slightly higher in protein, but left less to eat, meaning there were fewer calories of energy for native wildlife.[441] Another study looked to see if grazing negatively impacted the highly endangered pygmy rabbit in the northwestern U.S. Columbia River basin. Researchers reported that "cattle grazing in late summer through winter removed about 50 percent of the grass cover, and reduced the nutritional quality (e.g., increased fiber and decreased protein) of the remaining grass."[442]

Areas where rainfall is more plentiful seem to have more resilience to grazing of all types than arid ecosystems. In *Revolution on the Range*, White concluded that we could have cattle grazing across his specific ecosystem and find a balance. Ranchers in the United States control over half of western U.S. land, even more when you consider leased public lands. A 1994 estimate was that 70 percent of western U.S. lands were grazed by livestock.[443] Cattle grazing or not, this is an important decision.

The choice is this: Do we want to restore prairie ecosystems with their former bison, wolves, pronghorn, elk, mule deer, prairie dog communities, black-footed ferrets, and yes, grizzly bears on a landscape scale, or do we want an idealized and highly suspect grazing scheme that substitutes most of the former with cattle and sheep? To make room for grazing, what's left of the abundance and composition of indigenous species will unavoidably be managed, hunted, and trapped as an additional insult to replacing the original herbivores with livestock. Are the progressive new ranchers and their livestock so wondrous that we would choose them over the indigenous grazers and co-evolved species? If we remember what we have lost because of livestock, the complete answer should be clear to environmentalists.

The Bison Realm

The plains bison and wood bison once ranged in their specific habitats from Canada to Mexico and eastward to the Appalachian Mountains.[444] There were an estimated 30 million bison in North America before European settlement.[445] Today, there are some 500,000, most of them fenced within commercial operations. In our self-appointed role as creator-gods, we polluted bison genetics with cattle genes to create beefalo, the commercial cattle/bison cross. Cattle genes have contaminated the genetics of most remnant bison populations. Only 15,000 are free ranging.[446]

Some of the free-ranging wood bison who migrate annually out of Yellowstone National Park are shot at the behest of cattle ranchers. They fear their cattle will be exposed to brucellosis infections, though that is contested. Bison also are shot while captive, hundreds of them at a time, for commercial meat sales.[447]

Because of differences in behavior, dietary choices, and grazing methods, bison grazing is different from cattle grazing. Bison create large wallows in the land for dry dust and wet mud rolling. Cattle are more selective in what they eat than bison. Bison crop plants closer to the ground than cattle. Bison spend less time eating than cattle, more in other activities.[448] They once supported an ongoing, large-scale nation of predators—wolves and grizzly bears, and the scavengers from many species. No rancher could tolerate that predation financially today. That is one reason we need to end that industry. Both bison and wolves co-evolved over at least the last 10,000 years. Their co-evolution as predator and prey created bison defense strategies that arose from the ongoing refinement of survival by natural selection. It does not take much to assume that the historic great buffalo migrations created a different pattern of seed distribution, resistance to diseases, and distribution of predators than the new rancher would produce. Bison certainly provided a different ecosystem for the now endangered black-tailed prairie dog communities being destroyed by current livestock grazing practices.

Recent news stories describe bison killing by hunters. On a recent day, members of the Cayuse tribe drove 600 miles from Oregon to kill bison accustomed to Yellowstone National Park (YNP) tourists. The Cayuse are from the Umatilla Confederation of three tribes. One of their kills in 2011 was a bison who earlier in the day was grazing in a no-shoot zone behind an YNP ranger's cabin. This tribal version of a canned hunt was a resurgence of tribal tradition, or so claimed the Cayuse hunters.[449] The Nez Perce tribe of current Idaho and Washington is another tribe that kills these bison under their treaty rights.[450] Other people see a different future.

Coincidentally consistent with the new human ecology vision,

Deborah and Frank J. Popper propose an open-range bison commons of immense size. It would be on the drier plains that cover 10 states in the western United States.[451] Their proposal could save many struggling farmers from financial ruin; they would be paid to restore native grasslands. As an additional benefit, farmers would not need to use fossil waters from ancient, diminishing underground aquifers.

As we end animal agriculture, we solve moral issues, remove the fences, and reintroduce bison without the cattle genes as part of a larger effort to restore ecosystems to a scale needed to address climate change, restore soils, and stem the loss of biodiversity. If invasive cattle or sheep are deemed good substitutes to the indigenous bison, why are the original bison, who bring additional benefits, not the best biocentric choice?

How Many?

The environmental community may wonder how many vegetarians and vegans there are. Determining how many vegans and vegetarians there are is confounded by survey margins of error, the sample size, and the tendency of survey respondents to define themselves as *vegetarian* when they are not. Some survey respondents call themselves vegetarian because they do not eat red meat but do eat chicken, duck, or fish. The Vegetarian Resource Group (VRG) corrected this self-identification problem in their 2006 third-party professional poll that now lists animal-origin products by name. VRG began asking respondents if they ever ate a disqualifying item like red meat, fish, chicken, dairy, eggs, and fish. Under the more precise polling questions, their 2011 poll found that about 2.5 percent are vegetarian and another 2.5 percent are vegan.[452] The 2010 U.S. census revealed there are over 312 million people in the United States. We are millions strong in the U.S. alone, and growing.

Millions of people have experienced a very personal awakening to the truth of our place on Earth. For environmentalists, the animal question must be faced head-on. Species rights must be accepted as a necessity for saving ecosystems. For species rightists, it is time to both understand and take the cause of deep ecology seriously.

We are in a competition. It is between what good people and organizations are accomplishing and the inertia of ecosystems in decline. I leave it to others to celebrate hard-won environmental victories and progress. I have only admiration for those accomplishments. But my task here is to convince you that we are not doing nearly enough to win the race. Not even close.

The catastrophe is already here. Ask the poor, the hungry, the poisoned, and, were it possible, the extinct. My perspective, and that of many people in the environmental community I have talked with, is that we have failed to do enough in time to prevent the global collapse of ecosystems and the human societies dependent upon them. As human ecology professor Lynn Robins often quipped some years ago in his lectures, "We are on a toboggan to hell." Author James Speth, Dean at the School of Forestry and Environmental Studies at Yale University, wrote that "Capitalism as we know it today is incapable of sustaining the environment."[453] He is one of the multitudes of scientists who are convinced that our future is bleak.

Paddling Up the River of Denial

Advocates for change carry on because we cannot do anything else but try. Giving up is not an option. If we are going to stop the destruction of all that is sacred, we need to know what it will take to change our course; we need to know *all* of the goals that, if achieved, will actually allow Earth and us to survive and thrive. We *can* salvage a future. How good it will be for the remaining individuals from other species is up to us. There is still treasure worth saving.

Environmentalists, those speaking up for individuals from all species, vegan NGO communities, conservation biologists, human ecologists, and those in the scientific communities have a duty to lead, but not by going halfway to the river to drink. We must go the full distance if there is to be hope. We must see the results of our changed human ecology in our lifetimes. Environmental, species rights, population, social and economic justice, and religious/spiritual NGOs have to be holding hands on the way forward toward a new human ecology. We complete one another.

Chapter 11:

Vegan Human Ecology/The New Ecosystem Niche for Humans

This new model of the biosphere moves us away from an outdated view of the world as 'natural ecosystems with humans disturbing them' and towards a vision of 'human systems with natural ecosystems embedded within them.' This is a major change in perspective but it is critical for sustainable management of our biosphere in the 21st century.

—*Encyclopedia of Earth*[454]

Vegan humans occupy a different ecosystem niche than carnist humans. It is vital for human ecologists, aid workers, conservation biologists, and environmentalists to appreciate this. Our vegan human ecology transforms every relationship we have with one another, other species, ecosystems, and the entire biosphere. Thriving on an exclusively plant-based diet, zero use of animal-derived products and services, and a steep reduction in our neo-predation are how we create a humane and environmentally sane future. Vegan human ecology describes our relationships as vegans to ecosystems.

Biodiversity will not be saved by setting aside reserves of habitat when those parcels are surrounded by a hostile, carnist human ecology. The large landscapes of Earth are the scales of perspective we need to consider when making local decisions. It is those large landscapes currently dedicated to animal agriculture that vegans *return* to ecosystems.

For example, black-tailed prairie dogs are now 2 percent of their original, vast population. Yet they still face hostility from livestock grazing interests.[455] According to the Nebraska Game and Parks Division, "It is estimated that in the late 1800s, some 700 million acres of North American rangeland were inhabited by prairie dogs [five species]. Habitat changes and extensive eradication efforts have reduced the acreage by about 90 to 95 percent from historic levels."[456]

Prairie dogs have lived under wartime conditions all during this time. It is like waging war on children.

Hunting businesses boast, "Bring plenty of ammunition and guns! Our average hunter shoots 500 to 1500 rounds a day!"[457] These commercial outfits and their hunting clients call prairie dogs *varmints*. Merriam-Webster's Dictionary defines varmints as "an animal considered a pest; *specifically*: one classed as vermin and unprotected by game law." Coyotes, ground squirrels, and many other species experience these recreational hunters' disdain for those who once shaped ecosystems. As these carnist human ecology recreational shooters kill individuals, they change the ecosystem. That is their purpose. They are clearing the way for cattle.

The animal agriculture community sponsors hate for prairie dogs. Ranchers view them as competitors for grazing resources. Aside from the grass prairie dogs consume, cattle and horses can step into their burrow openings and injure themselves. Botanical agriculturalists who grow the corn, soy, and other crops to supply the livestock industry usurp millions of acres of prairie dog habitat. Prairie dogs trim the vegetation around his and her dwelling burrows as they always have. If that vegetation is young corn plants, it will be a loss to the botanical farmer.

From a NPR report, we get a snapshot of animal agriculture's attempt to make prairie dogs ecologically meaningless. Endangered black-footed ferrets depend upon prairie dogs as prey. One rancher, Larry Haverfield of Logan County, Kansas, has allowed the prairie dogs to remain on his 6,000 acres as a way to support the reintroduction of the endangered ferrets. His ranching peers oppose him. One rancher said,

'There's not enough profit in ranching today—or farming either—that you can afford to have part of your property taken by something that is not gonna produce nothing for you,' explains Burt Summers, a retired rancher. Haverfield says he's doing what he can to keep the dogs off other people's property. But Logan County says that's not enough; the dogs must be killed. And if Haverfield won't do it, they will.[458]

The five species of prairie dogs in the United States are vital to prairie ecosystems because they are prey for many terrestrial and avian predators like fox and hawks. Prior to European settlement, prairie dogs were a defining presence. Our vegan human ecology is a powerful tool to end the power of ranchers to do their harm and makes possible societal support for prairie restoration. Long-term restoration efforts by conservation biologists will then be possible. The professional field of conservation biology has not been promoting anything like a vegan human ecology. It has to.

The stakes are as high as they can be. As a biologist and president of Stanford University's Center for Conservation Biology, Paul Erlich reflects common wisdom about the choices we are making now, the last choices we will ever have, when he writes, "The fate of biological diversity for the next 10 million years will almost certainly be determined during the next 50–100 years by the activities of a single species. That species, Homo sapiens, is [approximately] 200,000 years old."[459]

Like similar findings in other publications, a report from the Organization for Economic Co-operation and Development (OECD) titled "Livestock and Climate Policy: Less Meat or Less Carbon?"[460] we are told that our dietary choices play a crucial role in greatly reducing the GHGs tied to climate change. The following is true for industrial agriculture *and* small plot livestock holdings of one to several animals in least developed and developing countries:

> Livestock production occupies 70 percent of the world's agricultural land, yet it provides only 20 percent of the calories in the global diet. Around a third of the planet's arable land is committed to producing livestock feed; a proportion of edible calories are lost when converted in this way. This confers a sizeable opportunity cost against using land and other resources for livestock production when more food could be produced with the same resource.

That opportunity is realized in a vegan human ecology. OECD calculates that by replacing meat protein with veggie protein, we would cut agricultural GHG emissions in half.

Ecosystem destruction and social and economic injustice is caused not only by our diets, but also the leather seats we have in our cars and the leather shoes we wear. The Greenpeace International report titled "Slaughtering the Amazon"[461] documents how the Brazilian government invested billions of dollars in massive industrial livestock operations responsible for 80 percent of deforestation in the Amazon Basin. While profiting from that crime, that same government demanded international aid to save the same ecosystems. Stored in the standing Amazonian forest vegetation is 50 years' worth of the annual U.S. carbon emissions. Non-vegans are creating the demands for the soybeans to feed their meat-bearing cattle. Brazilian soybeans grown where forest once stood supply Brazilian and overseas livestock industries, notably Europe's. Brazilians who dare report illegal logging are executed or have to go into hiding.[462]

Greenpeace identifies five corporations operating in Brazil that control over half of the meat exports and the raw materials like hides taken in slaughterhouses. They are Bertin, JBS, Independência, Minerva, and Marfrig. These corporations send raw hides from Brazil to China and Italy, the first- and second-place producers of finished leather goods. The finished leather is used by U.S. manufacturers for car interiors. PETA reports that it takes up to 15 cowhides for each leather-clad car interior.[463] Specifically, seven cows for a Mercedes S-class interior and for a Rolls-Royce, 15. Citing an article in *The New York Times*, Ingrid Newkirk writes in her book *Making Kind Choices* that U.S. tanneries produce 58 square miles of cow leather for the U.S. car industry.[464] From forest to leather without a trace of buyers' remorse.

For non-vegans, human slavery is an additional byproduct of meat and leather: "In the process of investigating illegal deforestation, Greenpeace has found that four of the top five beef exporters—Bertin, Independência, JBS, and Marfrig—have acquired cattle from ranchers linked to forced labour."

The Greenpeace report names product brands that you will recognize. Leather products traceable to the big five corporations just cited include Adidas, BMW, Carrefour, Ford, Honda, Gucci, IKEA, Kraft, Nike, Tesco, Toyota, Wal-Mart, Eagle Ottawa that supplies BMW and Toyota, Boss, Geox, Gucci, Hilfiger, Louis Vuitton, Prada, railway companies SNCF and Thalys International, Wal-Mart (in Brazil at least),

Cia Brasiliera de Distribuição, Unilever, Colgate Palmolive, and Johnson & Johnson. It does not end there. The Brazilian-sourced leathers have been tracked as far as the UK National Health Service and the British, Dutch, Italian, Spanish, and U.S. military forces.

This commendable report details more tragedy than I have cited but the lack of a Greenpeace campaign to end carnism is striking. Greenpeace appears to support the current carnist human ecology. Stunning in its magnitude, Brazil's example of carnage is just one example of the power and size attained by animal agriculture industries. Their global power is beyond imagination. Only consumers possess a greater power to stop them. Vegans, bless our hearts, should not be smug. Though way ahead of the game, it is important to remember that vegans are still predators through our neo-predation. We do it at a dramatically reduced level, but our mega, presence, and economic predations still send species to extinction.

Choosing a vegetarian diet instead of a vegan one, as I did without excuse for over three decades, continues the cruelty and environmental destruction. Vegetarians are still part of carnism. Vegetarianism is useless for achieving sustainability. Egg and dairy industries are inseparable from meat production industries. Like the meat-centered choice, a dairy and egg vegetarian diet requires high inputs of fossil fuel energy and water, pollutes the environment, creates habitat loss, and produces GHG emissions. A report created for the Swedish Ministry of Agriculture notes that "The GHG emissions from dairy production are similar to that of beef production ..." in a study of the European Union market that included imports.[465] The well-documented cruelty saturating the dairy and egg industries remains untouched by the vegetarian choice. Stopping at the vegetarian platform does not approach what the vegan human ecology does for ecosystems and the rights of individuals from other species.

Conversion

The vegan human ecology takes ecosystems out of the animal foods business. Though there are an endless number of compelling reasons to do this, it helps to know why veganism delivers the best nutrition to the most people using the least amount of resources. We know that species we domesticated for food production metabolize their food energy to keep warm, breathe, pump blood, grow bones, skin, fur, and hair, and move about. When we give cattle, chickens, pigs, and others plant crops to eat, only a small percentage of the food value they consume, soybeans and corn for instance, will be turned into edible animal products. To quantify this loss, we compare how much grain a cow, chicken, or other species eats to produce an edible animal product. The input of grains to the output of animal products is the *conversion ratio*. So if it takes 10 pounds of grain to produce one pound of edible animal product, the ratio is 10:1. Though I do not touch on it in this book, there are similar calculations that show how much more food can be produced on an acre of land in a vegan diet versus a carnist diet all while using a fraction of other ecosystem services like clean water.

Getting agreement about what the conversion ratio is for each species would seem to be an easy task. But it is not for a number of reasons. I will avoid using the term animal *feed* because it is carnist language that creates the illusion that animals are mechanical things that we supply with feed, not food they taste, chew, swallow, feel, digest, metabolize, and excrete. Try saying human feed and you will get my point.

Everyone agrees that chickens convert grains into flesh and eggs more efficiently than cattle. Beyond that, we find honest differences about what those conversion ratios are because of the many variables in the way meat is produced and how the weight of the animal product is measured. When corn prices are high, for instance, a western U.S. rancher with ecosystems available for grazing may leave cattle out on the range longer than when corn is cheaper. Animals raised for meat are fed a diversity of foods that change in quantity and type depending upon location and costs of production at any given time. The formulas for keeping animals until slaughter weight change to adapt to market conditions.

Conversion ratios can run higher and lower and change constantly even in the same producing feedlot or small farm source. Weather, costs of grain, the availability and condition of pasturage, access to byproducts of other industries—ethanol and corn sweetener production have as byproducts wet and dry distiller grains that can be fed to cattle—and the market niche the producer is trying to fill, all contribute to conversion ratios. Because of these complexities, the controversy of grain to edible meat ratios will likely continue. Experienced cattlemen and women will use different criteria such as *on the hoof* weight gains instead of edible product.

The USDA's February 2008 edition of *Amber Waves* considers these conversion factors: "... this analysis [about corn prices] uses upper-bound conversion estimates of 7 pounds of corn to produce 1 pound of beef [7:1], 6.5 pounds of corn to produce 1 pound of pork [6.5:1], and 2.6 pounds of corn to produce 1 pound of chicken [2.6:1]."[466]

Others calculate conversion ratios differently. Here are other opinions about conversion ratios.

- Author M.R. Montgomery states in *A Cow's Life* that the ratio for cattle can be 1:1 over a lifetime.[467]

- In *The End of Food*, Paul Roberts writes that after inedible waste is considered, the conversion ratio is 20:1 for beef, 4.5:1 for pigs, and 7.3:1 for chickens.[468]

- Referring to his McDonald's meal, Michael Pollan in *Omnivore's Dilemma* estimated that it took 14 pounds of corn to produce a pound of beef by assuming half of the original individual from another species he was eating was inedible.[469]

- The nonprofit organization Sightline offers these conversion ratios: 7:1 "to produce a pound of boneless, trimmed pork; 3:1 for chicken; and, depending on how much time cattle spend grazing before entering a feedlot, about 5:1 for beef."

I believe Vaclav Smil, distinguished professor in the faculty of Environment at the University of Manitoba in Winnipeg, Canada, does justice to the range of ratios and addresses their complexity. He notes that there are different conversion ratios of grain and legume foods for *light* birds who are younger at slaughter than the average more mature chickens. He also explains that at least 10 percent must be added to account for birds who die before going to slaughter. For cattle, he adds the losses of conversion efficiency due to environmental stress, fetal growth, rates of metabolism, and calf lactation. Importantly, he considers the difference between the overall *body weight* gained per unit of grain food eaten versus the *edible weight*. He applies these factors to the conversion ratios for chickens, pigs, and cattle sold for slaughter in the United States.[470]

Smil's paper, "Typical efficiencies of meat production," is based on "USDA long-term statistics." *Long-term* is important because it averages the data out over time. He concludes that the conversion ratio for chickens is 4.5:1; for pigs, 9:1. Grain-fed cattle are the most inefficient of the three species with a ratio of 10:1.[471] So, *typical* does not mean always. Yet the waste is clear and would be foolish at half these ratios.

Stewart Rose, in *The Vegetarian Solution*, sums conversion ratios appropriately: "Meat, poultry, dairy, and eggs represent the end process of a great inefficiency.... Farm animals are, in reality, food factories in reverse."[472] This monumental waste of food and ecosystems alone is enough reason to abolish the slave trade that is animal agriculture.

We are asked to believe that buying grass-eating cattle is sustainable and somehow entirely humane. Neither claim is true. Small family farms sell high-priced meat to a small sector of people who can afford it. These businesses still usurp habitat unnecessarily; wildlife management policies remain oriented to protecting invasive livestock species that control and warp ecosystems, and the inhumanity of carnism itself is not stopped. There are innovative programs that attempt to reduce grazing impacts and improve degraded habitat. However, that is far less than restoring the carbon sequestering, biodiverse ecosystems, and native species that were cleared for animal agriculture.[473]

Under a vegan human ecology, we increase the amount of habitat and soil banking for future generations of species, including humans. With an abundance of ecosystems no longer harnessed to agriculture, wildlife management science and agency policies become oriented to ecosystem dominion for the first time in human history. Agencies are finally free to act biocentrically. We will insist on it.

A vegan human ecology transforms the world profoundly. It ends many and mitigates the rest of nearly every environmental problem we are creating with the current human ecology. We have been eating our way into the Earth's biological and physical reserves for a long time. The vegan human ecology releases the prairies, steppes, mountain meadows, savannahs, rainforests, alpine meadows, and river valleys from our multi-tongued predation. As veganists, we eat plant crops directly from the land instead of funneling it through ducks, goats, cattle, pigs, camels, rabbits, chickens, and sheep. Imagine how we will regain natural orders of value and recalibrate how the economic order weighs the value of life. We have within us the compassion and common sense that will protect the beauty of our existence.

Intact ecosystems, and only intact ecosystems, can sustain their own adaptive complexity, their own survival, and manage themselves for their own inherent ends. To do this they need space and fewer of us. Vegan human ecology practitioners slow, stop, and reverse a scenario described by Ellis and Ramankutty, where, in their view, we are not so much a part of ecosystems anymore as much as ecosystems are now "embedded" within human systems. I will not accept this outcome. Perhaps it is because the idea is so repugnant and terrifying to me. Yet we are undeniably in the act of making their statement come true. The juggernaut of the carnist current human ecology must be stopped.

Pay Up or Die

If we are able to stabilize and then decrease our populations, there are still billions of people, the *have nots* and the *have-somes*, who want to achieve a higher standard of living. Unfortunately for ecosystems and individuals from other species, their otherwise just quest for economic justice is based on an unsustainable and inhumane carnist model of human ecology. Like the haves, the have-nots strive for the same material culture models that have already taken us beyond Earth's carrying capacity. While billions of people remain mired in poverty and consume relatively little, the rest of us push ecosystems into bankruptcy. This is where the vegan new human ecology will benefit the poor.

The poor seek the fuller, richer life some of us already have and expect to maintain. How are we to overcome the immensity of these emerging human demands when it is so obvious that the Earth cannot support the resource exhaustion by the haves even before the desperately poor are served? We must take less, not more, overall. There must be less of humanity and more of nature.

The vegan aspect of the new human ecology starts immediately with the haves. We have easy access to vegan alternatives to carnism and enough material wealth where we can end it now. For the nutritionally denied, we address nutritional deficits with plant-based solutions and social entrepreneurship while working to create cultural acceptance and change in cultural dietary choices. Already, there are international aid organizations that have established this successful approach.

Would You Like Shoes or a Handbag with That Ecosystem?

The 2007 issue of *Species*, the newsletter of the Species Survival Commission from the International Union for the Conservation of Nature (IUCN), included this statement:

Sustainable use can often be a controversial concept. This is especially true among groups that oppose any consumptive use of wild animals, such as animal rights groups, but is also true among conservationists. This is in part because there are a range of different ideas packed into the terminology of 'sustainable use' and possibly also because the term itself can be misused.[474]

An article in the same issue of *Species* was about the industrialization of the American alligator. Perhaps without the editors' intention, it highlights the extremes that are considered under interpretations of sustainable use.

Faced with uncontrolled hunting of American alligator, the Louisiana Department of Wildlife and Fisheries (LDWF) found a way to keep ecosystems producing high numbers of alligators for the commercial trade and save the species from being endangered. To gain support and avert widespread poaching, the LDWF teamed with landowners and industry to industrialize wildlife. Alligator "farms" were given the right to collect 350 thousand eggs (recent quoted average) every year from wild alligator nests. In return, alligator farms agreed to place 60 thousand sub-adult alligators to "maintain wild alligator populations" and supply trappers and hunters. After industry hatches the wild eggs, they rear the young in captivity. After slaughter, the alligators are processed into meat, handbags, and other fashion accessories. Soon after this arrangement began, the larger businesses squeezed out the smaller alligator farms.

Some reflection was left out of this *Species* article that celebrated this public-private agreement. The alligator products industry has a predictable supply, but how does this affect ecosystems and alligators? Restoring the American alligator was a laudable achievement, but there are costs. Ten to 20 percent of alligator eggs survive to hatchling stage in the wild. Had those 350 thousand eggs been left there, the sub-adult alligators who hatched naturally would have been present from hatchlings to sub-adults in the ecosystem, unlike the farmed alligators who are released instantly as sub-adults into ecosystems. The naturally hatched would have been prey for other species but would also be predators who ate spiders, insects, snails, small birds, fish, and as the young alligators grew, additional species.[475] From egg to just under sub-adult, some 350 thousand alligators of this age class are not present in their food webs and ecosystem relationships. They are missing.

If the 350 thousand eggs are left in the wild, other species will have them for food or the eggs would decompose for reuse to the ecosystem. The department estimates there are nearly 2 million American alligators in their state. With the average female laying 35 eggs per year, roughly 10 thousand nests would be raided if completely emptied. All of this manipulation of one species in the ecosystem may seem insignificant, but is it?

Will alligator genetics and fitness change over time as artificially incubated alligators are returned to the wild without natural selection pressures? As we have seen, this happens in salmon hatcheries. Would the alligator survive today without the commercial industry, or would poaching return to feed this multi-million dollar carnist demand for hunting, shoes, and handbags?

Measured in dollars and alligators, the LDWF reports that "Louisiana alligator hunters currently harvest over 28 thousand wild alligators and farmers harvest over 280 thousand farm-raised alligators annually. Raw meat and hide values are estimated at over $11 million for the wild harvest and over $46 million for the farm harvest."[476] Louisiana's model is replicated throughout the American alligator's U.S. range. There are a reported 100 commercial farms housing 650,000 alligators *for the trade* in several states as of 2008.[477]

This is how individuals from other species pay for themselves, to justify their existence on a planet we dominate. Highly respected organizations like the IUCN celebrate this method of saving species. But their cheers are in the context and time when our species lacks a biocentric human ecology. It was not a vegan human ecology that made these alligators endangered 50 years ago; the cause was hunting and poaching. Vegans do not buy products that make alligator poaching worthwhile and we do not need alligator *farms*.

Biocentric-viewing new human ecologists appreciate the fact that 70 percent of female alligators were found to mate with the same partner in succeeding years. Mother alligators have a strong and protective maternal drive.[478] Recent "studies on alligator social behavior have demonstrated a significant degree of complexity in the species' ability to communicate vocally (through bellows and head slaps) and visually (through a complex series of body postures)."[479] Vegans oppose commercial farms and hunters extracting their version of value from these sentient beings. The brutality cannot be exaggerated.

Trappers hang baited hooks from trees and then leave for home. The alligator lunges, takes the bait, and hangs from the hook struggling, in agony, until the hunter makes his rounds. Since *gator* eyes shine brightly red in spotlights, recreational and guided hunting often occurs at night in the many states that encourage it. Killing an alligator, other than by hooks in trees, requires destroying his and her small brain. There is a lot of trauma involved because hunted alligators move and off-center gunshots are the result. In addition to guns, grappling hooks, harpoons, bows and arrows, hooked poles, snares, bow-fishing gear, spears, crossbows, and bang sticks are among the tools of the alligator hunters' trade that state wildlife agencies condone.[480]

Our Place or Theirs?

Our ancestors migrated over time as climatic, environmental, and social conditions changed. They migrated in times of need. Our need now is to realize how far-reaching our response to *Earth's needs* has to be; we should consider that self-directed relocation is as appropriate today as it was for our ancestors. Wherever we are extinguishing the capacities and biodiversity of ecosystems, we should drastically reduce human presence. In our deliberations, we should stop requiring wildlife to pay for themselves with trophy hunting safaris, stop allowing invasive livestock to take over habitat, and stop growing food for livestock; it is not the best and highest use of an ecosystem and the lives of individuals from other species. It is appropriate to question why so many of us live in areas that require more natural resources like energy to heat and cool our homes and supply transport for goods and services when another location might be more resilient and at less cost to the environment. We have been willing to relocate when natural disaster makes a place inhospitable, to move on when the dust bowl consumes the farm and when the encroaching sea melts the permafrost—after we have done the damage. Now, though able, we are refusing to move.

That is characteristic of ecosystems becoming embedded in human systems. Human supremacy overrides ecosystem supremacy. As a result, nonhuman species try to adapt to the impossible rate of change we create with our simultaneous imposition of the carnist current human ecology and our neo-predation. Ecosystem supremacy is destroyed when consumers of meat and dairy products divert 98 percent of the U.S. soybean most of that to feed livestock instead of people.[481] In a vegan human ecology, 98 percent of the land, energy, water, and habitat will not be used to grow those soybeans. We will instead return ecosystem supremacy to the species requiring it even while we increase our intake of plant-based nutrition. This is a critical change we are making. Only 12 percent of the Earth was under some form of official protection as of 2008.[482] Vegans release and protect ecosystems on a global scale.

Human Halitosis

Whenever we put an ecologically inappropriate and cruelly sourced food into our mouths, the stink rising from the ecological destruction and suffering it causes should be overwhelmingly obvious and objectionable. Carnists make food choices so extreme that they are causing the sixth of six global mass species extinctions. The first five waves of catastrophic extinction events were caused by changes in Earth's geophysical state—flood magma and volcanoes, the cooling of Earth's interior core over time, and large interstellar bodies impacting Earth from space. This time we are the cause. Our sixth mass destruction of biodiversity and abundance has a name: the Great Holocene Extinction.

Some 10,000 years ago, the Holocene[483] mass extinction era began as a sharp increase in humans erasing forever the existence of other species. Preeminent biologist and Harvard professor Edmond O. Wilson worries that the rate of species extinction is "… catastrophically high, somewhere between one thousand and ten thousand times the rate before human beings began to exert a significant pressure on the environment."[484] "… in other words, one thousand to ten thousand species per million [of total species] per year."[485] The estimated rate of extinctions during the next 50 years is projected to increase 10 times today's rate.[486] This rapid pulse of annihilation pokes holes in the web of life where each strand is important to the others. We are affecting some species more rapidly than others.

We are causing the extinction of amphibians "211 times the background extinction rate," which would increase to "as high as 25,000–45,000 times greater if all of the currently threatened species go extinct."[487] Extinctions were caused by early humans, too, including our indigenous and subsistence ancestors who expanded across continents. All of our ancestors started the decline of Earth's biodiversity that we continue today. Andrew P. Dobsen, in *Conservation and Biodiversity*, has made the observation that "there are almost no examples of sustained human use of natural resources that have not led to overexploitation and the near extinction of the exploited species."[488]

I find it disheartening that wildlife management, ecosystem science, conservation biology, research, and policy are not screaming madly in proportion to this unfolding tragic loss of biodiversity and ecosystems. Too often, those institutions and people act as if resigned to the inevitability of it and have become understandably overwhelmed. Is it because they are not willing to challenge their beliefs about dietary choices and human population? Despite the Great Holocene Extinction "spasm," those in science, the NGO community, and agencies who know what is happening seem oddly hobbled by personal inabilities to get around current human ecology worldviews, including the culture of carnism, or whatever it is holding them back. Together, they and we are failing to come to grips with our deteriorating circumstances, much less taking seriously a vegan human ecology or a comprehensive new human ecology.

Invest in Vegan Futures

What would a vegan new human ecology future look like? It will end the annual killing, by one official count, of 58 billion[489] domesticated individuals from other species. We will stop removing, in addition, wildlife by the tens of billions from ecosystems. We will not kill *bushmeat*, including primates, in tropical forests or crowd out the scimitar-horned oryx of the Sahara Desert with cattle.[490] We do not hinder essential foraging and socialization behaviors needed for other species' survival because we will not pursue them. Wild fish will increase, fish hatcheries will close, dams will be removed. Fish farms will lose investors. Crustaceans will not be trapped in *pots*; marine mammals will not drown in fishers' nets or be clubbed to death. Birds will migrate and land in refuges without being shot. The mass post-traumatic stress disorder we have caused in individuals from other species will wane. In the vegan present and future, we return up to 26 percent of ice-free land that livestock graze back to the species they now compete with. Our homes, cities, and croplands will be better designed for adapting to the presence of other species. We will move out of many areas as our human population declines. We have stopped feeding livestock 80 percent of the global crop of soybeans and at least half of the corn. A vegan ecology future alters the course of humanity and every species on Earth.

What would wildlife management and conservation biology look like in a vegan human ecology? In *Essentials of Conservation Biology,* conservation biologist Richard B. Primack summarizes conservation as having "two goals: first, to investigate human impacts on biological diversity and, second, to develop practical approaches to prevent the extinction of species."[491] What could they accomplish and how would the scientific community redress the loss of biodiversity and extinction of species in the context of a vegan new human ecology? How would their professions adapt and thrive if absent the biological demands from carnist human ecologies? When our vegan human ecology is the norm of our species, where would scientific inquiry be directed? What policies and management programs would evolve? What would world ecosystems look like without billions of chickens, goats, sheep, camels, cattle, and pigs? Without a vegan new human ecology, are wildlife and ecosystem agencies confident they can stop or even slow the Great Holocene Extinction? We are witnessing the answer as the extinctions and ecosystem declines increase. Indigenous species are surrounded by seas of us.

On the websites of environmental management agencies, in the introductory paragraph for the comprehensive plans they publish, in the opening statements at their public meetings, and in the scientific papers their staff originates, these agencies and biologists must address what it will actually take to stop the Great Holocene Extinction. They must tell us that biodiversity and ecosystem health is best served by reigning in corn, soybean, and livestock invasions and work to end animal agriculture. They must tell us to reduce our own populations. The vegan new human ecology is the conservation biologist's strongest ally. It slows and can stop the Great Holocene Extinction.

Stealing Food from Wildlife

Carnists take food directly from other species without necessity and in bewildering quantities. Long before we collapse the populations of prey that other species need, we alter their food webs. When we remove predators nearer the top of the food chain, it causes a ripple effect in many other predator-prey relationships. If a predator like a small shark species is decimated, their prey increases as long as environmental conditions support it. As that increasing prey grows in population, they feed more intensively on the species *below* them in the food chain. A cascade of rises and declines in the numbers of each species causes ripples throughout the food web of many more species. Soon, the composition and population ratios between species changes the ecosystem. This is likely regardless of the species removed and their place in their food chain and web.

Fishing directly on marine species is one way to do this. However, global warming and ocean acidification, both caused by our neo-predatorship, are others. Our neo-predation is just as effective as taking marine species out of the sea by fishing. Now, global warming and oceanic acidification, the results of our mega, presence, and economic neo-predatorship, seem poised to do even more damage than all the terrible practices of fishers combined.

Our current human ecology has altered the biosphere. As the oceans warm, species try to compensate by moving up or down in the water column or move distances toward anywhere cooler. Not all species can adapt at the same speed, if at all. A bird can move, but their prey may not have yet made the adjustment, and arrive too late for parents to feed their newly hatched chicks. Migrations are dependent upon temperatures, other aspects of weather, and food availability; they must be synchronized for the multitude of relationships between species. When we create climate change, it is another way in which we steal food from wildlife. We starve them by disrupting the synchronicity of their food chains.

Some of us have the power and technology to crush the competition for food that other species and people need. Fishers do this. In addition to the hunger fishers create by removing so much food needed by marine species, there is too little remaining in the oceans for many artisan and poor fishers to catch, eat, and survive. Large foreign fleet trawlers fish offshore from poor fishers' homes. About half of the developed world's wild-caught fish are imported from developing countries, many of which have poor to no effective regulation of factory ship operations off their coasts.

For their part, the artisanal fishers can be inadequately regulated as well. Still, they use smaller vessels, support local and regional economies, use less fuel per unit of fish caught, and require less investment, though waste can be high because of lack of refrigeration and transportation to market infrastructure. Spoilage is 30 percent in coastal and inland fisheries in underdeveloped economies. In some cases, there are agreements for fishing access by foreign, industrial fleets that are called distant water fishers. Unfortunately, the payment to the poorer developing country is often a small percentage of the foreign market value of the fish. The smaller countries being fished do not have the power to make it otherwise.[492]

The artisanal fishers have nowhere else to turn for food and income. While the complexities of benefits and losses of commercial fishing are weighed, the whole enterprise is unsustainable and in decline. Eighty percent of the global fish stocks are "considered to be fully or over exploited."[493] This is another example where a vegan new human ecology adopted by people in developed economies will benefit the poor. We will not be eating their fish. We leave fish for marine mammals, birds, biodiversity, and the artisanal fishers who have no other choices before them, yet.

Earth is traumatized. Vegan human ecology is the most ecosystem-friendly path we can take, provides phenomenally greater efficiencies of food production for humans, frees up vast areas of habitat, reduces greenhouse gas emissions, greatly reduces the petroleum, fertilizers, water, and other resources invested in food, eliminates the majority of cruelty we impose upon domestic and wild species, and reduces competition for food with other species and impoverished humans. We see everyone's quality of life improve. Life gets better for humans because we make it better for other species on land, in the air, and in the sea.

Chapter 12:

Transnational Private Property:
The New Commons

The tragedy of the commons develops in this way. Picture a pasture open to all. It is to be expected that each herdsman will try to keep as many cattle as possible on the commons. Such an arrangement may work reasonably satisfactorily for centuries because tribal wars, poaching, and disease keep the numbers of both man and beast well below the carrying capacity of the land.... Finally, however, comes the day of reckoning, that is, the day when the long-desired goal of social stability becomes a reality. At this point, the inherent logic of the commons remorselessly generates tragedy.... The only way we can preserve and nurture other and more precious freedoms is by relinquishing the freedom to breed, and that very soon.
    —Garrett Hardin, "The Tragedy of the Commons"[494, 495]

Ecosystems belong to the individuals of all species. Based on the premise of that ownership, individuals from all species must be considered in our human ecology. We are co-tenants with them, not their owners. And we are not self-aggrandizing stewards of resources. The way we now apply the concept of stewardship of living resources is saturated in anthropocentric self-importance. We must go beyond that concept and listen to the needs of other species. The importance of *their* well-being upon which we depend is at least equal to the importance of our own. Humanity, wonderfully attired in many cultures, is one species out of millions.

Ecologist Garret Hardin explained his "Tragedy of the Commons"[496] by using the example of a grassy field where people grazed their cattle. This field was the commons, a community-owned resource. Now that wars and disease did not hinder a net growth in human populations, "the inherent logic of the commons remorselessly generates tragedy." If one or a few people acted selfishly and grazed more cattle than could be ecologically sustained, that person would gain short-term but unsustainable benefit to the detriment of others. Eventually, everyone else—cattle, humans, and countless other species—would face the consequences of a ruined commons.

Hardin's solution to prevent this irresponsible behavior was self-interested ownership that would act to protect the resource. Commons as large as unregulated oceans and expansive landscapes can be plundered if no one has a vested owner's interest in the future productivity of the resource. However, their biological attributes have always had innate value before anyone began calling them *resources*. We have seen that, without owners to stop overexploitation, the ruthless economic activity of industries would operate for selfish short-term gain. They would ruin the commons as they move on to the next one. Whaling, logging, and fishing industries are examples of these tragedies that plundered the commons for profit and then moved on, leaving behind ravaged ecosystems.

Private ownership does not necessarily have to drive the harm to ecosystems and their individuals from other species; it is the type of human ecology being practiced that determines outcomes. Under the anthropocentric current human ecology, we try to regulate inevitable harm. Yet, there are limits to the public good that regulators can achieve. Since we are still exploring the complexities of how the biosphere works, regulatory competence is hobbled by insufficient knowledge. We are also clever and get around regulations either because we disdain them, or are driven by poverty to ignore them, that we end up destroying the commons anyway. Economic systems are addicted to unattainable endless growth and are thus a power that easily overwhelms our willingness to regulate ourselves. Under the current human ecology, this tragedy cannot be stopped by informed self-interested ownership because we are chronically unsustainable as a species. An alternative perspective and proposal is needed.

Multidimensional Tragedy

In the new human ecology, deteriorating ecosystems and suffering within those ecosystems are stand-alone tragedies of the commons. The entire biosphere is the commons that belongs to all species. Whether privately or publicly possessed by people, other species still own it. When our selfishness denies other species their fair share of resources that they need to thrive, a fair share that we would ask for ourselves, we create the crime Hardin described. Judging by the trends of extinction when ownership of resources and ecosystems remains an exclusive human right that excludes the rights of other species to that same ownership, biodiversity declines. The western black rhino was declared extinct while I wrote this book.[497]

In *Human Ecology*,[498] ecologist Gerald Marten tells us that "clear ownership" can prevent the tragedy of overexploitation of ecosystems, but it is not a guarantee. We also need, he notes, social institutional control that enforces limits to our behavior. There are cultural models studied since *Tragedy* was published that demonstrate how communal cultural agreements can avoid overexploitation.[499] Adds Patricia Townsend in *Environmental Anthropology*, "Anthropologists criticized the individualistic bias of the commons model, showing that property rights around the world are much more complex and embedded in historical and social contexts." In these contexts, she explains, several social mechanisms control access and establish responsibilities for use of the community commons.[500] In some instances, imposing private property rights over these traditional arrangements can cause the tragedy Hardin describes instead of prevent it.

Private Parts, Public Domain

The total area of large and small privatized land holdings in the U.S. is large enough to determine the fate of ecosystems. The goals, aspirations, worldviews, and the collective mindset of private and corporate *landholders* affect if not control the viability of ecosystems and species. They also control whether or not individuals from other species have rights to live on private-corporate lands. When landholders declare other species are not welcome or need to be reduced to ecological insignificance, they (often times we) create conflicts with wildlife. As our global population density increases, the social and cultural worlds of humanity are bunched together ever more tightly. Landholders everywhere must answer to their neighbors, the rest of humanity, individuals from all species, and ecosystems. We need landholders to act biocentrically.

Where regulatory institutions are strong, the rights of property owners are already constrained. Yet, those constraints are still insufficient to offset the unsustainable current human ecology regulators believe in. They allow abuse of ecosystems where there needs to be none, livestock grazing being the obvious candidate. A truly sustainable human ecology will redefine the rights and responsibilities of property owners. We no longer ask grazing businesses to accommodate wolves, eagles, beaver, songbirds, and amphibians. In this time of need, when we must stop the erosion of our survival, we are going to be really unreasonable: The invasive grazers must go. We must also remove the vast regions of plant crops that are grown for animal agriculture. Only in healthy ecosystems can the rights of native species be honored.

Private and public property provide ecosystem services that include nutrient recycling, biodiversity, climate buffering, genetic diversity, pollinators, and stable watersheds. They provide this locally but also receive those services from private and public resources that exist over the horizon. All properties are connected by ecosystems to other ecosystems and then the biosphere; properties benefit from watersheds, the biomes, the hydrology, and the health of species far beyond their property lines. Artificially segregating land into plats of private ownership on a map never changes that. We just act as if it does. When we endorse ownership that creates responsible self-interest with direction from societal institutions, what is perceived as good and profitable for the owner can still fall far short of giving the community of all species what it needs.

External to land ownership are the unsustainable demands we make on them. The economic incentives we offer landowners to give us timber, meat, gold, and energy dictates landowner behavior. We should not expect them to be far ahead of the cultural context that our demands create. When our human ecology changes so will they.

The Growing Global Village

Cooperating and competing economic systems create intimate human ecologies between us even when we live far apart. Our intimate human ecologies are global, massive, and paradoxically, also impersonal. We go from local to global when we export and import goods and services that create environmental impacts upon people, other species, and our shared ecosystems. Our individual impacts have spread to other continents. We have become so interdependent that we now have de facto use of each other's local commons and private land holdings, far apart as they might be.

Hardin wrote this about human population growth in 1968: "The only way we can preserve and nurture other and more precious freedoms is by relinquishing the freedom to breed, and that very soon." He was not shy about the need to "coerce" people into stopping population growth because it is so central to the issues about the abuse of the commons.[501] Hardin also believed that everyone must be equally advantaged or else those who act for the common good may die out at the hands of the shortsighted, selfish, and irresponsible elements who grab all of the resources to the detriment of others. He tempered his support of "coercion" by stating, "The only kind of coercion I recommend is mutual coercion, mutually agreed upon by the majority of the people affected."

Coercion is not a word we like. But in a crowded world where we are threatening the ecosystems that give us life, assumptions about land ownership, rights, and responsibilities must change. How we get there is an open question. Certainly, a new human ecology will dictate land and other resource ownership use.

The U.S. Department of Agriculture calculated that of 2.3 billion U.S. acres, "Private owners held 61 percent in 2002 (the last report year available at this writing), the Federal Government 28 percent, State and local governments 9 percent, and Indian reservations 3 percent."[502, 503] Agriculture accounted for 46 percent of U.S. land use.[504] Approximately 60 million acres was converted that year from land formerly used for pasture, range, and forestry to urban use. [505]

Landholders' rights are being squeezed by rapid ecosystem and social change. Many non-corporatized landholders are deeply knowledgeable and love the plot of Earth they call home. However, the idea of unlimited, do whatever you want with the land as a fundamental freedom is over. That attitude is vestigial, a holdover from when there were fewer people. As human populations increase, so does the complexity of living with each other and ecosystems. A ranch on a remote property is not remote. It remains tied to the interconnected ecosystems and economic systems around the world, all of which create our net impact on the biosphere.

The sum acreage of private holdings is not the whole story. Their locations are ecologically strategic. Encompassing some of the most biologically important areas, they control river valleys, grasslands, wetlands, migratory corridors, unique ecosystems, and resting and procreating habitat for individuals from other species. Some of us have more leverage to affect ecosystem outcomes. Landholders are in that class. They will experience disproportionate responsibilities as we alter the nature of our human ecology.

When 7 billion people stand on the Earth, a strange thing happens: Privately owned habitat and resources become needed by the world community of species as never before. That land and all of the connected ecosystem services are being pulled back into the public realm from the private. I do not know if this is equivalent to saying we are, in the process, making private ecosystem ownership a highly regulated public commons, or simply far more regulated private properties. Hungry people and everyone wanting a sustainable future will insist landowners act in their interests. Farming, like stock market trading practices, should alleviate hunger and never act to increase it, always increase protections for biodiversity and humane human behavior, not decrease them. We must insist that public policy about land ownership and our treatment of the commons follow this rule.

This Land is Our Land — and Theirs

In an interview conducted by Fred Bahnson for *The Sun* magazine, plant geneticist Wes Jackson had this wisdom to share:

> 'This tall-grass prairie we're standing on,' Jackson said, 'is nature's wisdom. Those research plots of ours' — he pointed down the hill — 'represent human cleverness.' Whatever agricultural breakthroughs

they might achieve down there, he wanted me to know, the unplowed prairie up here would always be the lofty, unattainable standard.[506]

Evidence of our foolishness is visible on the prairies. Animal agriculture's grazing and growing crops for livestock has decimated native bird populations. According to the U.S. Department of the Interior's *The State of the Birds*, "Of the 42 grassland species with sufficient monitoring data, 23 are declining significantly." They believe 55 percent of grassland birds are "showing significant declines" because their tallgrass prairie habitat is a mere 2 percent of what existed in the early 1800s. Animal agriculture is the cause. Notes the report, "Although birds may settle in pastures and haylands, frequent haying, burning, and overgrazing can create 'ecological traps' where birds try to nest but fail to raise their young."[507] Wes Jackson is attempting to respond to at least part of the problem.

Jackson founded the Land Institute in Kansas and conducts research hoping to grow grain crops without tilling the soil. Tilling every year for annuals that bear grain and legumes exposes soil to wind and water erosion and the loss of soil fertility. Long-rooted perennials mimic the prairie grasses. If we can replace annuals with no-till perennials, we would make an important step toward ending erosion. Summarizing Jackson's thoughts, Brahnson wrote, "He believes the loss of topsoil is the single greatest threat to our food supply and to the continued existence of civilization."... Said Jackson, "'First off, I don't think farmers are bad guys. I think this is a problem of agriculture itself.'"[508] We should be thinking of soil in our human ecology. Researchers David Pimentel and Nadia Kounang report that we lose about 75 billion tons of it worldwide each year from wind and water erosion. This loss is, in their estimation, "The greatest threat to providing food for a rapidly growing human population."[509] Land use and abuse issues are societal responsibilities.

Private property rights must be subservient to our collective responsibilities. They must provide for the long-term interests of people and species, even those who live on the other side of the planet. It does not matter whether they walk with human legs or antelope legs. In this smaller world, everyone counts and is accountable to the larger, all-inclusive whole.

Inverting Eminent Domain

As soon as we stop assuming that we have a right to claim, live in, and develop any ecosystem we choose, we can talk about the benefits of redistributing ourselves to minimize ecosystem impacts. Though marine reserves, parks, wilderness areas, and critical habitat areas are *set-aside* exceptions, they are not sufficient to counter the expanse of our current human ecology. We have to invert the scale of the set-aside approach. What does this inverted model look like? Like a national park system, but in reverse.

Most of us will remain where we already live. Cities will be the core areas of human occupation, while suburban areas serve as buffer zones that gradually give way to smaller sub-core towns and villages. Connecting these human habitat and resource support areas are trans-portation corridors that are linked to other urban center core areas. Like wilderness areas and national parks, there will be boundaries for these areas. We will retain sufficient resource and recreational areas suitable for our reduced and more sustainable human population. Crop growing areas will be far smaller because a vegan human ecology elimi-nates the need to feed livestock species. When we are closer to the urban core and buffering sub-cores, our population density will be higher.

This inverted land use model is admittedly utopian. Until now it would have been perhaps impossible to accomplish. But we are moved by the force of climate change and the unraveling of ecosystems. Some places will become more inhabitable, others less so. An additional help is our trend toward urbanization. The global human population living in cities is expected to increase to 70 percent by 2050.[510] Already, more than half of humanity has made the move to urban environments.

You may recognize the *inverting eminent domain* model as an inverted version of the Wildlands Project, now called The Wildlands Network. Its many advocates include The Rewilding Institute (TRI).[511] In what was once thought to be an unrealizable dream, TRI's Dave Forman describes the vision: "The Rewilding Institute believes that the minimum for rewilding North America is protection and restoration of Four Continental MegaLinkages ..."[512]

MegaLinkages are created by connecting and restoring ecosystems on a continental scale. They have core areas that are critical to the ecosystems. A key characteristic of rewilding is the presence of large carnivores, just as rewilding was first proposed by Michael Soule and Reed Noss.[513] In their version, core areas are surrounded by buffer zones. As we travel outward from those core areas, the number of human activities increases in the buffer zones. Core areas are connected to others by wildlife corridors. The corridors allow communities of species to travel from core to core. Continental in consideration, and ignoring political boundaries, immense areas of habitat have been painstakingly researched and mapped.

It is an ambitious vision that has been quickly supported, though still insufficiently, by progressive ecosystem-oriented professionals. The effort appears to be focused more on habitat than wholesale changes in human behavior when compared to what the new human ecology calls for, perhaps a necessity if they are to get the cooperation of landholders. Livestock grazing would be acceptable, for instance.

I believe their vision is being overtaken by the tsunami of rising human impacts. It needs a new human ecology to work and a populace that is more biocentric. In the inverted new human ecology version, the core areas are not for large carnivores, they are the urban, suburban, and rural areas where humans thrive. They are surrounded by *buffering areas of decreasing human activity* and *increasing ecosystem dominion*. That means other species have dominion there.

Ecosystem Dominion Is Our Goal

Implementation on this scale will enable ecosystems to renew their roles in the ongoing processes of evolution, migratory behaviors, natural dispersal, and thus genetic diversity, population stability, and a chance to preserve ecosystem processes and services that existed before the imposition of so many humans. Inverting the Wildlands proposal will give ecosystems and the biosphere the scale of human response that is required for their vision to succeed. The science is here.

Research revealed that connective corridors helped plants disperse and increased biodiversity.[514] However, it appears the current human ecology premise of the Wildlands Project model is that hunting, trapping, fishing, and animal agriculture would continue outside the innermost core wilderness areas. This is not true with vegan new human ecology and its companion, the inversion of human dominion. Ecosystem dominion, which is perhaps another way of saying biocentrism, should not scare us.

The Wildlands Network, Rewilding Institute, Center for Large Landscape Conservation, and others are leading us to rethink our approaches to sustainability and ecosystem integrity. They will not succeed, I believe, to the degree needed for our sustainability and stopping the Great Holocene Extinction event without a vegan new human ecology. Certainly, the injustice to species and individuals from other species would continue outside of their core areas under their proposal. And our behavior would fall short of its biocentric potential. The inverted eminent domain can return ecosystem supremacy; it can work if we couple it to the new human ecology. The barrier is whether enough people will embrace it, and accept it in time.

Part IV:

The Human Ecology of Managing Ecosystems

Chapter 13:

Recognizing the Corruption

The analysis finds that making a sustainability transition by 2050 is unlikely.... At the same time, the absolute growth in threats to Earth's life-support systems from the world's production and consumptions systems still exceeds the pace of the countering trends in reducing energy and material use, in reducing pollutants, and in controlling the unsustainable extraction of land and sea resources.[515, 516]

—Project Summary/Characterizing a Transition Toward Sustainability/Special Feature in the journal *Proceedings of the National Academy of Sciences of the United States of America*

While we grow a new human ecology in our personal lives, we will be challenging public institutions and NGOs that shape and implement public opinions, laws, and policies. Supporting the new human ecology requires that we petition ecosystem-affiliated agencies, NGOs, and their professionals, the scientists, advocates, reformers, field biologists, and the hands-on implementers of ecosystem management. We challenge them to take an introspective look at their work and ask them to compare what they are doing to what our living Earth needs. Will empathy, compassion, sustainability, love, and the future that biocentrism offers ever get their support?

Applied wildlife and ecosystem management is a social, scientific, political, cultural, and economic business. Cultural beliefs and political institutions decide which science is funded, which policy priorities and values are implemented, what goals are sought, and how scientific data is applied in the field. In this chapter and the next two chapters, I will briefly examine agency cultures and their professions by presenting examples of their work.

We are dealing with complex issues. However, the first thing we must do is pledge allegiance against our endless manipulation of Earth to satisfy unreasonable human demands. That much is obvious. But there is more. I preemptively apologize to anyone who may be offended by my generalizations about professions, agencies, organizations, and the dedicated people who work in all of them. I thank those who are already raising your voices to say *enough* of the carnist human ecology.

For the rest, we have to ask: Should ecosystem managers provide millions of acres of ecosystems so invasive species can needlessly graze and impact them? Should they supply abnormal numbers of huntable species by artificially imposing age and sex ratios while suppressing less-favored native species at the expense of ecosystems? Should they call for lowered human populations and an end to the animal agriculture that smothers ecosystems? When will they prioritize changing human behavior instead of ecosystems? Can we ever expect them to act more biocentric than anthropocentric?

Agencies are—they will point out correctly—constrained by legislative mandates to produce maximum sustained yields, alter the characteristics of ecosystems for perceived public demands, and serve the public instead of following a biocentric value system. But if it is not the agency wildlife professionals leaving their safe haven of publishing papers and work culture, who will question the basic premises of our diseased human ecology?

The seeming lack of resistance by agencies to the status quo is curious in light of a 1998 survey by the American Museum of Natural History. It revealed that 70 percent of biologists believed we are in the Great Holocene Extinction event. We are its cause. Where is their revolution to stop it?

Every one of us is propped up by the remnants of ecosystems. Ecosystem and wildlife management is no exception. This gives the illusion that wildlife management is truly in control of long-term outcomes—outcomes like biodiversity and human sustainability. There is progress in wildlife and ecosystems management, but not enough of it. It is not net progress because another force is at work to defeat it and it is called our current human ecology. Sectors of the profession have responded with the more adaptive and effective application of conservation biology, leaving behind single-species management that ignored larger ecosystem values.[517] But not everywhere.

Agencies still focus their resources on the private and commercial hunting, fishing, and trapping sectors, especially at the state level. They

demand greater than supply

also tweak ecosystems to produce livestock and the crops that feed them. This outdated approach is not about long-term human adaptation to ecosystems; it is about ecosystems adapting excessively to humans. That is the harm. Wildlife management culture is not responding as rapidly as we are altering them. We have created immense changes in the biosphere quickly compared to the evolution of agencies. This slowness is the result of their continued support of obsolete relationships with ecosystems and other species. Look at how they describe themselves.

State-level wildlife management agencies are the [enter a state] Department of Fish and Wildlife, ["State"] Department of Fish and Game, ["State"] Department of Natural Resources, and ["State"] Department of Conservation. At the federal level, we are presented with the Department of the Interior, including the Bureau of Land Management, U.S. Fish and Wildlife Service, National Park Service, Bureau of Indian Affairs, Minerals Management Service, and others; the Department of Commerce, including the National Oceanic and Atmospheric Administration/National Marine Fisheries Service; and the Department of Agriculture, including the National Forest Service, Wildlife Services aka Animal Damage Control, Animal and Plant Health Inspection Services, and National Organic Program. In the United States, these powerful agencies are given broad mandates over the fate of ecosystems and therefore us as well.

Asking and Offering

Before I describe the five reasons why state and federal wildlife management agencies ("agencies") cannot possibly provide the sustainable future they promise, we should appreciate how impossible we have made their task.

The complexity of policy-making, the difficulty of weighing and updating information, and the burden of creating consensus after integrating knowledge from several disciplines is required for agency effectiveness. We do not provide the resources agencies need for this monumental undertaking. Wrote famed biologist Edward O. Wilson in *Consilience,*

Only in imagination can we travel ... from the recognition of environmental problems and the need for soundly based policy; to the selection of solutions based on moral reasoning; to the biological foundations of that reasoning; to a grasp of social institutions as the products of biology, environment, and history. And thence back to environmental policy.[518]

Wilson's advice? "... a universal environmental ethic is the only guide by which humanity and the rest of life can be safely conducted through the bottleneck into which our species has foolishly blundered."[519] The universal environmental ethic embedded in the biocentric new human ecology I am proposing can, at minimum, buy us time to sort it all out.

Once our economic consumption and cultural demands surround, lay siege to, and fragment ecosystems, maintaining or restoring them to their original function, or that of 50 years ago, is not possible. We have already driven species to extinction; our ecosystems are literally full of holes. While we can take pride in the fact that the Cuyahoga River in Ohio no longer catches on fire, evidence points to a dramatic, growing, and cumulative decline of Earth's biological integrity. Countering human behavior, our current human ecology, with agency management takes more knowledge, political will, social consensus, a transformed economic system, and more human resources and money than we have.

Wildlife and ecosystem-related agencies are directed to appease the demands of the current human ecology. They are under constant pressure from many different constituencies. Only part of their legislated mandates is about patching up ecosystems under duress. The agencies are disproportionately influenced to an extreme by a hunting, trapping, and fishing community so intertwined with agency culture that agencies seldom dare to confront them. Agency program revenues and paychecks depend upon the sale of hunting and fishing licenses and federal distributions of taxes on firearms and other equipment. We can generally count on agency staff for their expertise, but like all of us, implementing knowledge can be tainted with personal bias.

Departments of Ecosystems, Flora, and Fauna

Why not ask these agencies to change their names? Some need to eliminate the words *game, fish*, and *wildlife* and replace them with words that are anthropocentrically neutral and biocentrically accurate. Appropriately, they would call themselves the [enter a state] Department of Flora, Fauna, and Ecosystems, with specialized subdivisions such as terrestrial, marine and fresh waters, soils, and atmosphere. But that is not the bias-free context I have experienced.

I was privileged to be on a panel of a few dozen scientists as a non-scientist representing the Progressive Animal Welfare Society in Washington State. Nearly everyone else was a wildlife management professional holding a Ph.D. or Masters degree who occupied a senior position in his and her agency, organization, or Tribe. It was there that I fully absorbed the fact how so many astute scientists could look at the same data about wildlife and come to completely different policy proposals. The practical side of this was that they disagreed whether or not the interpretation of data met the threshold for taking or not taking action. In this case, the action was the killing of California sea lions preying on steelhead at the base of the Ballard Locks built by the Corps of Engineers in Seattle.

The Washington Department of Fish and Wildlife (WDFW) had made a number of attempts to transport these sea lions far from the region, only to have them return. They tried to scare them with underwater noise and other methods. The underlying problem was that the salmon were stymied by an inadequate fish ladder and other design flaws in the dam that had not been updated in several decades. It was there that sea lions took advantage of the unnatural, concrete-walled habitat that had neither natural cover for migrating fish species nor gave them an easy time finding the fish ladder where they could escape to safety. The benefit of the panel was that we all discovered these and other factors responsible for salmon mortality at the locks. At its beginning, most panel members were for rubber-stamping lethal removal of sea lions, effectively scapegoating them for the harm the locks did to migrating salmon and steelhead. At its conclusion, more than half the panel still voted for lethal removal of sea lions, but the remaining scientists switched and supported the minority no-kill opinion report to Congress. In it we called for reengineering portions of the fish ladder and dam. Defensive at first, the Corps of Engineers eventually made many of those changes. On a wider scale, though, many agency cultures are mired in their need to be self-perpetuating institutions more attuned to human subcultures than allegiance to biocentric principles Earth needs to survive us.

Fish and wildlife agencies readily align themselves with self-described conservation organizations like the Wildlife Society, Wildlife Management Institute, and Safari Club International. Together, they proactively support and recruit more hunters. Those wildlife professionals most successful in their field may advance to teaching professions where they shape the biased cultural perspectives of the next generation of biologist-managers.

Minority Control and Oppression

Hunters are a special interest that heavily influences wildlife management policy. According to the latest, I believe most reliable report, "National Survey of Fishing, Hunting, and Wildlife-Associated Recreation," there were 12.51 million hunters age 16 years and older in the United States as of 2006.[520] Data about hunters and fishers is often unreliable, based on licenses sold and self-reporting surveys. This report, sponsored by the U.S. Department of the Interior, U.S. Fish and Wildlife Service, the U.S. Department of Commerce, and the U.S. Census Bureau, estimated there were 1.6 million hunters aged six to 15. The authors felt 12.51 million hunters for this given year represented an actual number of 18.6 million hunters who hunted at least once over five years from 2002 to 2006. However, they did not give the same consideration for the far larger number of wildlife recreation citizens who are not hunters, fishers, or trappers. So, I use their estimated 12.51 million hunters over the age of 16 for that year compared to just fewer than 300 million people populating the United States in 2006.[521]

The report's findings alarmed even the authors. They combined the adult and youth numbers for this statement: "... 41 percent of American hunters only participate[d] in one or two years out of the past five years."[522] In a 2010 addendum to the 2006 report, the U.S. Fish and Wildlife Service wrote, "From the perspective of a percentage of the total population, the decline in hunting and fishing is more pronounced.... the drop in participation rates of fishing [fell] from 21.0 percent in 1991 to 13.1 percent in 2006. Participation rates for hunting fell from 7.4 percent to 5.5 percent."[523]

Why do 94.5 percent of us, non-hunters all, passively allow this powerful minority to control agencies and the character of ecosystems? The composition of wildlife communities, the abundance or lack of abundance of species, the impacts this has on plant communities and other animal species, and the entirety of ecosystems, all are shaped by management decisions intently focused on meeting the demands of the hunter, trapper, and fisher lethal take minority.

And the people who head these agencies are of the same minority culture. U.S. Fish and Wildlife Service Director H. Dale Hall opened the above survey with this statement: "I find duck hunting with friends in a bottomland hardwood swamp or fishing with my kids on an Oregon river bolsters my spirit and reminds me why I care about conservation and our wildlife heritage."[524] His words give him credibility to the falling minority of hunters and recreational fishers in the United States. According to his agency bio, "... [Hall] managed the Service's activities relating to the northern spotted owl, desert tortoise, endangered Hawaiian birds, and other listed species.... more than 300 new species were placed under ... the Endangered Species Act and nearly $200 million in environmental contaminants cleanup settlements were reached ..."[525] While this list of accomplishments was won by his agency, NGOs, court cases, Congress, agency staff enforcing the law, and the voting public, we are certain he has a love for his vocation. What I question is what he and all of us could have accomplished in the presence of a vegan new human ecology and how much time we have lost in preventing damage from the current human ecology.

Influence and control by the 5.5 percent hunting minority is an artifact of history. In the past, most people lived in rural areas on small family farms. Hunting and fishing supplemented their food resources and rural culture. Now that most people live in urban areas, agencies have yet to reflect our new priorities. Boards of game and fish are powerful, politically appointed panels that establish and implement agency policies. This is a power granted to them by state legislatures. They do not reflect the public at large who neither hunt nor fish. While the number of hunters declined by 1.5 million from 1996 to 2006, wildlife watchers increased by 13 percent over the same period.[526]

Appointing vegans to state boards of "game" would be seen as problematic since the purpose of these boards is to manage wildlife through the encouragement of hunting. Vegan ecologists would confront the bases of wildlife management at every turn. Advocating the removal of all invasive livestock, replacing hunting with ecosystem predator-prey relationships over time as a new human ecology takes hold, and advocating for the return of apex predators in ecologically meaningful numbers would create constant friction. We cannot expect to find a foothold as vegans, yet. But this is just the beginning. Everyone can appreciate that the 94.5 percent of non-hunters should be proportionally represented on boards of flora, fauna, and ecosystem agencies. We will demand biocentric policies.

Entrenched pro–hunting and trapping advocates are armored with their access to hundreds of millions of dollars of revenue from government licensing and taxation kickbacks. Money gives them and their minority the power to reinforce their own view of the current human ecology through media and the actions they take at their agency workplace. They clearly have the upper hand and control the message. I have not seen how the question was written, but according to a 2006 Southwick survey conducted on behalf of the Association of Fish and Wildlife Agencies (AFWA),[527] "More than 7 out of 10 Americans approve of recreational hunting." Another survey was conducted in the same year by Responsive Management that, like Southwick, is regularly employed by wildlife management-oriented agencies. They found a 78 percent public approval rating from a random sampling of 813 people.[528] The public attitudes they measured were shaped by the agencies who paid for the survey. It's an instance where they wanted to see how well they were selling their worldview to us. That's all. Remove the agency funds used to perpetuate the educational propaganda about hunting, trapping, and fishing, and watch public opinions and poll results change.

AFWA makes it clear that they and their members do not just influence hunting and trapping, they are the driving force behind its promotion and attempts at expansion. They are enmeshed in carnist culture. Leadership and change for the moment will have to come from nonprofit environmental and species rights organizations, not the agencies. They are hard at work justifying and imprisoned by the legislated status quo.

In a report titled "Hunting in America/An Economic Engine and Conservation Powerhouse,"[529] the AFWA markets their industry. They cite the economic benefits of hunting that generates retail sales, retail tax revenues, jobs, and license revenues. They emphasize that $9.2 billion dollars of revenue was raised at the local, state, and federal levels. Yet this revenue could just as well be spent on football, tourism, trekking, nature education camps, or any other activity to generate jobs, retail sales, and tax revenues. There is no special case here. The AFWA is not printing money. Disposable income not spent on hunting will be spent somewhere else.

There *is* a special case created when hunters and trappers buy licenses and when hunters pay excise tax on equipment. The Federal Aid in Wildlife Restoration Act of 1937, aka the Pittman-Robertson Wildlife Restoration Act,[530] imposes a tax on guns, ammunition, bows and arrows. Wildlife management agencies count on these revenues. It is another example of turning a natural order of value into an economic one, though they would not see it that way. The "Hunting in America" report states that the total annual excise taxation amounts to $280 million, an insignificant player when distributed over 50 states. It also estimates that U.S. state wildlife agencies raised $725 million in 2006 from the sale of hunting licenses. Those revenue streams will be more difficult to replace.

And what about the AFWA claims that hunting is a $9.2 billion industry? This tally is for the entire United States. Compare that to the arts and culture sector in Washington State alone that generated nearly $2 billion dollars in business activity, 29,000 jobs, and $78 million dollars in tax revenue in 2009.[531] One non-hunting sector. One state.

Spend my tax dollars to preserve and expand the ecosystem services

I have been getting for free. I have not been paying for clean air and water, pollination, and all that ecosystems provide us. Tax me for using them. Protect them. Use the revenue to help us with sustainability. That is the highest priority, not the perpetuation of hunting by a small sector of the population. Our lives and all economic activity depend on ecosystems. But that is not we get.

The Washington Department of Fish and Wildlife (WDFW) recently released this typical statement: "This month ... fish hatchery crews will finish stocking more than 20 million fish in Washington waterways ... At least 300,000 anglers are expected to turn out for the big day.... 200,000 other fish [from other] species—including walleye, tiger muskie and bass—stocked in 12 waters ..."

Walleye, tiger muskie, and bass are non-native fish species; WDFW plants them to raise money.[532] A freshwater fishing license brings in $26 each to the department. Lakes throughout the state are put to service, not for ecosystem restoration (tiger muskie are also used to prey on other invasives), but to fund the agency and appease recreational fishers. The agency also advertises when it is going to release jumbo trout grown in hatcheries for recreational fishing.

As we bear witness to unraveling ecosystems and declining biodiversity is this what we need? Wildlife professionals do invaluable, often difficult work. They contribute to the protection of species and ecosystems. However, we need agencies to prioritize ecosystem integrity and biodiversity for their intrinsic value instead of disfiguring ecosystems for animal agriculture, hunting, trapping, and fishing. These agencies should be employed by ecosystems instead of those who buy licenses.

The rest of us are supposed to be satisfied by the *free ride* we get as a secondary outcome of managing wildlife for harvest. The first part of wildlife management is dedicated to ensuring the perpetuation of species while providing a huntable surplus. The second part completes the first: Wildlife and ecosystem managers use hunting to shape species composition to achieve related economic and biological goals. So while the agencies manipulate ecosystems for hunters and trappers, they also employ hunters to protect crops and animal agriculture, reduce wildlife-vehicle collisions, and control invasive species, or at least the

double standard.

ones they do not favor. Instead of the agencies being burdened by the expense of doing this alone, the hunters pay a nominal fee to do it for them. That is a difficult relationship to change because the current human ecology, with its attendant animal agriculture and the crops grown to feed it, creates the demand for warping ecosystems far more drastically than is necessary; this is how departments then justify their bowing to the hunting minority. They see it as a partnership at all levels. The new human ecology can break this hunter-agency embrace.

When was the last time you received educational material from wildlife management agencies about ecosystem services and our duty to protect and pay for them? Non-hunting organizations, citizens, and NGOs and their staff scientists represent the public majority. Why are they not the majority that sets wildlife management policies? It is this non-hunting majority that pays hundreds of millions of dollars allocated in the federal budget for the Departments of Commerce, Agriculture, and Interior that fund wildlife management. State agencies do not live on license fees alone; general funds collected from state taxpayers are used as well. We will not be represented in these matters and we will not end this prejudicial manipulation of ecosystems until we change our personal human ecology. Agencies operate in the social and political culture we create and the ecosystems we harm. When our new human ecology sharply curtails the *need* for management by hunting and trapping, we will get the representation from agencies we and ecosystems deserve.

Ecosystem and Wildlife Management Schemes

We are searching for material sustainability and have not yet found it. Unwilling to distinguish between the excesses of what we think we want and deserve and our true needs, our predations upon the environment remain wildly out of control. Wildlife and ecosystem management agencies and NGOs cannot overcome the ferocious inertia of our unceasingly destructive human demands, beliefs, and practices.

Ecosystems are energy-intensive, complex physical and biological behemoths. As human ecologist Garrett Hardin noted, "The basic insight of the ecolate citizen is that the world is a complex of systems so intricately interconnected that we can seldom be very confident that a proposed intervention in this system of systems will produce the consequences we want."[533] With a great deal of time and effort, we can disrupt ecosystems, and we can influence and alter them to favor us over all other species. But we do not have the ability to replicate them nor control the multitude of fluctuating biosphere variables. We are inept in managing their infinite minutiae, the environmental wealth we inherited.

Intact, healthy ecosystems have within them the abilities to harness inputs from solar energy, biochemical processes, and create physical structure, biological communities, nutrient cycles, and the results of all these factors interacting with one another. The innate abilities of Earth dwarf our efforts to control with confidence her reactions to what we have done. We live for the hope that ecosystems have enough remaining function to heal sufficiently.

Restoration can be done successfully, as long as we remember what *successful* means in this context. In one telling study that reviewed 240 projects to restore ecosystems, the authors found that 83 recovered by meeting 94 different criteria, 90 had partial recovery, and 67 showed no recovery at all.[534] The authors cautioned that defining recovery was an elusive goal. It does not necessarily mean a state of pre-human exploitation with all of the original species and relationships returned. Some of the restoration may only have achieved a past state of human alteration.

Optimistically, there could be more recovery coming if the studies had run long enough to find it. The authors expressed optimism: "The message of our paper is that recovery is possible and can be rapid for many ecosystems, giving much hope for humankind to transition to sustainable management of global ecosystems." However, as their media release notes, "... if societies choose to become sustainable, ecosystems will recover ..." That is the key. *If we choose to become sustainable.* The current human ecology is not sustainable; the new human ecology has a chance at becoming so. No chance—or a chance.

Seattle Was ...

Scientists have a hard time establishing the starting point in time to compare ecosystems as they were to what they are today. One hundred years ago? Ten thousand? We may never realize what is missing biologically and aesthetically, what we already have lost forever. I was stunned to learn what was lost during the past 100 years in Seattle.

From David Williams' *The Street-Smart Naturalist, Field Notes from Seattle*, I learned that of 58 species of plants botanists collected 100 years ago, none grow in Seattle today. This was associated with the destruction of local old-growth forests, prairies, bogs, and springs. Williams notes there are still 200 species of spiders and an estimated 1,500 species of beetles in this city along with 54 species of dragonflies in the surrounding King County. Several microclimates exist within two miles of where I live not far from the city center.[535] Who knew? For that, and more, I am fortunate.

I can see bald eagles fly directly in front of my hillside window. Beavers build lodges around the corner from my view. Raccoons amble by my door. But I also have watched the remnants of urban and suburban forest disappear along with the thick undergrowth of native and invasive plant species that served as cover for wildlife. In the past 15 years that I have lived in this spot, I no longer see several species of birds. There are fewer raccoons. A few months ago in mid-winter, Hal stopped neighbors down the street from directing a powerful jet of cold water against a very young raccoon. He or she was clinging to the end of a branch screaming in terror 20 or more feet above the ground. The neighbors could not understand why we insisted they stop. They did.

Chapter 14:

Limits to Human Agency Abilities

... within two decades [Aldo] Leopold's manifesto [*A Sand County Almanac*–1949] became the intellectual touchstone for the most far-reaching environmental movement in American history. ... The most obvious reason for the initial lack of public interest in Leopold's ideas was their truly radical nature. What he proposed would have necessitated a complete restructuring of basic American priorities and behavior. ... Leopold's philosophy abruptly curtailed the accustomed freedom with which Americans had hitherto dealt with nature.

—Roderick Frazier Nash, *The Rights of Nature*[536]

The Five Insufficiencies

Ecosystem recovery and management needs, at minimum, five supportive resources. Wildlife and ecosystem management agencies ("agencies") cannot give us long-term biodiversity and maintain ecosystem integrity because doing so requires the following:

1) **Sufficient knowledge** of the phenomenal complexity of the biosphere.

2) **Political will and social consensus** capable of bringing us forward toward sustainability, including fair distribution of resources.

3) **Economic systems** that protect and heal ecosystems. Our current economies do not reflect the innate, biocentric natural order of value when pricing the goods and services derived from ecosystem services.

4) **An appropriate human ecology** that prevents ecosystem decline, engenders ecosystem recovery, stops our wanton cruelty and disregard for individuals from other species, is biocentric, and moves us toward sustainability.

5) **Access to sufficient resources and human effort** in both capital investment and social dedication to biocentric agency management. Agencies are failing to define our relationships to ecosystems and individuals from other species as a moral issue. We are neglecting to legislate and fund alternative futures for the agencies.

These insufficiencies are not within agency control. Some are not their responsibilities. The five insufficiencies are the external environment, the context in which agencies operate. When they, NGOs, and the rest of us realize we lack sufficiency in every one of these critical abilities, perhaps we will see that our current human ecology needs an overhaul to help mitigate them as part of reforming who they are and what they do. My complaint is that wildlife management agencies are not confessing the coming future they do not control.

The First Insufficiency: Sufficient Knowledge

Our knowledge base, that of both scientific and traditional indigenous experience, is not adequate. The state of ecosystems is always changing, so what we do know can become outdated. An additional challenge is accessing the knowledge that already exists. For example, researchers from Northwestern University examined a database of nearly 23 million scientific papers. Their goal was to help overwhelmed scientists and other researchers better understand which journal publications are most relevant to their needs. For each of 2,267 journals, they charted how many citations each paper received during that period. They then developed a model that allowed them to compare journals covering 200 fields of academic study.[537] The researchers believe that this data will help the scientific community find which studies have the most impact and are most relevant to their work.

Confounding the problem is the complex nature of the scientific community itself. In *The Revenge of Gaia*, James Lovelock ponders why scientists were so slow in responding to climate change. He writes, "They were not wholly to blame, for science itself was handicapped in the last two centuries by its division into many different disciplines, each limited to seeing only a tiny facet of the planet, and there was no coherent vision of the Earth."[538]

By one estimate, biological knowledge doubles every five years.[539] That means we knew about half as much five years ago as we do today. There is an estimated 500 thousand to 750 thousand species believed to be living in the United States. Only one-third to one-half has been discovered. Of the undiscovered and often the discovered, we know nothing of their roles in ecosystems, their relationships and interdependence with other species, or how much our future depends upon them. We do not know their population health or trends.

A 2011 paper calculated there are approximately 8.7 million species on Earth.[540] Another analysis estimated there may be 15 million species of plants, animals, bacteria, and fungi on Earth, or 100 million. No one knows.[541] For the 8.7 million species approximation, the paper's authors wrote, "... our results suggest that some 86 percent of existing species on Earth and 91 percent of species in the ocean still await description."[542] They also estimated that "describing Earth's remaining species may take as long as 1,200 years and would require 303,000 taxonomists at an approximated cost of US $364 billion."[543] We are reshaping the entire Earth without sufficient knowledge and humility.

Agencies are often directed by law to use *the best available science* in their policies and decisions. The implication is that we will learn more. We may come to different conclusions in the future; today, we may be making a mistake. Decisions are made. Then we unsustainably demand ecosystem services like children whacking at a piñata full of candy. We do not hesitate because in our ignorance, we do not know what we are doing.

The Second Insufficiency: Political Will and Social Consensus

Political will is unlikely to change agency behavior and culture because the majority of people who elect legislatures reflect the state of public consciousness and unconsciousness about alternatives to agency practices. Agencies are not likely to rise above this. In fact, they perpetuate it because they seem unwilling to revolt against carnism and its control of ecosystems. A revolt would entail a different worldview (biocentrism), progressive vision, and risk to their careers.

Social will to effect change requires public effort, real or perceived discomfort, and consistent motivation. Making people uncomfortable by telling them that *they*, not somebody else, must change is like promising to raise taxes and then wanting their vote. Social support for the current human ecology is still in control of our institutions. People hinder change by electing and appointing others like themselves to office.

Corruption, especially in impoverished economies, and pressure upon governments everywhere to meet an endlessly growing demand for jobs and economic growth undermine whatever political will and social consensus there may be for a sustainable human ecology. Sometimes it is visible. During U.S. President George W. Bush's time in office, science was funneled through the politically conservative gatekeepers of the White House. There, scientific reports and recommendations were rewritten to align with conservative political ideology. Julie Cart of the *Los Angeles Times* reported,

> The Bush administration altered ... The *original* draft of the environmental analysis [regarding the environmental impacts of grazing on public lands that] ... warned the new rules would have a 'significant adverse impact' on wildlife. The Bush White House removed that phrase: 'The [Bureau of Land Management] now concludes that the grazing regulations are 'beneficial to animals.'[544]

Corporations have taken up the conservative cause to the same effect. Seeking to keep their control of public opinions, they effectively abuse

willingly ignore but this is justified in u blocking

science and block legislation essential to our survival. In 2012, Nina Fedoroff, the president of the American Association for the Advancement of Science (AAAS), was quoted as being "scared to death" by corporate power whose agenda is anti-science whenever it restricts their activities.[545]

As long as social consensus, political institutions, and corporations lack a biocentric respect for ecosystems, we will not get changes in wildlife and ecosystem management agencies. As much as agency employees' love of the Earth makes them concerned, they are not going to change until our new human ecology reaches a critical mass of social and political support and forces it upon them.

The Third Insufficiency: Economic Systems That Protect and Heal Ecosystems

Ecosystems are finite, so our demands upon them must have boundaries. Our economic systems must parallel those boundaries. If we claim that we are a natural, legitimate species with rights to life, it follows that our economic systems should reflect our natural relationships to ecosystems and respect their capacities and limits. In addition to biological limits, we recognize we have an equal economic obligation to eliminate the suffering we impose on individuals from other species. Economic systems should adapt to ecosystem priorities, not the other way around.

Our present economic systems that represent and attempt to legitimize our unsustainable behaviors are running amuck. When we change the natural order of value that is defined by relationships between species within ecosystems to an economic order of value that is defined within our economic systems, we seem to forget which one comes first. We do not need to be economists to see the problems this creates.

The cheapest products and services are often the most harmful to the biosphere. Products and services that are more sustainable, morally responsible, and less damaging should cost less than environmentally destructive, immoral, and harmful choices. Products and services that pass costs of toxic pollution and terrible working conditions onto ecosystems and impoverished people should be priced out of existence. People of impoverished and modest means are faced with choices that should not exist: Merchandise that costs less at the store cost the Earth more. From the accumulated costs that Earth has absorbed from our behavior, we have a debt owed her that we are unable to repay. We see it in the loss of ecosystems and species.

When 100 percent unbleached, recycled toilet paper costs more than toilet paper that is chemically bleached and produced from virgin resources, the economic system fails us. As a result, we are pressed by our household budgets to choose the cheapest, cruelest, and most environmentally harmful products. In *Ambio: A Journal of the Human Environment*, James Galloway estimated that the "external costs of US agricultural production (e.g., the cost of damages to people and ecosystems, government control, and clean-up processes not borne by producers or consumers) total between USD 9.4 and 20.6 billion per year."[546] These costs are the damages that wildlife and ecosystem management agencies are trying to repair.

The duty of business is to reveal these *true costs* to consumers. Call it cost transparency. The role of consumers is to provide the demand and pay a higher price for the *good* products as often as possible. This is our investment. When it is painful for us to pay the higher price, we must remember the true costs of what we are buying and Earth pays for. The role of government is to lead, educate, and provide incentives for sustainable living through legislation, regulation, taxation, and policy.

New human ecology adherents strive to not buy products that, in their making, cause injustice, unsustainability, and cruelty wherever it is found. Our economic systems have to stop producing those byproducts. Fish, wildlife, and ecosystem management agencies are left with cleaning up our mess. That mess is more than they can fix.

The Fourth Insufficiency: An Appropriate Human Ecology

Agencies are trying to accommodate the current human ecology that is too destructive to manage. The Seven Results I have proposed are what an *appropriate* human ecology can accomplish. It provides an environment where reformed agencies will be able to succeed in becoming biocentric agencies. In *Hope*, I have put the most emphasis on a vegan human ecology. Though agencies require the entire new human ecology to succeed, our food choices create the relationships we have with other species more than any other factor.

As we end carnism, wildlife management agencies will be free to respond adaptively to the changes and opportunities this creates in ecosystems. The new human ecology frees agency resources, restores funding from the general public, eliminates agency dependence on the 5.5 percent hunting minority, and clears a path for a biocentric agency culture. As long as our human ecology remains unsustainable and anthropocentric, wildlife and ecosystem–related agencies will not succeed in saving ecosystems or biodiversity. A vegan human ecology will produce a historic change in how agencies approach their work.

The Fifth Insufficiency: Access to Sufficient Resources and Human Effort

We do not operate ecosystems. We do not supply their power, their nutrients, or their rainfall. Agencies cannot provide or control anything close to the inputs that make ecosystems and biodiversity work. If we pump greenhouse gasses into the atmosphere for over 200 years, agencies and their biologists are observers, not controllers. In the 1990s, our carbon emissions were growing at 0.9 percent annually.[547] During the past 10 years, they have grown faster than ever at 3.5 percent per year. Today, we are adding an average of 2.2 parts per million CO_2 to the atmosphere per year, "more than double the [rate of] increase in the 1960s."[548] Global warming is here as a result.

Agencies did not ask for global warming nor can they stop it. About a quarter of the CO_2 coming from our burning fossil fuels and other activities is absorbed by the world's oceans.[549] The trapped CO_2 acidifies the marine waters so that organisms are less able to build shells and exoskeletons.[550] According to the Natural Resource Defense Council (NRDC), the oceans have become about 30 percent more acidic over the past 250 years after absorbing approximately 530 billion tones of our CO_2.[551]

We should not expect agencies to have sufficient funding and human resources to overcome our irresponsible human ecology and then control long-term ecosystem health. They are in a unique position to educate us and help us achieve biocentric sustainability. And, as an editor reviewing this book noted, "They are in a unique position to show us by example."[552]

As we and agencies look on, global warming has dramatically melted and thinned the Arctic and Antarctic polar ice caps. Ice reflects solar energy (heat) back into space. Without ice, the darker water absorbs the sun's solar radiation and warms the oceans. Warmer water, more ice melt, more solar absorption, warmer water, more ice melt.

The presence and timing of ice cover affects the presence and timing of phytoplankton that are a foundation of the world's food webs. Most marine species are ultimately dependent upon them. Agencies do not control any of this. They cannot make polar ice.

It is the biosphere that will do most of the work, not agencies, once we stop spewing greenhouse gasses in excess. The sun will power the repair of ecosystems if we do not push them too far, not fish, wildlife, and ecosystem management agencies, or the scientific community. It is the bacteria, the seas, the green vegetation, and the rain that can restore us. We have been so confident that we can repair and control ecosystem outcomes sometime in the future that we continue to sabotage and cripple the very natural systems able to do the repairing. Earth could achieve the quickest return to her abundance of biodiversity if we simply vacated the planet.

Should we always let nature take her course and believe that will be the best situational outcome? No. But as long as those five generalized inabilities and insufficiencies exist, agencies, governments, and institutions will be unable to manage their way to sustainability attendant with healthy ecosystems and abundant biodiversity. The result will not sustain 7 billion people equitably, much less the 9.3 billion expected in 38 years. The agencies know this, I believe. I have listened to their professionals, scientists, and career environmental NGOs who say, usually *off the record*, that they are deeply pessimistic about our survival. They see a less habitable world where far fewer people and species survive.

What Wildlife Management Allows: The Canned Hunt

Fish and wildlife agencies on several continents allow private businesses to raise exotic and native wildlife species. These businesses charge fees to hunters who then kill those species while confined on fenced private and leased land. This is *canned hunting*. Though some biologists are concerned, this development should not be a surprise. Professional wildlife management culture is infected with beliefs and values that make canned hunting inevitable.

In a canned hunt, a person toting a gun or bow and arrow has paid a fee that is correlated to the kind of species he or she wants to kill. In exchange for a few hundred to tens of thousands of dollars not including airfare, taxidermy fees, and other incidentals, the hunter enters a fenced-in area that can be small or extend to thousands of acres. He or she then kills any number of mostly exotic species who are individuals often native to other continents. Lions, giraffes, water buffalos, impala, jaguar, and many others are killed this way. Some are shot at watering holes in a parched land while others are baited with piles of meat and killed as they eat.

I was surprised to learn the extent of this practice in the United States and its danger to ecosystems. One study estimated that 21 to 45 percent of exotic big game species in North America are not behind effective fences.[553] An Internet search for "exotic trophy hunt Texas," for example, opens the door to you if you want to see this cowardly business in action.

Exotic Texas

[handwritten annotation: How does this reinforce human domination of animals?]

The Texas Parks and Wildlife Department (TPWD) sells raffle tickets to hunters hoping to win "Big Time Texas Hunts" that "... offer hunters the chance to win one of seven exclusive hunting trips on some of the finest private ranches and prime wildlife management areas in Texas."[554] One of the prizes was a chance to kill exotic species: "... sable antelope, gemsbok oryx, scimitar-horned oryx or common waterbuck. Hunters may choose to shoot the exotic game with a modern rifle, muzzleloader, archery or crossbow." This is a state agency in the

253

business of canned hunts. It appears all U.S. wildlife management agencies hold raffles of one sort or another as well as use other marketing tools to fund their departments and promote the growth of hunting.

TPWD's website informs us that there is a high purpose to the research the raffle will fund because "proceeds go to benefit wildlife conservation and research on Mason Mountain WMA [wildlife management area]." The department acquired the once-private exotic *game ranch* in the Mason Mountain Wildlife Management Area where there are 14 types of exotic species surrounded by an eight-foot-high fence. The raffle is funding research about the impacts that African, yes African, wildlife has on Texas habitat. African species have escaped into Texas ecosystems. So while TPWD holds lotteries to fund this and other research, the department does not stop private businesses from holding more canned hunts. According to the department's press release, they raised "about $704,507 in gross revenue to support wildlife research, habitat management, and public hunting."[555] Four of the 17 prizes were licenses to hunt exotic species. Their assistance in corrupting biological wealth boggles the mind.

I was initially encouraged to see on the TPWD website the inference that ecosystems are the appropriate management perspective: "Single species deserve less attention, while the system in which they thrive requires more...." However, this statement is soon betrayed. The TPWD supports Texas' historic decimation of ecosystems by livestock grazing and broad use of fire as a management tool. What is obvious is that TPWD's business is to keep the hunting and animal agriculturalist economies running. The department pointedly remarks,

> The key to managing natural resources is to use a holistic approach, where all of [Aldo] 'Leopold's Tools' (cow, plow, ax, fire, and gun) are applied to develop and maintain healthy ecosystems.... Knowing how that system functions, and applying the techniques with which that system developed (e.g., moderate cattle grazing, prescribed burning, hunting) is imperative for its continued existence.[556]

Aldo Leopold and his contemporaries revolutionized the way in which wildlife management science perceived human relationships with other species and their ecosystems. But he died 63 years ago. Does anyone think that if alive today he would be giving the same prescription without modification in this vastly different world? Would he more likely be an advocate for reforming our human ecology and leap ahead of TWPD practices that are stuck in a tar pit from the past? Would Leopold rebel at the continued deep loss of biodiversity in the presence of today's wildlife management?

Eighty-four percent of Texas is privately owned farm, ranch, and forest.[557] TWPD may never bring to these entrenched interests what Leopold undoubtedly would bring to the profession today: to restore as best as possible dominating characteristics of original ecosystems. How do Texas wildlife professionals think he would feel about canned hunts against African exotic species and their agency-sponsored perpetuation in Texas?[558] What would Leopold say about the Texas human population increasing 22 percent, an additional 4,290,847 people, between 1997 and 2007? The Texas A&M Institute of Renewable Natural Resources believes it will increase another 6,500,000 by 2020. They estimate that 270 acres of land is lost for every one thousand additional Texans.[559]

Exotic Africa

In Africa, there are canned and trophy hunts where lions and elephants are killed with bow and arrow. Others prefer silencers on their firearms.

A canned hunt business in South Africa named Quaggasfontein uses silencers on guns, alleging that this preserves the environmental experience of its clients, including photographers. Their website advertises that "We are proud of the tame nature of the wild animals ... in order that game may be viewed and photographed in their natural habitat at close distance." The hunters with silencers must appreciate this as well since they select from the same population of individuals. There are 22 species on a "private reserve," which means the targets cannot escape. The Quaggasfontein website reveals how commercializing wildlife controls a large swath of ecosystem and predator-prey relationships:

> Surplus animals are sold for breeding purposes and the gender ratio
> is usually two or three male animals in a parcel of ten. Consequently,
> we allow a limited amount of hunting in order to reduce the
> numbers of those male animals where the bachelor herd sizes have
> become too large and/or to eliminate older animals—male or
> female—that would naturally have fallen prey to predators like lion
> and leopard.[560]

God forbid lions and leopards would spoil the money the proprietors
make on their *farm*. Anyone can spend days on the Internet and just
scratch the surface of the canned hunting sector. It is rampant in both
developed and emerging economies.

Like African, Texan, and other canned hunts, the large fenced-off
areas fragment habitat and risk introducing exotic, invasive wildlife.
This commercialization also usurps wildlife management agencies for
narrow interests. Wildlife is effectively privatized.[561] Some of these
businesses operate on smaller parcels and ensure that lazy hunters feel
like heroes.

At a single Texas operation I picked at random on the web, the
owners offer, on one thousand fenced acres, for a fee ranging from
$2,000 to $15,000 dollars, addax, American bison, aoudad sheep, axis,
blackbuck, blesbok, Fallow deer, gemsbok, common lechwe, nilgai, Pere
David's deer, pure Nubian ibex, red stag, sable, scimitar oryx, water
buffalo, Watusi, wildebeest, yak, zebra, white-tailed deer, Catalina goat,
Corsican sheep, four-horn sheep, painted desert sheep, Texas Dall
sheep, mouflon sheep, red sheep, elk, bison cow, and "exotic does." All
individuals from other species are described as "trophy class."[562]

These businesses may bolster their commercial wildlife ranching
operations with leased federal land that doubles for livestock
production. In Idaho, Juniper Mountain Elk ranch states on their
website:

> Juniper Mountain Elk ranch ... offer[s] big game animals like bison
> and elk ... we also include hunts for coyotes, rabbits, badgers, geese,

ducks, pheasants, sage grouse, sharptail grouse, grey partridge, Hungarian partridges, and doves.... Our elk ranch has over 11,000 acres of high fence. Our sheep ranch, however, covers almost 400,000 acres of forest, BLM, state land and private land...[563]

The hunting community imposes additional selfish priorities beyond canned hunts. Under pressure, wildlife management agencies license hunters to decimate wolf packs to ecological insignificance so there will be more elk, moose, and caribou to kill. Similarly, on a reclaimed Skagit River delta in Washington State, restoration of river estuaries is needed to save endangered Chinook salmon. This restoration is opposed by some hunters so that 14-year-olds can continue killing pheasants. When they oppose restoring Chinook's habitat, they are also impacting endangered Southern Resident orca whales who favor and need Chinook salmon over other species they eat.[564]

New Human Ecology and Wildlife Management

Agencies accept and ensure that ecosystems are perpetually dependent upon hunting and trapping to manage populations. They will correctly point out there would be many more conflicts and costs to the public if their hunting and trapping tools were taken away suddenly. Beyond that generality, they exploit fear with incomplete considerations of alternatives. A 2005 report by the International Association of Fish and Wildlife Agencies (IAFWA), titled "Potential Costs of Losing Hunting and Trapping as Wildlife Management Methods," was funded by the U.S. Fish and Wildlife Service with input from the Fur Institute of Canada. It went to lengths to explain how much their agencies depend upon hunting and trapping to keep conflict with wildlife at bay.

They warn that:

- Deer-automobile accidents result in over $1 billion in damage annually.
- Wildlife damage to households amounts to $633 million. This includes money spent by house owners to prevent wildlife

damage.

- Beavers, woodchucks, and other species cause millions of dollars in damage each year to roads, bridges, dams, water drainage systems, and electrical utilities in both the United States and Canada.
- Crops and livestock losses from wildlife in the United States totaled $944 million in 2001.
- Wildlife cause close to $750 million in damage to the timber industry. However, the timber industry projected that with no animal damage management, their loss would be approximately $8.3 billion.[565]

The report claims that if hunting and trapping were stopped a virtual Armageddon of conflicts with wildlife against human interests would ensue and cost "$70.5 billion from all forms of health, structural, agricultural, and other forms of wildlife-related damages annually." This non-biocentric perspective forgets that we cause most of the conflicts through our current human ecology.

The report's assumptions include a sharp increase in car-wildlife collisions, disease outbreaks in people and other species, an increase in crop and livestock damage, and more critters entering and damaging human homes. However, this scenario is misleading for a number of reasons.

Their roughly estimated $70.5 billion figure includes the figure for the estimated damage from wildlife conflicts already occurring, not the amount of increase. The authors cite an approximately 221 percent increase in costs to mitigate wildlife conflicts if hunting and trapping were ended. They frequently refer to a survey of wildlife agencies that reports no amount of budget increase would allow them to control wildlife issues without their enlisting hunters and trappers. Let us examine their doomsday outlook.

It appears the authors begin with a base of about $31.3 billion *conflict* dollars. They propose that if all public hunting and trapping were to stop in the United States, it would cost an additional $39.2 billion dollars to the U.S. economy. The report also presumes this flood of new conflicts would lessen the public goodwill toward wildlife and reduce them to the status of pests.

Undoubtedly, if we were to continue with the
ecology, conflict seems likely to increase to some ex
assumptions and predicted problems are based on th(
acceptance of the current human ecology replete with   ug
human populations, animal agriculture, the massive ɔotanical
agriculture that feeds animal agriculture, unfettered human
colonization of wildlife habitat, and people unwilling to change their
behavior to reduce conflict with wildlife.

Though the sooner the better, hunting and trapping is going to end
over time as a process, not overnight. There are three things to consider
in our human ecology: *what it has done, what it is doing,* and *what it could
do.* Our human ecology has evolved over time. In our preliminary
successes as a species, we have altered ecosystems, most of which will
not be recoverable to a pre-human-impacted state. That is *what our
human ecology has done.*

We have clearly crossed a line where our mega, presence, and
economic neo-predations now are additional impacts to our original
hunter, fisher, and animal agriculturalist human ecologies. That is *what
our human ecology is doing.*

What could our human ecology do? We can reduce our population and
eat lower on the food chain in a vegan new human ecology. Expanses
of ecosystems are released from our grip. This opens the way for a
considerable reestablishment of predator-to-prey and herbivore-to-
plant community relationships in ecosystems. Invasive livestock
species can be removed and thereby end those conflicts with predators.
Vast landscapes are made available to restoration. Crop damage from
wildlife will be massively reduced because we will stop growing the
majority of crops now cultivated for livestock food. We do not farm
ecosystems for their wildlife to appease hunters.

Conservation biologists can then begin their lifelong efforts to
restore biodiversity, stop soil erosion, and end the agricultural
pollution from fertilizer, pesticides, and herbicides. Fewer people and
intelligently designed or retrofitted homes and fenced communities
will prevent more conflicts with wildlife. Engineers and government
can retrofit roads. We can change our driving habits and the archi-

_ure of our highway system to lessen collisions with other species and habitat fragmentation. We will retreat from our encroachments on wildlife habitat to reduce human-wildlife conflicts further. Unfortunately, the report seems intent on pushing our panic buttons when it could have recognized and promoted a more adaptive and preventative new human ecology. Their fear of challenging our behavior is palpable.

Beliefs enshrined in agency culture will continue to be represented in publications like "Potential Costs of Losing Hunting and Trapping as Wildlife Management Methods" until we take the lead and change our own behavior. That is the quickest route to meaningful reform in wildlife and habitat management. Wildlife management and ecosystem science has evolved over time. Managing from broader ecosystem and landscape perspectives instead of favored species is a recent phenomenon. In its history, wildlife management has both encouraged and stopped our excesses. Today, it is not adequately responding to our mega, presence, and economic neo-predations, nor has it lessened its support for hunting, fishing, and animal agriculture.

Not all conflict with wildlife will magically disappear in the new human ecology. It will decrease significantly as more of us change our ecological niche from carnist to veganist. As much as managers hate losing species to extinctions and want healthy ecosystems, they are abetting their demise instead, placing policy bricks in the road to long-term failure. They, like many environmental NGOs, have led us to believe their agencies can deliver us from our unsustainability under the non-adaptive current human ecology. That is a false, empty premise. We need agencies and the scientific community of wildlife professionals to become activist biocentric visionaries. Ecosystems cannot have it any other way.

We want to believe we can achieve sustainability with a minimum of effort, not the required maximum. Trial and error management is applied to ecosystems that are constantly changing. This can result in overexploitation when combined with less than optimal control of "harvest."[566] Wrote Thomas T. Struhsaker in "A Biologist's Perspective on the Role of Sustainable Harvest in Conservation,"

... the concept of sustainable harvest has often been equated with effective conservation. To the contrary, sustainable harvest is invariably an activity whose objective is the material welfare of a select group of humans. Sustainable harvest does not necessarily have anything to do with conservation of species except in a coincidental and passive way.[567]

Struhsaker has 35 years of experience in tropical conservation. From the new human ecology perspective, he is indicating for us the transparent inability of agencies to counter the immensity of human impact and agency anthropocentric bias that is driving ecosystem change beyond all reasonable biological and moral constraint. More important is that you and I control this state of affairs through the human ecology we choose to live.

Chapter 15:

Establishing Relationships

At the same time that rites of passage can describe the critical passage of a whole culture to a new way of life, they also—and much more commonly— are explicitly transformative procedures designed to carry an initiate through profound encounters with the darkest aspects of existence. They begin with a separation from the old way of life. The initiate is then taken into a threshold period and often a holding place, where the stripping away continues until the old identity is dissolved. This is the fertile void, the place of death and rebirth.

—Paul H. Ray and Sherry Ruth Anderson, *The Cultural Creatives*[568]

We are all vulnerable, threatened, and endangered. Countless species are. Yet nowhere in the mountain of paperwork and years of costly agency administration and NGO dedication to creating policies and decisions meant to protect ecosystems and people, nowhere have I seen a vegan human ecology alternative proposed. During my environmental and species advocacy as an employee of NGOs, the idea was unthinkable. Recently, for the first time in my life, I was able to do this in my comments that addressed WDFW's wolf management plan. I had to represent my own organization, Green Vegans, before I had the chance to do it. Our new human ecology requires us to get agencies and NGOs to accept the legitimacy of a vegan human ecology. We do not need to look far to find candidates where this change is crying out to be heard. Here is a sampling of dishonest relationships conducted under fish and wildlife management agencies and the carnist culture in which they are embedded.

Killing Wolves

In 1995 and 1996, Idaho Fish and Game (IDFG), with concurrent state legislation, supported federal efforts to reintroduce the gray wolf.

Attached to this support was an agreement that ensured wolves would play relatively minor roles in ecosystems compared to hunters and ranching interests. Idaho insisted that the U.S. Fish and Wildlife Service list the wolves as a nonessential population south of Interstate 90 and that Idaho would be the agent to manage them. In return, on May 4, 2009, the federal government removed wolves from the Endangered Species Act protections in this and, as part of a larger decision, other areas. Wolf hunting season under state control opened September 1, 2009, some four months later.

At the time, Idaho estimated there were about 1,000 wolves in the state, and were expanding at a rate of 22 percent per year without recreational hunters pursuing them. IDFG intended to kill 220 wolves the first season that spanned 2009–2010; their overall goal was to limit wolves in Idaho ecosystems to 520. IDFG opened for business and sold 10,700 wolf tags (permits) as of September 1, 2009, at $11.75 each for Idaho residents and $186.00 for non-residents. The adjoining state of Montana set its 2009 quota at 75 killed with 2,600 permits sold on the first day of sales. There were an estimated 1,650 gray wolves in the northern U.S. Rocky Mountains then.[569, 570, 571, 572]

Robert Millage, a real estate agent, was the first to have a recorded kill in Idaho. As Associated Press reporter Todd Dvorak quoted him, "'It was really an adrenaline rush to have those wolves all around me, howling and milling about after I fired the shot.'" Hunting guides seemed to reflect the same belief system. "'Any success we have with wolves will be more of a happenstance sort of thing,' said Richard Huff, a guide for Silver Spur Outfitters and Lodge near Grangeville … 'But I can tell you if I see one it's going to be adios.'"[573]

I checked out IDFG's data that year for the Sawtooth wildlife management area that consisted of units 33, 34, 35, 36, and 39. These were the units that had the highest number of wolves; 55 were slated to be shot to death there.

Elk hunting is a recreational business where seasons are available in much of the state. According to their data, 903 elk were taken by hunters, under 9,349 elk permits for the Sawtooth area alone. Additionally, there was a controlled hunt in at least unit 39 where 967 additional permit holders took 250 more elk. Unit 39 is also where the largest number of elk, 508, was killed by hunters in 2008. I have not looked into whether the 2,009 muzzle loaders and bow and arrow hunters who killed 147 elk in Sawtooth are part of the general total for 2009, or in addition to it. But the point is already made: Wolves are killed to produce recreation for hunters, including those who get thrills in killing wolves with arrows.

While such opinions reflect the current human ecology doctrine of human supremacy, ecosystems are not being discussed. Coyotes, fully capable of killing deer and elk,[574] grow in numbers and range when not suppressed by wolves.

Elk are herbivores who shape the plant communities they browse. When wolves are reintroduced and elk numbers reduced, willows along riverbanks recover and support increased biodiversity. Aspen[575] and cottonwood[576] have shown the same response as willows. That is not foremost, if at all, in the minds of the hunting corps. They are intent on killing more prey than wolves at every point of their belief system. Those hunters will not act like wolves as agents of the ecosystem.

Many hunters seek elk trophies and remove the best of the gene pool. Others seek those age and sex classes of elk artificially structured by wildlife managers that promise recreation and meat for their license-paying clients. In a study done on the Yellowstone elk population that extends into Idaho and Montana, wolves were found to select calves and older females (mean age 13.9 years) with no to low reproductive abilities. Hunters, on the other hand, killed much younger females (mean age 6.5 years), which is their prime age for reproduction. [577] When human hunting controls these biased outcomes, they also alter the food web and community of species. The dominant selection pressures that shaped species over the millennia now come from humans, not other ecosystem forces.

I have not found discussion on the IDFG website that speaks to the impacts that will result from several thousand hunters shooting at wolves, chasing them even while they are pregnant and seeking locations for their dens. Like our families, their pack social cohesion is stressed or obliterated. These are the selection pressures IDFG and hunters create.

Researchers describe agency wolf control bluntly. To summarize other studies, and concluding that the same generalities apply to Australian dingo *control* as they do to wolves, A.D. Wallach and his co-authors published "More Than Mere Numbers: The Impact of Lethal Control on the Social Stability of a Top-Order Predator." They wrote that consideration must be given to social structure, not just numbers killed by or on behalf of agencies:

> The control of wolves fractures their social structure, which may lead to changes in age composition, group size, survival rates, hunting abilities, territory size and stability, social behavior, genetic identity and diversity. Controlled populations tend to have a higher proportion of young, breeding pairs and litters, due to the loss of pack structure which regulates breeding. ... [and] that the effect of control on abundance was neither consistent nor predictable.[578]

The researchers go on to describe "aberration of pack social traditions" and losses to their hunting skills. What social fracturing really means is that these wolves are suffering emotional and physical trauma. The bonding of wolves is as strong an emotion we will find. This is as true in Montana as it is in Idaho.

As of February 13, 2012, Montana Fish, Wildlife, and Parks (MFWP) reports 162 wolves killed although there are additional mortalities from other causes.[579] After several court challenges temporarily stopped most wolf hunting,[580] an unprecedented act of Congress removed Northern Rocky Mountain Gray Wolves from protections under the Endangered Species Act.[581] For the 2011–2012 season, Idaho Fish and Game set the Sawtooth quota at 60 dead wolves, but for most of the state, left the quota wide open.[582,583] Trapping, shooting from aircraft, and baiting are allowed. Idaho allows the trapper three days before returning to the trap.

Do not expect IDFG to stop wolf killing on its own; the 1938 ballot initiative that created the department requires the agency to supply a "surplus" of huntable species.[584] Political and economic considerations, not biocentric principles, warp ecosystems in Idaho.[585] Separately, federal agents will continue killing wolves at the behest of animal agriculturalists.

The Alaskan Aerial Wolf Killers

"Alaska's constitution requires that Alaska's resources, including its fish and wildlife, be managed for the maximum benefit of Alaskans." That is the opening sentence for the Alaska Department of Fish and Game's (ADFG's) publication, "Understanding Predator Management in Alaska." A brief mention is given to the fact that "The Alaska Board of Game and ADF&G are required by Alaska's constitution and state law to manage predators and prey for all user groups in Alaska."[586] This establishes the foundation for their extreme attitudes toward ecosystems and wildlife.

The Alaska Constitution does not allow wildlife management policies to be different for people living in subsistence in the wilderness from urbanite hunters. Both feed the demand for unspeakable treatment of wolves—and bears. Predator controls are mandated when demand from both rural and urban hunters exceeds supply, that "fish and wildlife be managed for the maximum benefit of Alaskans." Immense areas are affected.

Legions of hunters, trappers, and the staff of ADFG wound and kill wolves from low-flying airplanes and chase them down with snowmobiles. Fleeing wolves struggle in the snow to escape while others are caught in the immorality of snares and leghold traps.

Some of these wolves live in protected areas. For instance, after traveling a short distance out of Denali National Park's boundaries, they immediately lose their protection. A trapper named Coke Wallace killed a Denali National Park alpha female wolf belonging to the Toklat pack within a few hundred feet of the park's boundary. Biologist Gordon Haber had studied this pack for 40 years; he returned the next day to the site where the wolf was murdered. Haber reported that the female's mate, the alpha male, kept returning to the site, howling from the ridge.[587] Haber died soon after in a plane crash in the same area while studying his beloved wolves. I started the Greenpeace Alaska office that funded one of his papers, so I know first-hand the ugliness of ADFG and its board of game.

The Toklat River area in Denali National Park is a magnificent place to be and one of my favorite places on Earth. I think of the sad existence of a single trapper who did so much harm with so little consciousness, and the pain and the injustice he perpetuated on wolves. But the ADFG has licensed members of the public to kill wolves on their behalf for a long time. Decades ago, I attended a public ADFG board meeting on a proposal to initiate a *temporary* program to shoot wolves from aircraft. Their reason then was as it is now: to increase the numbers of huntable individuals from other species like moose and caribou, including in areas accessible to urban hunters along highways. The meeting was held in Fairbanks where I represented Greenpeace Alaska. For my testimony in opposition to their proposal, one board member said he would like to see my head mounted on his wall at home. Part of my response was that this program, once started, would become habit. I wish I had been wrong.

Winter after winter, wolves everywhere endure our persecution. They are killed, and they are traumatized by seeing their pack mates and pups wounded and dying in pain. They are unable to defend themselves from our relentless occupation and pursuit. Snow cover allows aircraft to track a wolf pack's trail in minutes what it takes wolves days to create.

Bears fare no better. They are baited with garbage and then shot. Cubs and adults can be snared, and they can be chased by aircraft that land before hunters shoot them.[588] ADFG encourages the use of heavy-gauge cable snares against black and grizzly bears and their cubs. They are trapped by one paw with *bucket snares*. A bucket filled with rotting meat is secured partway up a tree. When the brown bears and black bears reach into the bucket, the snare triggers and cable grabs them. Cubs are not protected after the first year and they, too, share in their mother's horrific struggle. If regulations are followed, the trapper/hunter is supposed to check the trap daily, but that can stretch from an early morning check the first day to a late evening check the next day. Regulations, under "intensive management," allow license-holders to shoot bears, including mothers with cubs, from aircraft. This was stipulated by the Alaska legislature. As reported in the *Los Angeles Times*, "State game officials have argued for even stronger tactics against predators because they say traditional bear hunts—which often target large males—fail to eliminate the females and cubs that they say must be eradicated if there are to be meaningful declines in predator populations."[589] That is what ADFG does to produce more moose and caribou for out-of-state hunters, Alaskan city dwellers, and the indigenous and non-indigenous people who live in *the bush*.

Imagine yourself suddenly being snared. You experience the fear and panic of this unknown, foreign attack that grabs you and does not ever let you go. Larry Aumiller, a 30-year veteran biologist and manager of the famed McNeil River State Game Sanctuary, has witnessed snaring: "'I helped snare bears in the 1970s [for radio-tracking] and it produced images that I still find in my dreams. When snared, brown bears go absolutely crazy with fear and tear up everything within reach.'"[590] Millions of wolf and bear years of evolution have no way of responding to get free. Then there is the pain as the snares tighten around their legs and even necks. Bears, if snared by the leg, will be exhausted and parched in the desperate fight. They will also chew off their own foot to escape.

The ADFG, like other wildlife management agencies, also encourages the use of wire snares that, with cruel and grotesque insensitivity to natural selection and humane issues, painfully strangle so-called furbearers to death. The agencies also ensure steel-jawed leghold traps do their evil as well.

Steel-jawed leghold traps most often grab a limb above a foot and tighten, like the snares, with every frantic effort to pull away and flee. The victim, an individual from another species, will struggle this way for hours and days as dehydration, hunger, and exhaustion compete with each other. Wildlife agencies, their staff, and their licensed killers conspire to create this lazy, nonselective human natural selection pressure that lives in the carnist human ecology. It is morally repugnant, indefensible, and should never have been endorsed and elevated as a *tool* by wildlife biologists. These are crimes against species, and only a corrupted agency and employee culture would allow it.

Some wildlife professionals and hunters abhor ADFG's aerial killing. And, there is criticism from the scientific community over ADFG intensive management schemes.[591] They are not objecting to killing ecosystem predators to increase the number of targets for human hunters, but they do feel a moral disgust when it is done against their worldview belief in fair chase. One of the best writers who kill wildlife is Ted Williams. He is not afraid to confront agencies and gun-centered organizations when they violate his sensibilities. In *Audubon* magazine he heaped scorn on ADFG and then-Governor Sara Palin's board of game: "'Even cubs and lactating sows are being targeted.... Six [board of game] members belong to an anti-predator, trophy-hunter-funded outfit called the Alaska Outdoor Council, and the seventh is Palin's close friend ... The lucky bears get shot before they starve.'"[592]

I cannot help but compare the corruption of human values Williams describes with an interview then-Governor Palin conducted around Thanksgiving. She was touring a turkey-killing farm. In the background throughout her interview, a worker was clearly cutting the throats of turkeys and putting them upside down into funnels while the hapless individuals flapped their wings in slowly diminishing strokes as if trying to fly away from their death. The clueless, nonplussed Palin took no notice. This symbolic expression of her worldview, culture, and religious beliefs makes her the poster adult for the carnist current human ecology. Her worldview is not new; it just did not die a natural death after infecting people looking at the world like John Haines.

From *The Art of Pulling Hearts*, by John Haines, we read of his past Alaskan life,

> ... I caught a neighbor's dog in a coyote snare. He was long dead when I found him, the wire drawn up so tightly around his neck that his head was nearly severed from his body. The snow and torn brush gave evidence of a terrible struggle. ... my regret over it was so keen that I set no more snares on the river close to home.[593]

To my understanding, he believes it is terrible when he kills a neighbor's dog this way but not individuals from other species; he will not trap close to home, but he will continue to do it farther away.

Move Over, Alaska

Wildlife management agencies support the physical and psychological suffering their hunters and trappers cause individuals from other species. This is present at all levels of wildlife management and includes the U.S. federal government. When the U.S. Geological Service (USGS) produced the *Furtakers Educational Manual*, they were clear about their insensitivity to suffering.

The biologists write, "When trapping beaver, plan your sets so that the beaver will drown.... In shallow water it may be necessary to wrap the trap chain through the spring of the trap to eliminate slack which would enable the beaver to reach the surface."[594] Is there no moral grounding in wildlife agency policies? A 2006 survey of wildlife conservation professionals found that among the biologists polled, "Respondents were divided on whether to outlaw leghold traps; 46 percent favored outlawing use of the leghold trap, 39 percent opposed outlawing its use, and 15 percent had no opinion."[595]

How do they feel about relentless packs of dogs running down terrified cougars until they flee up a tree? A hunter then shoots the treed cougar while casually standing nearby. This is another tool that wildlife and habitat agencies promote.

Agency staff time and skills are employed to create both great and awful endings. Were they to renounce carnism and embrace a vegan new human ecology, the profession would be profoundly different and far more effective, not at animal factorying wildlife, but protecting ecosystems for the rest of us. For too long, agencies have managed for the well-organized minority of hunters, trappers, fishers, and animal agriculturalists. Environmental NGOs are not reforming those relationships.

More on Species vs. Individuals

Most mainstream environmental non-governmental organizations (NGOs) appear to agree with wildlife management agencies' outlook that individuals from other species should be given scant consideration. In this view, species and select populations are worthy of protecting with policy and management goals. Species and populations count, individuals not very much. So, killing individuals for *sport* is not questioned. Wildlife management seems conditioned to ignore the pain and suffering of individuals because it sees species, not the physical and emotional suffering of individuals. Any lingering moral implications that should be bothering them are kept at bay with the willed ignorance about the sentience of wildlife.

In "What are 60 warblers worth? Killing in the name of conservation,"[596] authors John A. Vucetich and Michael P. Nelson address this issue. They found that over a 10-year span, there were just 14 articles in several conservation science journals they reviewed that had the words *ethics* or *ethical* in their title or used the terms as search keywords. Nearly absent were discussions about whether research and applied conservation were ethical. They also found that conservation professionals made errors in logic about the subject. This made weighing the ethics of their research more difficult.

The authors confirmed that individuals from other species do have inherent value and that value must be compared to the expected value the research would have for other species. They write, "The fundamental, yet apparently overlooked, point is that judging the ethical rightness or wrongness of killing in the name of conservation is very difficult precisely because both populations and individuals are valuable (Leopold 1949). If only one were valuable, the ethical solution would be substantially simpler."

Wildlife and ecosystem management professionals can reconcile Leopold's dilemma. I believe they must now become the advocates, inside and outside of their agencies, for radical changes in our human ecology that elevates the status of individuals.

Individuals Are Important

Individuals of highly socialized species can have specialized duties and knowledge. Prairie dogs take turns as sentinels; wolf packs and orca pods depend upon a rich culture and social cooperation to survive. They are strengthened by their shared, lifelong experiences together. Their accumulated knowledge becomes a synergistic wholeness. Lion prides, though they may have relatively high turnover in coalition males, depend upon specialized roles of each member. Parents of young have roles across species. We can assume individuals possess varying abilities to raise the young. These are individuals belonging to their cultures where language, learned norms of behavior, and relationships evolve and continue to reshape their kind from one generation to the next. In our own insufficiency, we focused on managing for species to the exclusion of individuals. This dismisses the importance of the complexity and uniqueness of individuals within species. Predictably, their joy and suffering are not counted in agency policies either.

Alpha male and female wolves lead the pack in teamwork yet others can initiate spontaneous pack activities. Individuals cooperate in rearing young, defending territory, and killing prey. Matriarchal elephants lead the herd to water, safety, and food by using their irreplaceable experiential knowledge accumulated over decades. The older, experienced females are more successful than any other member in leading the herd to alternative foraging areas during drought. They know which water sources and mineral salts are closest at hand. As reported in "Matriarchs as Repositories of Social Knowledge in African Elephants," researchers found that

> ... the possession of enhanced discriminatory abilities by the oldest individual in a group can influence the social knowledge of the group as a whole.... Our findings imply that the removal of older, more experienced individuals, which are often targets for hunters because of their large size, could have serious consequences for endangered populations of advanced social mammals such as elephants and whales.[597]

These differences make individuals important for their roles in the herd, pack, flock, and school. Individuals contribute uniquely, perhaps irreplaceably, to the larger, local, and regional populations and over time the species itself. Specific individuals can provide benefits of experience in foraging and defense and the cohesiveness of leadership. Individuals of species less dependent on social structure are also important.

Their individually unique possession of genetic traits is tested by natural selection pressures; each one holds the possibility he or she can survive and make irreplaceable contributions to the gene pool of their species. Individuals are important because they are not created equal. The superior gene traits of individuals will not be obvious to those seeking to kill them for *sport* nor to those managing them. The importance of the individual to the population and species is true at all times but is simply more easily described in highly social species.

Hunters remove genetic material that nature would not. This is a recognized issue. But consideration of the interests of individuals from other species is not what traditional wildlife management is about. Agency bias is on hunter demands that create fragile, artificial ecosystems that are made dependent upon regular human intervention. When wildlife management agencies remove predators to appease animal agriculture and the hunting community, they release prey populations to grow beyond the carrying capacity of the host ecosystem. This guarantees they will call in hunters who will then claim how ecosystems need them to kill. The TDPW brags they have more deer per acre than any place in the country. Now hunters can argue that deer have to be killed to save those ecosystems, after paying fees to run the department.

Agencies, Animal Rights, and Vegans

There has been friction between mainstream elements of the wildlife management profession and the species rights communities. I will be broad brushing both camps here to make a point. There are progressive biologists who see the world far differently than their predecessors. And there are species rights advocates who understand the concerns of agency professionals.

Wildlife-related agencies can be frustrated because, from their perspective, they see their work and passion undercut by species welfarists and rightists. The welfarists and rightists see heavy-handed disregard for suffering and needless killing intentionally created by wildlife management culture. It is often described in the simplest of terms as: Wildlife managers value species while the rightists and welfarists value individuals.

It does not help when Michael Hutchins, president of The Wildlife Society, founded in 1937 and the largest U.S. organization of wildlife management professionals, dismisses and stereotypes animal welfare and rights communities. He writes in the journal, *Conservation Biology*,

> As a conservationist, I reject animal rights philosophy. This unrealistic and reductionist view, which focuses exclusively on individual sentient animals, is not a good foundation for the future of life on our planet and does not recognize the interrelationships that exist among various species in functioning ecosystems. It is time to face up to the fact that animal rights and conservation are inherently incompatible and that one cannot be an animal rights proponent and a conservationist simultaneously.[598]

He was responding to an essay by Gad Perry and Dan Perry titled "Improving Interactions between Animal Rights Groups and Conservation Biologists."[599]

Gad Perry and Dan Perry acknowledged there are differences between the wildlife profession and species rightists. However, they were also reminding everyone that any chance for agreement should be explored to benefit ecosystem outcomes. Perry and Perry called for a better understanding of the other side by everyone involved. This can be underappreciated by state-level wildlife agencies that share the hunter carnist culture so exemplified by The Wildlife Society's policies. I say that as someone who has had an appreciation and enriched collaboration with wildlife professionals even when we disagreed. Just what is it that animal rightists and new human ecology proponents do for wildlife professional managers?

As I earlier referred to, when species rightists are vegans, or at minimum, vegetarians in transition to veganism, they occupy a different place in the food chain and therefore a different niche in ecosystems. Our plant-based diet and rejection of animal agriculture produces a far smaller environmental footprint than carnism. We make far fewer demands upon ecosystems compared to carnist believers of the current human ecology. Wildlife and ecosystems management professionals gain more ecosystem from a vegan human ecology than they ever dreamed of recovering.

Vegans do not hunt or fish, so the day we stopped consuming other animals, we stopped lead- poisoning bottom-feeding ducks, loons, and other species who ate leaded buckshot and lead weights from fishing lines. We believe your agency funding should be consistent and come from the general tax revenue because ecosystems are everyone's responsibility. You do not have to prostitute yourselves by selling tickets (tags) and holding raffles. You should not raise money as if you were the PTA holding a bake sale.

You deserve more respect than that. We support the reintroduction of large carnivores as part of the rewilding process overseen by conservation biologists. The reintroduction of these predators is made possible because the livestock grazing industry is no longer an economic interest controlling ecosystem outcomes and wildlife management goals and strategies. We support the recovery of salmon and marine mammals because we do not kill fish and other prey, preferring to leave them for indigenous predators who need them to survive. We are happy at the thought of millions of spawned-out salmon who, in their natural decomposition, die high in the mountains and leave vast amounts of nutrients for ecosystems and other species. We know this is not waste.

When we stopped killing and eating fish, we also stopped killing seabirds and turtles who are hooked and drowned in commercial fisheries. Millions of tons of bycatch is no longer killed and thrown back into the sea. Vegans use less water to produce their food. We demand a fraction of the irrigation water taken from river ecosystems and underground aquifers. Because we are species rightists, we are ripe for growth as humans who demand the following:

- Healthy ecosystems that are abundant in life
- Sustainability
- Organic food production
- An abrupt reduction of nitrogen fertilizer, herbicide, and pesticide use
- Economic systems that protect biodiversity

Despite real concerns wildlife management agencies and species rightists have about our past and current differences, the new human ecology is different. We are transforming our relationships with ecosystems to increase their stability and health, and to make those relationships healthier than anything your agencies are proposing or capable of accomplishing. Vegan human ecology has more power to protect ecosystems than any minority of hunters whose licensing fees are your source of funding. There are millions of us in the United States alone. We are evolving to prevent harm and heal ecosystems, and we believe you will, too.

We have a lot to learn about the species with whom we share our ecosystems. We look forward to the day when conservation biologists and other professions publish papers, discuss policies, envision, and implement their findings in the context of the vegan new human ecology. This will change your profession. You will enable *us* to change, solve problems, and provide the research that will make our new human ecology strategies more effective. Whether it is deer, ocelots, field mice, geese, warblers, beetles, or orca whales, vegan new human ecology practitioners create possibilities and opportunities for wildlife and ecosystem–related professionals. The individuality within other species is important; not all are created adaptively equal for evolution. There is nothing I can think of in the new human ecology that is inherently contradictory to biocentrism. We strive to create honest relationships.

More on Un-Natural Selection

When elephants are hunted for their large tusks, they are removed from the gene pool. Ecosystems are denied their progeny. In addition to reducing the tusk size of the generations that follow, this travesty has increased the number of male elephants not having tusks at all. Since large *tusker* African elephant males, as trophy hunters know them, have been killed off, their gene for big tusks has been made rarer. Matthew Scully, author of *Dominion*, includes this quote, from Douglas Chadwick's 1992 book, *The Fate of the Elephant*: "In 1979, 'it took 54 elephants to get a ton of ivory. Now, with mature tuskers all but non-existent and females the prime target, it took 133 elephants and left an average of 55 orphaned calves and young juveniles to die later.'"[600]

Fred Allendorf and Jeffry Hard point out in their paper, "Human-induced evolution caused by unnatural selection through harvest of wild animals," that

> ... the frequency of elephants (*Loxodonta africana*) without tusks increased from 10 percent to 38 percent in South Luangwa National Park, Zambia, apparently brought about by poaching of elephants for their ivory. Similarly, trophy hunting for bighorn sheep (*Ovis canadensis*) in Alberta, Canada caused a decrease in horn size because rams with larger horns had a greater probability of being removed from the population by hunting.[601]

The authors cite additional cases that indicate genetic evolution can be altered through loss of genetic variation from human predations. The selection pressures of human hunting and fishing is intense. It is common sense that any species living under unnatural wartime conditions will become a different species. Wildlife management is insisting species adapt to ecosystems whose chief characteristic is war; humans chase, kill, terrorize, and disrupt and destroy social relationships needed by individuals from other species, in addition to our displacing them with our exploding human populations. Safe passage migratory routes to water and food are denied them as they run from one hostile attack to the next.

Hunters employ agencies to carry out their belief that they are simply replacing other top predators. It is not that simple. "Humans have persecuted apex predators for millennia," begins one review of this idea in a paper titled "The Rise of the Mesopredator," published in the journal *BioScience*.[602] The authors reviewed the complex dynamics of apex predators, their prey, and the effects that eliminating them—for example, wolves and mountain lions in the United States and wild dogs and lions in Africa—have on ecosystems. Coyotes become mesopredators (medium-sized predators) who are *released* when we eliminate their competition, the apex predators such as wolves. The mesopredator coyotes then grow in number and range in the absence of wolves.

In Sub-Saharan Africa, lion and leopard populations have been decimated; this *released* olive baboons who then raided human crops and threatened children. The authors argue that mesopredator releases affect prey and the ecosystem differently than the original apex cougars, wolves, leopards, and lions. The effects can be profound, and result in changed relationships from insects, to lizards, to birds, to antelope. Widespread elimination of apex predators like grizzly bears has had measurable effects in the United States: "60 percent of mesopredators ranges have expanded, whereas apex predator ranges have contracted" during the past 200 years. The resulting explosion of coyote numbers meant that in 11 states alone coyotes accounted for 75 percent to 95 percent of mammals killed by federal animal control from 1950 to 1998.[603]

According to the authors, this is likely happening around the world because of the human penchant of eradicating top predators. But just as mesopredators do not replicate apex predators in ecosystems, neither do humans. From the same paper, "... it is exceptionally difficult to replicate the full ecosystem effects of apex predation ... interactions between predators result not only in direct killing but also in avoidance behavior and defensive group formation. Fear of predation can therefore have an even stronger impact on food webs than the killing itself ..."[604] The researchers noted that living with apex predators can be the best way to suppress problematic mesopredators. This requires us to change our attitudes about predators like wolves and bears.

Parallels are evident in oceans. Industrial shark fishing kills off the large sharks, who eat the smaller sharks. The smaller sharks, skates, and rays increase in the absence of their larger competitors. They then prey in greater numbers on shellfish like oysters, clams, and scallops, wreaking havoc in the marine ecosystem.[605] Whether it is commercial fisheries or hunting, individuals from other species are dying, but not from the natural causes they had adapted to over millions of years. They are dying from us, a single species predator among millions. That is emblematic of the relationships we choose to have with other species.

The enormity of the carnage we are perpetuating is impossible to exaggerate. In just one coastal area of the world, offshore of Namibia, South Africa, and Angola, fisher bycatch includes "some 34 thousand seabirds and 4 thousand 2 hundred sea turtles every year..."[606] In the coastal waters of South Africa, 7.8 million sharks are caught accidentally by the innately inhumane and immoral longline fishery. Imagine the true event: An albatross swallows a baited hook and is dragged through the water until she drowns. That is human natural selection at work. What wildlife professions offered that albatross, and us, is the same. Unsustainability and no survivable future. We need wildlife management agencies that will create honest relationships between us and all other species. Honest relationships start with individuals.

Chapter 16:

Wildly Out of Control

Rather than enhancing wild populations, facilities engaged in captive breeding [of marine mammals] tend merely to create a surplus of animals who may never be released into the wild and are therefore only used to propagate the industry. .. In captivity, natural feeding and foraging patterns are completely lost. Stress-related conditions...develop.... Wild-caught marine mammals gradually experience the atrophy of many of their natural behaviors... Viewing captive animals gives the public a false picture of the animals' natural lives. Worse yet, it desensitizes people to captivity's inherent cruelties—for so many captive marine mammals, the world is a tiny enclosure, and life is devoid of naturalness.

—Naomi A. Rose, Ph.D., E.C.M. Parsons, and Richard Farinato.
The Case Against Marine Mammals in Captivity[607]

Relationships

We typically do not witness what individuals from other species experience in the wild at the moment wildlife management strikes them. To help us understand how important it is for us to comprehend this, we can look at what we can see. Though now dead, the life of Qannik, a beluga whale confined to a tank in a zoo, is a memorial to those still in captivity. The unjust relationship between this beluga and us can remind us also that there are sentient beings we call wildlife. In this case, sentience is on stage, in a small pool.

Qannik the beluga whale died in his pool at the Point Defiance Zoo and Aquarium (PDZA) in 2009. He had been shipped from Shedd Aquarium in Chicago to PDZA in Tacoma, Washington. Zoos and aquaria habitually pluck their captive individuals away from the scant social relationships they may have been allowed to establish with others of their kind before being flown to yet another prison. Beluga whales are intensely social. In the wild, beluga whales congregate in groups numbering in the hundreds and thousands. Their vocalizations and echolocation sounds in the wild, often audible above the water, are a wonder to hear.

Belugas are actually dolphins. We call them whales only because of their larger size. They produce sounds for social communication and echolocation for navigation and finding prey. At PDZA and other aquaria around the world, belugas, orca whales, pilot whales, dolphins, and porpoises are housed in pools whose walls are hard surfaced. As Qannik experienced, their sonic expressions of language and echolocation do not travel into the watery depths as they would in the wild. Instead, every sound they make bounces off the concrete walls of the watery jail cells their captors provide them. Walls are what they see with their echolocation; captivity is what they feel. It is a sterile world.

Captivity is correlated to the early deaths of Cetaceans in marine entertainment exhibits.[608] Pro- and anti-advocates, including scientists, start from different worldviews and often disagree on this point. According to, "The Case Against Marine Mammals in Captivity,"

> Fierce debate continues over the issue of mortality rates and longevity, especially of whales and dolphins, in captivity. The most conclusive data are for orcas; their annual mortality rates are significantly higher in captivity than in the wild. The mortality data related to live captures are more straightforward—capture is undeniably stressful and, in dolphins, results in a six-fold increase in mortality risk during and immediately after capture.[609]

Belugas can live for 50 years in the wild; Qannik died a few months short of nine years old.[610] Death, in many respects, means freedom from the life-long deprivations and suffering captives endure in tanks. Zoo and aquarium visitors pay admission to see them because they do not understand what captivity means even though it is in front of them. The wildlife management profession certainly is not letting us know.

Uninformed parents and school teachers brought a steady stream of children to PDZA. Neither teachers, nor parents, nor the children experienced Qannik as a whole beluga. PDZA perpetuated the belief that captivity is a healthy relationship with individuals from other species. Putting Qannik on display told children we had a right to confine him in a small, never changing pool that provided only a narrow view of the sky. Qannik never saw the horizon. Instead of horizons that would change every day in the wild, instead of free-ranging freedom, Qannik felt only walls rising in all directions. He was denied all the possibilities of experience he needed and deserved. He had no rights as an individual from another species. This corrupted education prepared the children to love captivity at SeaWorld and aquaria around the world. They believed their parents and teachers.

Lolita, an orca whale captive at Miami Seaquarium, has not seen a horizon since taken from her mother in 1970. Like Qannik, she is environmentally starved. She is the slave who enriches Arthur Herz, Chairman of the holding company, Wometco, and the stock-holding board of directors of the Miami Seaquarium. Orca Network is an organization located near Lolita's home waters where she was captured in Penn Cove in the San Juan Islands of Washington State. They and others are working to free Lolita and return her home. Tokitae is the name they prefer; Lolita is her commercial stage name. Orca Network has this to say:

> Lolita's birthright is the L25 matriline of the 'L' pod of the Southern Resident orca community in the Pacific Northwest. Lolita's mother is believed to be L25, Ocean Sun, approximate age 82, who still resides with Lolita's family swimming freely in the open waters where Lolita was captured. Lolita continues to use the calls that only her family, the L25 subpod, uses. ... Lolita has been alone (aside from a few dolphins) for 30 years, performing two shows a day for tourists.... Lolita has resided in what is the smallest and oldest orca tank in North America. The tank is merely one-and-a-half-times her size ...[611]

She has been swimming in the same circle for 42 long years. Orca Network posts that some 13 members of Tokitae's family (Lolita is her stage name) were killed at her capture when she was about four years old. Her pool is 12 to 20 feet deep. She is 22 feet long.

For decades, the Department of Agriculture's Animal and Plant

Health Inspection Service (APHIS) has refused pleas to condemn the size of Lolita's tank. They have opted to not deduct the space a concrete island takes up in the middle of Lolita's watery cell. The standards are already so inadequate that they are cruel in and of themselves and demonstrate agency blindness to sentience and suffering by individuals from other species.

The Miami Seaquarium perpetuates ignorance. This is passively accepted by a Florida school system that busses thousands of young minds to learn about Lolita. I have watched the kids watch Lolita's show. The children get splashed and hear some interesting facts about the sight in front of them called an orca whale. But they are not inoculated with values that would condemn her confinement. There is no room for questioning as the loud music and circus showmanship of the trainers distract and entertain the children with Lolita's tricks. They exit the Miami Seaquarium turnstile clueless to what Lolita is experiencing.

Stripped of their natural environment and social life, captive individuals from other species are ghosts. Only in the company of their kind in the wild can orcas, belugas, and other species express innate and complex behaviors, a rich social life, and the relationships that give meaning to their lives. Orcas generally stay with their mother's pod for life. We took Lolita away from her mother and her pod.

To anyone who thinks this captivity is a good thing and worth the disfigured educational value, I say drain Qannik's and Lolita's pools. Then imagine yourself being kidnapped without warning, taken away from all you know, and imprisoned there for the rest of your life. The only activity you are allowed is a routine of unnatural acts like balancing a trainer on your snout. You get treats for that.

When the uneducated public comes to view *you* from above your tank, what would they learn about your depth and complexity? Without your social context of your family and friends, without seeing your normal, complex, and adaptive behavior, what would we learn about you? As we poolside tourists watch you take food from your captors' hands, what would we comprehend? How many endless days of walking in circles in your tank would it take before you were no longer you?

Of course, you are not in that tank. Lolita is. Her natural order of value is barely visible in this economic prostitution that you, our dear Tokitae, are made to bear, by Wometco, Inc., and its board of directors including Arthur Hertz. They have assaulted you and stolen your freedom. Like SeaWorld, they are thieves profiting off of your stolen life.

Aquaria that keep whales in captivity are circuses. They, too, imprison individuals from other species in small spaces. Traveling long distances over land, *their* captives endure grueling show schedules as they are taken from place to place by train and truck. Imagine what it is like to have the body, mind, and innate needs of a tiger or lion locked in a small space behind bars or an elephant in chains? The only APHIS agency requirement for tigers and lions is that they be able to stand up and turn around in their cages. I have yet to hear or see a fish and wildlife agency protest this either, perhaps because only species, not individuals, count in their professional concerns.

From Tank to Hunting

Valuing species but ignoring the plight of individuals is a theme full of meaning within mainstream wildlife management. Killing wildlife for recreation requires the same worldview that celebrates putting whales in captivity. If wildlife management responded to the morality of our relationships with individuals from other species, killing would not be the priority, managing human behavior would. Wildlife management does not concern itself with sentience. It is attentive to species and significant populations of species as best as it can. However, when it concerns their relationships to individuals, it operates like the controllers of Qannik and Lolita confined in tanks.

Ethology, the study of nonhuman species' behavior, is opening our sensibilities. We are seeing what is possible in other species and realize how crippled we are by our lack of understanding. Perhaps ethology will have an influence on wildlife and ecosystem managers eventually. Cognitive ethologist[612] Marc Bekoff has written that this field of science is important for many reasons:

I argue that cognitive ethology is the unifying science for under-standing the subjective, emotional, empathic, and moral lives of animals because it is essential to know what animals do, think, and feel as they go about their daily routines in the company of their friends and when they are alone. It is also important to learn why both the similarities and differences between humans and other animals have evolved.[613]

Agencies and environmental NGOs rarely consider individuals. That is why they do nothing for individuals in captivity.

Relationships and Bowhunters Afield

Linda Hatfield wrote "Report on Bowhunting" when she was the Executive Director of HOWL (Help Our Wolves Live). She reviewed and summarized 24 studies and found "A 1988 report to the Montana Department of Fish, Wildlife, and Parks indicated that of 2,370 bowhunters who hit an elk with an arrow, only 49 percent actually retrieved their prey." A study in Texas revealed a wounding rate of over 50 percent. An unpublished report indicated a bowhunting wounding rate of 53 percent in Minnesota.[614] The rate of wounded and lost individuals from other species shot with one or more arrows is highly contested. Terrain, weather, and licensing requirements are variables affecting study results.[615] Though many self-reported surveys confirm high rates of loss, other studies and field surveys set the loss, on average, at 13 percent.[616] Updated, thoroughly controlled studies are hard to find.

In a 1998 study, researchers radio-collared 80 male white-tailed deer who were subsequently shot at by bowhunters exclusively. Twenty-two deer were shot with arrows. Of them, 11 were recovered. Of the 50 percent who were wounded, "3 (14 percent) of the 22 deer shot by hunters died and were not recovered.... these estimates indicate that approximately 4 percent of adult males in the population die from archery related wounds annually and are never recovered."[617] That leaves the 36 percent walking wounded who suffered from their wounds.

Bowhunters *choose* their method of killing. Humaneness is not the reason. Guns provide for greater accuracy at distances while an arrow loses altitude in a short distance, dropping approximately 9.5 feet at 50 yards. Muzzleloaders hunt with vintage guns that are not as accurate as modern weaponry. Wildlife management agencies encourage both bow and muzzleloader hunting. They set aside special seasons and areas so this sector can experience a specific recreation. Agencies and hunters continue despite knowing they will cause more wounding, suffering, and loss than other hunting methods. Their values are on display.

On December 28, 2009, a tragic fiasco unfolded before witnesses. It involved a dozen or more bowhunters ineptly trying to kill a herd of elk as stunned motorists and an employee of the Washington Department of Fish and Wildlife (WDFW) looked on. The elk were trapped in an enclosure of barbwire fencing that bordered a heavily traveled highway. The bowhunters surrounded the trapped elk. As the panicked herd of 70 ran from one end to the other of the fenced beef ranch pasture whose grass attracted the elk, the bowhunters fired dozens of arrows. With arrows sticking out of them, at least one elk had his or her entrails dragging below his or her belly. This could have been caused by an arrow or from an unsuccessful attempt by the elk to jump over the barbed wire fence while trying to escape the torment. Quoted in the *Skagit Valley Herald,* a state wildlife official witnessing this obscenity, said, "'This is not hunting,' slowly shaking his head as the men with bows circled the panicked animals. As distasteful as he found the scene, Allen acknowledged that the elk kill in Johnson's pasture is completely legal."[618] Judging from radio and newspaper commentary afterwards, it disturbed at least some of the hunting community.

WDFW followed up with their version of "sharing the public's concern" and commented that the bowhunters did not act in accordance with the department's Hunter's Code of Conduct.[619] Speaking on KUOW public radio in Seattle, the head of the district's wildlife enforcement office gave an excuse: The bowhunters were not thinking clearly and things just got out of hand. Because wildlife management agencies double as the chamber of commerce for the hunting minority, we should not be surprised. To his credit, a person calling himself a master bowhunter gave the opinion that half of bowhunters lack the proper skills to kill elk.[620] I do not know if the female matriarch who led the herd was killed but the assault by hunters against elk continues.

Artificially introduced by WDFW to build the Nooksack herd for hunting, the elk are accustomed by their own traditions to use river valleys for browsing. Cattle, orchards, non-ranching new homes, and cars now dominate their homeland. Hunters want to "eliminate" and kill more cougar and the returning wolves they blame for driving the elk into the valley. Green vegans work to eliminate bow hunting and all practices that hunters use to kill.

Agency Responses

Birds

The U.S. Department of Agriculture's Animal Damage Control (ADC) was renamed Wildlife Services (WS) as a public relations ploy. I refer to them as ADC/WS as a form of resistance to their new name. They employ a wide variety of tactics against individuals from other species: hunting, den destruction, poisoning, trapping, noise harassment, chilling them to death, and aerial shooting from small, low-flying aircraft. ADC/WS supports ranchers and hunters, but it also improves safety at airports by dispersing birds attracted to habitats surrounding runways. In addition, they remove invasive species that threaten indigenous species, and in 2008 monitored 42 diseases, including rabies and plague, that are dangerous and fatal to livestock, companion individuals from other species, humans, and wildlife.

ADC/WS was founded in 1915 as a function of the Bureau of Biological Survey. This agency is notorious because of what it is willing to do to wildlife on behalf of agriculture (botanical and animal) and hunting. Within two years following the agency's founding, its employees had killed over 34,000 coyotes and 110 bobcats in addition to other species.[621] poisoning of species —affects other species

To its credit, ADC/WS has increased its research to find less lethal methods to reduce, prevent, and mitigate the conflicts we create with other species. For instance, dogs are trained to keep predators away from livestock in an effort to reduce or eliminate the use of poisons.

Still, this is not much of a change compared to their overall impact on wildlife. Their agency's legacy of offensives against native and invasive species is reflected in the numbers: For fiscal year 2009, ADC/WS dispersed 27,651,169 individuals from other species and killed/euthanized/removed and destroyed 4,138,765 others.

Among the dead are 1,046,120 Brown-headed Cowbirds, 27,292 beavers, 10,588 American crows, 571 river otters, 199 common barn owls, 65 American White Pelicans, 380 Mute Swans, 33,803 feral swine, 1,259,716 starlings, 1,775 bobcats, 17,935 Double-crested Cormorants, 19,694 Zebra Doves, 568 Northern and 4,013 Red-crested Cardinals, 569 badgers, 484 Great Blue Herons, 1,017 Horned Larks, 339 cougars, 13,292 raccoons, 896 Western Meadowlarks, 445 black bears, 711 Cliff Swallows, 965,892 Red-winged Blackbirds, 2,345 foxes, 81,711 coyotes, 23,804 ground squirrels (total of various species), 480 gray wolves, 1,013 feral cats, and 3,863 common ravens. This is a partial accounting of 37 pages of affected species.[622] I have not been able to find statistics about the wounding and crippling rate.

Many of these species are native to North America. Regarding the million-plus Brown-headed Cowbirds they killed, the Washington State University Extension Service attributes this to Richard A. Dolbeer, ADC/Wildlife Services Project Leader for the Denver Wildlife Research Center: "Damage to Crops: This species can cause damage to ripening sorghum, sunflower, and millet. Cowbirds consume some livestock feed, but often glean waste grain and seed from dung. Overall damage is usually minor."[623] Before European arrivals of humans to North America, native cowbirds used to follow the great migrations of bison. There were abundant songbird populations even though cowbirds parasitize other bird species. Now they are attracted to livestock feedlots.

DRC-1339 is an avicide (a bird-killing substance) still in use by ADC/WS. Though more selective than other poisons, it is harmful to a broad range of species. Researchers at the USDA National Wildlife Research Center reported, "... DRC-1339 is moderately toxic to even the least sensitive species."[624] The poisoning of non-targeted species includes crows, ravens, gulls, starlings, sparrows, blackbirds, and rock doves.[625]

The agencies claim this is a humane poison because the birds often go into a coma without showing evidence of convulsions. This compound affects the kidneys that as they are damaged cause uric acid to build up in the body. In humans, kidney failure results in an inability to excrete waste and regulate body chemistry. Heart failure, inflammation of the pericardium, fluid in the lungs, a decreased red blood cell count that makes it hard to breathe, debilitating tiredness, generalized swelling, and confusion are experienced.[626] Symptoms humans can talk about include "... burning of the mouth, throat, skin or eyes; nausea, possible vomiting and stomach pains."[627] How a bird might feel while enduring this slow death that takes 24–48 hours is not difficult to imagine. Who makes the poison to kill birds? Your friends at Purina who make "Starlicide Complete, pelleted bait used to control blackbirds and starlings in feedlots."[628] We are mammals, birds are not, but declining health and organ failure over one to two day's time is not, in a reasonable sense, a humane death.

Spraying Sodium Lauryl Sulfate (SLS) is another bird control tool ADC/WS has endorsed. SLS is the wetting agent found in our shampoos and hair conditioners. When used against blackbirds, starlings, and others, it is mixed with water and sprayed to wet the birds' feathers. Since the birds can no longer insulate themselves, they shiver and eventually die from hypothermia. SLS is used to kill European starlings, Red-winged Blackbirds, Common Grackles, Brown-headed Cowbirds, and blackbirds. In tests, birds died in as soon as 30 minutes when the ambient temperature was less than or equal to 41 degrees Fahrenheit.[629] Put yourself in their place by tapping into your empathy. How would you feel as you shivered to death?

Our vegan human ecology exerts a powerful, nontoxic, humane biological control of the Brown-headed Cowbirds, blackbirds, and starlings because we eliminate the feedlot habitat and much of the animal food croplands these birds use. Carnism is the source of the conflict; veganism is the cure, not avicides and other lethal controls. For the remaining conflicts, alternatives for reducing populations of birds are emerging. Innolytics is a company promoting their birth-control products for geese, ducks, and pigeons. Their OvoControl is classified as an unrestricted pesticide.[630]

Mammals

Relying on a 2004 survey of animal agriculturalists, the National Agricultural Statistics Service (NASS) determined coyotes killed an estimated 135,600 sheep and lambs while dogs and foxes killed an additional 34,000. "An estimated 155,000 goats were killed by predators—of all kinds." A 2005 NASS survey found that coyotes killed an estimated 97,000 head [of cattle] while dogs killed some 21,900 more, including calves.[631] ADC/WS has a solution.

For predators, the ADC/WS response of choice is sodium cyanide. Placing collars around the necks of livestock with a poison capsule attached is one way to get the cyanide into a predator's mouth. A different delivery system is the M-44 "ejector device." It targets coyotes, foxes, and feral dogs. Spring-loaded, the canids tug on the bait, activate a trigger, and the cyanide bursts directly into the targeted animal's mouth without spraying it up into their noses or eyes, at least as ideally intended, from the agency's point of view.[632] Since any coyote, wolf, fox, or feral and lost dog in the area will be attracted to the scented bait, this device is not selectively targeting a specific animal who may have killed livestock. Instead, M-44s are used to clear an area that is seen as more effective for socially behaving predators.

ADC/WS posts on their website that "The sodium cyanide quickly reacts with moisture in the animal's mouth, releasing hydrogen cyanide gas. Unconsciousness, followed by death, is very quick, normally within 1 to 5 minutes after the device is triggered. Animals killed by sodium cyanide appear to show no overt signs of distress or pain."[633]

Another agency, the U.S. Fish and Wildlife Service (FWS), has been using sodium cyanide for over 50 years "against coyotes in attempts to protect livestock, especially sheep."[634] FWS notes in one paper that "Clinical signs of acute cyanide poisoning in mammals last only a few minutes after ingestion and include rapid and labored breathing, ataxia [loss of muscle coordination], cardiac irregularities, dilated pupils, convulsions, coma, respiratory failure, and rapid death."[635] A 1991 FWS paper reported that intentional poisoning under controlled conditions gave a range for time to death. In 1988, they put dogs taken from shelters and coyotes in pens and then set out the M-44 devices. The average times to first symptoms were 32 seconds; falling down, 46 seconds; death, 127 seconds.[636] These times to symptoms and death represent lethal dosages under controlled conditions. Does 127 seconds pass quickly in this agony? And should we not care what happened to those who exceeded the average?

It is difficult to understand how ADC/WS could on their website make the claim that "Animals killed by sodium cyanide appear to show no overt signs of distress or pain." They leave out the suffering they cannot account for because the coyotes and foxes are not talking. In published, peer-reviewed papers, humans tell us what is happening.

Pesticide Action Network North America (PANNA) describes these symptoms of sodium cyanide poisoning, and refers to more than one authoritative source. PANNA's list of symptoms in humans includes the following:

Irritating to skin, eyes, and respiratory system. Bitter, acrid, burning taste. Constriction or numbness in the throat. Salivation, nausea and vomiting are not unusual. Anxiety, confusion, vertigo, giddiness, and often a sensation of stiffness in the lower jaw. Hyperpnoea [breathing abnormally deep and fast] and dyspnea [gasping for air]. Respirations become very rapid and then slow and irregular. Inspiration is characteristically short while expiration is greatly prolonged.... Unconsciousness, followed promptly by violent convulsions ... sometimes localized but usually generalized. Opisthotonos [the body is held in an abnormal posture and includes rigidity and severe arching of the back with the head thrown backward][637] and trismus [inability to open one's mouth] may develop. Involuntary micturition [urination] and defecation occur. Paralysis follows the convulsive stage.... The eyeballs protrude, and the pupils are dilated and unreactive. The mouth is covered with foam, which is sometimes bloodstained. The skin color may be brick red. Cyanosis is not prominent in spite of weak and irregular gasping.[638]

While some of the symptoms appear to occur after unconsciousness, much of it happens on the way there during ADC/WS's own stated 1 to

5 minutes time to death under controlled, not field conditions. ADC/WS is being dishonest by what they omit. They want us to believe cyanide poisoning is not a foul death and is not accompanied by extreme distress and pain. Their research limits the description to "shaking of the head, pawing at the mouth, rubbing the snout on the ground ..."[639] The agency leaves everything else out. In all of their evolution, coyotes and foxes on the ADC/WS hit list never had to face the torrent of abuse this poison causes.

I will include one more of the many substances ADC/WS uses. This time their targets are ground squirrels and similar species.

> For burrow treatment, [acrolein] ... is injected into the burrow opening that is then immediately sealed with soil. The vapor fills the burrow and causes lacrimation [tearing of the eyes] and severe upper respiratory tract irritation. Respiratory failure occurs quickly—usually in less than 1 minute—when a lethal dose is inhaled.... At low doses, acrolein has a pungent, offensive odor and immediately causes irritation to the eyes and throat.[640]

It is impossible to deliver a lethal dose of acrolein consistently under field conditions. According to a study posted on the USDA National Wildlife Research Center's website, "Efficacy of about 90 percent was reported for ground squirrels, but low efficacies of 5 percent for black-tailed prairie dogs and 59 percent for northern pocket gophers have been reported."[641] A lack of efficacy means, for instance in the case for black-tailed prairie dogs, 95 percent were gassed, suffered, and did not die.

Black-tailed prairie dogs are a keystone species indicative of the health of prairie ecosystems. But prairie dogs of all kinds are of no use to animal agriculturalists. And though there are international conventions against chemical warfare because it is so horrible, agencies ignore the ability of other species to suffer as we do. That is the economic predation aspect of neo-predation. Wildlife die and suffer whenever a person buys animal products from animal agriculturalists.

The biocentric view? Animal agriculture inserts invasive species—cattle, sheep, goats—into ecosystems. They are unnatural food resources for native species—wolves, coyotes, foxes. As a result, the native species' population densities, behaviors, movements, survival rates, natural selection pressures, and the ecosystem's species composition and abundance are affected. In addition, animal agriculture demands that agencies suppress apex predators such as wolves and grizzly and black bears. When their numbers are reduced, mesopredators like coyotes increase. ADC/WS seems to not be concerned about the impacts of animal agriculture feeding 443,500 substantially sized livestock individuals plus thousands of smaller ones to native predators.

As long as consumers demand meat, eggs, and dairy products, ADC/WS will remain out of control. Carnists, cowboy culture, animal agriculture, and the agencies doing their bidding resist vegan human ecology and in doing so threaten our ecological survival.

Hunter's Want a Medal of Honor

I have trekked for weeks at a time, have been charged by a grizzly bear intent on protecting her cub, was seriously tossed by a whale who flipped my kayak into the air like a toy, woke from a mid-day nap to see an Alaskan moose leg four feet from my head, and have been stranded on a rain-swollen river deep in the rainforest of Kalimantan while paddling a dugout canoe. None of it means anything about strength of character, bravery, or intelligence, especially intelligence. But in hunting culture and its magazines and websites, they want us to believe their pursuit is heroic bravery in the face of danger. They huff and puff themselves up on every page and in every photo.

Hunting media portray coyotes, badgers, cougars, bears, and lions as aggressive, fierce, snarling monsters with mouthfuls of teeth and paws bearing deadly claws. They make them appear as dangerous as possible. These mostly male enhancements are part of the big lie that hunting is a high-risk, manhood-making validation of self. Women, men, and children pose nearly the same in all photos: One or two hunters will show their gun or bow prominently while the dead elephant, coyote, white-tailed deer, wildebeest, or bear lies lifeless in front of their smiling, self-congratulatory faces. In a series of victory-lap photos, they will lift the head of the corpse if possible. If a large species like an elephant is their prize, they will rest a booted foot on the deceased and then look directly into the camera lens wearing a proud smile. They believe they are really something, even if the dead doormat to their pride is a lion less than two years of age.[642] This puffery is rampant in recreational hunting culture, more obvious with trophy hunters. We will not see humility in their faces. We will see nothing to indicate they have a clue to what they have done. In their imagined risk, to combat these dangerous individuals from other species, nothing but the best technology and firepower will do.

Hunters have a lot to choose from for their arsenal: night vision goggles, lasers mounted on powerful scopes, the outdoor equivalent of Fabreze that masks hunter scents, camouflaged all-terrain vehicles, computer-driven digital electronic "game" calls, GPS, cell phones, wireless remote cameras, and semi-automatic weaponry that looks like and performs as good as any weapon made for military applications and professional assassins.

Supporting this well-equipped army is an organization we have already visited, the International Association of Fish and Wildlife Agencies (IAFWA). Remember that they demonize NGOs who represent the non-hunting public. Their "2008 CITES Report" (CITES stands for the Convention on International Trade in Endangered Species of Wild Flora and Fauna) states, "The original intent of CITES was to ensure globally sustainable use of natural resources. However, today this arena is a place for extremists to promote preservation instead of conservation using emotional rhetoric instead of biological and scientific facts. Extremists will continue to be a threat to state management authority." Count me in.

In response to a request from one of these "radical" organizations for "equal time" with "the states" at the CITES conference, the report snorted, "The NGO did not comprehend (nor apparently care) that the CITES Technical Work Group was comprised of state agency personnel discussing wildlife management issues for which the states have statutory authority."[643]

NGOs are staffed with scientists, represent the non-hunting majority of citizens, and participate in similar conferences throughout the world.

IAFWA should be humbled, even shamed, by the fact they are unable to stop the loss of biodiversity and ecosystems in the presence of an unsustainable current human ecology that they endorse heart and soul. They fear the revolution we have brought; they fear having their world-views tipped over. They appear brittle when faced with biocentric consciousness. They do not like us caring about individuals from other species. Disagreeing with IAFWA is not anti-science; it is a debate concerning the foundations of worldviews, beliefs, goals, cultures, and methodologies.

Whale-killing governments of Japan, Norway, and Iceland rely upon the same defense as the IAFWA. They gloss over their targets as a harvest. Japanese agencies blame whales and dolphins for the decline of fishing. The Canadian Department of Fisheries and Oceans (DFO) has been blaming seals for the collapse of commercial fisheries species in the Maritime Provinces for a long time. Do not expect to hear IAFWA or the international community of scientists, including biologists, clamoring for the end of the infamous slaughter of dolphins documented in the movie, *The Cove*.[644] Every year, Japanese fishers herd dolphins into bays and then commence to stab them to death in front of their pod family members. Dolphins swim in their own blood. A few are trucked to aquaria to perform before tourists.

The same kind of hunt is repeated yearly in the Faroe Islands. Instead of dolphins, long-finned pilot whales, including mothers with their young, are herded into a bay and then stabbed and hacked to death as their family members see and hear their pod members' calls of pain and terror. These fishers, the people who purchase Faroese fish products, and the Faroese culture are the sponsors of these horrific crusades.[645] Perhaps the mercury contamination in dolphin and pilot whale flesh will stop these atrocities since it causes neurological disease, most sensitively in children. These cultural traditions are not unlike the traditions of the wildlife management agency culture.

More Agency Culture

Wildlife-related agencies and the professionals who work in them use the word *harvest* as frequently as they breathe. Harvesting refers to a season associated with the harvesting of plant crops in botanical agriculture. Wildlife agencies have advantaged themselves to this word to describe the economic and recreational killing machine they support. They use the term to soften, diffuse, cover up, and smooth over the killing, taking, betrayal, and violence of the act of hunting and the elimination of predators.

Killing sentient individuals with sensibilities that are similar to ours, but unique, is all the more unjust when we know it is unnecessary. How did it happen that the wildlife management profession is *not* continually decreasing violence toward species and their ecosystems?

Briefly—Selected Highlights

Professional wildlife management evolves. Yesterday's science, philosophies, management techniques, and goals are not the same as today's. Tomorrow's will be different, too. The history of wildlife management reflects our understanding of ecosystems and other species and our consideration of values and changing worldviews. According to the West Virginia Conservation Agency website,[646] that evolution roughly has been:

- the control of hunting followed by
- refuge establishment
- vermin control (reducing or eliminating competing nonhuman predators)
- restocking (game farming)
- environmental controls —habitat protection and development[647]

Conservation biology is a growing discipline. It seeks to preserve biodiversity, restore it to the extent possible, and address the causes of its loss. Preventing extinctions and understanding the cause of extinction are its priorities. They manage for ecosystem outcomes and try to avoid species management that subverts that goal. It draws on a far larger and more comprehensive perspective of academic disciplines than wildlife management considered in the past. Conservation biologists work with sociologists, economists, climatologists, and meta-ecosystem scientists.

Their work encourages biological complexity and maximized abundance in recovering ecosystems for their own sake while mitigating wildlife conflicts with humans. Conservation biology is not yet advocating a vegan human ecology, though its goals require it on the global stage.

While recognizing the impacts of agriculture, they are not doing nearly enough to confront human behaviors that tear through ecosystems. They are not confronting sufficiently hunters, fishers, and animal agriculturalists, human population, and all that is unsustainable about our current human ecology.

In 1990, biologist Daniel Botkin observed that environmentalists too often assumed that if only nature could be preserved, saved, then all would be well, that merely saving nature was all that was needed. He worried that this blind acceptance of nature "... tends to lead those concerned with conservation of the environment to emphasize the benefits of doing nothing and assuming that nature will know best."[648] After noting the need for large-scale ecosystems so nature could know her best, he comes down firmly on the benefits of management, including the systematic culling of elephants. Conclusion

We know that ecosystem services can be intensively managed to bear fruit for human needs. But we have forgotten our limits. Botkin seems right in that doing nothing, letting nature take her course, is not automatically a correct way to go, especially after we have disrupted things. Yet it also should be clear that we have been incapable of maintaining the net integrity of ecosystems, their services, their health, their sustainability, and their intrinsic beauty as a sacred value. We must manage ourselves first. It is the only way we can return to the evolutionary track of species and ecosystems where we knocked it off its wheels, and make natural processes more dominant than our impacts. Conservation biologists have to start managing *us* more effectively.

When I write that one of the Seven Results of the new human ecology is "healthy, intact ecosystems that dominate global landscapes and seascapes and require little to no human intervention," I am calling for management objectives to include limited human dominion. That requires there be fewer people, and it requires a vegan human ecology to help regain the scales of open spaces and restored habitat needed by elephants, wolves, and songbirds. What we need from managers and conservation biology is a reformation.

The new human ecology eliminates and reforms core goals and methodologies of wildlife and habitat management. Vegans do not need artificial propagation and manipulation of species for hunting and trapping. Nor do we need to shoot wolves from airplanes to create moose targets for urban hunters and aboriginal peoples.[649] We do not need fleets of ships to decimate marine mammals and fishes. Wildlife professionals and snipers will not be called upon to eliminate natural predators, nor poison ground squirrels living on prejudicially named rangeland that should only be called prairie ecosystem lying within a specific watershed. Buffalo will no longer be slaughtered as they migrate from protected areas in Yellowstone National Park to the land they own, land now usurped by ranchers and the carnist trade supporting them.

In vegan human ecology, there is an increased need for research and professionals who restore and monitor the health of recovering and rewilded land- and seascapes. Their ranks can, if they so choose, come from the next generation of farming and ranching families who no longer find animal agriculture profitable.

Spare Change

As I wrote earlier, cognitive ethology is the study of animal behavior in natural habitats. Its research is revealing the complexity of other species' emotional and physical needs. This includes wildlife. Not meeting their needs causes suffering. Hunting terrorizes them as readily as it would us. Like humans, individuals from other species experience trauma, including post-traumatic stress disorder (PTSD). When individuals from other species are chased, wounded, and their mates and socially important relationships are killed all around them, they are deeply traumatized. Capture and transport can readily damage the mental health of an individual from other species.[650]

These vulnerabilities are demonstrated by natural events as well. After an 8.0 earthquake in China, pandas were "Still haunted by the continuous aftershocks and landslides. They had to travel again toward the end of June to Kunming where they would spend two years to heal from their psychological trauma."[651] When parrots are captured and separated from their flock, which is the only social group that speaks their dialect, and when chimpanzees are confined to researcher's cages, we brutalize them. When we slaughter wolf packs and elephant herds, we rip apart deep, loving, needing, giving, and nurturing lives.

If we are tree-dwelling species who lose our forests, we have lost our homes and what we know. It does not matter if we are a common marmoset or a yellow warbler. If we are lake dwellers and our water becomes polluted with toxins that disrupt our endocrine systems, we cannot reproduce. We suffer while our community declines all around us. This is true whether we are seals, orca whales, or humans. When the land belonging to burrow-dwelling black-footed ferrets and greater prairie chickens has been plowed for food crops and grazed by domesticated species, their lives are over and their species endangered.

Emerging fields such as conservation medicine and wildlife psychology are attempting to understand the depth of harm we cause them and ourselves. As A.A. Aguirre and A. Gómez wrote, "Conservation medicine can be briefly defined as the practice of achieving ecological health ... to predicting, preventing and controlling the health implications of anthropogenic environmental change."[652]

It will be difficult for ecosystem management professionals to reorient their missions. While they work hard to restore fish runs, save endangered species, and allocate hunting quotas to a minority of consumers, they are trapped by political mandates to stay as they are. We are not so constrained. We have the power to change our personal relationships with other species and ecosystems. It is up to us. We must free the seas from our predatory factory fishing and our lands from animal agriculture. Habitat must be used to grow organic food for humans living within reasonable numbers while supporting the lichens, insects, bacteria, fungi, and all of the majesty of species' genetic diversity, an abundance that is allowed to move freely across the planet. Species will have eminent domain.

Spurred on by Rachel Carson's book, *Silent Spring*,[653] Senator Gaylord Nelson called for the first Earth Day[654] in 1970. Dennis Hayes expanded that to an international celebration in 1990. People around the world responded to environmental irresponsibility with the environmental movement. We became alarmed about the dangers of pesticides and herbicides and the decline of ecosystems. For today's agencies, biologists, and all of us, our current human ecology is everyone's "Silent Spring." Our current human ecology is poison.

We need a new story about our relationships with other species, and to turn from abuse and violence to healing and nonviolence. I believe with all my being that the vegan new human ecology, incomplete in its myriad of bioregional details, is the new story. It is the shortest route to, and our best chance for, sustainability. It is our best chance to adapt to today's ecosystems and is entirely doable. We require ecosystems agencies return to natural orders of value. We are looking for honest biocentric relationships between humans and all other species. If wildlife agency professionals continue perpetrating the current human ecology disaster, then nothing meaningful of ecosystems will remain. They will celebrate hunters who think they deserve medals of honor at a time we dishonor Earth. We will remain locusts, devouring the Earth, and feel immortal for a short time before eating ourselves out of our home.

Part V:

Impediments

Chapter 17:

Cultural Objections

Environmental contaminants coming to us from the south are a serious threat to the Arctic environment, to its living resources, to Inuit and to other indigenous peoples. These substances come into our lives through our diet. They strike at the very heart of Inuit society and culture, at the basis of our way of life. It is sometimes said 'That you are what you eat.' If this is true, then those who eat Inuit foods must be Inuit. Our foods do more than nourish our bodies. They feed our souls. When I eat Inuit foods, I know who I am. I feel the connection to our ocean and to our land, to our people, to our way of life ... When many other things in our lives are changing, our food remains the same, and they make us feel the same as they have for generations...[655]

—Inger Egede, Inuit Circumpolar Conference, 1995

More relevant to our security is the fact that poor countries will be the first to experience the impacts of climate change.[656]

—Ross Gelbspan, *Orion* magazine

We live within an estimated 10,000 human societies[657] that represent a difficult to determine number of cultures.[658] We speak some 6,700[659] to 6,809[660] languages. An estimated 20 percent of those human languages are dying. Patricia K. Townsend in her book, *Environmental Anthropology/From Pigs to Policies*, believes 3,000 languages will disappear in the next century.[661] Depending upon how we count them, we live in 189 to 195[662] political nation states.

Ecoregions, on the other hand, are geography-defined areas filled with a unique composition of species and their communities.[663] There also we find societies and cultures but they are nonhuman. Our global nation states span 867 distinct terrestrial ecoregions that abut an additional 232 marine waters ecoregions.[664]

Facing Ecosystem Collapse

Our cultures uniquely adapt to their external environments. When our environments change, so do our cultures, at least those that survive. When we do not adapt, we live unsustainably and in conflict with our host ecosystems. That is happening now, globally. We have become maladaptive not just as cultures here and there, but as a species. As we look for solutions to our unsustainability, we need to understand that Earth experiences us as a species first and less so as cultures. That is because there are so many of us creating a cumulative presence and impact upon the entire biosphere. Every human being creates environmental impacts.

For the first time, we have to respond as a species, not just as cultures, to address our unsustainability. No matter how far removed or small in number our culture's societies are, every person, group of persons, and variations of culture are actively contributing to the gross altering of the world's interconnected ecosystems.

My culture and your culture have not updated our human ecologies in response to the needs of a fast-changing biosphere. The debate over who must bear the responsibilities for the state of the Earth and people, the over-consumers or the over-populated, is a distraction while the world burns and starves. We are all uniquely responsible. Everyone's ancestors are accountable for starting and intensifying our species' decimation of biodiversity and ecosystems. There are no exceptions. Our populations have increased, as has our consumption of ecosystem services, transculturally.

Our ancestors began hunting species to extinction, especially those of large size, long ago. This human-caused wave of annihilation is the Great Holocene Extinction I referred to earlier. In *The Future of Life*, E. O. Wilson describes our most recent history:

The trail of *Homo sapiens*, serial killer of the biosphere, reaches to the farthest corners of the world. A few centuries after the Madagascan slaughter, another occurred in New Zealand. When the Polynesians came ashore in the thirteenth century they ... entered a vast biological wonderland.

The wonderland he describes included several species of flightless birds like the moa who ranged from turkey-sized to 330-pound giants nine feet tall. Within a few decades, the Maoris, "like the sweep of a scythe," hunted all of them to extinction, "and presumably the world's largest eagle with them." The New Zealand eagle had weighed an estimated 28 pounds.[665] By comparison, the average weights of mature male and female bald eagles in North America average eight to 15 pounds, respectively. Following the Maoris, the British colonists brought their rats while land-clearing further paved the road to extinctions. A procession of cultures devastated species one after the other. It was not a humane collection of human ecologies.

Language, spiritual practices, dietary choices, creation stories, art, shelters, gestures, the materials and technologies used, recreation, self-identity, and more live in our cultures. They reflect our interactions with our environments and one another. As John Grim reminds us in *Native North American Worldviews and Ecology,*

> From the pre-Columbian era to the present there have been not one but many Native North American worldviews and religious practices. Native spokespeople say that there are over five hundred distinct cultural traditions that still maintain sacred relations with the diverse terrains and life forms of the North American continent. Thus there are a variety of indigenous positions on ecological issues.[666]

Everyone's ancestors migrated to, occupied, and adapted to distinct habitats. Today, through the long reach of interconnected economies and climate change, the threats to ecosystems are growing more similar across cultures. Like it or not, smaller population cultural groups have been drafted into being responsible for the whole of humankind's increasing and cumulative impact. Rich and poor, indefensible over-consumers and low-scale consumers, all are drawn into the fray because we each have our varying degrees of impact that require responses.

All of us are accountable for the impacts of the goods we import as much as those we export. People "over there" are no longer over there; we are there and they are here because we import and export our ecosystem services and the impacts that go with them. Water is transported from one ecosystem internationally to another when the moisture in grapes and tomatoes is imported from a distant ecosystem—as were the soil nutrients. Water is drawn from a distant ecosystem and often contaminated where the product is made long before the product is shipped to us. We are party to that contamination far away.[667] Unseen people from equally unseen places purchase things, raw materials, and services that come from where we live. In turn, we do the same and create environmental and human impacts in places we will never know, see, touch, hear, or feel. And we cannot forget that individuals from other species are affected and often harmed everywhere in these human transactions. Through our personal, cultural, national, and global economies, we affect each other. We shape each others' human ecologies and the ecosystems that make life possible.

However unique we choose to be in our cultural responses to environmental collapse, we are all tasked to act. We share these challenges: ecosystem decline; disparities of income, health care, social and political freedom, and employment; a rising toxic burden in our bodies and environments; increasing and unsustainable human populations; rising and unsustainable human demands on ecosystems that exceed carrying capacity; climate change with its attendant acidification of marine waters; rising sea levels; declines of wildlife hunted as bushmeat; the suppression of apex predators; animal agriculture; armed civil conflicts that decimate defenseless wildlife and humans alike; evolving, border-crossing diseases; finite, insufficient, or wholly lacking potable water; the availability and costs of shelter; increasing threats to food security and affordability; access to financing at the community level; inadequate compassion and empathy; the continuing denial of resources to billions of people; and for all of us, a declining resource base.

All of it is inexcusable, and curable. In addition to all other species and ecosystems, the human poor are the first victims of ecosystem destruction, rising food prices, and political instability. In their poverty, over half of humanity already knows what suffering from ecosystem decline and economic injustice is about. They will benefit from the new human ecology like the rest of us. But they are also part of the problem. For instance, people dependent upon shifting agriculture burn forests to clear land for crops; this has a major impact upon ecosystems. It is estimated that shifting agriculture is responsible for one-third of the global burning of ecosystem biomass each year.[668] The ways we live and populate the planet are expressions of culture and the cause of our planet's declining health. Since everyone, everywhere is contributing to our collective downfall, it will take everyone everywhere to slow, stop, prevent, and then reverse it.

Can our sense of social and economic justice help us respond to environmental problems? Or as Grist writer Jonathan Hiskes titled one of his online postings, "Can Human Rights Be the Climate Movement's Moral Guide?"[669] It seems right, but how do we reconcile cultural practices if they have caustic effects on ecosystems? Our species' killing and obliteration spree must be turned off at the source. To succeed in this and become sustainably adaptive, we must overcome our resistance to cultural change.

Asking diverse human societies to agree to universal responses and accept new worldview beliefs is a cultural minefield. But we should pay attention to social anthropologist Kay Milton who wrote "Cultural Theory and Environmentalism":

> One of the clearest messages that anthropologists can give to environmentalists is that human beings have no 'natural' propensity for living sustainably with their environment. Primitive ecological wisdom is a myth, not only in the anthropological sense, as something whose truth is treated as a dogma, but also in the popular sense, as something that is untrue, a fantasy.

She gives several reasons why we want to believe otherwise and continues, "The analysis is inconclusive on the question of which transcultural perspective, globalist or anti-globalist, anthropocentric or ecocentric, holds out the best prospect for a sustainable future."[670]

Cultural buy-in makes change possible without coercion. But what if that does not happen? And what should our poorer neighbors do as we kill them with *our* unsustainable human ecology, when, with our massive contributions to GHGs we cause global warming and from that crop-killing drought, floods, and diseases arriving for the first time in newly warm areas? Christine MacDonald in *Green, Inc.* provides an example of another category of hard choices. In Africa, indigenous peoples are forcibly removed from ecosystems deemed more important as ecological reserves. She quotes World Conservation Society's Steve Sanderson as writing "'How do people live in fragile ecosystems? How can impoverished populations contribute to conservation?'" She tells us he has stated, "'... the global environmental movement has been 'hijacked' by advocates for indigenous peoples.... Forest peoples and their representatives may speak for the forest. They may speak of their version of the forest; but they do not speak for the forest we want to conserve.'"[671] Troubling and incendiary perspectives? Absolutely. Finding the balance between maintaining the viability of ecosystems and the indigenous who live within them will be as difficult as we and they can imagine. It will be the same for us. No society is immune to exceeding an ecosystem's carrying capacity to the detriment of other species living there. Many should move when that happens.

For emphasis, I repeat, there are so many humans living in so many cultures, that it is time to recognize that for issues concerning our human ecology, our species, *Homo sapiens*, is our primary identity, not our cultural or tribal group, not our nation. No one is excused from responsibility.

The new human ecology itself is susceptible to the spectrum of worldview beliefs and biases, including mine. Validation has to come not from my own and other cultures, but from its service to biodiversity, benefit to human welfare, cessation of unnecessary violence against sentient species, and expansion of healthier ecosystems.

While we may be rightly reluctant to insert human ecology values and beliefs into other cultures, it is important to remember that we already pledge an allegiance to near universal standards, and we are not afraid to say so. Humanity is uneven in its recognition of the rights of women, for instance. Discrimination prevents them an equitable access to education, social equality, their right to control the number of children they bear, and the right to refuse to be a child bride. In some shame-based, fundamentally religious cultures, women are blamed for being raped and then burnt alive or stoned to death. Slavery, the commercial bushmeat trade, and forced child labor are a few of the many cultural practices we are unafraid to openly oppose. Advocating for The Seven Results of the new human ecology when so much is at stake is not something we should be reluctant to do.

Outdated global cultural attitudes toward ecosystems and individuals from other species are woven into the norms of cultures. Tribal fish hatcheries are no different than nontribal fish hatcheries for the impacts they have upon wild salmon. Tribal and nontribal rodeos celebrate the same cruel treatments upon other animals as do the nontribal; they are both inherently cruel and disrespectful to individuals from other species. We must oppose rodeos regardless of cultural sponsorship. In North America, there is an Indian Rodeo Association covering the United States and Canada. In these events, bulls, horses, and calves are subject to abuse, injury, pain, and eventually, death. They are spared no indignity for the cause of cultural entertainment.

One Native American / U.S. cultural event I am acquainted with is the Omak Stampede Suicide Race in Omak, Washington. Competitors, many of them members of the confederated twelve Colville tribes, whip their horses to run at full speed over the edge of a steep slope. Race organizers call it a cliff. I measured it myself late one night under the cover of darkness and found it to be over sixty degrees steep on average. The horses bunch up as they struggle going down this sharp, narrow decline. They cannot see the ground directly in front of them, often collide, fall, and somersault with flailing hooves as they roll downward, pulled by the force of gravity. Despite the quarter-mile shortness of the race, horse legs and backs break. Death follows by euthanasia. If the horses survive the "cliff," they are whipped to run through the Okanogan River bed that is strewn with baseball-to-football and larger-sized boulders. It is here where more injuries in the near-dark occur. Horses have drowned in high water years.

As reported by Nick Timiraos of the *Wall Street Journal*, a rider stated, "Mr. Curry's strategy is to 'go so fast that you don't give your horse time to balk. There's no time to slow down. If you do you're dead or hurt, with 20 horses coming right over you,' he says."[672] I have witnessed the killing of horses at these races and the disregard for their welfare by the Colvilles and the "cowboy" representation of my own culture. Though well documented by myself and others, these abuses are not prohibited under Washington State law. The Suicide Race falls under the exclusions for customary agricultural practices. Though the commercial horse racing industry kills far more horses every year, and floods the market with unwanted "loser horses"—most go to slaughter—the Omak Suicide Race has a history of killing more horses per total races run. The otherwise good, multicultural people of Omak, the Colvilles that live there, and horse racing track enthusiasts are all blinded to these cruelties by their fossilized cross-cultural norms of approved brutality.

Notes *Native Peoples Magazine*, "Central to this tradition of raising and riding horses is the institution of rodeo. Indian rodeo is as much a part of Native American life and culture, perhaps more so in its historical reach, than say powwow dancing, yet is largely unrecognized outside its own circle of participants and fans."[673] The first sentence of their mission statement reads, "The All Indian Rodeo Cowboys Association acknowledges our Indian and western heritage, culture and tradition as we promote organized professional entertainment as rodeo." [674] The associations for Indian and non-Indians promote the same events: saddle bronc (horse), bareback bronc, bull riding, calf roping, and steer wrestling. Cultural differences do not change the nature of the relationships between people and sentient nonhumans at these events.

The reintroduction of horses to the North American continent by early Spanish explorers changed both tribal culture and their relation-ships with ecosystems. Though estimates vary widely, prior to European contact there were an estimated 4 to 7 million indigenous people who were altering landscapes in North America through the setting of fires to drive their prey to waiting hunters. They also used fire to create panic among bison who stampeded over cliffs to their injury and deaths.[675] There are earlier periods that involve everyone's ancestors elsewhere. It is the practices, regardless of culture, that must change. The new human ecology requires the end of all rodeos, all bullfighting, cock fighting, dog fighting, water buffalo fighting

(Vietnam), horse fighting (China), and the destruction of ecosystems and biodiversity regardless of the cultural context that encourages them. It is our species that must make universal changes to reduce harm to individuals from other species and ecosystems if we are to survive.

Global Cultural Responsibilities

When any of us from any culture consumes an extravagant quantity of resources compared to the poorest half of people on Earth, we have to be expected to lower it. If my consumption is 500 times the consumption of impoverished people, then I have 500 times the responsibility, roughly speaking. We *haves* have an abundance of options to create a greater per capita reduction in harm. It falls to us initially to do much of what Earth requires. As we bumble our way through figuring out what equitable consumption means, we will depend upon citizens, businesses, and government to create alternatives to our present way of doing things. Public transportation is an easy example as is taxing carbon at the source to reduce GHGs and shift us towards more sustainable energy sources. Recycling and composting in our homes and apartments are additional easy steps.

People are offended when their cultural norms are criticized. Pressing for a new human ecology as urgently as it is needed may feel like a confrontation, an attack on our deeply held cultural beliefs and practices. In his "Three Great Movements," deep ecology founder Arne Naess writes, "You say the deep ecology movement asks for a widening care so that nonhuman beings get more chance. But you should also support the increased care for the underprivileged humans."[676] Our new human ecology is premised on social and economic justice being one of our results. That speaks to all cultural expectations. What constitutes conflict and cultural imperialism will be in the eye of the beholder. Striking a balance that works and saves ecosystems is hard. Naess, committed to cultural justice, wrote that

> *Whereas self-determination; decentralization; local community; and think globally, act locally,* [his italics] will remain key terms in the ecology of human societies, the implementation of deep ecology changes

nevertheless requires increasingly global action in the sense of action across every border. And often, local communities or areas with scattered population are uncritically in favor of so-called development and must be forced to a more ecological responsible policy by central authorities. There are important limits to decentralization of ecologically relevant decisions.[677]

He is addressing the need for emphasizing biocentrism. The new human ecology incorporates that while being a practical and loving response to the threats all of us face. The process of most change is seldom popular throughout. But these changes will be attended by ongoing debates about whether the new human ecology is just one cultural archetype imposing itself upon others, or whether this is a co-evolutionary step where environmental necessity and a moral awakening require us to leave behind transcultural carnism and current human ecologies that imperil Earth and our societies. If we are able to celebrate the multitude of cultures on Earth today that are infused with carnism and destructive environmental outcomes, I certainly hope we can also rejoice in new human ecology cultures that are just as wonderful, diverse, strong, vibrant, and celebrated. Different? Yes. But if we fail to adapt to our rapidly changing environments, billions of us may die. If my culture and your culture and their culture do not alter our unsupportable and interconnected human ecologies, then we are doomed as is most of everything we love about Earth. We will lose cultures and languages that describe our links to the past and our places on Earth.

Competition between cultures, introduction of new belief systems, and responses to environmental change are in our cultural histories. Change will happen by either catastrophe or through our proactively making choices to avoid that end. Every person on Earth is now connected to the other by cause and effect.

More on Poverty

There are many, often complex, reasons why human poverty continues. They include lack of land rights, the lack of suitability for human occupation and crops, weather trends, political freedom, local access to markets and infrastructure, the availability of power, and access to knowledge, financing, and technology. These barriers can be overcome. Climate change makes it more difficult. A 2010 Oxfam media briefing includes this example: "Poor women farmers from Bangladesh to Malawi do not need scientists to tell them their weather is becoming more unpredictable or that their seasons are shifting. They are already struggling to cope with the consequences of not knowing when and what crops to sew."[678] Ominously, they predict that the poor "will bear 75–80 percent of the costs of harmful climate change ..."

Economist and author Jeremy Rifkin reminds us that those of us living in the northern hemisphere, especially Western countries, were enriched by our technological use of petroleum that created climate change. Yet, "... the effects of human-induced climate change are most pronounced in the southern hemisphere where the poorest of people live."[679]

The seemingly radical solution to poverty across cultures is not radical at all. We just have to stop living radically. Endless population growth is impossible. Reducing it must be a strategy to reduce poverty. If that seems too drastic a proposition, then we must think risking the deaths of billions of people from overpopulation and the assured extinctions of a multitude of species is a moderate, moral position to take. We have no choice but to find a global consensus about the basics of living. If we do not, there will be a desperate time in the near future when our children will have to do it.

The global community of nations lays charges against those who wage wars of aggression and genocide. Warrants for their arrest are issued. They are tried before international tribunals. They are criminals. When nations harm people beyond their borders through toxic pollution, exclusive and excessive consumption of natural resources, irresponsible policies and economic activities that cause food prices to rise unreasonably, the destruction of ecosystems, and produce unsustainable levels of harmful GHG emissions—these are as deadly as war and genocide. When nations behave this way, their crimes should be treated in the same manner. Charges should be brought, nations tried before tribunals, and sanctions imposed. Sanctioning nations that refuse to join and abide by international protocols to slow climate change, and whose pollution enters the ecosystems of others, is a necessary tool of international diplomacy.[680]

The documentary *From the Heart of the World: The Elder Brothers Warning*[681] leaves us with a message. It comes from the Kogi Indians, a pre-Columbian tribe of the Tairona civilization in the Sierra Nevada Mountains of present-day Peru. They came out of their self-imposed isolation to tell us in 1992 that we are destroying the natural world and its balance. They saw their life-giving snowpack disappear and their ecosystem change drastically 20 years ago. They refer to us as their Younger Brothers, and about us they say: "The Mother is being cut to pieces and stripped of everything... If they do not change their ways, the world will end."

Subsistence

True subsistence non-cash economy societies that live in relatively unaltered ecosystems are a minority but no less important portion of the total human population. However, most subsistence occurs within the context of at least partial cash economies. Poor families who tend small-plot farms, for instance, would be happy to increase their part in the cash economy if it were available to them. For billions of people, it is not. So they subsist, truly subsist on what they can glean from the Earth through whatever means available. They may possess a few chickens, goats, or cattle who are exploited to create an income. Whatever money they do get will go to food, education for their children, potable water, medicine to avoid death, and perhaps a cell phone that links them to market prices if they have crops to sell.

I will never forget the man in Sierra Leone, West Africa, who came into the one-room house I was visiting and asked to borrow a shovel he could not afford. He needed it to bury his four-year-old child. Until we *haves* fix our own Earth-destroying human ecology, we will sabotage the futures of the *have-nots* and *have-somes*. We will kill them with climate change while spending our cash on unsustainable consumption of global resources.

Subsistence comes in many degrees and varieties. Many Inuit who live in Greenland do not use their whaling quota from the International Whaling Commission primarily for direct food subsistence. Instead, they sell an estimated 25 to 50 percent of it. In a recent year, 223 humpback, minke, and fin whales went to over 100 supermarkets where anyone can buy it. The supermarkets sell the whale meat for 20 times what they paid to the Inuit.[682, 683] As of 2012, they are allowed to harpoon (strike) 211 whales.[684] Denmark, on Greenland's "aboriginal hunt" behalf, proposes that 1,344 whales from four whale species be killed between 2013 and 2018.[685] Greenland aboriginal targets include the massive fin whale, second only to the blue whale for sheer size and weight. They grow to 80 tons, 85 feet, and if not harpooned, can live for 90 years. Like everyone else on the planet, the Greenland Inuit place in the ecosystem has changed. They are participating in the cash economy and turning the natural order of value into the economic one. Climate change has already affected their key industry, shrimping and fishing. The actions of billions of other people have weakened Earth, global fisheries, and the whales the Inuit want to cash out.

People will for a time still rely heavily upon subsistence hunter, fisher, and animal agriculture models of human ecology. But they have as large a stake in the new human ecology as does everyone else. Even though isolated communities may be the last, if ever, to partake in a vegan human ecology, their abilities to catch, consume, and sell individuals from sentient species will be impacted by what the rest of us do to the biosphere. Our identities are tied to familiar foods. In a multicultural society and robust economy, we have choices. Where one's cultural identity is stronger, perhaps more isolated, and the food is procured in a partial subsistence economy, the more resistant to changes in diet a person may be. As Inuit Inger Egede said at the opening of this chapter, "When I eat Inuit foods, I know who I am." Yet, relationships to food, connections to place, and cultural beliefs surrounding them have already resulted in uncomfortable tradeoffs in some of the most troubled ecosystems.

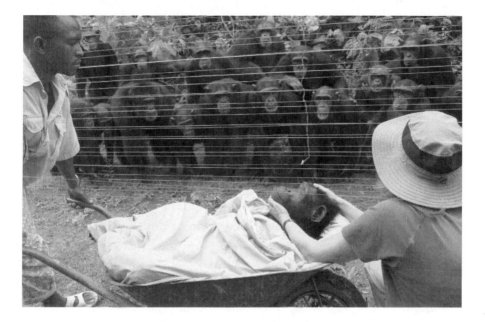

Dorothy's Funeral. Dorothy's mother was shot by a bushmeat hunter and then sold. After spending 25 years chained by her neck to the ground at a crude amusement park in Africa, Dorothy the chimpanzee was rescued and taken to Cameroon's Sanaga-Yong Chimpanzee Rescue Center. After living eight years there, she developed relationships with other chimpanzees, many who also were orphaned by the bushmeat trade. Dorothy died in 2008. These are the reactions of the chimpanzees who knew her. Photographed by Monica Szczupider, a volunteer at the center. © Monica Szczupider. 2008.

Bushmeat

Bushmeat is a term usually associated with African and warm tropics subsistence hunting of wildlife for food. It also includes the meat produced by large and commercialized hunting that generates cash income. Sometimes referred to as *wildmeat,* it is found in climates and cultures around the world.[686] Bushmeat includes marine and terrestrial species. Researchers Phil Clapham and Koen Van Waerebeek describe their findings:

Market surveys conducted in several South American and West

African coastal nations found that the sale and consumption of cetacean [whales, porpoises, and dolphins] and sea turtle products is common.... The main anthropogenic threat to six sea turtle species, three sirenians [manatees, dugongs] and an undetermined number of cetaceans may well be the bushmeat trade.[687]

In "Wild meat: the bigger picture," E.J. Milner-Gulland and others describe the extent of the trade: "Recent estimates of the annual wild meat harvest are 23,500 tonnes in Sarawak [Indonesia], 67,000–164,000 tonnes in the Brazilian Amazon, and 1 million–3.4 million tonnes in Central Africa." Some of this wildmeat is important to the poor living in remote places; they eat it directly, and may participate in the commercial trade for cash as well. The distinction between commercial and subsistence hunting is blurred. The paper reports that "25 tonnes of turtles exported every week from Sumatra, Indonesia, 1,500 forest rats sold per week in a Sulawesi market, and 28,000 primates hunted annually in Loreto, Peru, would not be considered bushmeat in the narrow sense of the word. Yet they are part of the same problem of overhunting of wildlife for human consumption."[688]

The authors find "The relationship between improved economic livelihoods and the demand for wild meat is not simple.... Ultimately, the current scale of hunting can only be lowered ... if ample, affordable nonwild fresh protein is available to large sectors of the population." Those alternatives are described as meat from livestock. As the market prices for domesticated meat sources increase or decrease, along with cultural preferences, so too does the commercial bushmeat trade.[689] There was no discussion of site-specific investigation of plant protein alternatives even though areas like the Amazon Basin in Brazil export phenomenal floods of protein-rich soy and other crops. In many bushmeat regions, peanuts, also a good source of protein, are already part of the local diet. However, cultural objections to changing dietary preferences and increasing human populations are emptying the forests. Carnism is a global disaster.

Resistance to changing our food preferences kills wildlife and ecosystems regardless of where we live, regardless of the economy, regardless of the availability of alternatives. The damage is still there.

The bushmeat trade for carnists in Africa is a cash economy that also supplies urban dwellers. It is a 2 billion dollar business that killed 8,000 endangered great apes in one year alone. Their dismembered lives and those of other species are flown to cities where they are consumed by urbanites relishing their past cultural lives.[690] The trade is abetted by logging roads that penetrate deep into areas that had been difficult to reach. As hunting pressures increase, the individuals from other species are disoriented when they are driven out of familiar homeland. As they are crowded into smaller and smaller plots of land, their peace, food, socializing, and shelter come to an ugly end by shotgun.

Michael McRae wrote "Road Kill in Cameroon." Published in *The Environment in Anthropology*, he describes how logging employees employ the subsistence hunters. Each hunter is provided with a shotgun and three cartridges. The hunter gets to keep every third kill. At the end of the day, the hunters and meat are picked up by the truck-driving loggers. The meat is smoked and then transported further by truck and airplanes to towns and cities. The author found that an average 12,500 pounds of bushmeat were being sold each week in the markets of Ouesso in Northern Congo.[691]

A World Wildlife Fund reported that "More than a ton of illegal bushmeat—including primate and elephant meat—was seized in the Congo Basin last week [2009] ... including remains from several protected species: gorillas, elephants, and chimpanzees." Law enforcement also confiscated over thirty rifles, some of them automatic assault weapons.[692] Authorities there believe that organized crime is supplying bushmeat in high volume to urban locations. Again, we find that cash hunting for bushmeat in impoverished places is difficult to discern from the direct subsistence consumption that feeds hungry families. There are too many people, too much logging, too little wildlife left, and poverty that the ecosystems have no responsibility for ending at this scale.

Organized crime and heavily armed rebel militias seeking cash crops have put lowland gorillas on their hit list. The United Nations and INTERPOL, the world's largest international police organization, believe that "Gorillas may have largely disappeared from large parts of the Greater Congo Basin by the mid-2020s ..." Within 20 years, lowland gorillas may not exist in most of their Congo Basin range.[693] Hunting creates another threat.

Hunting has a profound impact on the composition of species of trees in a forest. As fruit eaters are killed off, the trees have no means to distribute their seeds. If there are no other fruit-eating species that fulfill the same niche, the composition of the forests changes. In one study titled "Hunting reduces recruitment of primate-dispersed trees in Amazonian Peru," the authors found

In continuous, un-fragmented forests of southeastern Peru regularly hunted with firearms for 30–40 years, large primates are extirpated and medium-sized primates are reduced 61 percent compared with protected forests. At hunted sites seedlings and small juveniles (<1m height) of trees ... are reduced 46 percent ... compared with protected forests.[694]

In *Eating Apes*,[695] author Dale Peterson gives us a detailed, first-person accounting of the bushmeat trade in the Congo Basin. The story is achingly familiar: New roads create access into virgin ecosystems and impoverished indigenous people are enticed to hunt gorillas. In countries like Cameroon, bushmeat is legal if the hunter is licensed and taxes are paid on the corpses.

Like calves in the dairy industry, infant chimpanzees are byproducts of bushmeat hunting. Too small for meat value, they are sold in markets as toys for children, or "as experimental subjects for the Institut National de la Recherche Biomedicale...." Bush hunters have learned to kill the females first, and then hide from the protective silverback male. After a time, the hunter kills them off one by one. As Peterson describes, several cultures have a long history of killing and eating gorilla families. Before the introduction of modern firearms and larger populations of both forest and urban humans, the volume of killing was far lower. Gorillas and other species now face a culturally sponsored Armageddon. One hunter named Joseph estimated he kills "about fifty apes, a year, mostly gorillas" with demand rising during the Christmas holidays.

Dale estimated that "30 million people living in the cities and forests of the Congo Basin are consuming around 5 million metric tons of wild animal biomass per year." In the journal *Conservation Letters* we learn that "About 270 tonnes of illegal bushmeat could be passing through one of Europe's busiest airports each year...." There may be five tons of bushmeat passing through Paris Roissy-Charles de Gaulle Airport every day.[696]

We have a strong fidelity toward our traditional foods, even when we corrupt our appetites with foods high in sugar, fat, and salt. If our cultural taste preferences were flexible and affordable, there are innumerable foods from other cultural traditions that will support good health, if not a traditional identity and connection to the land. Outside food may not provide cultural continuity nor represent the relationships people have to place. Still, over time, food preferences do change.

We will find populations of people from other cultures who appear to live quite well as carnists deep within their particular ecosystems. Those limited exceptions will exist but they are not applicable to the rest of us nor does it reduce Earth's need for our species to change our behavior. There are peoples and places where some or much of the new human ecology will not yet work. That does not reduce the absolute need for it everywhere else. Improvements in our sustainability and humaneness are needed everywhere. There will be those who will change and those who never will.

I have experienced and appreciate the wonderful diversity of cultures and how the essence of cultural life is tied to what I am calling the current human ecology. I have smelled the smoke of home fires as food of all persuasions simmered in the light of kerosene lamps. I remember the people and their cultures. I also remember the individual people from other species. Their suffering and the wanton waste of their Earth is as real as ours; only the cultural contexts change.

The new human ecology is entirely human inclusive, but not passive. It is active, energetic, uplifting, fulfilling, and here for the entire marathon. Weighing in for and against other cultural practices will always be a sensitive issue. There is more room for humility than arrogance, but arrogance is ultimately what our current human ecology is about. Failing ecosystems will be the ultimate agents of cultural change if we do not ourselves change.

Cultural Approaches to Implementing the New Human Ecology

Discarding cruel and unsustainable acquired tastes and dietary habits and acquiring others intentionally and preemptively is a monumental challenge to our sustainability. For some international aid agencies, livestock are seen as the way to bring poor people out of poverty. Money from selling goats, eggs, milk, and the calves of cows are their standard approaches. From a new human ecology perspective, there are problems with this.

First, the pain of poverty is being transferred from humans to domesticated individuals from other species and ecosystems. Second, though increasing the standard of living for the poor is essential, as our net population increases, this will only increase the pain we shift to individuals from other species. From the first donated livestock will arise commercialized animal agriculture. People will seek to increase their wealth with more animals, more people will cut down forests to create pasturage, more predators will be killed, and grazing will compete with herbivorous wildlife. There is another way. We can instead develop non-animal alternatives to relieve poverty and hunger. This has already started to succeed.

Vegfam, founded in 1963, conducts emergency relief and aid programs that are

> Feeding The Hungry Without Exploiting Animals. Vegfam helps people overseas by providing funds for self-supporting, sustainable food projects and the provision of safe drinking water. We fund ethically sound plant-food projects, which do not exploit animals or the environment ...[697]

Similar organizations include HIPPO (Helping International Plant Protein Organisation) and Food For Life Global, "the world's largest vegetarian and vegan food relief organization ... With operations spanning 50 countries, the charity has served more than 100 million freshly cooked vegetarian meals throughout America, Asia, Africa, Australia and Europe." Hare Krishna Food for Life and Malnutrition Matters employ innovative technologies to process and distribute soy and other grains for aid relief operations.[698] A Well-Fed World is another vegan hunger relief organization. They combine hunger "and animal protection ... working with social justice groups to strengthen feeding, food production, and animal saving programs in the United States and globally."[699]

We could use a world where there is less violence. Veganism accomplishes that; carnism defeats it. I am weary of seeing chickens with their feet bound together and slung thoughtlessly over human shoulders. I do not want to see more goats and cattle having their throats cut by the side of the road and in markets. It is as disturbing to me as knowing there are human refugees being butchered, raped, and imprisoned in tribal, ethnic, and civil wars. Culture does not excuse any of it.

In a world where we blithely accept corporate commercialization of cultural food preferences, tastes, and values, I am willing to advocate for cultural practices consistent with a nonviolent new human ecology. Perhaps Coca Cola, Nestle, and other mega companies with a pockmarked social history will use their power to induce veganism globally. It is the most sustainable thing they can do.

Being Anthropocentric about Other Cultures

We protect and excuse cultures and subcultures of hunters, animal agriculturalists, sealers, and habitat destroyers because we or our ancestors are or have been them. Carnists have a real problem criticizing other carnists because it is hypocritical. They see other cultures as having inalienable rights to take nonhuman animals' lives on the same bases as their own rights. They do this because they believe we are at the pinnacle of creation or part of a relationship cosmology where one individual of a species gives himself up to us to be killed. We are unwilling to admit that individuals from other species are victims of violence that we readily recognize when it is perpetuated against women, children, and our elderly. A carnist from one culture approving the carnism in other cultures is useless to biocentric sustainability. Like-minded carnists from cultures around the world fall into this trap.

The herdsman still feels peace in the meadows, the farmer still sees the land yielding crops, the hunter his targets, and the commuter on his way to work will see most things as appearing normal. They may or may not see the slow motion unraveling of our natural Earth, the labored breathing of our interconnected ecosystems, the suffering. Drop all pretenses that the status quo human ecologies are working or will ever work again. They are failing. The new human ecology can be embraced because it works. And that will be good. Though many solutions will come from within our cultures, preserving biodiversity is more important than cultural traditions that destroy it. My culture will howl against the new human ecology as much as the others will.

Chapter 18:

Washing Away the Answers:
Green, Blue, Humane, and Religion Washing

> We stand at a critical moment in Earth's history, a time when humanity must choose its future. As the world becomes increasingly interdependent and fragile, the future at once holds great peril and great promise. To move forward we must recognize that in the midst of a magnificent diversity of cultures and life forms we are one human family and one Earth community with a common destiny. We must join together to bring forth a sustainable global society founded on respect for nature, universal human rights, economic justice, and a culture of peace. Towards this end, it is imperative that we, the peoples of Earth, declare our responsibility to one another, to the greater community of life, and to future generations.
>
> —Earth Charter Preamble, United Nations[700]

With the active and passive support of our economic, social, political, and religious institutions, we are hell-bent on a course of overpopulation and cataclysmic destruction of ecosystems. These are not the outcomes we intentionally want, but they are the result of the choices we are making. There are more chronically malnourished, destitute people on Earth today than the entire population of people who lived on Earth in the early 1800s. So while we make progress in reducing the global *percentage* of people living in extreme poverty, there are more in *absolute numbers*.[701] That is because the smaller percentage of poor on Earth is applied to a much larger world population of 7 billion people. More than half of humanity struggles to live from day to day even as some of us revel in material excess and quality of life. In this setting, we are exhausting what remains of Earth for poor and rich alike.

In this chapter, we look at how aggressive green washing, blue washing, humane washing, and religion washing frustrate our finding a just, sustainable, and humane human ecology that leads to human prosperity. These *washings* appeal to our wanting to do the right thing.

Washings are effective at making us think we have succeeded when we have fallen short of that goal. If we believe what the washings tell us, we lose our urgency go further into the truth of what we are doing to the planet, individuals from other species, and each other. Washings dumb us down and harm our character. They mislead us.

Can't Get the Dirt Out

Green, humane, blue, and religion washing paint thin veneers on products and services so they appear to have attributes that do not exist.

- Green washing claims or infers that the product or service is sustainably produced with minimal or no environmental impact when it is not the truth. The washing seeks to improve a product's environmental image, but its net environmental impact has changed little, or not at all.

- Humane washing gives us the false impression that producers have addressed the most important issues about the welfare of individuals from other species. Species' rights in the wild and within animal agriculture are not considered. It seeks to perpetuate carnism.

- Blue washing refers specifically to fishery sustainability. It is associated with NGOs guiding consumers in their choices of which fish to eat and not eat. It does not consider sentience.

- Religion washing is a general approval of human behaviors or choices based on religious beliefs. With few exceptions, it will not challenge carnism and other cultural beliefs about our relationships with other species, beliefs that are woven into the social fabric of religious institutions.

From green cars and houses to happy cows and contented chickens, we are misled into feeling justified and good about our purchases when we should not. These washings take advantage of our readiness to accept a flimsy accounting of the issues. If we believe a product is environmentally sustainable and humanely produced, we stop asking questions. We are given permission to consume even more of the product.

Claims that a car, detergent, or piece of meat is green, sustainable, or humanely raised are often compared to the worst choices, a gas-guzzler, toxic formula, or factory-farmed individual. Those are not the ultimate criteria we must use. Instead, we have to measure the sufficiency and the context of these comparisons. Will that car, detergent, or piece of meat really address critical environmental issues and the moral challenges we face? Is the suffering of individuals from other species no longer an issue in animal agriculture because they are uncritically certified as being *cage-free* and *humanely raised*? Or does product washing lead us into a false sense of accomplishment and stop us from changing our behaviors and choices? If the product is incrementally better, that may be a good improvement, but it is not the same as sufficient.

Greener, more sustainable, and more humane is not the same as restorative for ecosystems, truly sustainable, impact neutral, or humane in any sense of the word. We must not be careless about this. Sustainability and moral consumer conduct requires us to ask the right questions about products and services. "Environmentally friendly" printed on the label of a household cleaning product does not mean we should drink it or fish can swim in it.

Products and services are marketed to influence and manipulate our worldviews, our belief systems, and our values so they can get what they want from us, ownership of our behavior. We become co-conspirators to environmental ruin and the unjustified abuse of other species if we believe we are entitled to possess everything and buy into every lifestyle marketed to us.

Green Washing

A new or improved product or service can be better for the environment than a previous version, and it may be as good as it gets for the moment. However, it can also continue to create a net environmental loss. "Green" and "environmentally friendly" are not the same as neutral or restorative. "Greener" or "less-impacting" more accurately inform the consumer that the goods and services still harm ecosystems.

Coal can be called "Clean Coal" thousands of times in TV advertizing to justify continuing to use coal-fired power plants, but there is no explanation about the fact clean coal has not yet arrived, that there are still technological and financial obstacles, and that test projects are underway. We are guided away from how the Earth's skin is peeled back to strip mine coal. We only get the message, clean coal, so we relax.

It does not help the planet if we believe a car or house is "green" without prominent qualifiers. Hybrid SUVs fall into this category as do overly large, energy-efficient homes that are built on former farmland. In some ways they are greener than past offerings, but that message should not be overstated and mislead everyone into believing the new, lower levels of impact are suitable and sustainable green choices. Overly large homes still have to be heated, cooled, furnished, maintained, and cleaned; their surfaces of wood, metal, stone, paint, and vinyl stand over a large land footprint. Farmland is still lost and that is unacceptable.

Green and other "washings" are applied to entire corporations, not just single products. James Ridgeway, senior correspondent for *Mother Jones*, wrote in his blog about British Petroleum's rebranding "... to depict itself as a public-spirited, environmentally sensitive, green energy enterprise ... While making miniscule investments in things like solar power, biofuels, and carbon fuel cells that backed its PR claims, BP continued to work relentlessly to expand its oil and gas operations."[702] As we know, BP was a party to the disastrous oil spill in the Gulf of Mexico, the largest to date.

Author Christine MacDonald, in *Green, Inc.*, documents numerous cozy and questionable deals between environmental NGOs and industry. After green certifications are issued to businesses for adopting nominally better practices, the certifying NGO is given a donation. MacDonald cited a study from TerraChoice that found of one thousand products making environmental claims, "... all but one [were] misleading or flatly untrue. Nearly 60 percent of the products were guilty of 'the hidden trade-off"—they touted one environmentally friendly attribute but ignored other unfriendly considerations that cancelled out the positives."[703]

During a Christmas holiday season of marketing, advertisers told me that if I buy an SUV that gets 22 miles per gallon of gas, I am helping the planet. One television commercial featured a large truck plowing through a beautifully pristine, otherwise unblemished deep and powdery field of snow to the music of *The Nutcracker*. Suddenly, the truck leapt into the air in slow motion like a ballet dancer then smashed through a snowdrift. On the TV screen we read: "GMC 403 Horsepower Nutcracker." In 2011, *spirit* was a term used to sell me cars, cigarettes, and countless Christmas gifts. The true meaning of spirit, human spirit and spirituality, was a casualty.

Humane Washing

Humane-washing wants to remove the slaughterhouse from our minds. It is a campaign to replace the movement for species rights with a bare minimum of improved welfare. For example, when egg producers and sellers present themselves as humane businesses, this is what they omit when they humane wash *free-range* and *cage-free* egg production:

- for a number of reasons, these chickens seldom go outside of their shed to use their "free range,"
- their sensitive beaks are painfully cut off with a hot knife blade to prevent pecking,
- though not in cages, their densities per square foot in housing can be extremely high,
- grain fed to them is wasted by the inefficiencies of grains being converted to eggs,
- habitat and biodiversity is impacted in the growing of that grain,
- unnecessary water use and air and water pollution remain as a byproduct,
- the hatchery providing the chicks still kills all the males, routinely with great cruelty,
- claws and spurs will be cut off the chickens' feet and legs,

- and their chicken lives remain brutally short because they are killed when they become unprofitable egg-laying machines.

Humane washing deceptions run deep in the egg industry as they do throughout animal agriculture.

"Organic, grass-fed beef" and "small family farm" are humane washing phrases that lessen our concerns about the inhumane nature of meat production and the consequences for ecosystems and wild species. These subsets of animal agriculture are different, but those differences are limited and ultimately inconsequential for saving ecosystems or addressing the rights of other species headed to slaughter.

Calves are still kidnapped from their mothers, perhaps a few months after birth instead of a few days, and most are sold off at auction. The mothers and calves remain on the landscape as an invasive species, part of the millions of cattle grazing in the United States, at any given moment. And they are still killed at a very young age for thoughtless epicurean entertainment. Small family farms do not change that regardless of the farmed species in question or any romanticized ideas we may hold about animal agriculture. Examples are easy to find.

A physician and her "computer-pro" husband were featured in a *Seattle Metropolitan* magazine article full of praise for what they do: They specialize in selling lambs, among other species. We learn that

> Because meat from sheep born between February and March tastes best when slaughtered from July to October, Graham and Connolly are butchering them now. Welcome to lamb season…. for lamb to impart that sweet, slightly gamey taste, young sheep need to develop muscles by frolicking over grassy hills—maybe even chasing those [Easter] bunnies and chicks.[704]

After reminding us that lamb refers to sheep, individuals who are killed before they are less than one year old, the writer does not show an ounce of concern about what this means to lambs.

In a similar story, Oregon Public Broadcasting reporter Anna King focused on the hectic nature of raising sheep at lambing time. She quoted the business owners to demonstrate their perspectives, not the lambs':

> ... 'sometimes the mothers have trouble giving birth. And the sheep or lambs die as a result.... Now we have a pretty good system of emotional control.'... Eventually, these lambs and kids will be sold for pets or milkers. Some will end up on dinner plates.

Like all dairy, the kids and lambs were born to create milk that will be taken to be sold. In this story, the milk is "for the farmers' artisan French cheeses for another year."[705]

The animal agriculturalists who believe that breeding and raising an individual of another species organically in less restrictive confinement, but whose young life is violently taken by a trusted human, will tell us their handiwork is humane and environmentally sustainable. I call it one part humane washing and one part green washing because of the broad and deep moral lapses in what they and their customers fail to consider.

Humane washing and green washing animal agriculturalists want you to believe that making a few degrees of improvement in the lives of livestock is the right response to the humane and ecological nightmares surrounding industrial-scaled agribusinesses. After choosing to compare themselves to the worst standards available, the depraved and ecologically destructive practices of the industrialized animal agriculture empire, the small, family-operated animal agriculturalists want us to feel grateful about the changes they have made.

Objectively, they are still part of the livestock grazing that monopolizes 22 to 26 percent of the Earth's ice-free land area,[706] no matter how small scale they try to be. And while the injustice suffered by the nonhuman animals under their control may be reduced, the greater and most important parts of it continue. They and their offspring are exploited for a few years, sold off, moved, and then denied a natural life span before being killed.

When vegetarians settle for organic, locally produced dairy and egg products, instead of becoming organic vegans, they make the same green and humane washed-out mistakes as the carnists do. When vegetarians choose to eat organically, dairy cows and chickens are still spent, exhausted from being exploited, and then sent to slaughter. There are billions of slaughtered egg-laying hens and male chicks killed to make egg omelets. Vegetarians who consume these lives and the products taken from these individuals contribute significantly greater amounts of GHGs than vegans do; dairy products produce approximately the same amount of GHGs as does meat consumption. [707, 708] If we consume the milk that rightfully belongs to calves instead of soymilk, hemp milk, almond milk, and rice milk, we also pay for the artificial beginnings and endings of their short lives. There is a dead calf and exploited mother cow in every glass of milk and slice of cheese pizza. It is cows' milk, goats' milk, or some other type. Milk is never just *milk*. We have choices.

There is a major fork in the road as we consider one decision. Is it appropriate to support incremental changes in nonhuman animal welfare, or is it best to set a course straight to the abolition of using individuals from other species, domesticated and wild, for any purpose that harms them?

I do not have a right to speak on behalf of any nonhuman animal and tell you that it is OK to harm them. Thus, I cannot tell anyone that their incremental change is the best strategy to end that harm. But we know that change often comes gradually and small changes can lead to bigger ones. There is a reduction in harm and that is important. For many of us, going from carnist, to vegetarian, and then onto veganist was a process, not an instant event. Transforming our lifestyle to become more environmentally sustainable follows the same process.

However, now that I am on the other side as a vegan, I mourn the harm I did in my own incremental journey. The time I wasted, the suffering I caused, and the environmental destruction could have been avoided. I cannot undo those crimes. I am compelled to tell you to go vegan as quickly as you can. So what do we do when organizations campaign for incremental changes in animal welfare and environmental protections and not for the abolition of carnism and environmental devastation?

I generally withhold criticism on incremental changes in the welfare of nonhuman species as long as that incremental change is *clearly* and *publicly* stated as being a step towards near-term abolition. In addition, the organizations sponsoring incremental change must tell the public that abolishing these harms in our personal behavior is needed now. If an organization avoids the goal of abolition, opposes it, or denies it, they and their campaigns do not deserve your support. This also holds true for environmental organizations pushing us to change our environmental impacts incrementally. The danger, well underway in the campaign to improve the welfare of egg-laying hens, is that the incremental reforms insidiously become the goal. If animal welfarists and rightists agree to lock in industry-wide standards of care that, ultimately, are not humane, they've stopped even incremental reforms. And while they celebrate their victory, there's no mention of the immense environmental costs to ecosystems. There's not a single self-identified environmental organization willing to stop it. The industry of animal agriculture remains intact, and humane washing, green washing, and sustainability washings win the day. That type of animal welfare destroys species rights and ecosystems. That is unacceptable.

Blue Washing

Blue washing occurs when seafood suppliers infer their specific fisheries are sustainable and not over-fished. They do not address sentience and suffering in fish. Though bycatch will be a consideration, it is only when it becomes extreme that the fishery will be deemed unsustainable.

For a number of reasons, including a lack of reliable information, fishery advocates have difficulty determining what is sustainable. In a recent *New Scientist* editorial, we learn

> There is little consensus on what constitutes a 'sustainable' fishery.... while most schemes agree on high-profile species such as the Atlantic bluefin tuna, six organizations rank Atlantic halibut as a species to avoid, while Friends of the Sea and the Monterey Bay Aquarium recommend it as sustainable.[709]

The fishing industry is soaked in waste and cruelty. Ecosystems need fish. Marine mammals and birds need fish. The entire food web needs fish, but fishing can cut links out of food chains. Like the trade in "legal" ivory that gives cover for the illegal market, fisheries that are deemed sustainable give cover for the rest of the blue-washed industry. The concept is meant to help ecosystems, but the concept itself is blue washing.

At a 2010 CITES meeting, 150 governments failed to protect four species of heavily hunted sharks and bluefin tuna. There is little accounting in high-seas industrial shark fisheries. Millions of sharks are killed only for their fins that are the main ingredient in shark fin soup.[710] As long as the demand for shark fin soup and fish and chips— taken from spiny dogfish, a shark—continues, ecosystems will lose as many as 100 million sharks every year.

The legendary bluefin tuna can reach nearly nine feet in length, weigh up to 1,400 pounds, is able to swim at 25 mph per hour, and can dive to 3,280 feet below water. A single bluefin tuna sold for $736,000 in early 2012. At 593 pounds, that is $1,241 per pound, wholesale.[711] They are over-fished worldwide. What better way to demonstrate how our economic order of value has replaced the natural order of value of bluefin tunas in ecosystems?

Religion Washing

In a 1997 letter dated "Spring Equinox," environmentalist and species activist Benjamin White Jr. announced his founding of the Church of the Earth.

> My hope is to use the Church of the Earth as a direct challenge to the spiritual disease that infects us all.... I am not willing to put the little time I have left on this wonderful Earth into an effort unless it directly challenges the dominant mindset that holds that life on Earth is just stuff to use and people simply consumers ... think of the possibilities ...[712]

If organized religion and spirituality became what Ben's Church of the Earth sought it to be, many religious traditions would not busy themselves with religion washing. It may be the most intractable washing of them all.

Religious traditions, like other cultural practices, have rituals to make slaughtering a sentient being a good thing. Their rituals and underlying beliefs surrounding slaughter and food explain how individuals from other species, and ecosystems, are here for us to take. Some spiritual beliefs assume that individuals from other species give themselves up voluntarily to be eaten. Rituals include prayers of thanks to God or gods and blessing the food to be eaten. Kindness is required or implied, but this has failed to stem the universal abuses that species endure prior to and during slaughter. Where is the commandment that we should stop slaughtering and eating other sentient beings and conquering ecosystems when it becomes unnecessary for our survival?

Religious institutions have not kept up with what we are learning about the sentience of other species and their psychological and physical needs. With few exceptions, religions support the carnist current human ecology. Churches, temples, mosques, and synagogues are not controlling the arrogance of their members who are over-running and -consuming the Earth like there will be no tomorrow. As long as they give their blessings and religion-wash our arrogance, they will be the problem, not a solution.

Getting the religious to accept equality with, not supremacy over, ecosystems and other species may seem like an impossible task. As Karijn Bonne and Wim Verbeke noted in their paper on religious values and *halal* (Muslim) meat production, "Most religions forbid certain foods ... with the notable exception of Christianity, which has no food taboos."[713] Yet the biocentrism that equates the importance of all species also protects human welfare; it reduces poverty and suffering across the spectrum of species, including our own.

The care of the individual, method of slaughter, attitude during slaughter, and consumption are, for the religious, at least theoretically subject to religious regulation. Adherents want to believe that the meat being certified as halal, blessed, purified, or kosher, makes the violence and environmental destruction sanctified, but that is irrational. Violence, killing, suffering, and destruction do not disappear just because a religious tradition approves it. One study found that 14 percent of the 174 cattle studied in Muslim halal ritual cutting stood up again after their throats were cut. Eight percent took over 60 seconds to final collapse.[714] This was under ideal, controlled conditions. Jewish ritual also employs throat-cutting. Santeria, an old-world religion originating in Africa and practiced in much of the Caribbean, is just as barbaric.

I have walked along desert roads where goats were lined up for slaughter in front of prospective buyers and watched their throats cut. Who would choose this way to die for themselves? If religious tenets fail to be adaptable to and protect ecosystems and sentient beings, then the religion and its leaders must be held accountable.

Do we see the religious question the suffering and death of sentient beings to feed gluttony? Was there injustice in taking the life of the calf, lamb, chicken, and pig? Are ecosystems and our health harmed unnecessarily and unsustainably by these choices? If we find that there are reasonable and effective ways to meet our nutritional needs without the evil of slaughter and the annihilation of ecosystems, it makes no sense to cite feeble justifications based on spiritual and religious traditions from an era long gone. The vegan human ecology is a reformation because it offers new choices to old institutions.

We can choose, instead, a ferocious reawakening of the values already extolled by the world's religions and apply them to our relationships with all species. The Earth is at the center of our physical existence. The best chance we have for an increase in social and economic justice, for the greatest reduction in suffering, and the most effective path to sustainability will come from the new human ecology. It illuminates the sacredness of creation.

Happy Death, Happy Meat

Nothing Sweet on the Other Side of the Fence

Animal agriculturalists, chefs, and consumers desperately want to believe the myth that animal products labeled organic, humane, and sustainable are morally and ecologically defensible. They promote the *washings* as cover for their beliefs. They choose not to see the abusive and unsustainable nature of meat, dairy, and eggs. They pledge allegiance to an adjustment to factory farming, nothing more.

Passively accepting these beliefs, carnists take pride in eating "cage-free" eggs, hams from "free" pigs, cheese from the milk belonging to "humanely raised" cow's calves, and legs from "free" dead chickens. These consumers have become washed into believing that a little improvement in egg, meat, and dairy production has stopped the harm. They settle for the slight inconvenience of choosing and paying for a different box of eggs or a non-factory-farmed slab of meat. They believe in happy death, happy meat fantasies, and thus find escape from doing what is really needed. They avoid true and effective personal change.

Take for instance the boutique animal agriculturalist from Sweet Grass Farm who was featured in a National Public Radio (NPR) interview[715] to represent the organic, humane, and sustainable animal agriculture sector. I say boutique because at this small family farm buyers order meat months ahead of time at a cost reflecting the small scale, hands on effort of production. During the NPR interview, the husband of this farm family sounded terribly conflicted. He pasture-grazes Kobi Wagyu cattle and then lets them live a bit longer than normal by agribusiness standards before slaughtering them at a bit over two years of age. Sweet Grass Farm also allows calves to stay with their mothers a little bit longer than is customary in the business. In this interview, he talked about the spiritual crisis he suffers after killing so many sentient individuals of another species. At the end of each killing season, he has to go away and, I assume, recover his spiritual centeredness.

Like others of their generation of kinder animal agriculturalists, this family has worked hard to reform the industry. But the deepest harms remain. The emotional and spiritual angst he experiences at killing time demonstrates how animal agriculture is deeply destructive to both human and nonhuman at any scale. Arguably, his spiritual well-being, his most important guide, is telling him all he needs to know: Killing these Kobi Wagyu beings is soul-sucking violence.

From the Sweet Grass Farm (SGF) website, we are told that he and his wife take in "...fall born heifers [young female cattle who have not been impregnated]. We raise them to breeding age and breed them using artificial insemination.... These heifers return to BRCC [Blue Rock

Cattle Company] as bred two year olds." The newly pregnant cows will be used to create more calves who will be separated from mothers. The calves' milk will go to dairy drinkers and eaters.

Tellingly, the comments posted on the SGF website are from meat-eating zealots who rave about the taste and quality of the meat. Little is said about their other motivations that likely include the advertized claims of organic, humane, and sustainable production. It strikes me how much more they are not valuing.

On Sweet Grass Farm, the owners let the growing calves live a bit longer than the eighteen-month to two-year standard of industrial production, not to grant a few months reprieve before slaughter, but to improve the meat's taste. SGF lets its customers know that "The most flavorful tender beef of any breed comes from animals that are truly mature.... We focus on quality and harvest no animal before *it* (my italics) is truly ready, usually 28 to 32 months." The owners take pride in letting the calves see their mothers through a fence for a while after they are forcibly separated. But Amy Hatkoff in her book *The Inner World of Farm Animals* cites the research of Joe Stookey and his group at the University of Saskatchewan. They have studied attempts to reduce the stress of forced mother–calf separation. They examined the "'fence line weaning'" described on the SGF website and found "'the cows are visibly upset by the separations'" and use vocalizations to express that stress. We can bet our own lives that the mother cows' body language, body chemistry, and eyes provide additional evidence about the depth of a mother's anguish.

In this industry, no matter where you go or what you read, it all comes down to celebrating taste over the innate worth of sentient life. Taken to its bare essentials, they force the births of complex mammals then brutally kill them at 18 to 32 months of age to please gluttonous gullets. No matter the size of farm, its location, organic or not, animal agriculture artificially impregnates social animals with sentient awareness and kills them and their calves in short order. Every one of them will experience herd mates missing as they are taken away for slaughter, if they are allowed herd behavior at all. Their lives are full of broken attempts at social bonding. Remember Michael Pollan's steer, number 534. Compared to confined animal feedlot operations (CAFOs),

Sweet Grass Farm is a castle of reform, but only when compared to the hell of purely industrial animal agriculture.

There is no reform like abolition. Putting lipstick on the carnist omnivore movement will not save it from the vegan alternative. We will wear it down and strip it of its green and humane washings. From a vegan human ecology perspective, animal agriculture, including good intentions like Sweet Grass Farm, is a crime on many levels once more deeply examined.

Chef

Tamara Murphy is a renowned Seattle chef and restaurant owner. As a fan of Sweet Grass Farm, she takes the organic, humane, and sustainable myth a bit further. She decided to become personally involved in the beginning and end of pigs' lives. The piglets she bought were born and raised on Sweet Grass Farm. Murphy periodically checked on the piglets through the short time it took them to reach one hundred pounds. Then she took their lives. She blogged about this on her website and was interviewed by the *Seattle Post-Intelligencer*: "Last week, she [Tamara Murphy] was able to hand-feed them organic apples to help finish off the flavor of the rich, dark, 'almost creamy' meat of the pigs … the meat from four of the pigs will be served up in an eight-to-twelve course 'Life of a Pig' dinner…."[716]

I do not have to explain the dark, bizarre, self-serving worldview that has Murphy celebrating this as "The Life of a Pig." It was the death of four young pigs. Her choice of title is more befitting a Halloween horror movie about an ax murderer. As quoted in the article, the Sweet Grass Farm family is just fine with this because "… she [the wife and her husband] are at peace with the dichotomy of the piglets' lives, the fact that farmers put in backbreaking efforts to keep them alive and healthy and content, and yet they were created for the purpose of dying." Their belief in the pigs existing "for purpose of dying" is part of their worldview and by inference perhaps their religion-washed belief system about food.

Prior to slaughter, the reporter described how the young "animals were solid and energetic and playful as they romped around their outdoor pen, tufted tails curled proudly tight." The story almost ended for me with a quote from Tamara Murphy's blog postings as a chef and human being: "The 'Life of a Pig' feast," wrote Murphy, "allows us the opportunity to recognize, appreciate and honor the farmers, the sustainable process in which these animals were raised and the exact reason for which they were raised. I, for one, am very grateful." In this thoroughly anthropocentric accounting, she is the center of all purpose, the reason for all existence, and in control. To question the necessity and morality of their actions would violate their worldview about sentient beings whose flesh is "the exact reason for which they were raised." This is why they had to wash the whole enterprise with humane and sustainable mythology.

Murphy and the Sweet Grass Farm owners were wrong to do this. Theirs is a nostalgia that fails to wake up from its coma. The pigs' brief lives were sliced up, pushed into the mouths of diners who paid $50 dollars for the flesh they did not need. It was a taste for indulgence. Those diners, with their dollars, paid for the next insemination of the next sow mother to restart the process of artificially bringing piglets into being for the purpose of killing them. All of it is cold, calculated, premeditated, and profitable. For a brief time the next generation of piglets will play and then, in the beginnings of their young experience, be wasted. That is as good as animal agriculture and carnism gets.

Murphy's meat-as-entertainment-for-us rises again at "Burning Beast Three." Reporting for *The Stranger*, Bethany Jean Clement wrote, "Burning Beast Three: The Beastening/A Report from the World's Best Beast Feast in a Field." Clement described the "annual open-fire meat bacchanal held at Smoke Farm, an hour north of Seattle...." It is a fundraiser with the 400 tickets costing $75 dollars each used to support Smoke Farm, site of many charitable activities. Murphy organized the carnist gluttony and drink fest that in 2010 drew a dozen chefs and featured 14 kinds of "sustainable" meat. Reporter Clement noted that "The big tablefuls of grilled vegetables—corn and carrots, this and that—were not especially popular."[717] Everyone attending closed their eyes to the importance of who was burning. Tellingly, these sentient beings they were eating were called *beasts*.

Like-minded chefs and omnivores derive their pleasure and self-identity by creating intentional misfortune in other species. "Eat food. Not too much. Mostly plants." That is how Michael Pollan begins his book *In Defense of Food*.[718] He further advises, "Like, eating a little meat isn't going to kill you, though it might be better approached as a side dish than as a main." But in 2008 he praised food historian Betty Fussell's book *Raising Steaks*: "With an unflinching look at the ethical and environmental implications of modern meat, Fussell has certainly complicated steak eating, yet she somehow leaves you with a powerful hankering for a thick T-bone grilled rare." Perhaps that is why those who laude Michael Pollan appear to ignore his advice as if winking to say, "Sure, let's eat mostly plants." Somewhere in between his book and the response of high-profile omnivores like Murphy, they green- and humane-wash their behaviors all the way home.

Happy Media

Green, humane, and other washings could not exist without the unexamined support carnists get from the media. Our dietary choices are a hot topic for them as they eagerly wash the issues. Lacking balanced objectivity, high-profile writers limit their own horizons and those of their readers when the subject is carnism.

Before the magazine was closed by parent company Gaiam in 2009, *Conscious Choice* published a green- and humane-washed article titled "The Carnivore's Dilemma: Responsible meat eaters belly up to the offal truth."[719] As you may guess, *offal* is the author's intentional misspelling of *awful*. The story features a color photo of Chef Chris Cosentino holding a severed pig's head—the pig obviously less powerful and unable to stop his own murder—accompanied by the article squealing that humans should overcome their disgust over eating parts of slaughtered animals that have fallen out of style. Chris Cosentino is chef at Incanto restaurant in San Francisco whose specialty is offal.

"'An animal is giving its life for you to eat,' he insists. 'Do it justice and eat every last piece. It's just the right thing to do.'" Then the author pays homage to the "celebrated" Seattle chef, Tamara Murphy. This is how the carnist mind operates. They apply humane and green washing, call it sustainable, and then magically transform carnism into a solid moral and environmental choice. They offer no moral arguments for the necessity of this butchery, nor do they weigh the innate vale of their sentient victims.

Gaiam has since focused on its sales of eco-lifestyle, raising self-awareness, and yoga-related products. Searching the Gaia Life sales website in 2012, I found only a few products that urge consumers to eat animals. *Why Our Ancestors Were Not Vegetarians* by Arthur De Vany, Ph.D., is a book they featured. The author's quote on the Gaiam Healthy Living website included this tidbit: "But my question for you is this: Why would you want to be a vegetarian? ... There is no other way to obtain adequate calories. Otherwise, you have to eat so frequently and so much that you can't be very active."[720]

In "the food issue" of the magazine *GOOD*[721] writer Peter Rubin gives us his perspective in "Guess Who's Coming AS Dinner?" He reports uncritically and employs green and humane washing to describe small-time animal agriculturalists as sustainable and progressive: "More than organic, the small-farm movement is humane. Its animals are free-range, grass-fed, patiently raised; artisanal meats, resurrected from nearly extinct breeds." To prove his point, Rubin begins his first of several interviews with Paul Alward and Stephanie Turco, owners of Veritas Farm: "'Every time we sell a pig,' Paul Alward says, 'I'm refreshed by the fact that I took one ham away from the Smithfield pork company.'" Smithfield is the world's largest supplier of pig parts and products.

Curiously, in this article Alward is distressed by the veal industry that buys days-old male calves who are unwanted byproducts of the dairy industry. So much so that he goes to auctions about once a year and purchases them for between three and six dollars, then he raises these few calves more humanely than the veal industry would. What does Mr. Alward do with their lives after they are fattened to two years of age? He sells them to "beef farmers."

Rubin next interviews Ariane Daguin. She did not eat red meat for 13 years. Since her objections to animal flesh were described as the lack of quality and care in production, appearance, and taste, her concerns faded when those issues were settled to her satisfaction. Her satisfaction, not the individuals from other species she now slaughters. In fact, at the time the article was written, she was president of the meat company D'Artagnan that had revenues of $50 million dollars. One of her products is foie gras, "a process that is marred by two weeks of force-feeding." The article's author failed to describe the actual horrific forced-feeding program that enlarge goose and other fowl livers to grotesque size. Like others in her tribe, Daguin believes sentient beings are here for us to kill and eat. Rubin quotes her:

"'That's why they are here on Earth,' she says in a French accent that betrays her native Gascony. 'If you believe there is a God, and you taste a very good meat, there is no way that this animal was made with that taste so that it could live without us tasting it.'" Which washing dominates her statement?

What is interesting about Rubin's article is his focus on vegans and vegetarians who, like him, flopped back into carnism after a period of vegetarianism. The explanation, he infers, is that once vegan and vegetarian concerns are addressed, carnism works. He relieves himself of further exploration by diminishing the motives, the depth, and the complexity of vegan and vegetarian belief systems. He does this by continuing his interviews with Karma Glos.

Though she owns, with her husband, a farm that raises individuals for slaughter, she has the distinction of being a former "PETA activist" and vegan "in her younger days." In her role as overlord that she now occupies as an animal agriculturalist, the article continues, "'I made profound leaps in understanding,' she writes on the farm's website, 'when I stayed up all night to help a tired sow deliver piglets into the world … and when I killed my first chicken, by my hand, for my food.'" What was lost on her, and apparently writer Rubin, is that the sow was struggling because Karma and her husband, for their own enrichment, make pigs unnecessarily pregnant and others subservient, slaughtered captives to their enterprise.

Anthropocentric focus can blind the best of us and derail logic that could otherwise give us sight to see the obvious. In our youth, we all experimented with different identities, apparently as Karma Glos had.

She moved to a killing farm after abandoning her beliefs, deep or shallow, as a temporary vegan. That tells us about her, but not the selfish fascination she has with killing "her food."

Read "Crimes Unseen, The dark story of America's big slaughter-houses, and the effort to make butchers' grim work more humane"[722] in *Orion* magazine, as well as "Shortening the Food Chain," in the same issue.[723] The latter story is about "grass fed and locally slaughtered" alternatives that the writer makes look good by comparing them to the factory farmed livestock industry. Jason Houston, managing editor at *Orion*, writes a green- and humane-washed endorsement for the story, telling the reader that visitors can "see how the lambs or cows or pigs or chickens are treated, and then purchase a chop or steak or side of bacon ... This reconnection to food is happening in many places ... and it offers a way to support an honest and open agricultural system."

Ode magazine went as far as to declare, "Eat a burger, Save the World. Why the new fast food is good for you (and the planet)" on their front cover.[724] Says writer Mary Desmond Pinkowish, a proponent of the locavore movement: "For decades, fast food has been seen as emblematic of just about everything that's destroying our bodies and our planet. These fast-food restaurants are proving we can have our burgers—and feel good about them too." Just in case we had any lingering doubt about a vegan diet having any chance of being the better alternative, Pinkowish drives her point home with this dismissive: "Menus in these new establishments cater to people who want healthier, tastier food—and want it fast—but who may not be keen on tofu burgers." Will somebody please treat her to a good vegan restaurant?

Here is my question to these writers: How can you believe that your report and understanding of the concepts *humane, environment, sustainability,* and *health* is accurate when you ignore the obvious? When we stop eating meat, eggs, and dairy, every one of these issues will be addressed, and we will have at least the chance to heal ourselves and the planet. The best humane, environmentally green, sustainable, and healthy choices do not exist in animal agriculture. But the washing continues.

The Hole of It

The pervasive omnivore culture that dominates the media also rules consumer education and beliefs at otherwise progressive food outlets. Whole Foods Market and Puget Sound Consumers Coop (PCC) do a great job of fostering organic and local sourcing of food. They support smaller-scale producers, and they selectively try to work against green and blue washing—except for animal agriculture—where they also stumble over what is truly humane and biocentric.

Using standards found in the carnist current human ecology, these merchants approve of grass-fed beef and chickens and pigs fed a vegetarian (grain) diet. The nine-store PCC Natural Markets serve 45 thousand members. This financially successful business both mirrors and perpetuates the omnivore movement because they are following their customer base that is oriented to omnivore beliefs. While they feel free to remind their members to source food locally, they do not challenge their members' core beliefs about carnism and its unsustainability.

Their animal-based product selections are described as being humane and environmentally sustainable; they dwarf the variety of vegan selections. I see little evidence of critical thinking or discussion about the attributes of vegan human ecology there and at their non-coop competitor, Whole Foods Market. Both seem to be trying to please everyone without admitting—or by employing willed ignorance—to the unsustainability of carnist culture. They are comfortable in being at the forefront of organic and socially just food production, but not on vegan environmental and vegan humane issues. Both merchants recently made an amazing effort to label product shelves helpful to gluten-intolerant customers, but not vegans. Their practices are not rational; they are cultural.

These merchants represent carnist culture; though they are upgraded to sustainability version 3.0, we need to be at 10. They still are based on the worldview that we have the right to steal the breath and life of sentient beings whenever we wish and they settle for the current human ecology. Whole Foods made a great vegan birthday cake for me recently, but at the same time, their newest Seattle store featured this sign over their meat counter: "Righteously Raised." Below it, body parts of many species, including bison, were there under glass. Another sign comforted customers that Whole Foods dealt directly with small operators who "know" their animals and produce the highest quality of meat. Whole Foods, like all other meat merchants, would have us forget that each of their refrigerated meat cases is just an additional room in the slaughterhouse. An abattoir under glass. Done. Finished. Their green, blue, and humane washing machines have cleansed our concerns.

We are being ushered into a room of forgetfulness they have built for us. There are wonderful things here. But they mean for us to forget what veganism does for ecosystems. In this marketing-inspired amnesia, we do not have to remember how we shoot wolves and poison coyotes and black-tailed prairie dogs; we are not concerned how we chill millions of birds to death; and we leave our empathy at the door by not caring about how we dehorn, castrate, punch holes in their ears, and burn brands into living cattle skins without anesthetics. Those ingredients are not on their labels. We hide behind the plausible denial these merchants provide us. We are free from remembering that most pigs' tails were cut off because we have been green, blue, and humane washed by the banners boasting the meat is organic, humane, and "certified." In this room, we are to forget we are grazing Earth's ecosystems in biblical proportions.

Karen Dawn reminds us in *Thanking the Monkey: Rethinking the Way We Treat Animals* (Harper, 2008) that "Organic dairy cow babies become organic veal. Their mothers, when no longer highly productive, become organic hamburgers." Someday, perhaps soon, everyone will realize that green, blue, and humane washing is not sustainable. It is nothing more than washing one's hands of responsibility.

Animal agriculturalists and the consumers who support them turn against the sentient beings under their control. Killing individuals from other species who are conditioned to trust us as we feed and shelter them, or as they move freely in our presence during hunting's off season, shows just how abruptly inconsistent we are in these relationships. Morally defensible behavior in relationships of trust requires us to be consistently nonviolent. Turning violent after establishing trust is called betrayal.[725] This primal betrayal of trust is so obvious that only willed ignorance can deflect it. Take for instance that we betray pigs by the tens of millions in the United States every year.

Marine biologist and animal behaviorist Lyall Watson, in *The Whole Hog*, describes one of his many encounters with pigs.

> The boar's response was instantaneous and reciprocal. He panted back, and I remembered that this was the way a pet bushpig in Africa had greeted me as a child. I replied once more in kind, and when the boar's long look softened, I knew for certain what I had already begun to suspect. I was looking at an ape in swine's clothing.[726]... My contention is that present knowledge already shows that pigs can and do distinguish between self and non-self and that they are able to comprehend quite complex circumstances, and respond to them in meaningful, perhaps even conceptual, ways. Pigs process thoughts. They understand 'if, then' situations, they apply previous experience to novel circumstances, and they interact with their environments, and with each other, as though they are conscious of the consequences.[727]

It is strange, even unforgiveable, how we act unconsciously in the business of eating. People who kill individuals from other species for food believe they have adequate justification and lack a murderer's sense of remorse over their betrayal. Tamara Murphy's *food* and Michael Pollan's *food* had no choice. For consumers of boutique animal agriculture, and for omnivorous chefs and an uncritical media, this is about the palate's taste buds in their mouths. Justice does not live there.

Consumers who believe that buying animal products from smaller family farms is sustainable are celebrating too quickly. In at least one 2011 study, grass-fed cattle were found to produce far more CO_2 per pound of carcass weight than "more efficient" factory farm production. Animal waste and resource use were higher in grass-fed production systems as well. The study considered several countries, including the United States. Though counterintuitive, this included subsistence-level herding in developing areas of the world.[728]

Green, blue, humane, sustainability, and religion washings are popular yet unsustainable time-wasting detours that maintain our bizarrely inconsistent behaviors toward other species and ecosystems. Though I have not seen him apply the term *green washing* to the omnivore movement, in *Hot, Flat, and Crowded*, Thomas L. Friedman evaluates the term *green revolution*: "That's not a revolution. That's a party. We're actually having a green party. And, I have to say, it's a lot of fun. I get invited to all the parties. But in America, at least, it is mostly a costume party. It's all about *looking* green—and everyone's a winner."[729]

How can omnivores who hide behind green and humane washing believe that less suffering is good, but ending it entirely is not best? How can any animal agriculturalist, large or small in scale, state that their claimed increase in sustainability is good, but much, much more sustainability gained in a vegan human ecology is not best? The humane washing and green washing animal agriculturalists and blue washing fishers cannot on their best day come close to the environmental, humane, and moral sustainability of a vegan new human ecology.

It lifts my heart to hear when people understand this. In a letter to the editor of *The Sun Magazine*, Geraldine King Hitt wrote, "I am still open to whatever changes will help me think and live better. My most recent change was to become a vegan and to quit eating for entertainment." She was 77 years old at the time.[730]

I meet good people like you everywhere I go. You live the Golden Rule principle of loving others as you would be loved. Love, compassion, consciousness, and self-awareness are at the core of the new human ecology because they are essential to our healthy relationships. As author and scientist James Speth wrote not long ago, "... today's challenges require a rapid evolution to a new consciousness.... It suggests that today's problems cannot be solved with today's mind. That should give us pause, for we know that changing minds can be slow and difficult."[731] Is it possible for the new human ecology to be your new mind?

Part VI:

Hope

Chapter 19:

This Is the Hope

At some critical point, the realization will set in that we share a common planet, that we are all affected, and that our neighbor's suffering is not unlike our own. At that juncture recriminations and retributions will be of little avail in addressing the enormity of the crisis at hand. Only by concerted action that establishes a collective sense of affiliation with the entire biosphere will we have a chance to ensure our future. This will require a biosphere consciousness.[732]

—Jeremy Rifkin, *The Empathic Civilization*

The New Human Ecology: Seven Results and How You Can Achieve Them

There is immense suffering in the destruction of ecosystems. They are alive. The suffering of billions of individuals from other species is inseparable from what we do to their ecosystems. We have had hundreds if not thousands of years of opportunity to create a different world than the one we have shaped today. We could and should have sought coexistence instead of ruthless dominion despite our ancestors' struggle to survive. For those of us alive today, and perhaps for a time those of the next generation, this is the last experience we will have of any semblance of nature. This is the last experience of its kind. As we use up nature, it collapses.

The new human ecology can prevent that collapse. We have choices to make about how we are going to conduct ourselves. Given our declining resource base and the ridiculous number of people we have produced, the odds of our succeeding at this late start are not that great. But we must try to save what is left and restore what is restorable. We *can* create the Seven Results.

Since we have overrun Earth with our consumption, numbers, and presence, we have only remnants of living systems to save, and often, not their wholeness. We have driven too many species to extinction and destroyed too much of the structural integrity of ecosystems to claim we are at a critical moment, or that we have but a few more years to change. We passed that critical point morally and ecologically some time ago; when we arrived at that threshold is debatable. But it can be measured by the reduction of ecosystem health and integrity, the wholesale subjugation of landscapes, atmospherescapes, and seascapes to human purposes, and our arrogant dismissal of the needs of individuals from other species, including their right to life without enduring suffering at our hands. Who can claim that we have done enough to live honorably in these matters?

Once a species no longer exists, we forget about them. Except in rare moments of imagination, we have no easy way to remember that they were ever here. Once an extinction has drifted for a generation or two, we do not feel so much or care about the radical thing we have done. After enough time passes, it is as if they never existed.

Change

This is the to-do chapter. It is the time to talk about the joy of change. We are creating hope out of the goodness we find within ourselves and driven by the innate value of all species and ecosystems. They surround us and cheer us on invisibly and silently. We have learned about the importance and difficulty of protecting ecosystems. While we should celebrate our successes, there are two reasons we are not winning the struggle: Not enough of us are engaged in preventing the harm we are doing to Earth, and we have not agreed on universal principles and methods to achieve equally universal goals like the Seven Results. We can change that.

The premise behind the new human ecology and its Seven Results is simple: Life needs from us not one new behavior, but many. A single toxic element in a stream can kill all life. If one of the Seven Results is missing, the others will be ineffective. If we add 2.3 billion more people to Earth in 38 years, we will continue to lose ecosystems at an accelerating rate; billions of people already here will live in poverty forever.

The Seven Results are the goals of the new human ecology. We change our behaviors to create them. For most of us:

- The first fast track to the Seven Results is created when we change what we consume, from the organic grains we choose to the hair products we buy. We stop eating meat, eggs, and dairy, and discover the thousands of plant species to eat. We stop buying SUVs. We choose smaller homes and change how we heat and cool them. We stop buying leather shoes and leather car interiors. We boycott businesses that imprison orca whales.

- The second fast track is to stop making babies. One child at most can be enough for each family. We must reduce our populations now; slowing or leveling off population growth is not a sustainable, humane, and biocentric option.

- The third fast track is our love, empathy, and compassion. It will deliver us to social and economic justice as it will to species' rights. Do not underestimate its power to sustain us as we learn how to change our human ecology. We will wake up to the needs of impoverished people and invest in their desire to be in control of their lives.

That is the abbreviated way we create hope.

The Seven Results Revisited

In chapter 1, I described the Seven Results we must create if we are to thrive ecologically and morally as a species. Here they are revisited:

1) Healthy, intact ecosystems that dominate global landscapes and seascapes and require little to no human intervention

2) A vegan, organic, and humane consumer lifestyle oriented to sustainable efficiencies and relationships

3) Social and economic justice for all with transparency in public and corporate institutions

4) An immediate, negative population growth based on natural attrition

5) Economic systems that are ecologically sustainable and restorative, enable social and economic justice, moral, humane, and operate within the new human ecology

6) An increase in empathy, love, and compassion toward all beings and ecosystems

7) Appropriate, sustainable, and equitable consumption of goods and services

All Seven Results are required to create the new human ecology.

Each of the Seven Results has a synergistic effect on the other six. They feed and strengthen one another to create a solid new human ecology. Moving to a vegan ecosystem niche and steeply reducing human populations may feel like radical steps, but consider how radically unsustainable and harmful we are living today. The Seven Results signal a de-radicalization of our current human ecology. They are direct and pragmatic goals. Life will be better for us because it will be better for all species.

Getting agreement on the details of each of the Seven Results will be a challenge. Vested economic interests and powerful institutions are, like us, innately resistant to cultural and personal change. Social and economic justice, one of the Seven Results, sounds good, but there will be vivid disagreement about how we achieve it. The bigger the change, and this is big, the more we will tend to avoid it and find reasons to reject anything outside of our comfort zones, worldviews, and ideologies. We are strong enough to do this.

We are walking away from the carnist, morally inept, current human ecology because it leads directly to a future none will be able to bear, a future no good soul would choose. If we make the right choices, we may be able to create an environmentally sustainable and humane future, but only if there is a consensus that there exist some universal human values and behaviors that are adaptable to ecosystems on the scale Earth needs.

The Seven Results are purposefully and by necessity broad. Yet they assume that specific human behaviors will be needed to produce them. How we achieve each of the Seven Results will be a creative process. Those few billions of us who have access to wealth and resources have the greatest ability and responsibility to implement the Seven Results immediately. That does not exclude what can be done in the presence of poverty. For all of us, rich and poor, this is our species' moment, our era.

Population: The Ethics of Carrying Capacity for Humans

I look at Earth's carrying capacity for humans as existing on two levels: local and non-local. Local is the ecosystem where we physically live. Perhaps the majority of our impacts to ecosystems and relationships with other species and people occur at and near where we reside. It depends on our lifestyle choices. We also create non-local impacts upon ecosystems and relationships with other species and people in places far from our homes. From a distance, we affect and limit carrying capacities in places populated by other people and ecosystems.

Vegan chocolate is delicious. However, if we buy non-organic chocolate that is not certified for paying cocoa workers a living wage (Fair Trade), we have poisoned their ecosystem and reduced the quality of life for others who are a hemisphere away. We also have reduced the carrying capacities of the ecosystem for humans and all the other species where the cocoa is grown. That is just one transaction. Add together all the resource transactions from all places and we get our species' demand upon Earth's total carrying capacity for us. Other species need room in the ecosystems to survive. They have rights to exist and flourish in meaningful numbers as much as we do. Reducing our population can make that possible.

The carrying capacity for humans can be measured in a few ways: our total population (local and global), our aggregate local and global consumption of ecosystem services, the general health of ecosystems, and the diversity and abundance of other species. If we know these, we may then get some idea of the number of people that a given amount of habitat can sustainably support at an acceptable social and economic standard of living while maintaining maximum biodiversity and abundance.

As part of the population and carrying capacity discussion, we need to define what *enough* is. Enough people, enough personal consumption, enough petrochemical-fueled travel, enough individual wealth, and enough of everything we do that affects every species' and ecosystems' long-term sustainability. Depending on culturally relevant middle-class living standards, enough may vary a lot, or not so much.

I must repeat this: The United Nations projects our population will reach 9.3 billion in the year 2050 before social and economic changes are *expected* to cause a decline. Tied to a population of 9.3 billion is the assumption and acceptance of the inevitable suffering and loss we will cause for individuals from other species, species, other people, and ecosystems.

How acceptable is it to us that multitudes of other species will be reduced to biological insignificance? How many individuals will die, and in what manner? Starvation? Thirst? Depression? How many more intricately social elephants will suffer the trauma of seeing their family herd gunned down because there are too many desperate people, poor people, encroaching upon their habitat? How many wolves will have their social relationships ripped from their packs as they are gunned down because people insist on eating animal products? How many individuals from other species will be homeless when we cut down their forests for lumber and palm oil plantations? For us and other species, quality of life counts. Apes have it. Amazon otters have it. Snow leopards have it. Pikas and Ganges River dolphins have it. The now extinct Great Auks, Passenger Pigeons, and Steller Sea Cows had it.

Our new human ecology means we are becoming a different kind of human being. We are fulfilling our capacities to be just, compassionate, and— realistic. We honor life when we keep our own populations relatively low, our quality of life high, and other species far more abundant than now.

In *Requiem for Nature*, John Terbough, Research Professor Emeritus and Director, Center for Tropical Conservation, reminds us that

> ... sustainable development is currently unobtainable. Certainly, sustainable growth is not being practiced by any society that lives in the modern money economy.... to equate sustainable development with the perpetuation of biodiversity is a mistake. Sustainable development means development, just as sustainable use means the exploitation of natural resources.[733]

If common sense has us agreeing that endless growth of human impact is wrong, then we must look to our own lives to stop it. The Seven Results are our minimum goals. We could add more: the absence of war and civil conflict, a world that prioritizes cultures of nonaggression and peace, the elimination of nuclear weapons, and policies that guarantee citizens everywhere the rights to control and own food resources. The possibilities for good are limitless.

The New Human Ecology: What It Will Do

The new human ecology can be the transformation of human behavior all of Earth has waited for. We are the people to do it. It is an adaptive revision, a reformation of the outgoing current human ecology. As our new human ecology replaces the current human ecology, person-by-person, we begin to restore Earth.

The Seven Results created by the new human ecology change nearly everything. The sun will rise and set on a different Earth. In review:

- Vast landscapes now subjected to grazing and growing food for livestock is released from animal agriculture. It is restored over time to the extent possible by conservation biologists in service to a biocentric vegan human ecology.

- Some of that land will be banked and rotated with other croplands. This allows the land to lie fallow, rested, and then rotated back into production. Soil erosion and pollution are sharply reduced. Sustainably grown, organic food becomes more reliably available. Banked cropland held in reserve provides stability in times of unforeseen need and climate change. Botanical agriculture is in; animal agriculture is out.[734]

- Conceivably, fewer people on Earth and the efficiency of botanical agriculture will allow lower food prices and raise food availability to people who are now denied the right to adequate nutrition for whatever reason. Botanical agriculture will seek to end hunger locally by growing food locally.

- We will reduce our greenhouse gas emissions immediately by 18 to 51 percent.

- Other human pressures on ecosystems decrease and allow them to trend toward recovery.

- Demand for irrigation water decreases dramatically. We will slow or stop the depletion of fossil water taken from aquifers. Water pollution drops, quality increases.

- Wherever agriculture is dependent upon oil imports, we reduce those imports and the global environmental impacts from petroleum extraction, refining, and transport. Petrochemicals are no longer used to grow crops fed to livestock.

- Vegan diets will create better human health. This should result in lower health care costs that are a social burden on personal and national economies. With better health, our quality of life increases.

- We stop the intentional impregnation of billions of domesticated individuals from other species, the torment of their enslavement and denial of their innate needs, and their early, violent deaths. The slaughter falls precipitously and then screeches to a halt in a relatively short time.

- The science and implementation of wildlife and habitat management is transformed; its mission is socially shaped to become more biocentrically oriented. Control by the small minority of people who hunt, fish, and trap is ended. Once invasive livestock are removed, grazing lands will be restored as close as possible to indigenous wildlife habitat and other ecosystem services. The profession will need far more people than present in response. Wildlife slaughter and population manipulation will drop sharply.

- A steady state economy will create ecosystem-based human economic systems. We closely examine the differences between the natural order of value and the economic order of value in our pricing of goods and services.

- Animal agriculture is the largest consumer of pharmaceuticals. When it ends, these drugs stay out of ecosystems.

- Livestock fences will be removed. Wild herds of indigenous wildlife can reoccupy habitat and have room to migrate long distances. Ecosystem keystone species like black-tailed prairie dogs will not be cruelly persecuted on behalf of animal agriculture.

- There are no new ghost nets, those fishing nets that break away from vessels, drift with oceanic currents, and continue to trap fish, turtles, marine birds, and marine mammals.

- We stop bottom trawling that destroys benthic (seabed) marine ecosystems. Since vegan human ecology does not require fish, it ends the trashing of millions of tons of unwanted bycatch (non-targeted species), eliminates shark finning that is decimating shark populations, stops the killing of octopi, and ends the drowning of dolphins and turtles.[735]

- Many dead zones like the one in the Gulf of Mexico are created by agricultural runoff. A vegan human ecology supports restoration to that and similar ecosystems.

- We finally create a moral code of behavior that is based upon biocentric innate value; it is more consistently applied to all individuals of all species and ecosystems.

- In our cultural expectations, we act out of empathy, love, and compassion to support societal goals for social and economic justice not only for us, but for all people.

A study titled "Evaluating the environmental impact of various dietary patterns combined with different food production systems" compared the environmental impacts of a vegan diet to vegetarian, omnivore, and a mainstream Italian "regular" diet. It used the following criteria: carcinogens, respiratory organics, respiratory inorganics, climate change, ozone layer, ecotoxicity, land use, minerals, fossil fuels, and acidification/eutrophication (the excess nutrients in a body of water that results in oxygen depletion and the death of species). The vegan diet was the winner. An organic vegan diet shone even brighter. [736]

Scientists and NGOs are losing hope of restoring truly wild, self-regulating ecosystems; the new human ecology restores that hope. The new human ecology refuses to allow our irresponsible behavior of the past become the model for our future. We are freeing ourselves from the worldviews, beliefs, habits, and industries that are ruining Earth like a permanent eclipse of the sun. We refuse to be hunter, fisher, and animal agriculturalist predators. We pledge to get our mega, presence, and economic neo-predations under control. This is our time. We are leaving the current human ecology behind and embracing the new. The new human ecology is the foundation, but not the completed home. But it does answer the question, "What can I do to create hope?"

pine forests ready to burn from Canada's Pacific coast to the Maritime Provinces, in the white nose disease that is decimating bats, and the disappearing populations of amphibians and bees.

If you are not already vegan for environmental and moral reasons, you and I go through each day seeing different things. If you are intent on having several children, we do not see the same future. Everywhere I turn, I see needless suffering in the markets where I buy food, at birthday parties, on the street, on TV, in the newspapers, in casual conversation, virtually everywhere I look, including the words coming out of our mouths.

We are never excused from the responsibilities of our consumption. The stories behind the products we consume motivate us, pain us, outrage us, empower us, and too often overwhelm us. Do not wait for perfection in the new human ecology or the Seven Results; you will not find it because this is a public and very human work in progress. It is waiting to be creatively applied to what we do with our lives. And it takes time that we do not have.

In impoverished northeast Brazil, mothers put rocks in boiling water, telling their starving children to wait, "the food is cooking," so their children will stop crying and fall asleep, exhausted in their long anticipation of a meal that does not exist.[738] In a region south of their home, food is exported. There, the Brazilian rainforest has been obliterated on a massive scale for the industrial production of soybeans. Those soybeans are given to cattle in Brazil and also shipped long distances to feed the livestock of the European meat industry. This is a tragedy that originates in warped economic systems and profit taking, part of the worldviews that do not recognize the natural order of value in people and ecosystems.

We do not need more dire predictions; we need to act. Hunter, fisher, and animal agriculture models are no longer adaptive and of no use to our survival. In fact, the reformation of our dietary choices in a vegan new human ecology is as important as the development of agriculture and the domestication of other species some 10,000 years ago. I do not exaggerate.

Anticipate the joy you will give the world—and receive. Take time to restore yourself, because the reality I have described to you about our current human ecology, the state of Earth and her species, is overwhelming. Yet there is beauty all around us.

Listen to raindrops, the voice of falling snow, music you love, and your heart. Take extra time and focus on being with the people you love and doing the things that fulfill you. Get out and experience nature, even if you only can open a window. Feel at peace, and know that you are doing something profoundly good. After all of the dark I have described in this book, you are the light in this story

You are the hope.

References

Recommended NGOs and Links

Green Vegans / The New Human Ecology - www.greenvegans.org
Vegan Outreach - www.veganoutreach.org
Earth Island Institute – www.earthisland.org
United Poultry Concerns - www.upc-online.org
The Vegan Society - www.vegansociety.com
Farm Sanctuary - www.vegforlife.org/earth.htm
Vegfam relief organization - www.vegfamcharity.org.uk
Food for life - http://www.ffl.org/
A Well Fed World - www.awellfedworld.org/feeddirect
Amboseli Elephant Trust - http://www.elephanttrust.org
HumaneMYTH.org (Deconstructing the Myth of Humane Animal
    Agriculture) - http://www.humanemyth.org/index.htm
Tribe of Heart - http://tribeofheart.org/
E - The Environmental Magazine - http://www.emagazine.com/
TerraMar Research - http://terramarresearch.org/
Daily Climate - www.dailyclimate.org

End Notes

1) Dicke, M., Agrawa, Anurag A., Bruin, Jan. 2003. Plants talk, but are they deaf? TRENDS in *Plant Science* Vol.8 No.9 September 2003. (p. 403) http://www.eeb.cornell.edu/agrawal/pdfs/2003/dicke-2003-ts-plants-talk.pdf. Accessed 3/5/2012.

2) Baldwin, Ian T., Kessler, André., Halitschke, Rayko. Volatile signaling in plant–plant–herbivore interactions:
what is real? *Science* 10 February 2006: Vol. 311 no. 5762, pp. 812–815. DOI: 10.1126/*Science*.1118446. http://www.faperta.ugm.ac.id/newbie/download/pak_tar/biochemistry/plantherbivoreinteraction3.pdf. Accessed 3/5/2012.

3) Population Reference Bureau, http://www.prb.org/Articles/2002/HowMany PeopleHaveEverLivedonEarth.aspx. Accessed 12/6/2011.

4) Marten, Gerald G. *Human Ecology/Basic Concepts for Sustainable Development.* Earthscan Publications Ltd. London, UK. 2001.

5) Wilson, Edmund O. *The Future of Life.* Borzoi Book/Published by Alfred A. Knopf. 2002. (p. 3) "The totality of life, known as the biosphere to scientists and creation to theologians, is a membrane of organisms wrapped around Earth so thin it cannot be seen edgewise from a space shuttle, yet so internally complex that most species composing it remain undiscovered. The membrane is seamless. From Everest's peak to the floor of the Mariana Trench, creatures of one kind or another inhabit virtually every square inch of the planetary surface. They obey the fundamental principle of biological geography, that wherever there is liquid water, organic molecules, and an energy source, there is life."

6) Speth, James Gustave. *The Bridge at the End of the World /Capitalism, the Environment, and Crossing from Crisis to Sustainability.* A Caravan Book. 2008. (p. 36) "Nothing–not national or international laws, global bioreserves, local sustainability schemes, or even 'wildlands' fantasies–can change the current course....The broad path for biological evolution is now set for several million years. And in this sense the extinction crisis – the race to save the composition, structure, and organization of biodiversity as it exists today– is over, and we have lost."

7) Wilson, Edmund O. *The Future of Life.* Borzoi Book/Published by Alfred A. Knopf. 2002. (pp. 10–11)

8) Female Genital Cutting (FGC) is an invasive cultural practice that removes part or all of the external female genitalia. This act is dangerous, yet it is very common in Africa and parts of Asia and the Middle East. http://www.care.org/newsroom/specialreports/fgc/index.asp . Up to 140 million girls and women worldwide are currently living with the consequences of FGC. There are an estimated 3 million girls in Africa at risk of undergoing female genital cutting every year; this number soars when girls at risk all around the world are added into the figure. FGC causes serious psychological and health complications. The practice is often done under unsanitary conditions, and without anesthesia. The average age of girls forced to undergo FGC is between 4 and 12. There are no health benefits of FGC.

9) Joy, Melanie. "From Carnivore to Carnist: Liberating the Language of Meat." *Satya Magazine*, September 2001. http://www.satyamag.com/sept 01/joy.html.

10) Joy, Melanie. *Why We Love Dogs, Eat Pigs, and Wear Cows /An Introduction to Carnism.* Conari Press. 2010. (p.18)

11) Ralston III, Holmes. *Environmental Ethics/Duties to and Values in The Natural World*. Temple University Press. 1988. (pp. 60–61)

12) Ralston III, Holmes. *Environmental Ethics/Duties to and Values in The Natural World*. Temple University Press. 1988. (p.47)

13) Regan, Tom. *Defending Animal Rights*. University of Illinois Press. 2001. (p. 21) and p. 35. In contrast to Rolston's comments, Regan writes, "When a system is unjust to the core, respect for justice demands abolition."

14) Fussell, Betty. *Raising Steaks/The Life and Times of American Beef*. Harcourt of Houghton Mifflin Harcourt. 2008.

15) Pollan, Michael. *Omnivores Dilemma/A Natural History of Four Meals.* Penguin Books. 2006.

16) Illinois Soybean Association. http://www.ilsoy.org/index.cfm?pageID=90. Accessed 9/19/2011.

17) Cohen, Joel M. How Many People Can the World Support? Stated Meeting Report. "This presentation was given at the 1806th Stated Meeting, held at the House of the Academy in Cambridge on December 10, 1997." He also has a book of the same title, "*How Many People Can the Earth Support?*" W. W. Norton & Company (1995).

18) http://www.census.gov/population/international/data/idb/worldhis.php.

Accessed 11/27/2011.

19) http://www.un.org/News/briefings/docs/2011/110503_Population.doc.htm.
     Accessed 11/27/2011.

20) The Millennium Development Goals Report. 2009. United Nations. New
     York. http://mdgs.un.org/unsd/mdg/Resources/Static/Products/Progress20
     09/MDG_Report_2009_En.pdf. Accessed 1/30/2010.

21) Foreman, Dave. *Rewilding North America/A Vision for Conservation in the 21st
     Century.* Island Press/The Center for Resource Economics. 2004. [page 61
     that cites Aldo Leopold, "The Round River–A Parable," in *Round River: From
     the Journals of Aldo Leopold* (Oxford University Press, New York, 1972), 165].

22) Conversation: David Orr discusses ecological instruction in the 21st century.
     Earth Island Journal. FindArticles.com. 11 Jan, 2010. http://findarticles
     .com/p/articles/mi_hb6393/is_4_22/ai_n29399120/. *Earth Island Journal.*
     Winter, 2009. www.earthisland.org.

23) Marten, Gerald G. *Human Ecology/Basic Concepts for Sustainable Development.*
     Earthscan Publications Ltd. London, UK. 2001.

24) Schlaepfer, Martin A., Runge, Michael C., Sherman, Paul W. Ecological and
     evolutionary traps. *TRENDS in Ecology & Evolution.* Vol.17 No.10 October
     2002. http://www.esf.edu/efb/schlaepfer/PDFs/Ecologicalpercent20andper
     cent20Evolutionarypercent20Traps.pdf.

25) Daily, G. C., Alexander, S., Ehrlich, P. R., Goulder, L., Lubchenco, J., Matson,
     P. A., Mooney, H. A., Postel, S. L., Schneider, S. H., Tilman, D., Woodwell, G.
     M., 1999. Ecosystem Services: Benefits Supplied to Human Societies by
     Natural Ecosystems. *Issues in Ecology.* http://www.sierraforestlegacy.org/
     Resources/Conservation/FireForestEcology/ForestEconomics/Economics-
     Daily97.pdf. Accessed 1/27/2010.

26) Living Beyond Our Means: Natural Assets and Human Well-being.
     Statement from the Board. March 2005. A report for the United Nations
     General Assembly. (in its Statement of the Board) http://www.millenniu-
     massessment.org/documents/document.429.aspx.pdf. Accessed 1/07/2010.

27) http://www.cascadiaresearch.org/WSeattle-ER.htm. Accessed 3/25/2011.
     And a follow-up email.

28) Examination of gray whale from west Seattle reveals unusual stomach
     contents but no definitive cause of death. Cascadia Research.
     http://www.cascadiaresearch.org/WSeattle-ER.htm. Accessed 4/20/2010.

29) College of Human Ecology. Kansas State University. http://www.humec.k-

state.edu/about/history-humec.php. Accessed 11/10/2009.

30) http://www.societyforhumanecology.org/.

31) Ethology is the study of nonhuman species' behavior.

32) Bekoff, Marc. "Redecorating Nature: Reflections on Science, Holism, Community, Humility, Reconciliation, Spirit, Compassion, and Love." *Human Ecology Review*, Vol. 7, No. 1, 2000. (p. 60–67) http://www.humane-cologyreview.org/pastissues/her71/71bekoff.pdf.

33) http://www.queensu.ca/philosophy/People/Faculty/smithmick.html. Accessed 7/23/2011.

34) Smith, Mick. "The 'Ethical" Space of the Abattoir: On the (In)human(e) Slaughter of Other Animals." *Human Ecology Review*, Vol. 9, No. 2, 2002. (p.49–58)

35) Berry, Thomas. *The Dream of the Earth*. Sierra Club Books, San Francisco, CA. 1988. (p. 37)

36) University of California–Berkeley. "Doomsday messages about global warming can backfire, study shows." *ScienceDaily*. 19 November 2010. 3 December 2010. http://www.sciencedaily.com/releases/2010/11/1011170942 48.htm.

37) Advocating Meat Reduction and Vegetarianism to US Adults. Humane Research Council. 2007. http://www.humanespot.org/system/files/HRC_Veg_Study_2007.pdf.

38) Marten, Gerald G. *Human Ecology/Basic Concepts for Sustainable Development*. Earthscan Publications Ltd. London, UK. 2001.

39) Townsend, Patricia K. *Environmental Anthropology / From Pigs to Policies*. Second Edition. Waveland Press. 2009, 2000. (p. 70)

40) U.S. Census Bureau. http://www.census.gov/. Accessed 2/21/2011.

41) Allison, I., et al. The Copenhagen Diagnosis, 2009: Updating the World on the Latest Climate Science . The University of New South Wales Climate Change Research Centre (CCRC), Sydney, Australia, p. 60 www.copen-hagendiagnosis.com. Accessed 12/5/2009.

42) http://co2now.org/Current-CO2/CO2-Now/annual-co2.html. Accessed 1/23/2012.

43) http://co2now.org/Current-CO2/CO2-Widget/. Accessed 3/7/2012.

44) http://co2now.org/Current-CO2/CO2-Now/. NOAA-ESRL. Accessed 7/30/2012.

45) Ramankutty, N., Evan, A. T. , Monfreda, C., and Foley, J. A. 2008. Farming

the planet: Geographic distribution of global agricultural lands in the year 2000. *Global Biogeochem. Cycles*, 22, GB1003, doi:10.1029/2007GB002952.

46) Pimentel, David and Kounang, Nadia. 1998. Ecology of Soil Erosion in Ecosystems. *Ecosystems* (1998) 1: 416–426. http://www.ciens.ucv.ve:8080/generador/sites/ProVeg/archivos/Seminariopercent201percent20Nuria ngel.pdf. Accessed 12/14/2010.

47) Newsletter of the Species Survival Commission. International Union for the Conservation of Nature/IUCN. *Species 48:* July–December 2007. http://cmsdata.iucn.org/downloads/species_48_web.pdf. Accessed 11/22/2009.

48) International Union for the Conservation of Nature. Wildlife in a Changing World: An analysis of the 2008 IUCN Red List of Threatened Species. http://cmsdata.iucn.org/downloads/wildlife_in_a_changing_world.pdf. Accessed 11/20/2009.

49) IUCN. Extinction crisis continues apace. November 3, 2009 press release. http://www.iucn.org/about/work/programmes/species/red_list/?4143/Extinction-crisis-continues-apace. Accessed 12/5/2010.

50) Baker, Scott C. and Clapham, Phillip J. 2004. Modeling the past and future of whales and whaling. *Trends in Ecology and Evolution*. Vol. 19, No. 7.

51) http://www.unfpa.org/swp/. Accessed 10/30/2011.

52) "2050: A third more mouths to feed." September 23, 2009. FAO Media Center. http://www.fao.org/news/story/en/item/35571/icode/. Accessed 2/4/2010.

53) Turner II, B.L., et. al. 2007. The emergence of land change science for global environmental change and sustainability. Proceedings from the National Academy of Science U.S. *PNAS*, vol. 104, no. 52. December 26, 2007. www.pnas.org_cgi_doi_10.1073_pnas.0704119104. http://www.pnas.org/content/104/52/20666.full.pdf. Accessed 10/22/2009.

54) Diamond, Jared. *Collapse/How Societies Choose to Fail or Succeed*. Penguin Books, Publishers. NY, NY. 2005. (p.6, soft cover)

55) Foreman, Dave. *Rewilding North America/A Vision for Conservation in the 21st Century*. Island Press/The Center for Resource Economics. 2004. (introduction). Bullets added.

56) Friedman, Thomas L. *Hot, Flat, and Crowded / Why We Need A Green Revolution – And How It Can Renew America*. Farrar, Straus, Giroux. 2008. (p. 27) He cites Conservation International frequently, including their extinction estimate. (p. 141) Bullets added.

57) Edwards, Andres R. *The Sustainability Revolution / Portrait of a Paradigm Shift.* New Society Publishers. 2005. Bullets added.

58) Goodall, Jane and Bekoff, Marc. *The Ten Trusts / What We Must Do For the Animals We Love.* Harper Collins. 2002.

59) Speth, James Gustave. *The Bridge at the End of the World / Capitalism, the Environment, and Crossing from Crisis to Sustainability.* A Caravan Book. 2008. (p. 45)

60) Myerson, George. *Ecology and the End of Postmodernity.* Totem Books (USA). 2001. Though much of this essay goes beyond my background of referencing earlier writers on the subject, this quote struck me as a reverberation of what the new human ecology is trying to settle.

61) Goodland, Robert and Anhang, Jeff. Livestock and Climate Change: What if the key actors in climate change are…cows, pigs, chickens? *World Watch.* November/December 2009. (p. 10-19) (possibly citing FAO statistics). http://www.worldwatch.org/files/pdf/Livestockpercent20andpercent 20Climatepercent20Change.pdf. Accessed 11/17/2009.

62) Goodland, Robert and Anhang, Jeff. Livestock and Climate Change: What if the key actors in climate change are…cows, pigs, chickens? World Watch. November/December 2009. (pp. 10–19) http://www.worldwatch.org /files/pdf/Livestockpercent20andpercent20Climatepercent20Change.pdf. Accessed 11/17/2009.

63) Food and Agriculture Organization of the United Nations (FAO); Livestock's Long Shadow; Environmental Issues and Options. 2006. ftp://ftp.fao.org/docrep/fao/010/a0701e/a0701e00.pdf.

64) Food and Agriculture Organization of the United Nations (FAO); Livestock's Long Shadow; Environmental Issues and Options. 2006. ftp://ftp.fao.org/docrep/fao/010/a0701e/a0701e00 pdf. Accessed 11/17/2009. "In all, livestock production accounts for 70 percent of all agricultural land and 30 percent of the land surface of the planet."

65) Read, Andrew J.; Drinker, P.; Northridge, S. 2006. Bycatch of Marine Mammals in U.S. and Global Fisheries. *Conservation Biology.* Vol. 20, No. 1, pp. 163–169. "The preponderance of gill-net vessels in the global fleet, coupled with the known high bycatch rates of marine mammals in gill-net fisheries in the United States, suggests that most of the world's cetacean and pinniped bycatch occurs in gill-net fisheries… For example, Zhou and Wang (1994) estimated that 3.5 million gill nets were in use in China in the

early 1990s." http://www.nero.noaa.gov/prot_res/atgtrp/ai/gr/10.pdf. Accessed 10/11/2009.

66) http://www.grist.org/article/sour-milk. Accessed 10/11/2009.

67) What is Poverty? The World Bank. http://web.worldbank.org/WB SITE/EXTERNAL/TOPICS/EXTPOVERTY/EXTPA/0,,contentMDK:20153855 ~menuPK:435040~pagePK.

68) Human Development Report 2010. http://hdr.undp.org/en/media/ HDR_2010_EN_Complete_reprint.pdf.

69) World Bank. Food Price Watch. http://www.worldbank.org/food crisis/foodpricewatch/april_2011.html. Accessed 7/30/2010. "Global food prices remain high, partly due to increasing fuel prices, and the World Bank's Food Price Index is around its 2008 peak. Since June 2010, an additional 44 million people fell below the $1.25 poverty line as a result of higher food prices."

70) The Millennium Development Goals Report. 2011. United Nations. New York. http://www.un.org/millenniumgoals/pdf/percent282011_Epercent29 percent20MDGpercent20Reportpercent202011_Bookpercent20LR.pdf

71) http://www.worldbank.org/foodcrisis/food_price_watch_report_feb201 1.htm. Accessed 3/12/2011.

72) High Commodity Prices: Impact on poor people. World Bank. http:// web.worldbank.org/WBSITE/EXTERNAL/EXTDEC/EXTDECPROSPECTS/ GEPEXT/EXTGEP2009/0,,contentMDK:22002680. "… For very poor people, reducing consumption from already low levels even for a short period has severe long-term consequences. Higher food prices during 2008 alone may have increased the number of children suffering permanent cognitive and physical injury due to malnutrition by 44 percent."

73) The Millennium Development Goals Report, 2011. United Nations. New York. http://www.un.org/millenniumgoals/pdf/percent282011_Epercent29 percent20MDGpercent20Reportpercent202011_Bookpercent20LR.pdf

74) Conflict, Security, and Development. World Development Report. 2011. http://wdr2011.worldbank.org/fulltext. Accessed 2/24/2012.

75) *ScienceDaily.* July 27, 2008. "Riley E. Dunlap, PhD, of Oklahoma State University and Richard York, PhD, of the University of Oregon compared results from four large cross-national surveys, each conducted in several dozen nations ranging with differing economic statuses. Representative samples of citizens were surveyed in each nation." http://www.

sciencedaily.com/releases/2008/07/080725114548.htm. Accessed 12/5/2010.

76) http://www.unfpa.org/swp/. Accessed 10/30/2011.

77) McKee, Jeffrey K. 2009. Contemporary Mass Extinction and the Human Population Imperative. *Journal of Cosmology*. 2009, Vol 2, pages 300-308. Cosmology, October 27, 2009. http://journalofcosmology.com/Extinction 104.html. Accessed 2/22/2010.

78) Smail, Kenneth J. 1997. Beyond Stabilization: The Case for Dramatically Reducing Global Human Numbers. *Politics and Life Sciences. PLS*, 16(2), 183–192. Beech Tree Publishing. UK. http://www.jstor.org/pss/4236335. Accessed 3/2/2011.

79) http://www.census.gov/ipc/www/popclockworld.html.

80) Weisman, Alan. *The World Without Us*. Picador/Thomas Dunne Books/St. Martin's Press. 2007. (p.349)

81) Howmany.org. "That is 1 billion more people every 12 years." http://www.howmany.org/big_picture.php. Accessed 4/22/2010. "Every year about 135 million people are born and 55 million people die..."

82) Fahrenthold, David A. *Washington Post* Staff Writer. When it Comes to Pollution, Less (Kids) May Be More. September 15, 2009 http://www.washingtonpost.com/wp-dyn/content/article/2009/09/14/AR 2009091403308_pf.html.Accessed 12/16/2009.

83) Murtaugh, V. and Schlax, Michael G. 2009. Reproduction and the carbon legacies of individuals. *Global Environmental Change*. 19 (2009) 14–20. doi:10.1016/j.gloenvcha.2008.10.007. http://blog.oregonlive.com/environm ent_impact/2009/07/carbonpercent20legacy.pdf. Accessed 12/16/2009.

84) http://www.vhemt.org/.

85) Hawken, Paul. *Blessed Unrest / How the Largest Movement in the World Came into Being and Why No One Saw It Coming*. Viking. Published by the Penguin Group. 2007. (p. 33)

86) Center for the Advancement of the Steady State Economy (CASSE). http://steadystate.org/.

87) Czech, Brian and Daly, Herman E. 2004. "In My Opinion: The steady state economy—what it is, entails, and connotes." *Wildlife Society Bulletin*. 2004, 32(2):598–605. http://steadystate.org/files/SSE.pdf. Accessed 10/20/2009.

88) Hawken, Paul. *The Ecology of Commerce*. Harper Business / Harper Collins. 1993. (p. 75, 27 and preface)

89) Rifkin, Jeremy. *The Empathic Civilization / The Race to Global Consciousness In*

a World In Crisis. Jeremy P. Tarcher/Penguin, publishers. 2009. (p. 593, 616)

90) Kumar, Satish. 2008. "Nonviolent Change, a Good Idea." *Conservation Biology.* Volume 22 Issue 2. 2008. (p. 239–240)

91) Christensen, Jennie R. et al. 2005. Persistent Organic Pollutants in British Columbia Grizzly Bears:
Consequence of Divergent Diets. *Environmental Science and Technology.* Vol. 39. No. 18. 6952-6960. Published on the web 08/04/2005.
http://www.raincoast.org/files/publications/papers/POPs-in-BC-grizzlies. pdf. Accessed 4/22/2010.

92) Ramsussen, Larry L. "Cosmology and Ethics." Union Theological Society. page 173 in *Worldviews and Ecology: Religion, Philosophy, and the Environment.* Mary Evelyn Tucker and John A. Grim, Eds. 1997. Associated University Presses, Inc. Third printing, 1997. Orbis Books.

93) Tucker, Mary Evelyn and Grim, John A., Eds. *Worldviews and Ecology: Religion, Philosophy, and the Environment.* 1994.Preface, page 12. Associated University Presses, Inc. Third printing, 1997. Orbis Books.

94) Devall, Bill and Sessions, George. *Deep Ecology.* Gibbs Smith, publisher. Peregrine Smith Books. 1985. (p.42)

95) Devall, Bill and Sessions, George. *Deep Ecology.* Gibbs Smith, publisher. Peregrine Smith Books. 1985. (p.42). The authors are in turn citing, Kuhn, Thomas, *The Structure of Scientific Revolutions,* 2nd ed. (Chicago: University of Chicago Press, 1970).

96) Devall, Bill and Sessions, George. *Deep Ecology.* Gibbs Smith, publisher. Peregrine Smith Books. 1985. (p.42)

97) Mason, Jim. *An Unnatural Order / Uncovering the Roots of Our Domination of Nature and Each Other.* Simon and Schuster, publishers. 1993. (p.22)

98) Scully, Matthew. *Dominion: The Power of Man, the Suffering of Animals, and the Call to Mercy.* St. Martin's Griffin, NY 10010. 2002. (p. 90)

99) Francione, Gary L. *Introduction to Animal Rights / Your Child or the Dog?* Temple University Press. 2000. * Francione writes that the originator of the term speciesism was Richard D. Ryder in *Victims of Science: The Use of Animals in Research.* London: Davis-Poynter, 1975.

100) Lyman, Howard F. with Glen Merzer. *Mad Cowboy / Plain Truth from the Cattle Rancher Who Won't Eat Meat.* Scribner, NY. 1998. From opening paragraph, Chapter 1. To learn more, go to http://www.madcowboy.com/.

101) *Peaceable Kingdom, The Journey Home.* Created by Tribe of Heart.

http://www.peaceablekingdomfilm.org/.

102) Guisepi, Robert, Editor. *Agriculture and the Origins of Civilization: The Neolithic Revolution.* International World History Project. http://history-world.org/agriculture.htm. Accessed 1/05/2010.

103) http://www.wdexpo.org/index.php?s=advertising. Posted 3/2/2009.

104) The Dairy Checkoff Program is managed by Dairy Management, Inc. (DMI). http://www.dairycheckoff.com/DairyCheckoff/AboutUs/About-Us. Accessed 12/16/2009.

105) http://www.dairycheckoff.com/NR/rdonlyres/5EA6B565-74DE-4FE1-9F71-6722904D392C/0/DairyCheckoffBrochureLoRes.pdf. Accessed 12/16/2009.

106) http://www.wdexpo.org/index.php?s=advertising. Accessed 12/16/2009. Posted 6/2/2009. "This month, McDonald's launched a campaign aimed at boosting McCafe espressos that will thereby boost milk sales. In total, McDonald's invested more than $1 billion in store remodeling and equipment costs, and $100 million a year in advertising and marketing support for the new beverages. Dairy producers, through the dairy checkoff, supported the McCafe launch by Providing consumer data and insights on milk and specialty coffee Assisting McDonald's on the introduction of specialty coffees and nationwide sampling efforts to build local awareness of McCafe espresso beverages "This is just the beginning," Rovey said. "The dairy checkoff is entering into a longer-term agreement with McDonald's that could lead to new milk and dairy menu options, including yogurt smoothies, espresso drinks, new cheeseburgers, and new single-serve, flavored milk options."

107) U.S. Department of Agriculture Economic Research Service. Briefing Rooms. http://www.ers.usda.gov/Briefing/Dairy/Background.htmm. Accessed 12/13/2010.

108) http://www.dairycheckoff.com/NR/rdonlyres/5EA6B565-74DE-4FE1-9F71-6722904D392C/0/DairyCheckoffBrochureLoRes.pdf. Accessed 12/16/2009. "Pizza offerings at schools remain a popular item among students - nearly 25 percent of school meals include pizza."

109) http://www.dairycheckoff.com/NR/rdonlyres/5EA6B565-74DE-4FE1-9F71-6722904D392C/0/DairyCheckoffBrochureLoRes.pdf. Accessed 12/16/2009.

110) www.veganoutreach.org. Accessed 8/8/2011. They do wonderful work.

111) According to the Animal Law Coalition, "Until this past year the United States Department of Agriculture interpreted the federal Twenty Eight

Hour Law, 49 USCS § 80502, so that most farm animals did not receive the protections of this law, the nation's first federal humane law. Under the law, animals must be humanely offloaded after 28 hours in transit on a 'common carrier,' 'vessel transporting animals,' or 'vehicle.'" The animals can then eat, drink and rest for at least five hours. http://www.animallaw coalition.com/farm-animals/article/202. Last accessed April 29.

112) Veal Defined. Veal Information Gateway. http://www.veal.ca/. "This article was created by veal.ca but can be freely published." Accessed 4/28/2009.

113) Veal Defined. Veal Information Gateway. http://www.veal.ca/. "This article was created by veal.ca but can be freely published." Accessed 4/28/2009.

114) http://www.veal.ca/veal-farming-in-canada/. Accessed 1/31/2010.

115) Home page and "A Future in Veal" web page. http://www.provitello.com/ Accessed 4/28/2009. The website link for this quote no longer works but was: A future in veal. Provitello offers dairies another option for their ... veal calves a year in Canada it has a U.S. processing operation near Utica, N.Y., and ...
http://www.provitellofarms.com/wp-content/plugins/article2pdf/ article2pdf_getfile.php?p=YS1mdXR1cmUtaW4tdmVhbA==&r=10ed6d&d= L3RtcA .

116) http://en.wikipedia.org/wiki/Dairy_cow. Accessed 4/28/2009. "[Milk] Production levels peak at around 40 to 60 days after calving. The cow is then bred. Production declines steadily afterwards, until, at about 305 days after calving, the cow is 'dried off', and milking ceases. About sixty days later, one year after the birth of her previous calf, a cow will calve again. High production cows are more difficult to breed at a one-year interval. Many farms take the view that 13 or even 14-month cycles are more appropriate for this type of cow. Dairy cows will continue to be productive members of the herd for many lactations. Ten or more lactations are not uncommon. The chances of problems arising, which may lead to a cow being culled, are however, high; the average herd life of US Holsteins is today fewer than three lactations. Left to their own schedules, dairy cows can have a life expectancy of twenty-five years or more; the average dairy cow lives three to four years before being sent to slaughter."

117) U.S. Department of Agriculture Economic Research Service. Briefing Rooms. http://www.ers.usda.gov/Briefing/Dairy/Background.htmm. Accessed 12/13/2010.

118) http://www.dairyfarmingtoday.org/DairyFarmingToday/Home. Accessed 4/28/2009.

119) Lovenheim, Peter. *Portrait of a Burger as a Young Calf / The Story of One Man, Two Cows, and the Feeding of a Nation.* Harmony Books, publisher. 2002.

120) http://www.ers.usda.gov/Briefing/Dairy/Policy.htm. Accessed 3/07/2012.

121) Eisnitz, Gail A. *Slaughterhouse / The Shocking Story of Greed, Neglect, and Inhumane Treatment Inside the U.S. Meat Industry.* Prometheus Books. Amherst, New York. 1997. (p. 188)

122) Demick, Barbara. *Los Angeles Times.* "Close-up: How China's Dairy Experiment Soured." January 9, 2009. http://seattletimes.nwsource .com/html/nationworld/2008607200_chinacow09.html. Accessed 11/3/2009.

123) Human Development Report. 2010. Media Release. November 4, 2010. http://hdr.undp.org/en/media/PR1-HDR10-overview-E-rev6.pdf. Accessed 3/17/2011. The media release figures differed substantially from the report itself ("About 1.7 billion people—fully a third of the population in the 104 countries included in the MPI—are estimated to live in multidimensional poverty, more than the estimated 1.3 billion who live on $1.25 a day or less.") so I am using those from the report, next citation.

124) Human Development Report. 2010. http://hdr.undp.org/en/media /HDR_2010_EN_Complete_reprint.pdf. (p. 21)

125) UN News Service. UN reports progress towards poverty alleviation, urges increased support for the poorest. July 7, 2011. http://www.un.org/apps/ news/storyasp?NewsID=38965&Cr=MDGs&Cr1=. Accessed 7/23/2011.

126) The Millennium Development Goals Report. 2011. United Nations. New York. http://www.un.org/millenniumgoals/pdf/percent282011_Epercent29 percent20MDGpercent20Reportpercent202011_Bookpercent20LR.pdf

127) The Millennium Development Goals Report 2011. United Nations. New York. http://www.un.org/millenniumgoals/pdf/percent282011_Epercent29 percent20MDGpercent20Reportpercent202011_Bookpercent20LR.pdf "By 2015, the number of people in developing countries living on less than $1.25 a day is projected to fall below 900 million."

128) http://web.worldbank.org/WBSITE/EXTERNAL/NEWS/0,,print:Y~is CURL:Y~contentMDK:21882162~pagePK:64257043~piPK:437376~theSiteP K:4607,00.html. "Updated February 17, 2010: The Chen and Ravallion (2008) research reported below still stands as the latest comprehensive estimate of poverty in developing countries." Accessed 7/30/2011.

129) http://web.worldbank.org/WBSITE/EXTERNAL/TOPICS/EXTPOVERT
Y/EXTEMPOWERMENT/0,,contentMDK:20040961~isCURL:Y~menuPK:48
6417~pagePK:148956~piPK:216618~theSitePK:486411,00.html. Accessed
7/31/2011.

130) Population Reference Bureau. http://www.prb.org/pdf11/2011population-
data-sheet_eng.pdf Accessed 7/31/2011.

131) Human Development Report. 2011. http://content.globalmarshallplan.org
/ShowNews.asp?ID=2860. Accessed 7/24/2011.

132) Human Development Report. 2011. http://content.globalmarshallplan.org/
ShowNews.asp?ID=2860. Accessed 7/24/2011.

133) The Millennium Development Goals Report. 2009. United Nations. New
York. http://mdgs.un.org/unsd/mdg/Resources/Static/Products/Progress
2009/MDG_Report_2009_En.pdf.

134) Human Development Report. 2010. http://hdr.undp.org/en/media/HDR_
2010_EN_Complete_reprint.pdf.

135) Population Reference Bureau. 2011 World Population Data Sheet.
http://www.prb.org/Publications/Datasheets/2011/world-population-data-
sheet/data-sheet.aspx.

136) Population Reference Bureau. 2009 World Population Data Sheet. © 2009
Population Reference Bureau http://www.prb.org/pdf09/09wpds_eng.pdf.
Accessed1/31/2010.

137) "World Population to reach 10 billion by 2100 if Fertility in all Countries
Converges to Replacement Level." Press Release. May 3, 2011. Revising
World Population Prospects: The 2010 Revision. (www.unpopulation.org).
http://esa.un.org/unpd/wpp/Other-Information/Press_Release_WPP2010
.pdf. Accessed 7/31/2011.

138) Weiss, Kenneth. "Slowing Population: Would It Curb Climate Change?" *Los
Angeles Times.* October 10, 2010. Accessed 12/3/2010. http://latimesblogs.
latimes.com/greenspace/2010/10/global-warming-overpopulation-climate-
change.html?utm_source=feedburner&utm_medium=feed&utm_campaign
=Feedpercent3A+GreenspaceEnvironmentBlog+percent28Greenspaceperce
nt29. "The U.S. Census Bureau estimates that U.S. population of 310 million
will swell to 439 million by midcentury..."

139) Bremner, Jason et al. Population Reference Bureau. September 2009.
Population bulletin 64.3 2009. Vol. 64, No. 3. World Population Highlights.
Key Findings from PRB'S 2009 World Population Data Sheet.

http://www.prb.org/pdf09/64.3highlights.pdf. Accessed 10/25/2009. "Africa's population will double by 2050, increasing by 24 million people per year."

140) Weiss, Kenneth. "Slowing Population: Would It Curb Climate Change?" *Los Angeles Times*. October 10, 2010. Accessed 12/3/2010. http://latimes blogs.latimes.com/greenspace/2010/10/global-warming-overpopulation-climate-change.html?utm_source=feedburner&utm_medium=feed&utm _campaign=Feedpercent3A+GreenspaceEnvironmentBlog+percent28Green spacepercent29. "The U.S. Census Bureau estimates that U.S. population of 310 million will swell to 439 million by midcentury..."

141) The Millennium Development Goals Report. 2011. United Nations. New York. http://www.un.org/millenniumgoals/pdf/percent282011_Epercent 29percent20MDGpercent20Reportpercent202011_Bookpercent20LR.pdf

142) Human Development Report 2010. http://hdr.undp.org/en/media /HDR_2010_EN_Complete_reprint.pdf.

143) The State of Food Insecurity in the World. 2008. Towards the Summit commitments; Policy responses: effective and sustainable? "Increases in food and agricultural production and productivity will be essential for meeting further increases in effective demand in the years to come. An estimated 80 percent of the increase in global food production must come from growth in crop yields. To this, the new demands for feedstock for an expanding bioenergy sector should be added." ftp://ftp.fao.org/ docrep/fao/011/i0291e/i0291e04.pdf. , "About two-thirds of the 3 billion rural people in the world live off the income generated by farmers managing some 500 million small farms of less than 2 hectares each.... Small-scale farming constitutes about 80 percent of African agriculture, producing largely staple foods."

144) Mapes, Linda. Reporter. *Seattle Times*. "Winter wren: little bird, big song." February 24, 2010. Professor emeritus of biology at the University of Massachusetts Amherst. http://seattletimes.nwsource.com/html/localnews/ 2011179036_wren25m.html?syndication=rss. Accessed 5/17/2010.

145) Krulwich, Robert. "Look Up! The Billion-Bug Highway you can't see!" National Public Radio. Morning Edition. July 15, 2010. http://www.npr. org/templates/story/story.php?storyId=128389587&ft=1&f=1001. Accessed 12/5/2010.

146) Joyce, Christopher. Reporter. "High Above, Insects Travel On Sky

Superhighways." February 5, 2010. National Public Radio. http://www. npr.org/templates/story/story.php?storyId=123330735&sc=nl&cc=nh-20100205. Accessed 2/5/2010.

147) "Remembrance of tussles past: paper wasps show surprisingly strong memory for previous encounters." Story posted on Physorg.com cites the work of graduate student Michael Sheehan and assistant professor of ecology and evolutionary biology Elizabeth Tibbetts. September 22, 2008. http://www.physorg.com/news141308727.html. Accessed 5/17/2010.

148) Mozingo, Joe. Reporter. "The Secret Life of Seals." Los Angeles Times. March 5, 2010. http://www.latimes.com/news/local/la-me-sanmiguel5-2010mar05,0,4769217.story?track=rss&utm_source=feedburner&utm_medi um=feed&utm_campaign=Feedpercent3A+latimespercent2Fnewspercent2F local+percent28L.A.+Times+-+California+percent7C+Local+Newspercent29 &utm_content=Google+Reader. Accessed 5/17/2010.

149) Navy NW Training Complex DEIS. 2009. http://www.nwtrangecom plexeis.com/Publicpercent20DEISpercent20files/Chapterspercent201 /Resource_Section_8_Sea_Turtles.pdf.

150) *Miami Herald*. April 15, 2009. Cited from http://www.biological diversity.org:80/news/center/articles/2009/miami-herald-04-15-2009.html.

151) Peckham, S. Hoyt et al. High mortality of loggerhead turtles due to bycatch, human consumption and strandings at Baja California Sur, Mexico, 2003 to 2007. *Endangered Species Research*. Preprint, 2008. Published online October 13, 2008. doi: 10.3354/esr00123. http://brd1.ucsc.edu/Tinker/Tim'sper cent20PDF's/peckham_etal_2008.pdf. Accessed 12/5/2009.

152) Platt, John. "Report: 21 percent of Africa's freshwater species threatened with extinction." *Scientific American*. September 7, 2010. http://www.scien-tificamerican.com/blog/post.cfm?id=report-21-percent-of-africas-freshw-2010-09-07. Accessed 12/3/2010.

153) Newsletter of the Species Survival Commission. International Union for the Conservation of Nature/IUCN. *Species 48:* July–December 2007. http://cmsdata.iucn.org/downloads/species_48_web.pdf. Accessed 11/22/2009.

154) Newsletter of the Species Survival Commission. International Union for the Conservation of Nature/IUCN. *Species.* "Overall, 114 of the world's 394 primate species are classified as threatened with extinction on the IUCN Red List™." *48:* July–December 2007. http://cmsdata.iucn.org

/downloads/species_48_web.pdf. Accessed 11/22/2009.

155) Newsletter of the Species Survival Commission. International Union for the Conservation of Nature/IUCN.

Species. 48: July–December 2007. http://cmsdata.iucn.org/downloads /species_48_web.pdf. Accessed 11/22/2009.

156) Newsletter of the Species Survival Commission. International Union for the Conservation of Nature/IUCN. Species 48: July–December 2007. http://cmsdata.iucn.org/downloads/species_48_web.pdf. Accessed 11/22/2009.

157) Clanin, Amy. "Orangutans Barely Hanging On: Can They Survive the Spread of Oil Palm Plantations?" The Wildlife Professional. Winter 2008. A publication of the Wildlife Society. "98 percent of the forest [in Indonesia] may be destroyed by 2022." The 98 percent quote is cited in this article as coming from the United Nations Environment Program. http://www.wildlifeprofessional-digital.org/wildlifeprofessional/2008 winter/?pg=38&pm=1&u1=friend#pg38. Accessed 1/03/2010.

158) Timmons, Michael. "Jungle Traffic / Investigating the Live Animal Trade." Rattle the Cage Productions. http://www.rattlethecage.org/elephant _traffic.htm. Accessed 1/03/2010.

159) Newsletter of the Species Survival Commission. International Union for the Conservation of Nature/IUCN. Species. "After a major assessment of Mexican and North American reptiles, 723 were added to the IUCN Red List™, taking the total to 738 reptiles listed for this region. Of these, 90 are threatened with extinction." 48: July–December 2007. http://cmsdata. iucn.org/downloads/species_48_web.pdf. Accessed 11/22/2009.

160) Putting Meat on the Table: Industrial Farm Animal Production in America. A Report of the Pew Commission on Industrial Farm Animal Production. 2008. http://www.ncifap.org/_images/PCIFAPFin.pdf. Accessed 11/17/2009. "...the ratio of fossil fuel energy inputs per unit of food energy produced averages 3:1 for all US agricultural products combined. For industrially produced meat products, the ratio can be as high as 35:1."

161) Pimentel, David. Ethical Issues of Global Corporatization: Agriculture and Beyond. 2004. Poultry Science. 83:321–329.

162) Livestock Slaughter. 2010 Summary. April 2011. United States Department of Agriculture. National Agricultural Statistics Service. http://usda. mannlib.cornell.edu/usda/current/LiveSlauSu/LiveSlauSu-04-25-2011.txt.

Accessed 7/31/2011.

163) http://law.psu.edu/_file/aglaw/Animal_Welfare_Final.pdf. Accessed 10/13/2011. Humane Methods of Slaughter Act (HMSA) requires these individuals be unconscious before being cut or hoisted. This is poorly enforced because of the speed of the kill line, lack of inspectors, and inconsistent results from the methods of rendering them unconscious. Slaughterhouse workers consistently report the butchering of individuals who are still alive.

164) World Preservation Foundation. http://www.worldpreservationfo undation.org/blog/news/the-food-crisis-and-too-much-meat/. Accessed 7/31/2011. "Each year we use 67 billion farm globally for meat, milk and eggs, the majority in industrial-scale farms. At the same time, the livestock population is set to double in the face of growing demand for meat and dairy products, particularly from developing countries such as China and India."

165) Goodland, Robert and Anhang, Jeff. Livestock and Climate Change: What if the key actors in climate change are...cows, pigs, chickens? *World Watch*. November/December 2009. http://www.worldwatch.org/files/pdf/Livestock percent20andpercent20Climatepercent20Change.pdf. Accessed 7/31/2011. "The report also states that 21.7 billion head of livestock were raised worldwide in 2002, while many nongovernmental organizations report that about 50 billion head of livestock were raised each year in the early 2000s."

166) World Bank. Agriculture and Rural Development. http://web.worldbank .org/WBSITE/EXTERNAL/TOPICS/EXTARD/0percent2Cpercent2Ccontent MDK:20452726~pagePK:148956~piPK:216618~theSitePK:336682percent2C0 0.html. Accessed 7/31/2011. "In total, livestock make use of more than two-thirds of the world's surface under agriculture, and one-third of the total global land area."

167) Forero, Juan. Reporter. National Public Radio. Argentine Cattle No Longer Just Home on the Range. 9/14/2009. http://www.npr.org/templates /story/story.php?storyId=112767649&ft=1&f=1001. Accessed 12/16/2009.

168) Livestock Impacts on the Environment. *Spotlight* / 2006. FAO. Agriculture and Consumer Protection Department. http://www.fao.org/ag/magazine /0612sp1.htm. Accessed 2/21/2010. "some 700 million people keep farm animals and up to 40 percent of household income depends on them." ... According to the FAO, "Despite its wide-ranging environmental impacts,

livestock is not a major force in the global economy, generating just under 1.5 percent of total GDP [Global Domestic Product]. But the livestock sector is socially and politically very significant in developing countries: it provides food and income for one billion of the world's poor, especially in dry areas, where livestock are often the only source of livelihoods. 'Since livestock production is an expression of the poverty of people who have no other options,' FAO says, 'the huge number of people involved in livestock for lack of alternatives, particularly in Africa and Asia, is a major consideration for policy makers.'"

169) Allison, I., et al. The Copenhagen Diagnosis, 2009: Updating the World on the Latest Climate Science . The University of New South Wales Climate Change Research Centre (CCRC), Sydney, Australia, 60 pp. www.copenhagendiagnosis.com. Accessed 12/5/2009.

170) Boyce, Daniel G., Lewis, Marlon R. and Worm, Boris. 2010. Global phytoplankton decline over the past Century. *Nature.* Vol. 466|29 July 2010| doi:10.1038/nature09268. http://www.fmap.ca/ramweb/papers-total/Boyce_etal_2010.pdf.

171) *e! Science News* was built and is maintained by Michael Imbeault, PhD student in Retrovirology & Bioinformatics. http://esciencenews.com/articles/2009/12/22/man.made.carbon.dioxide.affects.ocean.acoustics Accessed 1/05/2010.

172) http://www.pmel.noaa.gov/co2/story/What+is+Ocean+Acidification%3F Accessed 1/27/2012.

173) Gore, Al. *Our Choice/A Plan to Solve the Climate Crisis.* 2009. Published by Rodale, Inc.

174) Dietz, Thomas, Eugene A Rosa, and Richard York. 2007. Driving the ecological footprint. *Front Ecol Environ;* 5(1): 13–18. http://stirpat.bizland.com/frontiers.pdf. Accessed 8/5/11.

175) Global Footprint Network. "Do We Fit the Planet?" http://www.footprint-network.org/en/index.php/GFN/page/world_footprint/. Accessed 8/05/2011.

176) Bremner, Jason et al. Population Reference Bureau. September 2009. Population bulletin 64.3 2009. Vol. 64, No. 3. World Population Highlights. Key Findings from PRB'S 2009 World Population Data Sheet. http://www.prb.org/pdf09/64.3highlights.pdf. Accessed 10/25/2009.

177) Moussaieff Masson, Jeffrey and McCarthy, Susan. *When Elephants Weep: The Emotional Lives of Animals.* Delta/Dell Publishing, Bantam Doubleday Dell

Publishing Group, Inc. 1995. (p.192)

178) The State of Food Insecurity in the World. FAO. 2008.

179) Fabiosa, Jacinto F. et al. 2009. Land Allocation Effects of the Global Ethanol Surge: Predictions from the International FAPRI Model. *Working Paper 09-WP 488/* March 2009. Center for Agricultural and Rural Development Iowa State University Ames, Iowa. http://www.card.iastate.edu/publications /dbs/pdffiles/09wp488.pdf. Accessed 11//03/2011.

180) Oxfam International Media Briefing. November, 2010. Ref. 08/20/10. http://www.oxfam.org/sites/www.oxfam.org/files/oxfam-cancun-media-briefing-2010.pdf. Accessed 12/5/2010.

181) Roberts, Paul. *The End of Food*. Houghton Mifflin Company. 2008. (p.153, 174)

182) "More heat waves: increase of extremes due to climate change." 10/24/2011. Pottsdam Institute for Climate Impact Research. http://www.pik-potsdam.de/news/press-releases/mehr-hitzewellen-extreme-sind-folge-des-klimawandels. Accessed 2/21/12

183) Slaughtering the Amazon. Greenpeace International. 2009. http://www. greenpeace.org/raw/content/international/press/reports/slaughtering-the-amazon.pdf for the executive summary. The full report is in four parts, starting with part 1: http://www.greenpeace.org/international/assets /binaries/slaughtering-the-amazon-part1.

184) Webster, Donovan. The Devastating Costs of the Amazon Gold Rush. *Smithsonian Magazine.* February 2012. http://www.smithsonianmag .com/people-places/The-Devastating-Costs-of-the-Amazon-Gold-Rush.html#. Accessed 2/21/2012.

185) http://en.wikipedia.org/wiki/Interoceanic_Highway. Accessed 4/24/2011.

186) Garcia-Navarro, Lourdes and Poole, John. Reporters for National Public Radio. "Traveling Down the Amazon Road." http://www.npr.org/templates /story/story.php?storyId=112489035. Accessed 4/8/2010.

187) The Tallgrass Prairie Alliance is a multi-agency and cattle rancher organization ostensibly to protect a prairie ecosystem. There are a number of indications on their website that tell me they are trying to avoid endangered species listings. http://www.fws.gov/mountain-prairie/pfw/kansas/ks7.htm. Accessed 10/10/2009.

188) *The State of the Birds.* 2009. North American Bird Conservation Initiative, U.S. Department of the Interior. http://www.stateofthebirds.org/

pdf_files/State_of_the_Birds_2009.pdf. Accessed 12/5/2010. Humane Research Council Spotcheck #1015. www.humanespot.org

189) Dinner, Simon D. Surf or turf: A shift from feed to food cultivation could reduce nutrient flux to the Gulf of Mexico. *Global Environmental Change.* 17 (2007) 105–113.http://yosemite.epa.gov/sab/sabhap.nsf/e1853c0b6014d3658 5256dbf005c5b71/0172ca7b30bd023a8525729f004e3729/$FILE/Donner07.pd f. Accessed 12/06/2009.

190) Diaz, Robert J. and Rosenberg, Rutger. Spreading Dead Zones and Consequences for Marine Ecosystems. *Science* 15 August 2008:Vol. 321. no. 5891, pp. 926 – 929 DOI: 10.1126/science.1156401. http://www.science mag.org/cgi/content/abstract/321/5891/926. Accessed 12/06/2009. Abstract only.

191) National Science Foundation. Special Report. SOS: Is Climate Change Suffocating Our Seas? http://www.nsf.gov/news/special_reports/dead zones/climatechange.pdf. Accessed 12/06/2009.

192) Population Reference Bureau. 2009 World Population Data Sheet. © 2009 Population Reference Bureau. http://www.prb.org/pdf09/09wpds_eng.pdf. Accessed1/31/2010.

193) Rice, Susan E. 2006. The Threat of Global Poverty. *The National Interest;* Spring 2006; 83; Research Library. http://relooney.fatcow.com/00_New _1539.pdf. Accessed 3/17/2011. Cited percentage varies, but hovers around 50 percent.

194) Pollan, Michael. *Omnivores Dilemma / A Natural History of Four Meals.* Penguin Books. 2006.

195) Pollan, Michael. *Omnivores Dilemma / A Natural History of Four Meals.* Penguin Books. 2006. (p. 10-11)

196) Phelps, Norm. *The Longest Struggle / Animal Advocacy from Pythagoras to PETA.* Lantern Books. 2007. (p. 7, 8)

197) Singer, Peter and Mason, Jim. *The Way We Eat and Why Our Food Choices matter.* Rodale. 2006. (p.250)

198) "What causes it? ... The genetics of meat birds has changed dramatically in the last ten years. Today's broilers grow much faster, eating less feed. The growth of the heart and lungs has not increased in size proportional to the increase in body weight and breast meat yield. The rapid growth of the bird means more oxygen demand, requiring more work out of the heart and lungs." http://www.millerhatcheries.com/InformationFactSheets/Disease_

Info/Ascites%20(waterbelly)_in_Meat_Chickens.htm. Accessed 12/14/2011.

199) Pollan, Michael. *Omnivores Dilemma / A Natural History of Four Meals*. Penguin Books. 2006. (p. 80)

200) Pollan, Michael. *Omnivores Dilemma / A Natural History of Four Meals*. Penguin Books. 2006. (p. 7)

201) Pollan, Michael. *Omnivores Dilemma / A Natural History of Four Meals*. Penguin Books. 2006. (p. 68)

202) Pollan, Michael. "No Bar Code." *Mother Jones*. May/June 2006. http://motherjones.com/environment/2006/05/no-bar-code.

203) United Poultry Concerns. http://www.upc-online.org/freerange.html. Accessed 8/8/2012.

204) "Livestock impacts on the environment." *Spotlight*. 2006. http://www.fao.org/ag/magazine/0612sp1.htm. Accessed 10/09/2009.

205) "Livestock impacts on the environment." Spotlight. http://www.fao.org/ag/magazine/0612sp1.htm. Accessed 10/09/2009.

206) Lavigne, D.M. 2003. Marine Mammals and Fisheries: The Role of Science in the Culling Debate. pp 31-47. In: *Marine Mammals: Fisheries, Tourism and Management Issues* (N. Gales, M. Hindell and R. Kirkwood eds.). Collingwood, VIC, Australia: CSIRO Publishing, 446 pp.

207) Pollan, Michael. *Omnivores Dilemma / A Natural History of Four Meals*. Penguin Books. 2006. (p. 6)

208) Myers, B.R. "Hard to Swallow." *The Atlantic*. September 2007. http://www.theatlantic.com/doc/200709/omnivore. Accessed 11/24/2009.

209) Jeffery, Clara. "Michael Pollan Fixes Dinner." *Mother Jones*. March/April 2009.

210) Pollan, Michael. *Omnivores Dilemma / A Natural History of Four Meals*. Penguin Books. 2006. (p. 232)

211) Pollan, Michael. *Omnivores Dilemma / A Natural History of Four Meals*. Penguin Books. 2006. (p. 306)

212) Singer, Peter. *Animal Liberation*. Second Edition. The New York Review of Books. Distributed by Random House. 1975, 1990.

213) Singer, Peter. *Practical Ethics*. In *The Animal Ethics Reader*. Armstrong, Susan A. and Botzler, Richard G., editors. Second Edition. Routledge / Taylor and Francis Group, publisher. 2008, 2003. Chapter 4. (p. 45)

214) Singer, Peter. "Does Helping the Planet Hurt the Poor?" *Wall Street Journal*. January 22, 2011. http://online.wsj.com/article/SB10001424052748703779

704576074333552233782.html?mod=WSJ_LifeStyle_Lifestyle_6. Accessed 11/06/2011.

215) Regan, Tom, *Empty Cages / Facing the Challenge of Animal Rights*. Rowman & Littlefield Publishers, Inc. 2004.

216) "The rights view can apply compensatory principles to animals (the East African black rhino, for example) whose numbers are in severe decline because of past wrongs (for example, poaching of ancestors and destruction of habitat). Although the remaining rhinos have no greater inherent value than the members of a more plentiful species (rabbits, say), the assistance owed to the former arguably is greater than that owed to the latter. If it is true, as I believe it is, that today's rhinos have been disadvantaged because of wrongs done to their predecessors, then, other things being equal, more should be done for the rhinos, by way of compensatory assistance, than what should be done for rabbits." So, using broad strokes, this is how I think the rights view can account for our intuition that we owe more to the members of endangered species of animals than we owe to the members of more plentiful species. I failed to make this argument in the first edition of *The Case*—one of many omissions, I'm sure." http://arzonetran scripts.wordpress.com/2011/05/20/professor-tom-regan-interview/. Accessed 11/06/2011.

217) Donovan, Josephine. *Feminism and the Treatment of Animals: From Care to Dialogue*. In *The Animal Ethics Reader*. Armstrong, Susan A. and Botzler, Richard G., editors. Second Edition. Routledge / Taylor and Francis Group, publisher. 2008, 2003. Chapter 5. (p. 47, 48,52)

218) Devall, Bill and Sessions, George. *Deep Ecology*. Gibbs Smith, publisher. Peregrine Smith Books. 1985. (p.75)

219) Pollan, Michael. *Omnivores Dilemma/A Natural History of Four Meals*. Penguin Books. 2006. (p.322)

220) BirdLife International 2009. *Gallus gallus*. In: IUCN 2011. IUCN Red List of Threatened Species. Version 2011.1. <www.iucnredlist.org>. Downloaded on 13 August 2011.

221) Pollan, Michael. *Omnivores Dilemma/A Natural History of Four Meals*. Penguin Books. 2006. (p. 327)

222) Hanh, Thich Nhat. *Going Home/Jesus and Buddha as Brothers*. Riverhead Books / Penguin Putnam, Inc. 1999. Next paragraph is.

223) Pollan, Michael. *In Defense of Food/An Eaters Manifesto*. Penguin Group,

publisher. 2008. (p.164-165)

224) Foer, Jonathan Safran. *Eating Animals*. Back Bay Books / Little Brown and Company. New York. 2009. (p. 196, 197, 199, 244)

225) Scully, Matthew. *Dominion/The Power of Man, the Suffering of Animals, and the Call to Mercy*. St. Martin's Griffin, publisher. 2002. (p. 28, 43)

226) Goodland, Robert and Anhang, Jeff. Livestock and Climate Change: What if the key actors in climate change are...cows, pigs, chickens? *World Watch*. November/December 2009. (p.10-19) (possibly citing FAO statistics). http://www.worldwatch.org/files/pdf/Livestockpercent20andpercent20 Climatepercent20Change.pdf. Accessed 11/17/2009.

227) Gore, Al. *Our Choice. A Plan to Solve the Climate Crisis*. Published by Rodale, Inc. 2009.

228) *An Inconvenient Truth*. 2006. DVD. A documentary on global warming featuring Al Gore. Davis Guggenheim, director.

229) Brown, Lester R. "World Facing Huge New Challenge on Food Front". 4/16/2008. http://www.earth-policy.org/Updates/2008/Update72.htm . Accessed 4/28/2009. Copyright © 2008 Earth Policy Institute.

230) Brown, Lester R. *Outgrowing the Earth: The Food Security Challenge in an Age of Falling Water Tables and Rising Temperatures*. NY: W.W. Norton & Co. 2005. Earth Policy Institute. http://www.earth-policy.org/images/uploads/book _files/outch03.pdf. Accessed 6/20/2010.

231) Chickens and Eggs / 2008 Summary Agricultural Statistics Board. February 2009 2 NASS, USDA. http://usda.mannlib.cornell.edu/usda/current/Chick Egg/ChickEgg-02-26-2009.pdf. Accessed 1/09/2010.

232) http://wiki.answers.com/Q/What_is_the_lifespan_of_a_chicken and http:// www.backyardchickens.com/media/L-5323.pdf.

233) Davis, Karen, PhD. *Poisoned Chickens Poisoned Eggs*. Book Publishing Company. Summertown, Tennessee. 1996. (p.55) Revised and updated 2009.

234) University of Delaware (August 1, 2007). Chickens Dieting To Help Delaware Waterways. *Science Daily*. http://www.sciencedaily.com /releases/2007/07/070731175846.htm. Accessed 4/16/2009. The subject of the story was the reduction of phosphorus in chicken waste.

235) MacDonald, James M. The Economic Organization of U.S. Broiler Production. *Economic Information Bulletin* No. 38. Economic Research Service, U.S. Dept. of Agriculture. June 2008. http://www.ers.usda.gov/publi cations/eib38/eib38.pdf.

236) Olkowski, A.A. and Classen, H.L. Ascites in Broiler Chickens from a Welfare Point of View. Department of Animal & Poultry Science, University of Saskatchewan, Saskatoon, SK, S7N 5B5, Canada. Cited from http://www.eatwild.com/animals.html.

237) Davis, Karen, PhD. *Poisoned Chickens Poisoned Eggs.* Book Publishing Company. Summertown, Tennessee. 1996. (p. 94). Revised and updated 2009.

238) America's Soybean Farmers Form Partnership With DPI. April 9, 2009. "Delmarva Poultry Industry, Inc. (DPI), the non-profit trade association for the broiler chicken industry, whose members include farm families that grow chickens, four chicken companies, hundreds of poultry company employees, and hundreds of suppliers of products and services..." http://www.dpichicken.org/index.cfm?content=news&subcontent=details&id=334. Accessed 1/09/2010.

239) http://www.dpichicken.org/index.cfm?content=news&subcontent=details&id=348. Dated September 16, 2009. Accessed 1/09/2010.

240) Bellotti, Stephanie. The Fouling of the Chesapeake Bay by the Delmarva Peninsula's Booming Poultry Industry. http://www.uvm.edu/~gflomenh/VTLAW-EcoEcon/papers/termpercent20papers/Belloti-term.doc. Citing Sims, J.T. and F.J. Coale, Solutions to Nutrient Management Problems in the Chesapeake Bay in *Agriculture, Hydrology, and Water Quality* 171-192 (P.M. Haygarth and S.C. Jarvis, ed., 2002).

241) Bellotti, Stephanie. The Fouling of the Chesapeake Bay by the Delmarva Peninsula's Booming Poultry Industry. http://www.uvm.edu/~gflomenh/VTLAW-EcoEcon/papers/termpercent20papers/Belloti-term.doc. Accessed 1/09/2010.

242) Siefert, Ronald L. et al. 2004. Characterization of Atmospheric Ammonia Emissions from a Commercial Chicken House on the Delmarva Peninsula. *Environmental Science & Technology* 2004 38 (10), 2769-2778. http://pubs.acs.org/doi/abs/10.1021/es0345874. Accessed 1/09/2010.

243) Rimer, Sara. "In Maine, Egg Empire Is Under Fire." *New York Times.* August 29, 1996. http://www.nytimes.com/1996/08/29/us/in-maine-egg-empire-is-under-fire.html?sec=&spon=&pagewanted=all.

244) Jalonick, Mary Clare. *Huffington Post.* AP. 8/22/10. "Egg Recall: Supplier Austin 'Jack' DeCoster Has History of Health, Safety Violations." http://www.huffingtonpost.com/2010/08/22/egg-recall-supplier-viola-

tions_n_690400.html. Accessed 1/10/2011.

245) Davis, Karen, PhD. *Poisoned Chickens Poisoned Eggs.* Book Publishing Company. Summertown, Tennessee. 1996. (p.8) Revised and updated 2009.

246) Masson, Jeffrey M. *The Face on Your Plate: The Truth About Food.* W.W. Norton & Company. 2009. (p. 164)

247) Personal Communication. When I asked about the use of the phrase, he responded, "I think you are right, that is the first time I used it. I believe it belongs to me, but who knows? Just about everything has been said by somebody, somewhere, sometime!" April 17, 2010.

248) Brown, David, reporter. *The Washington Post.* "Rats surprise scientists by not acting like 'rats'." "In a simple experiment, researchers at the University of Chicago sought to find out whether a rat would release a fellow rat from an unpleasantly restrictive cage if it could. The answer: Yes.

The free rat, often hearing distress calls from its compatriot, learned to open the cage and did so with greater efficiency over time. It would release the other animal even if there wasn't the payoff of a reunion with it.

The successful release of the caged rat led to what strongly resembled a triumphal celebration between the two.

Astonishingly, if given access to a small hoard of chocolate chips, the free rat would usually save at least one treat for the captive, which is a lot to expect of a rat." http://seattletimes.nwsource.com/html/nationworld/2016971412_rats09.html. Accessed 12/13/2011.

249) Phelps, Norm. *The Longest Struggle / Animal Advocacy from Pythagoras to PETA.* Lantern Books. 2007. (p. 9)

250) Armstrong, Susan A. and Botzler, Richard G., editors. *The Animal Ethics Reader.* Second Edition. Routledge / Taylor and Francis Group, publisher. 2008, 2003. (p. 2, introduction).

251) World Wildlife Fund. "Pulp and palm oil the villains in Sumatra's global climate impact and local elephant losses." http://www.panda.org /index.cfm?uNewsID=125780. Posted 26 February 2008. Accessed 12/15/2010.

252) Bekoff, Marc. Individual Animals Count: Speciesism Doesn't Work. Blog. Animal Emotions. Posted at *Psychology Today,* online. http://www.psycholo-gytoday.com/blog/animal-emotions/200908/individual-animals-count-speciesism-doesnt-work. Accessed 12/17/2009.

253) Bekoff, Marc. *The Emotional Lives of Animals.* 2007. New World Library,

publisher. (p. 131, 134)

254) Balcombe, Jonathan. *Pleasurable Kingdom / Animals and the Nature of Feeling Good*. Macmillan, publisher. 2006.

255) Viegas, Jennifer. Lobsters and Crabs Feel Pain, Study Shows. March 27, 2009. Discovery Channel. http://www.msnbc.msn.com/id/29915025/. Accessed May 4, 2009. Excerpts from the web page: "Ripping the legs off live crabs and crowding lobsters into seafood market tanks are just two of the many practices that may warrant reassessment, given two new studies that indicate crustaceans feel pain and stress... The findings add to a growing body of evidence that virtually all animals, including fish, shellfish and insects, can suffer." ..."All of the crabs survived the experiments and were later released back into their native habitat. Elwood and Appel gave small electric shocks to some of the crabs within their shells. When the researchers provided vacant shells, some crabs — but only the ones that had been shocked —left their old shells and entered the new ones, showing stress-related behaviors like grooming of the abdomen or rapping of the abdomen against the empty shell... If crabs are given medicine — anesthetics or analgesics — they appear to feel relieved, showing fewer responses to negative stimuli.... Another study led by Patterson, however, found that when humans twisted off legs from crabs, the stress response was so profound that some individuals later died or could not regenerate the lost appendages."

256) Fish May Actually Feel Pain and React To It Much Like Humans Do. *ScienceDaily*. http://www.sciencedaily.com/releases/2009/04/090430161242.htm. Retrieved January 5, 2010. Story sourced from Nordgreen et al. Thermonociception in fish: Effects of two different doses of morphine on thermal threshold and post-test behaviour in goldfish (Carassius auratus). *Applied Animal Behaviour Science*, 2009; DOI: 10.1016/j.applanim.2009.03.015.

257) Scientific Opinion of the Panel on Animal Health and Welfare on a request from European Commission on General approach to fish welfare and to the concept of sentience in fish. The *EFSA Journal* . 2009. 954, 1-26. Last updated September 22, 2009. Adopted January 29, 2009. http://www.efsa.europa.eu/EFSA/efsa_locale-1178620753812_1211902344910.htm. Accessed 1/06/2010.

258) Regan, Tom. *Defending Animal Rights*. University of Illinois Press. 2001. (p. 42-43)

259) http://kerulos.org/. Accessed 1/17/2010.

260) Wildon, Michelle. "Where Food Comes From." *Audubon*. March-April. 2011/Vol. 113, Number 2. (p. 10)

261) http://animalbehaviour.net/JudithKBlackshaw/Chapter3c.htm. Accessed 3/21/2012.

262) Anderson, Jennifer. "An Underwater Rescue." *Animal Times*. Spring, 2008. People for the Ethical Treatment of Animals. www.peta.org.

263) Talbot, Margaret. "Birdbrain." *The New Yorker*. May 12, 2008.

264) Ice Stories. Dispatches From Polar Scientists. http://icestories.explor atorium.edu/dispatches/big-ideas/arctic-seals/ and for * audio, go to http://www.dosits.org/gallery/intro.htm. Accessed 2/02/2010.

265) Cava, Marco della, reporter. "Birds, boats threatened by the Great Pacific Garbage Patch." *USA Today*. 11/15/2009. http://www.usatoday.com/life/ lifestyle/2009-11-16-plastiki16_VA_N.htm?csp=34&utm_source= feedburner&utm_medium=feed&utm_campaign=Feedpercent3A+usatoday -NewsTopStories+percent28News+-+Top+Storiespercent29&utm_ content=Google+Reader. Accessed 11/15/2009.

266) Derraik, Jose G.B. The pollution of the marine environment by plastic debris: a review. *Marine Pollution Bulletin* 44 (2002) 842–852. PII: S00 2 5- 32 6X(02)0 0 22 0 -5. http://homepages.ihug.co.nz/~jderraik/Publications/ Derraikpercent202002percent20-percent20Plasticpercent20pollution.pdf. Accessed 11/16/2009.

267) Munro, Margaret. Postmedia News as posted in *The Vancouver Sun*. "Researchers find more plastic in the guts of Arctic seabirds." March 5, 2011. http://www.vancouversun.com/technology/Researcherspercent20 findpercent20morepercent20plasticpercent20gutspercent20Arcticpercent20 seabirds/4390662/story.html. Accessed 3/11/2011.

268) Wildlife-Vehicle Collision Reduction Study: Report to Congress. August, 2008. http://www.tfhrc.gov/safety/pubs/08034/exec.htm. Accessed 11/9/2009.

269) Durbin, Dee-Ann, Associated Press reporter. "Vehicle-animal collisions soaring." *Seattle Post-Intelligencer*. 11/18/2004.

270) U.S. Department of Transportation, Federal Highway Administration, Office of Natural Environment. April 2000. http://www.fhwa.dot.gov/ environment/wildlifecrossings/intro.htm.

271) U.S. Department of Transportation. Report to Congress: Best Practices

Manual: Wildlife Vehicle Collision Reduction Study. Chapter 1.1; October, 2008. http://www.fhwa.dot.gov/environment/hconnect/wvc/index.htm. Those species are the "Lower Keys marsh rabbit, Key deer, bighorn sheep (peninsular California), San Joaquin kit fox, Canada lynx, ocelot, Florida panther, red wolf, American crocodile, desert tortoise, gopher tortoise, Alabama red-bellied turtle, bog turtle, copperbelly water snake, eastern indigo snake, California tiger salamander, fatwoods salamander, Houston toad, Audubon's crested caracara, Hawaiian goose, and Florida scrub jay."

272) Clapham, Phil and Ivashchenko, Yulia. 2009. A Whale of a Deception. *Marine Fisheries Review*. 71(1); pp. 44-52.

273) Ollikainen, Rob. "Whale Killed in Illegal 2007 Hunt is Identified." *Peninsula Daily News*. May 7, 2009.

274) Calambokidis, J., Klimek, A., and Schlender, L. Summary of collaborative photographic identification of gray whales from California to Alaska for 2007. Cascadia Research, 218½ W 4th Ave., Olympia, WA 98501. http://www.cascadiaresearch.org/reports/Rep-ER-07-Final.pdf. Accessed May 7, 2009.

275) Borodin, R.G. et al. 2012. Rationale of subsistence and cultural needs for Gray whales and Bowhead whales by indigenous people of Chukotka (Russian Federation) in 2013-2018. IWC/64/ASW 6 Agenda items 6.1.2 and 6.2.2. http://iwcoffice.org/cache/downloads/cbhug8kbt0oo80kkg084ksgk4/64-ASW%206.pdf. Accessed 7/30/2012.

276) Celebrated oceanographer scientist Sylvia Earle, among many accomplishments, served as the chief scientist at the U.S. National Oceanic and Atmospheric Administration (NOAA). (http://www.achievement.org/autodoc/page/ear0bio-1). Chapter quote is from an interview Steven Colbert conducted with her 10/14/2009 on the show, The Colbert Report, Comedy Central television. http://www.comedycentral.com/colbertreport/full-episodes/index.jhtml?episodeId=252149. Accessed 10/14/2009.

277) Ehrlich, Paul R. and Ehrlich, Anne H. 1990 (original publication, *The Population Explosion*). I'm referencing "Why Isn't Everyone as Scared as We Are?" in Daly, Herman E. Introduction to *Essays toward a Steady-State Economy* for *Valuing the Earth / Economics, Ecology, Ethics*. Edited by Herman E. Daly and Kenneth N. Townsend. The MIT Press. 1993.

278) http://www.masaikenya.org/. Accessed 5/14/2009.

279) http://www.bluegecko.org/kenya/tribes/maasai/. Accessed 5/14/2009.

280) The estimate of Maasai population before 1890 was around 45,000. By the mid-1920s their population was estimated to be 50,000. In the 1948 census the Maasai numbered 107,309, and Talbot's most recent figure was 117,000 (Talbot 1964: 105). http://lucy.ukc.ac.uk/EthnoAtlas/Hmar/Cult_dir/Culture.7860

The 500,000 figure is from http://www.maasai-association.org/maasai.html that states: "The Maasai people of East Africa live in southern Kenya and northern Tanzania along the Great Rift Valley on semi-arid and arid lands. The Maasai occupy a total land area of 160,000 square kilometers with a population of approximately one half million people. However, many Maasai see the national census as government meddling and often miscount their numbers to census takers." On the same web page, there is more elaboration about Maasai censusing: "It is estimated that 1 million Maasai people live in Kenya and Tanzania. Please note that most Maasai doubt these numbers. Many Maasai see the national census as government meddling and often miscount their numbers to census takers. Some people want to be counted ten times while others refused to be counted. Tanzania does not conduct census based on ethnicity, which makes it difficult to estimate Maasai living in Tanzania." UNPO, Unrepresented Nations and Peoples Organization, also cites 900,000 but also states the population is in decline: http://www.unpo.org/content/view/7920/125/.

281) MacDonald, Mia. "The Dilemma of Development." In the anthology, *The Way of Compassion*. Edited by Martin Rowe. Stealth Technologies, publisher. 1999. (p. 96-97)

282) J. O. Ogutu, H.-P. Piepho, H. T. Dublin, N. Bhola, R. S. Reid. 2009. Dynamics of Mara–Serengeti ungulates in relation to land use changes. *Journal of Zoology*. Vol. 278, Issue 1. p. 1-14. DOI: 10.1111/j.1469-7998.2008.00536.x. [Abstract only]. http://onlinelibrary.wiley.com/doi/10.1111/j.1469-7998.2008.00536.x/abstract. Accessed 3/22/2012.

283) IRLI Blog. ILRI; Dynamics of Mara-Serengeti ungulates in relation to land use changes. Posted 2009. International Livestock Research Institute. http://regionalplan.wordpress.com/2009/06/12/ilri-dynamics-of-mara-serengeti-ungulates-in-relation-to-land-use-changes/. Link to rest of article not working. Accessed 3/21/2012.

284) Weisman, Alan. *The World Without Us*. Picador/Thomas Dunne Books/St.

Martin's Press. 2007. (p.103)

285) http://baraza.wildlifedirect.org/2009/07/20/alarming-rise-in-elephant-and-rhino-poaching/. Posted online July 20, 2009. Accessed 10/24/2009.

286) http://www.africanconservancy.org/about/documents/Facts.pdf. Accessed 10/24/2009.

287) World Wildlife Fund. Several sources cite approximately these same numbers though some believe it reasonable to think that there are far fewer than 500,000. Given the record rise in illegal poaching for ivory, we may be losing 8 percent of the total African elephant population annually (Wasser, Samuel K. et al. Combating the Illegal Trade in African Elephant Ivory with DNA Forensics. 2008. *Conservation Biology.* Volume 22, No. 4, 2008).

288) http://www.iucnredlist.org/documents/attach/12392.pdf. Accessed 11/8/2011.

289) Kenya Television Network. "Lion Killed, Three Locals Injured In Loitoktok" http://www.standardmedia.co.ke/ktn/?videoID=2000058717. Accessed 7/23/12.

290) Kenya Television Network. "Lion Killed, Three Locals Injured In Loitoktok" http://www.standardmedia.co.ke/ktn/?videoID=2000058717. Accessed 7/23/12.

291) Kenya: Morans Injured in KWS Scuffle Over Elephants. *The Star.* Kurgat Marindany, reporting. 20 July 2012. http://allafrica.com/stories/2012 07201311.html. Accessed 7/24/12.

292) Wasser, Samuel K. et al. 2008. Combating the Illegal Trade in African Elephant Ivory with DNA Forensics. 2008. *Conservation Biology.* Volume 22, No. 4, 2008.

293) Muruthi, Philip. Human Wildlife Conflict: Lessons Learned From AWF's African Heartlands. July 2005. African Wildlife Foundation. The disturbing photo of Odile the African elephant with Maasai spears hanging from her face is the cover image of this report. http://www.awf.org/documents /AWF_Human_Wildlife_Conflict.pdf. Accessed 2/13/2010.

294) Martin, Glen. "The lion, once king of vast African savanna, suffers alarming decline in population." *San Francisco Chronicle,* 10/0/2005. Accessed on SFGate.com 10/10/2007.

295) Muruthi, Philip. Human Wildlife Conflict: Lessons Learned From AWF's African Heartlands. July 2005. African Wildlife Foundation. http://www. awf.org/documents/AWF_Human_Wildlife_Conflict.pdf. Accessed 2/13/2010.

296) BBC News. 6/23/2003 http://news.bbc.co.uk/go/pr/fr/-/2/hi/africa/301 2630.stm. Accessed 10/10/2007.

297) The Maasai migrated into the Great Rift Valley several hundred years ago (~500 years) and after a long history of taking land from other cultural groups by warfare, were first decimated by British colonialism, then disease, and later had much of their land taken. More land was seized for national parks. Since Maasai did not originally hunt much wildlife, it was bountiful in their presence. Now, with less land to graze, and other populations of non-Maasai pressing for the same land, there is the additional several-fold increase in Maasai numbers as well. For a self-described explanation of current lion killing by Maasai, go to http://www.maasai-association.org/lion.htm/. Accessed 5/14/2009.

298) http://lionguardians.wildlifedirect.org. Wildlife Direct: "Through Wildlife Direct we aim to reach a global community of people concerned with the survival of wildlife in Africa, and other tropical regions. The goal is simple, to support field conservation by enabling an enormous community of people around the world to learn about the challenges and support projects of their choice with just a little bit of money. We encourage our online community to support basic field costs through donations. Accessed 10/24/2009.

299) Loibooki, Martin et al. 2002. Bushmeat hunting by communities adjacent to the Serengeti National Park, Tanzania: the importance of livestock ownership and alternative sources of protein and income. *Environmental Conservation.* 29: 391-398. Cambridge University Press.

300) www.wcs.org/international/Africa/kenya/predatorsinkenya is no longer available as of 10/24/2009.

301) http://www.laikipia.org/general-information/general-information/wildlife-management.html. Accessed 10/24/2009.

302) http://yubanet.com/enviro/Three-More-Lions-Killed-In-Kenya—-Authorities-Issue-Alarm.php. October 19, 2009. Accessed 10/24/2009.

303) For additional web-based access to the issues that will continue to unfold, visit the following websites: http://www.awf.org/documents/AWF_Human_Wildlife_Conflict.pdf ; http://www.kws.org/amboseli.html ; http://www.globalchange.umich.edu/webprojects/w00_maasai.htm ; http://www.fao.org/Wairdocs/ILRI/x5552E/x5552e05.htm ; http://www.pubmedcentral.nih.gov/articlerender.fcgi?artid=60090 ;

http://www.newworldencyclopedia.org/entry/Maasai ;
http://www.int-res.com/articles/esr2008/6/n006p067.pdf.

304) http://lionalert.org/Lionpercent20Releasepercent20Program.pdf. Accessed 10/24/200.

305) http://www.iucnredlist.org/apps/redlist/details/15951/0 . Accessed 11/9/2011.

306) Antunes A, Troyer JL, Roelke ME, Pecon-Slattery J, Packer C, et al. 2008 The Evolutionary Dynamics of the Lion *Panthera leo* Revealed by Host and Viral Population Genomics. *PLoS One*. Genet 4(11): e1000251. doi:10.1371/journal.pgen.1000251 http://www.plosgenetics.org/article/info: doipercent2F10.1371percent2Fjournal.pgen.1000251. Accessed 10/24/2009.

307) Barley, Shanta. Kenya's lions could vanish within 10 years. *NewScientist*. 12:53 20 August 2009. "Research by the University of Chicago's Field Museum of Natural History and KWS suggests that on average each lion eats livestock worth around $270 a year. "On the other hand, given the size of Kenya's tourist industry and the central importance of lions to tourist satisfaction, each of Kenya's 2000 surviving lions may be worth upwards of $17,000 per year in tourist revenues," says Bruce Patterson, curator of mammals at the museum."

308) Goldenberg, Suzanne. *Brisbane Times* (Australia). "From jungle king to trophy rug: US hunters turn sights on lions." March 2, 2011. http://www.brisbanetimes.com.au/environment/animals/from-jungle-king-to-trophy-rug-us-hunters-turn-sights-on-lions-20110302-1ber7.html. Accessed 3/11/2011.

309) Barley, Shanta. Kenya's lions could vanish within 10 years. *NewScientist*. 12:53 20 August 2009.

310) Population Reference Bureau and African Population & Health Research Center. 2008 Africa Population Data Sheet. http://www.prb.org/pdf08 /africadatasheet2008.pdf. Accessed 12/07/2009.

311) CRS (Congressional Research Service). Report for Congress. International Illegal Trade in Wildlife: Threats and U.S. Policy. 2008. http:// ncseonline.org/NLE/CRSreports/08Jun/RL34395.pdf. Accessed 10/14/2009.

312) Wasser, Samuel K. et al. 2008. Combating the Illegal Trade in African Elephant Ivory with DNA Forensics. 2008. *Conservation Biology*. Volume 22, No. 4, 2008.

313) Wasser, Samuel K. et al. 2009. "The Ivory Trail." *Scientific American*

Magazine. July, 2009.

314) http://www.eia-global.org/News/PR_ElephantPoachingAndIvoryTrade OutOfControl.html. http://www.eia-global.org/PDF/report—OpenSeason —Species—mar10.pdf. Accessed 11/9/2011.

315) Now Orion Entertainment. http://www.orionentertainment.com/. Accessed 1/31/2012.

316) Bowhunting Elephants. *Outdoor Life.* http://www.outdoorlife.com /photos/gallery/hunting/bowhunting/2008/10/bowhunting-elephants . Uploaded to the *Outdoor Life* magazine website October 9, 2008. Accessed 9/7/2009

317) "Lions that are roaming in fenced areas of 2,000—20,000 ha are hunted on foot. There is always a member from Nature Conservation in attendance to ensure that these Lions are not drugged, and that the hunt is completely ethical, fair and legal. This way we can assure you of a good quality animal in advance, on a 7 x day safari." http://www.kukuzans.co.za/. Accessed 9/8/2009.

318) Scully, Matthew. *Dominion / The Power of Man, the Suffering of Animals, and the Call to Mercy.* St. Martin's Griffin, publisher. 2002. (p. 53, 57)

319) Brown, Lester R. Letter mailing I received at my home announcing the publication of his book, *World on the Edge: How to Prevent Environmental and Economic Collapse.*

320) Population Reference Bureau and African Population & Health Research Center. 2008 Africa Population Data Sheet. http://www.prb.org/pdf08/afri cadatasheet2008.pdf. Accessed 12/07/2009.

321) Alexander, Robert R. Modeling species extinction: the case for non-consumptive values. *Ecological Economics.* 35 (2000) 259–269. http://www. landecon.cam.ac.uk/up211/EP09/reading/session3/alexander_2000.pdf. Accessed 12/07/2009.

322) Feely, Richard A., Sabine, Christopher L. and Fabry, Victoria L. 2006. Carbon Dioxide and Our Ocean Legacy. A "Brief" posted on the NOAA website. http://www.pmel.noaa.gov/pubs/PDF/feel2899/feel2899.pdf. Accessed 11/10/2011.

323) http://climate.nasa.gov/evidence/. Accessed 11/10/2011.

324) Cooley, Sarah R. et al. 2009. Anticipating ocean acidification's economic consequences for commercial fisheries. *Environ. Res. Lett.* 4 024007 (8pp) doi: 10.1088/1748-9326/4/2/024007.

325) http://www.fao.org/docrep/014/am859e/am859e07.pdf. Accessed 11/10/2011.

326) FAO Fisheries and Aquaculture Department. Food and Agriculture Organization of the United Nations. Rome, 2009. The State of World Fisheries and Aquaculture - 2008 (SOFIA). ftp://ftp.fao.org/docrep/fao/011 /i0250e/i0250e01.pdf. Accessed 10/30/2009.

327) Agnew DJ, Pearce J, Pramod G, Peatman T, Watson R, et al. 2009 Estimating the Worldwide Extent of Illegal Fishing. *PLoS ONE* 4(2): e4570. doi:10.1371/journal.pone.0004570. http://www.plosone.org/article/citation List.action?articleURI=infopercent3Adoipercent2F10.1371percent2Fjournal .pone.0004570. Accessed 12/29/2009.

328) Peckham, S. Hoyt et. al. 2007. Small-Scale Fisheries Bycatch Jeopardizes Endangered Pacific Loggerhead Turtles. *PLoS ONE*. 2007; 2(10): e1041. Published online 2007 October 17. doi:10.1371/journal.pone.0001041. http://www.ncbi.nlm.nih.gov/pmc/articles/PMC2002513/. Accessed 10/31/2009.

329) Worldwatch Institute. Fish Farming Continues to Grow as World Fisheries Stagnate. http://www.worldwatch.org/node/5444. Accessed 11/10/2011.

330) Safina, Carl. Scorched Earth Fishing. *Issues in Science and Technology*. April 9, 1998. University of Texas at Dallas.

331) Lewison, Rebecca L. et al. 2004. Understanding impacts of fisheries bycatch on marine Megafauna. *TRENDS in Ecology and Evolution.* Vol.19 No.11 November 2004. http://bycatch.env.duke.edu/publicationsandreports/Lew ison2004.pdf. Accessed 10/30/2009.

332) http://gcaptain.com/jensen-design-worlds-largest/?40049&utm_source =feedburner&utm_medium=feed&utm_campaign=Feed:+Gcaptain+(gCapt ain.com. Posted on 2/14/2012. Accessed 2/21/2012.

333) Crowder, Larry B. and Mycro, Ransom A. (Principal Investigators). 2001. A Comprehensive Study of the Ecological Impacts of the Worldwide Pelagic Longline Industry. First Annual Report to the PEW Charitable Trusts. http://www.gotmercury.org/downloads/Pew_Longline_2002.pdf. Accessed 10/31/2009.

334) Tasker, Mark L. et al. 2000. The impacts of fishing on marine birds. ICES Journal of Marine Science, 57: 531–547. 2000 / doi:10.1006/jmsc.2000.00714. http://icesjms.oxfordjournals.org/content/57/3/531.full.pdf. Accessed 11/10/2011.

335) Tasker, Mark L. et al. 2000. The impacts of fishing on marine birds. *ICES*

Journal of Marine Science, 57: 531–547. 2000. doi:10.1006/jmsc.2000.00714 "Overall, there is no scientific evidence that a cull of any marine predator has enhanced a commercial fishery venture …."

336) Kelleher, K. 2005. Discards in the world's marine fisheries. An update. *FAO Fisheries Technical Paper. No. 470.* Rome, FAO. 2005. 131p. http://www.fao.org/docrep/008/y5936e/y5936e00.htm. Accessed 10/30/2009.

337) NOAA/NMFS. U.S. National Bycatch Report. http://www.nmfs.noaa.gov/by_catch/BREP2011/Executive%20Summary.pdf. Accessed 11/10/2011. Data posted as of date accessed.

338) Alverson, Dayton L. et al. 1994. A Global Assessment of Fisheries Bycatch and Discards. FAO Fisheries Technical Paper 339.

339) Davies, RWD, et al. 2009. Defining and estimating global marine fisheries bycatch. *Marine Policy* (2009), doi:10.1016/j.marpol.2009.01.003. http://www.sciencedirect.com/science/journal/0308597X.

340) DeMaster, Doug et al. 2001. Predation and Competition: The Impact of Fisheries on Marine-Mammal Populations Over the Next One Hundred Years. *Journal of Mammalogy*, 82(3):641-651, 2001.

341) Dulvy, Nicholas K. et al. 2008. You can swim but you can't hide: the global status and conservation of oceanic pelagic sharks and rays. *Aquatic Conserv: Mar. Freshw. Ecosyst.* (2008). DOI: 10.1002/aqc.975 http://www.lenfestocean.org/publications/Pelagic_Sharks_paper_final_version.pdf. Accessed 10/30/2009.

342) FAO Fisheries and Aquaculture Department. Food and Agriculture Organization of the United Nations. Rome, 2009. The State of World Fisheries and Aquaculture - 2008 (SOFIA). ftp://ftp.fao.org/docrep/fao/011/i0250e/i0250e01.pdf. Accessed 10/30/2009.

343) Clarke, Shelley C. et al. 2006. Global estimates of shark catches using trade records from commercial markets. *Ecology Letters*, Volume 9 Issue 10, Pages 1115 – 1126. 2006a.

344) Hoelzel, A.R. 2001. Shark fishing in fin soup. *Conservation Genetics* **2:** 69–72, 2001. http://www.dur.ac.uk/a.r.hoelzel/hoelzelCGshark.pdf. Accessed 10/30/2009.

345) Clarke, Shelley C. et al. Identification of Shark Species Composition and Proportion in the Hong Kong Shark Fin Market Based on Molecular Genetics and Trade Records. *Conservation Biology.* Volume 20, No. 1, 201–211. Society for Conservation Biology. DOI: 10.1111/j.1523-

1739.2006.00247.x

346) MAC's 2008 Year in Review. January, 2009. Maine Animal Coalition.

347) Tribuzio, Cindy et al. 2008. Research, Biology, and Management of Sharks and Grenadiers in Alaska. Alaska Fisheries Science Center. Quarterly Report. April/May/June 2008. Content stated as provisional.

348) People For The Ethical Treatment of Animals (PETA). Take A Closer Look At Fish. www.fishinghurts.com; www.peta.org.

349) Tribuzio, Cindy et al. 2008. Research, Biology, and Management of Sharks and Grenadiers in Alaska. Alaska Fisheries Science Center. Quarterly Report. April/May/June 2008. Content stated as provisional.

350) http://seagrant.uaf.edu/news/96news/03-01-96_Grenadier.htm. Accessed 1/21/2011.

351) Preisser EL, Bolnick DI. 2008. The Many Faces of Fear: Comparing the Pathways and Impacts of Nonconsumptive Predator Effects on Prey Populations. *PLoS ONE* 3(6): e2465. doi:10.1371/journal.pone.0002465. http://www.plosone.org/article/citationList.action;jsessionid=E8707960C95 3547409108D9A37FABD56?articleURI=infopercent3Adoipercent2F10.1371 percent2Fjournal.pone.0002465. Accessed 12/29/2009.

352) http://www.abcbirds.org/abcprograms/policy/collisions/index.html. Accessed 11/10/2011.

353) Harris, Richard. NPR. Scientists Tune In To The 'Voices Of The Landscape.' March 12,2011. http://www.npr.org/2011/03/12/134425597/scientists-tune-in-to-the-voices-of-the-landscape. Accessed 3/13/2011.

354) Helmut Haberl, Karl-Heinz Erb and Fridolin Krausmann (Lead Authors); Mark McGinley (Topic Editor). 2008. "Global human appropriation of net primary production (HANPP)." In: Encyclopedia of Earth. Eds. Cutler J. Cleveland (Washington, D.C.: Environmental Information Coalition, National Council for Science and the Environment). [First published in the Encyclopedia of Earth March 14, 2008; Last revised December 10, 2008. Accessed 1/12/ 2009].

355) Blake S, Deem SL, Strindberg S, Maisels F, Momont L, et al. 2008. Roadless Wilderness Area Determines Forest Elephant Movements in the Congo Basin. *PLoS ONE* 3(10): e3546. doi:10.1371/journal.pone.0003546. http://www.plosone.org/article/info:doi/10.1371/journal.pone.0003546. Accessed 12/30/2009.

356) Blake S, Deem SL, Strindberg S, Maisels F, Momont L, et al. 2008. Roadless

Wilderness Area Determines Forest Elephant Movements in the Congo Basin. *PLoS ONE* 3(10): e3546. doi:10.1371/journal.pone.0003546. http://www.plosone.org/article/info:doi/10.1371/journal.pone.0003546. Accessed 12/30/2009.

357) Weilgart, L.S. 2007. The impacts of anthropogenic ocean noise on cetaceans and implications for management. *Can. J. Zool.* 85(11): 1091–1116 (2007) | doi:10.1139/Z07-101.

358) Noren, D.P. et al. 2009. Close Approaches by Vessels Elicit Surface Active Displays by Southern Resident Killer Whales. *Endangered Species Research*; Vol.8: 179–192. http://www.nwfsc.noaa.gov/research/divisions/cbd/marine _mammal/documents/norencloseapproachespresentation.pdf. Accessed 10/12/2009.

359) Gaydos, Joseph K.. NOAA/NMFS Killer Whale / Oil Spill Workshop. October 11-12, 2007. Notes of meeting. http://www.vetmed.ucdavis. edu/whc/seadoc/pdfs/kw_mtg_notes_oct07.pdf. Accessed 2/13/2010.

360) NOAA, 2004. Noise Symposium. (p. 17)

361) Maender, Gloria. 2003. Invaders Have Fewer Parasites, Giving Them Competitive Edge Over Native Animals and Plants. *Sound Waves*. Vol. FY2003, No.8. Feb.-Mar. 2003. U.S. Geological Survey. http://soundwaves .usgs.gov/2003/03/. Accessed 10/31/2009.

362) Mooney, H.A. and Cleland, E.E. 2001. The evolutionary impact of invasive species. *PNAS* May 8, 2001 vol. 98 no. 10 5446-5451. doi: 10.1073/pn as.091093398. http://www.barrierecheck.net/nocolor.php?url=http://www. pnas.org/content/98/10/5446.full. Accessed 10/31/2009.

363) Whitty, Julia. Listen to the Lionfish. *Mother Jones*. January/February 2009.

364) Pimentel, David, Zuniga R., Morrison D. 2009. Update on the environ- mental and economic costs associated with alien-invasive species in the United States. *Ecological Economics*, Volume 52, Issue 3, 15 February 2005, Pages 273-288. Online 29 December 2009. http://protectyourwaters.org /news/data/EconomicCosts_invasives.pdf. Accessed 10/31/2009.

365) http://www.fao.org/ag/magazine/0612sp1.htm.

366) Van Soest, Peter J. 1982. *Nutritional Ecology of the Ruminant*, Second Edition. Cornell University Press. 1994. Original edition, 1982. (p. 1)

367) Stewart, Kelley M. et al. 2002. Temporalspatial Distributions of Elk, Mule Deer, and Cattle: Resource Partitioning and Competitive Displacement. *Journal of Mammalogy,* 83(1):229–244, 2002. http://wwws.isu.edu/depart-

ments/bios/CV_Pub/Bowyer/CV_pdfs/Stewartpercent20etpercent20al.perc ent202002.pdf Accessed 11/20/2009.

368) Cryderman, Kelly. *Vancouver Sun.* Canwest News Service. August 10, 2009.

369) Van Soest, Peter J. 1994. *Nutritional Ecology of the Ruminant,* Second Edition. Cornell University Press. 1994. Original edition, 1982. (p. 4)

370) Bengtsson, Janne, Ahnström, Johan, and Weibull, Ann-Christin. 2005. The effects of organic agriculture on biodiversity and abundance: a meta-analysis. *Journal of Applied Ecology.* (2005) 42 , 261–269. doi: 10.1111/j.1365-2664.2005.01005.x. http://bie.berkeley.edu/files/bengston05.pdf. Accessed 11/4/2010.

371) D.G. Hole et al. 2005. Does organic farming benefit biodiversity? *Biological Conservation* 122 (2005) 113–130. http://www.ecosensus.ca/Hole2005.pdf. Accessed 11/4/2010.

372) Benton, Tim G., Vickery, Juliet A. and Wilson, Jeremy D. 2003. Farmland biodiversity: is habitat heterogeneity the key? *TRENDS in Ecology and Evolution.* Vol.18 No.4 April 2003. http://www.ask-force.org/web/Organic/Benton-Farmland-Biodiversity-2003.pdf. Accessed 11/4/2010.

373) Parris, K. M., M. Velik-Lord, and J. M. A. North. 2009. Frogs call at a higher pitch in traffic noise. *Ecology and Society* 14(1): 25. http://www.ecologyand-society.org/vol14/iss1/art25/. Accessed 1/08/2010.

374) Kozel, Scott M. New Jersey Median Barrier History. Last web update 6/21/2004. http://www.roadstothefuture.com/Jersey_Barrier.html. Accessed 5/15/2009.

375) http://www.bts.gov/publications/national_transportation_statistics/ht ml/table_01_11.html. Accessed 3/30/3012 and U.S. Department of Transportation, Federal Highway Administration. For the year 2007. http://www.bts.gov/publications/national_transportation_statistics/html/ta ble_01_11.html. Accessed 5/22/2010.

376) U.S. Department of Transportation, Federal Highway Administration, Office of Natural Environment. April 2000. Publication No: FHWA-EP-004.http://www.fhwa.dot.gov/environment/wildlifecrossings/overview.ht m. Accessed 5/15/2009.

377) Clevenger, Anthony P. and Kociolet, Angela. 2006. Highway Median Impacts On Wildlife Movement and Mortality. Western Transportation Institute College of Engineering; Montana State University. A report prepared for the State of California. Department of Transportation Office of

Materials and Infrastructure Research October 6, 2006. Research Report Number F/CA/MI-2006/09. http://www.dot.ca.gov/hq/research/ researchreports/reports/2006/median_barrier_final_report.pdf.

378) Environmental Services Office. Washington State Department of Transportation. Guidance on Placement of Concrete Barriers. October 2002. Found in Environmental Procedures Manual M31-11. March 2006. Exhibit 436-5.

379) Robbins, Jim. Thinking Anew About a Migratory Barrier: Roads. *New York Times*, 10/14/2008. http://www.nytimes.com/2008/10/14/science/14road. html?_r=1. The article describes, among other things, how Interstate 90 blocks the return of a recovering population of grizzle bears to former habitat on the other side of the road where they were hunted to local extinction "50 years ago to protect sheep."

380) Briggeman, Kim. Wildlife to Roam Free. Unique Crossing Near Evaro Will Allow Cars, Animals to Harmonize. *Missoulian.* August 19, 2009 http://www.missoulian.com/news/local/article_e2490eb0-8d48-11de-abb7-001cc4c002e0.html. Accessed 12/15/2009.

381) (Trombulak, Stephen C. and Frissell, Christopher A. 2000. Review of Ecological Effects of Roads on Terrestrial and Aquatic Communities. *Conservation Biology*, Vol. 14, No. 1 (Feb., 2000), pp. 18-30. http://roadecology.ucdavis.edu/pdflib/TTP_289/W08/Trombulakpercent20andpercent2 0Frissellpercent202000.pdf. Accessed 10/21/2009.

382) Montagne , Renee. NPR's Morning Edition. "Ford Motor Co. Is Prepared For Gas Prices To Rise." March 3, 2011. http://www.npr.org/2011/03/03 /134222010/William-Clay-Ford-Jr. Accessed 3/11/2011.

383) Cascadia Research Collective. "Injured whale in south Puget Sound - Update through 6 December 2010." http://cascadiaresearch.org /InjuredWhale-SPS-1Dec10.htm. Accessed 1/23/2011.

384) Betz, Sarah et al. 2010. Preventing Vessel Strikes to Whales in the Santa Barbara Channel /An Economic Analysis and Risk Assessment of Policy Options for Reducing Vessel Strikes to Endangered Whales. University of California Santa Barbara / Bren School of Environmental Science & Management.

385) I wrote this statement without considering how the term, *natural order,* might be seen from varying perspectives both philosophical and otherwise. It is an observation I think obvious to many. I have since seen it described

as relationships between beings as well as the order of the universe organized by innate rules. In addition, when I did an online Wiki search for natural order and natural law, this is the overview I found: "In philosophy, the natural order is the moral source from which natural law seeks to derive its authority. It encompasses the natural relations of beings to one another, in the absence of law, which natural law attempts to reinforce. ... Natural law or the law of nature (Latin: lex naturalis) is a theory that posits the existence of a law whose content is set by nature and that therefore has validity everywhere.[1] So, yes, it seems obvious that economic values have replaced and largely eliminated the natural law of right conduct in our human ecology we once derived from our perceptions of a natural order. We are beginning to realize that folly and trying to backtrack and are now experimenting with ways to create economies that follow ecosystems by enacting, for instance, taxing reforms and carbon caps and trades.

386) Galloway, James N.et al. 2007. International Trade in Meat: The Tip of the Pork Chop. *Ambio.* Vol. 36, No. 8, December 2007. Royal Swedish Academy of Sciences. http://ambio.allenpress.com/archive/0044-7447/36/8/pdf/i0044-7447-36-8-622.pdf. The Aral Sea, located between Uzbekistan and Kazakhstan once the fourth largest lake on the planet but shrank in no small part due to the diversion of rivers used to irrigate crops, like cotton. There a lot more to read on this disaster.

387) Turner II, B.L. et al. The emergence of land change science for global environmental change and sustainability. Proceedings from the National Academy of Science U.S. *PNAS,* vol. 104, no. 52. December 26, 2007. www.pnas.org_cgi_doi_10.1073_pnas.0704119104. http://www.pnas.org/content/104/52/20666.full.pdf+html. Accessed 10/22/2009.

388) Galloway, James N.et al. 2007. International Trade in Meat: The Tip of the Pork Chop. *Ambio.* Vol. 36, No. 8, December 2007. Royal Swedish Academy of Sciences. http://ambio.allenpress.com/archive/0044-7447/36/8/pdf/i0044-7447-36-8-622.pdf.

389) Food and Agriculture Organization of the United Nations (FAO); Livestock's Long Shadow; Environmental Issues and Options. 2006. ftp://ftp.fao.org/docrep/fao/010/a0701e/a0701e00.pdf. Accessed 11/17/2009. "70% of previous forested land in the Amazon is covered by pastures...and feedcrops cover a large part of the remainder."

390) Slaughtering the Amazon. Greenpeace International. 2009. http://www.

greenpeace.org/raw/content/international/press/reports/slaughtering-the-amazon.pdf for the executive summary. The full report is in four parts, starting with part 1: http://www.greenpeace.org/international/assets/binaries/slaughtering-the-amazon-part1.

391) Galloway, James N.et al. 2007. International Trade in Meat: The Tip of the Pork Chop. *Ambio*. Vol. 36, No. 8, December 2007. Royal Swedish Academy of Sciences. http://ambio.allenpress.com/archive/0044-7447/36/8/pdf/i0044-7447-36-8-622.pdf.

392) Goodland, Robert and Anhang, Jeff. Livestock and Climate Change: What if the key actors in climate change are...cows, pigs, chickens? *World Watch*. November/December 2009. (p. 10-19) (possibly citing FAO statistics). http://www.worldwatch.org/files/pdf/Livestockpercent20andpercent20Climatepercent20Change.pdf. Accessed 11/17/2009.

393) Food and Agriculture Organization of the United Nations (FAO); Livestock's Long Shadow; Environmental Issues and Options. 2006. ftp://ftp.fao.org/docrep/fao/010/a0701e/a0701e00.pdf. Accessed 11/17/2009.

394) T. Gresh, J. Lichatowich, P. Schoonmaker. 2000. Evidence of a Nutrient Deficit in the Freshwater Systems of the Pacific Northwest. *Fisheries*. January (2000). "The number of fish now returning to these rivers has a biomass of 11.8-13.7 million kg."

395) WDFW Fishing Rule Change. February 9, 2011. Anglers must retain hatchery steelhead in upper Columbia and its tributaries.

396) H. Araki, B. Cooper, M.S. Blouin. 2007. Genetic Effects of Captive Breeding Cause a Rapid, Cumulative Fitness Decline in the Wild. *Science*. Vol 318 OCTOBER 5 (2007).

397) Shogren, Elizabeth. Reporter. "Byproducts of Urban Life Smother Chesapeake Bay." National Public Radio. Broadcast 12/24/2009. http://www.npr.org/templates/story/story.php?storyId=121588652&sc=nl&cc=nh-20091225. Accessed 12/27/2009.

398) King, Anna, Reporter. "Scientists Step Lightly To Study Northwest's Desert Crust." 3/24/2010. Northwest News Network. KUOW Public Radio. http://www.kuow.org/program.php?id=19804. Accessed 5/16/2010.

399) Mason, Jim. *An Unnatural Order: The Roots of Our Destruction of Nature*. Lantern Books. 2005. (p. 277)

400) *Animal People*. Merritt Clifton, Editor in Chief. An independent newspaper. Editorial: Donor defense in a desperate cause. December, 2003 (last

paragraph which is still used on the organization's web page). Though I would question some of the broader statements for some clarification in this long editorial, I believe this quote illustrates one of the key points I'm making about the downside of alleviating the plights of species while ignoring the individuals. Enviros will fail if they do not a include individual human and nonhuman beings alike. http://www.animalpeoplenews.org/03/12/editorial1203.html.

401) Vining, Joanne. 2003. The Connection to Other Animals and Caring for Nature. *Human Ecology Review*, Vol. 10, No. 2, pp. 87- 99. 2003. http://www.humanecologyreview.org/pastissues/her102/102vining.pdf. Accessed 1/06/2010.

402) http://www.psp.wa.gov/

403) Puget Sound Partnership Discussion Paper: Habitat Protection and Land Use. July 11, 2008. http://www.psp.wa.gov/downloads/ACTION_AGEN DA_2008/TopicPapers/07-11_08HLUPaper.pdf. Accessed 8/14/09.

404) Puget Sound Partnership Discussion Paper: Habitat Protection and Land Use. July 11, 2008. http://www.psp.wa.gov/downloads/ACTION_AGEN DA_2008/TopicPapers/07-11_08HLUPaper.pdf. Accessed 8/14/09.

405) http://www.epa.gov/pugetsound/pdf/Summary_Population_Health _Indicator.pdf. Accessed 8/21/2011.

406) Puget Sound Partnership. Puget Sound Action Agenda. Protecting and Restoring the Puget Sound Ecosystem by 2020. December 1, 2008. http://www.psp.wa.gov/downloads/ACTION_AGENDA_2008/Action_Ag enda.pdf. Accessed 1/11/2010.

407) Devall, Bill and Sessions, George. *Deep Ecology*. Gibbs Smith, publisher. Peregrine Smith Books. 1985. (p.3)

408) Rifkin, Jeremy. *The Empathic Civilization/The Race to Global Consciousness In a World In Crisis*. Jeremy P. Tarcher/Penguin, publishers. 2009. (p. 468-469).

409) Feeney, John. 'Earth Needs Our Renewed Attention to Human Population Growth." *Population Press*. Fall, 2007. Vol. 13; No. 7. A publication of Blue Planet United. www.populationpress.org. Accessed 11/18/2009.

410) Bandura, Albert. 2007. Impeding ecological sustainability through selective moral disengagement. *Int. J. Innovation and Sustainable Development*, Vol. 2, No. 1, 2007. http://des.emory.edu/mfp/Bandura2007MDEcology.pdf with thanks to Population Press for posting excerpts, alerting me to this must-read paper. www.populationpress.org.

411) Mayer, Judith. "Borneo Project: Burning for Biofuels." *Earth Island Journal.* Spring, 2008. www.earthisland.org.

412) Palmer, Mark. International Marine Mammal Project: Saving Dolphins. *Earth Island Journal.* Spring, 2008. www.earthisland.org.

413) Mark, Jason. From the Editor/Food for Thought. *Earth Island Journal.* Spring, 2008. www.earthisland.org.

414) Spangenberg, Joachim H. et al. 2009. The DPSIR scheme for analyzing biodiversity loss and developing preservation strategies. Editorial. *Ecological Economics* 69 (2009) 9–11. doi:10.1016/j.ecolecon.2009.04.024.

415) Quinn, Daniel. *Ishmael.* Bantam Books/Random House. 1992. (p. 105-110)

416) Humane Research Council. www.humanespot.org.

417) Devall, Bill and Sessions, George. *Deep Ecology.* Gibbs Smith, publisher. Peregrine Smith Books. 1985. (p.75)

418) Naess, Arne in *The Ecology of Wisdom/Writings by Arne Naess.* Alan Drengson and Bill Devall, editors. Counterpoint Press. Berkeley, CA. 2008. (p. 105)

419) Bateson, Melissa et al. 2011. *Current Biology,* Volume 21, Issue 12, 1070-1073, 02 June 2011 Copyright © 2011 Elsevier Ltd All rights reserved. 10.1016/j.cub.2011.05.017. http://www.cell.com/current-biology/abstract/S0960-9822%2811%2900544-6. Accessed 6/25/2011. Thanks to Brandon Keim (Wired Science) and Marc Kekoff (*Psychology Today* blog, Animal Emotions) for alerting me to this paper.

420) Angier, Natalie. *New York Times.* "So Much More Than Plasma and Poison." June 6, 2011, quoting David J. Albert, a jellyfish expert at the Roscoe Bay Marine Biological Laboratory in Vancouver, British Columbia. Thanks to Marc Bekoff (*Psychology Today* blog, Animal Emotions) for alerting me to this paper.

421) Garm, Anders, Magnus Oskarsson and Dan-Eric Nilsson. 201.1 Box Jellyfish Use Terrestrial Visual Cues for Navigation. *Current Biology.* Volume 21, Issue 9, 10 May 2011, Pages 798-803.
Thanks to *Psychology Today* blog, (Animal Emotions) for alerting me to this paper, and Angier, Natalie. *New York Times.* So Much More Than Plasma and Poison. June 6, 2011for reporting on it.

422) Whitehead, H., Rendell, L., Osborne, R.W., Würsig, B. Culture and Conservation of Non-Humans with Reference to Whales and Dolphins: Review and New Directions. In *The Animal Ethics Reader.* Second Edition. Armstrong, Susan A. and Botzler, Richard G., editors. Routledge / Taylor

and Francis Group, publisher. 2008, 2003. Chapter 22. (p. 181)

423) Becker, Jasper. Chronicle Foreign Service. *San Francisco Chronicle*. June 24, 2002. http://www.sfgate.com/cgi-bin/article.cgi?file=/chronicle/archive/ 2002/06/24 /MN180160.DTL. Accessed 8/20/09.

424) It was probably thirty-five years or so ago that I read this letter, so I can't give you a date or issue number. It just stuck with me as something that was so wrong because it was so shameful. http://www.alaskamagazine.com.

425) U.S. Geological Service. "Do not use small traps as the beaver will pull out of them, and will become trap wise and much harder to catch. When trapping beaver, plan your sets so that the beaver will drown. The surest way to do this is through the use of a drowning wire. In shallow water it may be necessary to wrap the trap chain through the spring of the trap to eliminate slack which would enable the beaver to reach the surface." There are many types of underwater sets. Some will kill more quickly than others. http://www.npwrc.usgs.gov/resource/mammals/furtake/beaver.htm. Accessed 8/20/09.

426) 2008 Wisconsin Trapping Regulations. http://dnr.wi.gov/org/land/ wildlife/regs/08TrappingRegs.pdf. Accessed 1/09/2010.

427) Dawn, Karen. *Thanking the Monkey*. 2008. HarperCollins Publishers. (p.105)

428) Washington Department of Fish and Wildlife. Stream Habitat Restoration Guidelines: Final Draft. Beaver Re-introduction Guide. 2004. http://wdfw. wa.gov/hab/ahg/shrg/13-shrg_beaver_reintroduction.pdf. Accessed 1/09/2010. Citing Naiman, R. J., C. A. Johnston, and J. C. Kelly. 1988. Alteration of North American streams by beaver. *Bioscience* 38: 753-762.

429) Outwater, Alice. From chapter 2, Nature's Hydrologists in, *Water: a natural history*. Copyright 1996 by Alice Outwater. Website of Shawnee River Watershed Association. http://www.shawsheen org/Beavers/Natural_ History_of_Beavers/natural_history_of_beavers.html. Accessed 8/21/09.

430) Connelly, Joel. Columnist. "Undaunted, they fight for the Montana way of life." *Seattle Post-Intelligencer*. 10/6/2004. (p. A2)

431) White, Courtney. *Revolution on the Range / The Rise of a New Ranch in the American West*. Island Press/Shearwater Books. 2008. (p. xix)

432) I will be using the term bison for all individuals called buffalo in the U.S. Buffalo, though used in common reference in the U.S., only exist as "true buffalo" in Africa and Asia.

433) Towne, E. Gene, David C. Hartnett, and Robert C. Cochran. 2005.

Vegetation Trends in Tallgrass Prairie From Bison and Cattle Grazing. *Ecological Applications* 15:1550–1559. [doi:10.1890/04-1958].

434) Collins, Scott L. et al. 1998. Modulation of Diversity by Grazing and Mowing in Native Tallgrass Prairie. *Science Magazine.* Vol. 280:745-747. 1 May 1998. http://www-personal.ksu.edu/~jblair/Collins%20et%20al%20 Science%201998.pdf. Accessed 11/27/2010.

435) Plumb, Glen E. and Dodd, Gerald L. 1993. Foraging Ecology of Bison and Cattle on a Mixed Prairie: Implications for Natural Area Management. *Ecological Applications.* Vol. 3, No. 4 (Nov., 1993), (p. 631-643). http://www.jstor.org/pss/1942096. Accessed 11/27/2010.

436) Hart, Richard H. 2001. Plant biodiversity on shortgrass steppe after 55 years of zero, light, moderate, or heavy cattle grazing. Plant Ecology. Volume 155, Number 1, 111-118, DOI: 10.1023/A:1013273400543.

437) Donahue, Debra L. *The Western Range Revisited /Removing Livestock From Public Lands to Preserve Biodiversity.* University of Oklahoma Press. 1999. (31)

438) Donahue, Debra L. *The Western Range Revisited /Removing Livestock From Public Lands to Preserve Biodiversity.* University of Oklahoma Press. 1999. (157, 250)

439) Jones, Allison. 2000. Effects of Cattle Grazing on North American Arid Ecosystems: A Quantitative Review. *Western North American Naturalist.* 60(2), © 2000, (p. 155–164) https://ojs.lib.byu.edu/ojs/index.php/wnan/ article/viewFile/396/262. Accessed 11/27/2010.

440) Curtin, Charles G. 2002. Livestock Grazing, Rest, and Restoration in Arid Landscapes. *Conservation Biology.* Vol. 16, No.3. June 2002. (p. 840-842).

441) Welch, Craig. "WSU Study Examines When Cattle, Wildlife Mix." *Seattle Times.* 6/27/2011. Page B1. http://seattletimes.nwsource.com/html/localnews /2015435240_grazing27m.html. Accessed 6/28/11.

442) Siegel Thines N.J., Shipley L.A., Sayler R.D. 2004. Effects of cattle grazing on ecology and habitat of Columbia Basin pygmy rabbits (Brachylagus idahoensis) (2004) Biological Conservation, 119(4), pp. 525-534. http://www.sciencedirect.com/science/article/pii/S0006320704000187. Accessed 6/28/2011.

443) Fleischner, Thomas L. 1994. Ecological Costs of Livestock Grazing in Western North America. *Conservation Biology*, Volume 8, No. 3, September 1994. (p. 629—644). http://www.prescott.edu/faculty_staff/faculty/tfleis-chner/documents/Ecol.CostsofLivestockGrazing.pdf. Accessed 11/27/2010.

444) http://en.wikipedia.org/wiki/American_Bison. Accessed 11/27/2010.

445) Matlack, Raymond S., Kaufman, Donald W., Kaufman, Glennis A. 2001. Influence of Grazing by Bison and Cattle on Deer Mice in Burned Tallgrass Prairie. *Am. Midi. Nat.* 146:361-368.

446) http://en.wikipedia.org/wiki/American_Bison. Accessed 11/27/2010.

447) http://www.buffalofieldcampaign.org/.

448) Matlack, Raymond S., Kaufman, Donald W., Kaufman, Glennis A. 2001. Influence of Grazing by Bison and Cattle on Deer Mice in Burned Tallgrass Prairie. *Am. Midi. Nat.* 146:361-368.

449) Templeton, Amelia. NPR. "Back To Tradition, Bringing Home The Bison." February 26, 201.1. http://www.npr.org/2011/02/26/134060177/back-to-tradition-bringing-home-the-bison&sc=nl&cc=nh-20110226. Accessed 3/12/2011.

450) Volz, Matt. Associated Pres. "Idaho tribe probing claim of waste in bison hunt." *Seattle Post-Intelligencer.* http://www.seattlepi.com/national/1110ap_us_bison_hunt_tribe.html. Accessed 3/12/2011.

451) http://en.wikipedia.org/wiki/Buffalo_Commons. Accessed 11/27/2010.

452) http://www.vrg.org/journal/vj2011issue4/vj2011issue4poll.php. Accessed 2/07/2012.

453) Speth, James Gustave. *The Bridge at the End of the World / Capitalism, the Environment, and crossing from Crisis to Sustainability.* A Caravan Book. 2008. (p. 63, 71)

454) Ellis, Erle and Navin Ramankutty (Lead Authors); Mark McGinley (Topic Editor). 2008. "Anthropogenic biomes." In: *Encyclopedia of Earth.* Eds. Cutler J. Cleveland (Washington, D.C.: Environmental Information Coalition, National Council for Science and the Environment). First published in the Encyclopedia of Earth November 26, 2007. Last revised August 29, 2008. Retrieved 1/19/2009. http://www.eoearth.org/article/Anthropogenic_biomes, http://creativecommons.org/licenses/by-sa/2.5/.

455) Wiens, John A. 2008. Landscape ecology as a foundation for sustainable conservation. *Landscape Ecol.* DOI 10.1007/s10980-008-9284-x. http://leml.asu.edu/jingle/Web_Pages/LE_Website/PDFs/Landsc_conservation/Wiens-2009-LE-as-foundation-for-sustainability.pdf. Accessed 11/10/2009.

456) Nebraska Game and Parks Commission. Nebraska Wildlife Species. http://www.ngpc.state.ne.us/wildlife/prairiedogs.asp. Accessed 2/4/2010.

457) Dakota Hunting Trips webpage. http://dakotahuntingtrips.com/prairiedo-

gandcoyotehunts.html on which is listed http://www.dakotahunt ingtrips.com/antleradventures.html. Accessed 2/4/2010.

458) Brady, Jeff. Reporter. Outlaw Prairie Dogs Find Refuge with Rancher. December 5, 2006. National Public Radio – All Things Considered. http://www.npr.org/templates/story/story.php?storyId=6582517. Accessed 2/4/2010.

459) Erlich, Paul R. and Pringle, Robert M. 2008. Where Does Biodiversity Go From Here? A Grim Business-As-Ususal Forecast and a Hopeful Portfolio of Partial Solutions. *PNAS*. August 12, 2008. vol. 105, suppl. 1, pp. 11579–11586· www.pnas.org_cgi_doi_10.1073_pnas.0801911105. http:// www.pnas.org/content/105/suppl.1/11579.full.pdf+htm. Accessed 1/09/2010.

460) Livestock and Climate Policy: Less Meat or Less Carbon? Round Table on Sustainable Development.
John Stephenson, Principal Advisor. OECD. SG/SD/RT(2010)1. 2/11/2010. Citations omitted. http://www.oecd.org/dataoecd/22/3/46512036.pdf. Accessed 2/9/2012.

461) "Slaughtering the Amazon." Greenpeace International. 2009. http://www. greenpeace.org/raw/content/international/press/reports/slaughtering-the- amazon.pdf for the executive summary. The full report is in four parts, starting with part 1: http://www.greenpeace.org/international/ assets/ binaries/slaughtering-the-amazon-part1.

462) Phillips, Tom. "Amazon Defenders Face Death or Exile." *The Guardian*. 2/12/2012. http://www.guardian.co.uk/world/2012/feb/12/brazil-amazon- rainforest-activists-murder. Accessed 2/21/2012.

463) http://www.peta.org/feat/mercedes/FleshFreeCars.asp. Accessed 5/4/2010.

464) Newkirk, Ingrid. *Making Kind Choices*. St. Martin's Griffin, publisher. 2005. (p. 27)

465) Sonesson, Ulf et al. 2009. Food Production and Emissions of Greenhouse Gasses / An overview of the climate impact of different product groups. Swedish Institute for Food and Biotechnology. Swedish Presidency of the European Union. http://www.se2009.eu/polopoly_fs/1.23297!menu/stand ard/file/foodproduction.pdf. Accessed 12/15/2009.

466) Leibtag, Ephraim. 2008. "Corn Prices Near Record High, But What About Food Costs?" *Amber Waves*, a USDA publication. February, 2008. http://www.ers.usda.gov/amberwaves/february08/features/cornprices.htm. Accessed 1/04/2009.

467) Montgomery, M.R. *A Cow's Life/The Surprising History of Cattle and How the Black Angus Came to be Home on the Range*. Walker & Company, publisher. 2004. (p. 144)

468) Roberts, Paul. *The End of Food*. Houghton Mifflin Company. 2008. (p.210)

469) Pollan, Michael. *Omnivores Dilemma/A Natural History of Four Meals*. Penguin Books. 2006. (p. 115)

470) Smil, Vaclav. 2002. Worldwide transformation of diets, burdens of meat production and opportunities for novel food proteins. *Enzyme and Microbial Technology* 30 (2002) 305–311. http://home.cc.umanitoba.ca/~vsmil/pdf_pubs/enzme1.pdf. Accessed 12/7/2009.

461) Smil, Vaclav. 2002. Worldwide transformation of diets, burdens of meat production and opportunities for novel food proteins. *Enzyme and Microbial Technology* 30 (2002) 305–311. http://home.cc.umanitoba.ca/~vsmil/pdf_pubs/enzme1.pdf. Accessed 12/7/2009.

472) Rose, Stewart. *The Vegetarian Solution / Your Answer to Cancer, Heart Disease, Global Warming, and More*. The Book Publishing Company. 2007. (p. 97)

473) Food and Agriculture Organization of the United Nations (FAO) http://www.fao.org/ag/magazine/0603sp2.htm.

474) *Species:* Newsletter of the Species Survival Commission. International Union for the Conservation of Nature/IUCN. *Species* 48: July–December 2007. http://cmsdata.iucn.org/downloads/species_48_web.pdf. Accessed 11/22/2009.

475) Louisiana Alligator Advisory Council. http://www.alligatorfur.com/index.htm. Accessed 4/5/2011.

476) http://www.wlf.louisiana.gov/frequently-asked-alligator-questions. Accessed 10/23/2011.

477) Elsey, R.M. and Woodward, A.R. 2010. American Alligator *Alligator mississippiensis*. Pp. 1-4 *in* Crocodiles. Status Survey and Conservation Action Plan. Third Edition, ed. by S.C. Manolis and C. Stevenson. Crocodile Specialist Group: Darwin. http://www.iucncsg.org/ph1/modules/Publications/ActionPlan3/01_Alligator_mississippiensis.pdf. Accessed 4/5/2011.

478) http://www.macroevolution.net/alligator-mating.html and http://en.wikipedia.org/wiki/American_alligator. Accessed 11/23/2009.

479) Elsey, R.M. and Woodward, A.R. 2010. American Alligator *Alligator mississippiensis*. Pp. 1-4 *in* Crocodiles. Status Survey and Conservation Action Plan. Third Edition, ed. by S.C. Manolis and C. Stevenson. Crocodile

Specialist Group: Darwin. Citing (Garrick *et al.* 1978; Vliet 1989). http://www.iucncsg.org/ph1/modules/Publications/ActionPlan3/01_Alligat or_mississippiensis.pdf. Accessed 4/5/2011.

480) http://www.biggamehunt.net/sections/Alligator/Alligator-Hunting-Big-Business-Across-the-South-08110704.html. Accessed 11/24/2009.

481) http://en.wikipedia.org/wiki/Soybean. Accessed 5/24/2011. And elsewhere.

482) The Millennium Development Goals Report. 2009. United Nations. New York. http://mdgs.un.org/unsd/mdg/Resources/Static/Products/Progress20 09/MDG_Report_2009_En.pdf. Accessed 1/30/2010.

483) http://en.wikipedia.org/wiki/Conservation_biology.

484) Wilson, Edmond O. *The Future of Life*. Borzoi Book/Published by Alfred A. Knopf . New York. 2002. (p. 14)

485) Wilson, Edmund O. *The Future of Life*. Borzoi Book/Published by Alfred A. Knopf. 2002. (p. 100)

486) Living Beyond Our Means: Natural Assets and Human Well-being. Statement from the Board. March 2005. A report for the United Nations General Assembly. http://www.millenniumassessment.org/documents/ document.429.aspx.pdf. Accessed 1/07/2010.

487) Wake, David B. and Vredenburg, Vance T. 2008. Are we in the midst of the sixth mass extinction? A view from the world of amphibians. Published online before print August 11, 2008.
doi: 10.1073/pnas.0801921105. AND *PNAS*. August 12, 2008. vol. 105 no. Supplement 1 11466-11473. http://www.pnas.org/content/105/suppl.1/ 11466.full. Accessed 2/22/2010.

488) Dobson, Andrew P. *Conservation and Biodiversity*. Scientific American Library. 2006. (p.119).

489) World Farm Animals Day. Based on their extrapolation of FAO statistics at www.faostae.fao.org . http://www.wfad.org/statistics/index.htm. Accessed 2/24/2010. This is in the general range of published estimates that I've seen.

490) http://www.worldwildlife.org/wildworld/profiles/terrestrial/pa/pa13 29_full.html. Accessed 10/23/2011.

491) Primack, Richard B. *Essentials of Conservation Biology*. Sinauer Associates, Inc., publishers. 1993. (p. 5)

492) Myikya, Stephen Mbithi. 2007. Globalized Out? A Case For Fish Trade in Developing Countries. OECD / Organization for Economic Co-operation and Development. TAD/FI/GLOB(2007)5. http://www.olis.oecd.org/olis/

2007doc.nsf/NEWRMSENGDAT/NT00000D76/$FILE/JT03224679.PDF. Accessed 2/24/2010.

493) Swartz, Wilf et al. 2010. Sourcing seafood for the three major markets: The EU, Japan and the USA.
Marine Policy. 34(2010)1366-1373. http://www.seaaroundus.org/rese archer/dpauly/PDF/2010/JournalArticles/SourcingSeafoodForTheThreeMaj orMarkets.pdf. Accessed 2/2/2011.

494) Hardin, Garrett. 1968. "The Tragedy of the Commons." *Science* 13 December 1968: Vol. 162. no. 3859, pp. 1243 – 1248. DOI: 10.1126/ science.162.3859.1243. http://www.garrethardinsociety.org/articles/art_ tragedy_of_the_commons.html. Accessed 1/09/2010. "The tragedy of the commons develops in this way. Picture a pasture open to all. It is to be expected that each herdsman will try to keep as many cattle as possible on the commons. Such an arrangement may work reasonably satisfactorily for centuries because tribal wars, poaching, and disease keep the numbers of both man and beast well below the carrying capacity of the land. Finally, however, comes the day of reckoning, that is, the day when the long-desired goal of social stability becomes a reality. At this point, the inherent logic of the commons remorselessly generates tragedy.… The only way we can preserve and nurture other and more precious freedoms is by relin-quishing the freedom to breed, and that very soon."

495) Hardin later had this to say about this statement: "As a result of discussions carried out during the past decade I now suggest a better wording of the central idea: Under conditions of overpopulation, freedom in an unmanaged commons brings ruin to all. When there is no scarcity, as is the case in a pioneer community with ample resources, an unmanaged commons may in fact be the best distribution device since it avoids the costs of management." In Hardin, Garrett. An Ecolate View of the Human Predicament. From a talk later developed into his book, *Filters Against Folly.* 1985. http://www.garrethardinsociety.org/articles/art_ecolate_view_hu man_predicament.html. Accessed 1/09/2010.

496) Hardin, Garrett. "The Tragedy of the Commons." *Science.* 13 December 1968: Vol. 162. no. 3859, (p. 1243 – 1248). DOI: 10.1126/science.162.3859.1243. http://www.garrethardinsociety.org/articles /art_tragedy_of_the_commons.html. Accessed 1/09/2010.

497) http://www.npr.org/2011/11/11/142245106/western-black-rhino-declared-

extinct. Accessed 11/11/2011.

498) Marten, Gerald G. *Human Ecology / Basic Concepts for Sustainable Development*. 2001. Earthscan Publications Ltd. London, UK. (p. 145)

499) Berkes, F., Feeney, D., McCay, B.J., and Acheson, J.M. "The Benefits of the Commons." In *The Environment in Anthropology*. Nora, Haenn and Richard R. Wilk, editors. New York University Press. 2006. Sourced from an original article in *Nature*, vol.340:91-93. Macmillan Magazines, Ltd.

500) Townsend, Patricia K. *Environmental Anthropology / From Pigs to Policies*. Second Edition. Waveland Press.2009, 2000. (p. 94)

501) Hardin, Garrett. The Tragedy of the Commons. *Science*. 13 December 1968: Vol. 162. no. 3859, pp. 1243 – 1248. DOI: 10.1126/science.162.3859.1243. "A Madison Avenue man might call this persuasion; I prefer the greater candor of the word coercion." http://www.garretthardinsociety.org/articles/art_tragedy_of_the_commons.html. Accessed 1/09/2010.

502) USDA. AREI Chapter 1.3: Land Ownership and Farm Structure. "Farm operators do not own all the land used in agriculture. According to the 1999 Agricultural Economics and Land Ownership Survey (AELOS), farmers held 58 percent of the land in farms in 1999 (USDA, 2001). These landowning farmers also made up 58 percent of the 3.4 million farmland owners." http://www.ers.usda.gov/publications/arei/eib16/Chapter1/1.3/. Accessed 2/25/2010.

503) http://www.ers.usda.gov/publications/EIB14/eib14j.pdf. Accessed 9/3/2011. Still referring to 2002 data.

504) USDA. Briefing Rooms, Overview. http://www.ers.usda.gov/Briefing/LandUse/. Accessed 2/25/2010.

505) USDA Briefing Rooms. http://www.ers.usda.gov/Briefing/LandUse/major-landusechapter.htm. Accessed 2/25/2010.

506) Bahnson, Fred. "Farmed Out." *The Sun*. Issue 418. October 2010. (p. 4-12)

507) North American Bird Conservation Initiative, U.S. Department of the Interior. *The State of the Birds*. 2009. http://www.stateofthebirds.org/pdf_files/State_of_the_Birds_2009.pdf. Accessed 12/5/2010. Humane Research Council Spotcheck #1015. www.humanespot.org.

508) Bahnson, Fred. "Farmed Out." *The Sun*. Issue 418. October 2010. (p. 4-12)

509) Pimentel, David and Kounang, Nadia. 1998. Ecology of Soil Erosion in Ecosystems. *Ecosystems* (1998) 1: 416–426. http://www.ciens.ucv.ve:8080/generador/sites/ProVeg/archivos/Seminariopercent201percent20N

uriangel.pdf. Accessed 12/14/2010.

510) 2050: A third more mouths to feed. September 23, 2009. FAO Media Center. http://www.fao.org/news/story/en/item/35571/icode/. Accessed 2/4/2010.

511) http://www.wildlandsproject.org/cms/index.cfm?group_id=1000 /. http://www.wildlandsproject.org/cms/page1089.cfm. Accessed 2/24/2010. http://rewilding.org/rewildit/about-tri/vision/. Accessed 2/24/2010.

512) http://rewilding.org/rewildit/the-science-behind-continental-scale-conservation/the-north-american-wildlands-network-four-megalinkages/. Accessed 2/11/2012.

513) Soule, Michael and Noss, Reed. 1998. "Rewilding and Biodiversity: Complimentary Goals for Continental Conservation." *WildEarth*. Fall 1998. http://academic.evergreen.edu/curricular/MES/rewilding.pdf. Accessed 2/11/2012.

514) Dean, Cornelia. "Research Shows That Plants Like a Path to Biodiversity." *New York Times*. Environment. September 5, 2006. Reporting on a Sciencemag.org article, "Corridors Increase Plant Species Richness at Large Scales." http://www.nytimes.com/2006/09/05/science/earth/05wild.html?_r=1. Accessed 3/4/2012.

515) Characterizing A Transition Toward Sustainability. Sustainability Science Project. Referring to Project summary documents: "Science and Technology for Sustainable Development." Special Feature in the *Proceedings of the National Academy of Sciences of the United States of America (PNAS)*. 8 July 2003. Research and Assessment Systems for Sustainability Program. 2003. Science and Technology for Sustainable Development. *Proceedings of the National Academy of Sciences of the United States of America (PNAS)*. Special Feature. 100(14) (8 July): 8059-8091. http://www.hks.harvard.edu/sust/transition.htm. Accessed 5/16/09.
Many relevant articles are found at the website for *The Proceedings of the National Academy of Sciences in the United States(PNAS)*: http://www.pnas.org/site/misc/sustainability.shtml. Accessed 5/16/2009.

516) Trends change from one year to the next. Some goals may be met based on present information, e.g. sanitation.. Update at http://www.un.org/millenniumgoals/poverty.shtml. Accessed 9/3/2011.

517) Conservation biology draws on many disciplines to understand and prevent species extinction by considering the many factors that cause it. Overwhelmingly, humans are the cause of extinction.

518) Wilson, Edward O. *Consilience / The Unity of Knowledge.* Vintage Books/Random House. 1998. (p. 10)

519) Wilson, Edmund O. *The Future of Life.* Borzoi Book/Published by Alfred A. Knopf. 2002. (p. 41)

520) U.S. Department of the Interior, Fish and Wildlife Service, and U.S. Department of Commerce, U.S. Census Bureau. 2006. National Survey of Fishing, Hunting, and Wildlife-Associated Recreation. Report is outsourced, so lead author was Rob Southwick of Southwick Associates. http://www.census.gov/prod/2008 pubs/fhw06-nat.pdf. Accessed 12/28/2009.

521) U.S. Census Bureau. American Community Survey 2006. Actual number reported is 299,398,485. http://factfinder.census.gov/servlet/STTable?_bm=y&-geo_id=01000US&-qr_name=ACS_2006_EST_G00_S0101&-ds_name=ACS_2006_EST_G00_. Accessed 12/28/2009.

522) Southwick Associates Newsletter. Winter 2011. And personal email from Southwick Associates, dated 1/27/2011.

523) U.S. Fish and Wildlife Service. National Hunting and Fishing Trends 1991–2006 / A Focus on Fishing and Hunting by Species. December, 2010. Richard Aiken. This does not reflect that "big game" hunting (mostly deer) was somewhat steady; the decline was driven by subsets of hunters, like those who kill squirrels and other "small game. http://library.fws.gov/Pubs/nat-survey2006-trends-fishing-hunting-1991-2006-focus-on-species.pdf. Accessed 2/8/2011.

524) U.S. Department of the Interior, Fish and Wildlife Service, and U.S. Department of Commerce, U.S. Census Bureau. 2006 National Survey of Fishing, Hunting, and Wildlife-Associated Recreation. Report is outsourced, so lead author was Rob Southwick of Southwick Associates. http://www.census.gov/prod/200 8pubs/fhw06-nat.pdf. Accessed 12/28/2009.

525) http://www.fws.gov/offices/H.DaleHall.htm. Accessed 2/8/2011. "... he managed the Service's activities relating to the northern spotted owl, desert tortoise, endangered Hawaiian birds, and other listed species. He was also responsible for the regulation of the region's wetlands, environmental contaminants, issues, and Federal water projects. Under his guidance, more than 300 new species were placed under the protection of the Endangered Species Act and nearly $200 million in environmental contaminants cleanup

settlements were reached with parties responsible for the pollution."

526) U.S. Department of the Interior, Fish and Wildlife Service, and U.S. Department of Commerce, U.S.
Census Bureau. 2006 National Survey of Fishing, Hunting, and Wildlife-Associated Recreation. Report is outsourced, so lead author was Rob Southwick of Southwick Associates. http://www.census.gov/prod/2008 pubs/fhw06-nat.pdf. Accessed 12/28/2009.

527) Hunting in America / An Economic Engine and Conservation Powerhouse. 2007. Association of Fish and Wildlife Agencies. Outsourced to Southwick Associates. Rob Southwick. "These were produced for the Association of Fish and Wildlife Agencies with funding from the Multistate Conservation Grant Program 2007."

528) "Public Opinion Sides with Hunters: Survey Shows Most Americans Think Hunting's OK." Results. 2006 Survey conducted by Responsive Management. Summarized by the Humane Research Council. Spot check #958. www.humanespot.org.

529) Hunting in America / An Economic Engine and Conservation Powerhouse. 2007. Association of Fish and Wildlife Agencies. Outsourced to Southwick Associates. Rob Southwick. "These were produced for the Association of Fish and Wildlife Agencies with funding from the Multistate Conservation Grant Program 2007."

530) http://wildlifelaw.unm.edu/fedbook/pract.html. Accessed 12/29/2009.

531) Sillman, Marcie. "On and Off the Dole." Culture Shock Series, Part 2. 2/10/2011. KUOW/National Public Radio. Marcie was quoting studies on the economic impacts of the arts at a time when the state was slashing its funding.

532) WDFW News Release. April 7, 2011. "Lakes stocked for big April 30 fishing season opener." Received by email, same date.

533) Hardin, Garrett. "An Ecolate View of the Human Predicament." From a talk later developed into his book, Filters Against Folly. 1985. http://www.garretthardinsociety.org/articles/art_ecolate_view_human_pre dicament.html. Accessed 1/09/2010.

534) Jones, H.P., Schmitz, O.J. 2009. Rapid Recovery of Damaged Ecosystems. *PLoS ONE* 4(5): e5653. doi:10.1371/journal.pone.000565.3. http://www. plosone.org/article/infopercent3Adoipercent2F10.1371percent2Fjournal.po ne.0005653. Accessed 8/21/09.

535) Williams, David B. *The Street-Smart Naturalist, Field Notes from Seattle*. West Winds Press, an imprint of Graphic Arts Center Publishing Company. 2005. www.gacpc.com.

536) Nash, Roderick Frazier. *The Rights of Nature*/A History of Environmental Ethics. The University of Wisconsin Press. 1989.(pp.63 and 73)

537) Stringer MJ, Sales-Pardo M, Nunes Amaral LA. 2008. Effectiveness of Journal Ranking Schemes as a Tool for Locating Information. PLoS ONE 3(2): e1683. doi:10.1371/journal.pone.0001683. http://www.plosone.org /article/info:doi/10.1371/journal.pone.0001683 Accessed 11/18/2011. AND Northwestern University. Media Release. New method ranks quality of scientific journals by field. 2/26/2008. http://www.eurekalert.org/ pub_releases/2008-02/nu-nmr022608.php. Accessed 2/11/2011.

538) Lovelock, James. *The Revenge of Gaia / Earth's Climate Crisis and the Fate of Humanity*. Basic Books, publisher. 2006. (p.5)

539) Kupfer, David. "The Sincerest Form of Flattery." An interview of Janine Benyus. *Sun Magazine*. September, 2009. Issue 405. Quoting from the intro-duction of that interview, http://www.www.thesun magazine.org/issues /405/the_sincerest_form_of_flattery. Accessed 8/31/09.

540) Mora C, Tittensor DP, Adl S, Simpson AGB, Worm B. 2011. How Many Species Are There on Earth and in the Ocean? *PLoS Biol* 9(8): e1001127. doi:10.1371/journal.pbio.1001127. http://www.plosbiology.org/article/info %3Adoi%2F10.1371%2Fjournal.pbio.1001127. Accessed 2/11/2012.

541) Dirzo, Rodolfo and Raven, Peter H. 2003. Global State of Biodiversity and Loss. *Annu. Rev. Environ. Resour*. 2003. 28:137–67. doi: 10.1146/annurev .energy.28.050302.105532. http://ecology.botany.ufl.edu/adveco/downloads /GlobalBiodiversityLoss2003DirzoRaven.pdf. Accessed 11/01/2009.

542) Mora C, Tittensor DP, Adl S, Simpson AGB, Worm B. 2011. How Many Species Are There on Earth and in the Ocean? *PLoS Biol* 9(8): e1001127. doi:10.1371/journal.pbio.1001127. http://www.plosbiology.org/article/info %3Adoi%2F10.1371%2Fjournal.pbio.1001127. Accessed 2/11/2012.

543) Mora C, Tittensor DP, Adl S, Simpson AGB, Worm B. 2011. How Many Species Are There on Earth and in the Ocean? *PLoS Biol* 9(8): e1001127. doi:10.1371/journal.pbio.1001127. http://www.plosbiology.org/article/info %3Adoi%2F10.1371%2Fjournal.pbio.1001127. Accessed 2/11/2012.

544) Cart, Julie. "Administration excised scientists' warnings in grazing report." *Los Angeles Times*. As printed in the *Seattle Times* / Nation and World.

6/18/2005.

545) McKie, Robin. Science Editor. *The Observer.* "Attacks paid for by big business are 'driving science into a dark era." 2/18/2012. http://www. guardian.co.uk/science/2012/feb/19/science-scepticism-usdomesticpolicy. Accessed 2/21/2012.

546) Galloway, James N. et al. 2007. International Trade in Meat: The Tip of the Pork Chop. *Ambio* Vol. 36, No. 8, December 2007. Royal Swedish Academy of Sciences. http://ambio.allenpress.com/archive/0044-7447/36/8/pdf/i0044-7447-36-8-622.pdf.

547) Schmid, Randolph A. Associated Press Science Writer. "Climate Warming Gasses Rising Faster Than Expected." February 14, 2009. http://www .newsvine.com:80/_news/2009/02/14/2435571-climate-warming-gases-rising-faster-than-expected.

548) CO2Now.org. http://co2now.org/Current-CO2/CO2-Trend/acceleration-of-atmospheric-co2.html. Accessed 2/12/2012.

549) http://www.pmel.noaa.gov/co2/story/Ocean%2BAcidification. Accessed 2/12/2012.

550) Joling, Dan. "Research finds higher acidity in Alaska waters." Associated Press. *Seattle Post-Intelligencer.* 8/24/2009. http://www.seattlepi.com/national/1501ap_us_acid_oceans_alaska.html?source=rss.

551) Ocean Acidification: The Other CO2 Problem. Natural Resources Defense Council. http://www.nrdc.org/oceans/acidification/. Accessed 3/22/2010.

552) Laura Lee Bennett

553) Butler, Matthew et al. 2005. Wildlife ranching in North America – arguments, issues, and perspectives. *Wildlife Society Bulletin.* 2005. (33)1:381-389. http://www.rw.ttu.edu/butler/pdf/Butler_et_al_WSB_33 (1)_381-389. pdf. Accessed 10/10/2009.

554) http://www.tpwd.state.tx.us/huntwild/hunt/public/btth/. Accessed 3/22/2010.

555) http://www.tpwd.state.tx.us/newsmedia/releases/?req=20091030a. Accessed 3/22/2010. "...to study the effects of African ungulates on local habitat, and interactions between exotic and native wildlife."

556) http://www.tpwd.state.tx.us/landwater/land/habitats/hillcountry/. Accessed 3/23/2010.

557) Texas Land Trends. Texas A&M Institute of Renewable Natural Resources / American Farmland Trust. http://www.texaslandtrends.org/Briefings/

Landuse.aspx. Accessed 3/23/2010.

558) http://www.tpwd.state.tx.us/huntwild/hunt/wma/find_a_wma/list/?id=14. Accessed 3/22/2010.

559) Texas Land Trends. Texas A&M Institute of Renewable Natural Resources / American Farmland Trust. http://www.texaslandtrends.org/Briefings/ LossOfAgLand.aspx. Accessed 3/23/2010.

560) "Quaggasfontein is a private game reserve where the wildlife and their environment are as important to us as our esteemed clients. We are proud of the tame nature of the wild animals and strive vigorously to maintain this state of affairs in order that game may be viewed and photographed in their natural habitat at close distance. http://www.qsafari.com/hunting.html. Accessed 9/8/209.

561) Butler, Matthew et al. 2005. Wildlife ranching in North America – arguments, issues, and perspectives. *Wildlife Society Bulletin*. 2005. (33)1:381-389. http://www.rw.ttu.edu/butler/pdf/Butler_et_al_WSB_33(1)_ 381-389.pdf. Accessed 10/10/2009.

562) Texas Safari Ranch. http://www.texassafari.com/hunting.html. Accessed 2/8/2011.

563) http://www.junipermountain.net/index.html. Accessed 12/29/2009.

564) Ryan, John. Reporter. Restoring the Skagit. KUOW Public Radio, Seattle, WA. 8/27/2009. http://www.kuow.org/program.php?id=18279. Accessed 12/29/2009.

565) Potential Costs of Losing Hunting and Trapping as Wildlife Management Methods. Updated May 25, 2005. Animal Use Issues Committee of the International Association of Fish and Wildlife Agencies. http://www. fishwildlife.org/pdfs/Outreachpercent202004percent20DCpercent20M-35-O.pdf. Accessed 12/28/2009. www.iafwa.org.

566) Hilborn, R. et al. 1995. Sustainable Exploitation of Renewable Resources. 1995. *Annu. Rev. Ecol. Syst.* 1995. 26:45-67. www.annualreviews.org/ aronline.

567) Struhsaker, Thomas T. 1998. A Biologist's Perspective on the Role of Sustainable Harvest in Conservation. *Conservation Biology*. Vol. 12, No. 4. August 1998. (p. 930-932) http://www.life.illinois.edu/ib/451/Struhsaker percent20(1998).pdf. Accessed 11/7/2009.

568) Ray, Paul H. and Anderson, Sherry Ruth. *The Cultural Creatives*. Three Rivers Press. New York. 2000. (p. 263)

569) http://fishandgame.idaho.gov/cms/wildlife/wolves/. Accessed 9/5/2009.

570) http://fishandgame.idaho.gov/apps/releases/view.cfm?NewsID=5049 Accessed 9/5/2009.

571) http://www.comcast.net/articles/news-science/20090831/US.Hunting. Wolves/. Accessed 9/5/2009.

572) http://fishandgame.idaho.gov/apps/releases/view.cfm?NewsID=5049 .

573) Dvorak, Todd. Associated Press. "Wolf hunt is on in Idaho - for now." Tue Sep 1, 7:14 PM EDT, as posted at http://www.comcast.net/articles/news-science/20090831/US.Hunting.Wolves/. Accessed 9/5/2009.

574) Gese, Eric M. and Grothe, Scott. 1995. Analysis of Coyote Predation on Deer and Elk during Winter in Yellowstone National Park, Wyoming. *American Midland Naturalist*, Vol. 133, No. 1 (Jan., 1995). (p. 36-43). http://www.jstor.org/pss/2426345. Accessed 1/02/2010.

575) Ripple, William J. and Larsen, Eric J. 2000. Historic aspen recruitment, elk, and wolves in northern Yellowstone National Park, USA. *Biological Conservation*. Volume 95, Issue 3, October 2000. (p. 361-370). doi:10.1016/S0006-3207(00)00014-8. Accessed 1/02/2010.

576) Beschta, Robert L. 2003. Cottonwoods, Elk, and Wolves in the Lamar Valley of Yellowstone National Park. *Ecological Applications*: Vol. 13, No. 5. (p.1295-1309). doi: 10.1890/02-5175. http://www.esajournals.org/doi/abs/10.1890/02-5175. Accessed 1/02/2010.

577) Wright, Gregory J. et al. 2006. Selection of Northern Yellowstone Elk by Gray Wolves and Hunters. *Journal of Wildlife Management*. (2006) 70(4). (p. 1070-1078).

578) Wallach, AD, Ritchie EG, Read J, O'Neill AJ. 2009. More than Mere Numbers: The Impact of Lethal Control on the Social Stability of a Top-Order Predator. *PLoS ONE* 4(9): e6861. doi:10.1371/journal.pone.0006861. http://www.plosone.org/article/info:doi/10.1371/journal.pone.0006861. Accessed 12/27/2009.

579) http://fwpiis.mt.gov/content/getItem.aspx?id=54632. Accessed 2/12/2012.

580) http://fishandgame.idaho.gov/cms/hunt/wolf/. Accessed 2/11/2011. "U.S. District Court Judge Donald Molloy in Missoula issued an order Thursday, August 5, that in effect returns the gray wolf in Idaho and the Northern Rocky Mountains to the protection of the Endangered Species Act. Wolves south of Interstate 90 in Idaho have reverted to management under a section of the Endangered Species Act known as the 10(j) rule, allowing

some flexibility to respond to livestock depredation and impacts on big game. Wolves north of Interstate 90 in Idaho were fully protected under the Endangered Species Act."

581) On April 15, 2011, President Obama signed the 2011 federal Budget Bill that included the following language: "Before the end of the 60-day period beginning on the date of enactment of this division, the Secretary of the Interior shall reissue the final rule published on April 2, 2009 (74 Fed. Reg. 15123 et seq.) without regard to any other provision of statute or regulation that applies to issuance of such rule. Such reissuance (including this section) shall not be subject to judicial review and shall not abrogate or otherwise have any effect on the Order and Judgment issued by the United States District Court for the District of Wyoming in Case Numbers 09-CV-118J and 09-CV-138J on November 18, 2010." IDFG Commission meeting minutes of May 19, 2011. Agenda item #14. http://fishandgame.idaho.gov/public/about/commission/2011/05_18_2011_agenda.pdf. Accessed 9/4/2011.

582) http://fishandgame.idaho.gov/public/hunt/?getPage=266. Accessed 9/4/2011.

583) http://www.spokesman.com/stories/2011/sep/04/montana-begins-wolf-hunt-season/. Accessed 9/04/2011.

584) http://fishandgame.idaho.gov/public/hunt/?getPage=265. Accessed 9/4/2011. "Why does Idaho need to control wolves, black bears and mountain lions where predation suppresses elk, deer, or moose populations? Idaho law, dating back to a 1938 ballot initiative, requires Fish and Game to manage for a surplus of elk, deer, and other wildlife for public harvest. When predation from wolves, mountain lions, or black bears has unacceptable impacts to other game populations, IDFG develops predation management plan to address the situation."

585) Smith, Christian A. and Sime, Carolyn A. Policy Issues Related to Wolves in the Northern Rocky Mountains. Transactions of the 72nd North American Wildlife and Natural Resources Conference. Held March 20 to 24, 2007 in Portland, Oregon. Wildlife Management Institute, an organization heavily into predator suppression and affiliated with Safari Club International and the Boon and Crockett Club, trophy hunters. https://www.wildlifemanagementinstitute.org/store/product.php?productid=16196&cat=251&bestseller=Y. Accessed 2/18/2011.

586) ADFG. 2007. "Understanding Predator Control in Alaska." http://www.

adfg.alaska.gov/static/home/about/management/wildlifemanagement/inte nsivemanagement/pdfs/predator_booklet.pdf. Accessed 2/13/2012.

587) Pemberton, Mary. Associated Press. "Alpha female wolf killed; mate howls for its return." *Seattle-Post Intelligencer*. 2/26/2005. (p. A2).

588) ADFG. 2006. Findings of the Alaska Board of Game. 2006-164-BOG. http://www.adfg.alaska.gov/static/regulations/regprocess/gameboard/pdfs /findings/06164bog.pdf. Accessed 2/13/2012.

589) Murphy, Kim. *Los Angeles Times*. "Alaska expands aerial shooting of bears." 1/18/2012. http://www.latimes.com/news/nationworld/nation/la-na-alaska-hunt-20120118,0,1078567.story?2344344234. Accessed 1/21/2012.

590) Sherwonit, Bill. "Alaska's newest wildlife experiment: Snaring and shooting brown bears." *Anchorage Press*. January 12, 2012. http://www.anchorage-press.com/news/alaska-s-newest-wildlife-experiment-snaring-and-shooting-brown-bears/article_70f96850-3d76-11e1-8de2-001871e3ce6c.html. Accessed 2/15/2012.

591) Sinnott, Rick. "Does science back up Alaska's policy of killing grizzly bears?" AlaskaDispatch. September 9, 2011. http://www.alaskadi spatch.com/article/does-science-back-alaskas-policy-killing-grizzly-bears. Accessed 2/13/2012. "Rick Sinnott is a former Alaska Department of Fish and Game wildlife biologist." See also scientists' letter to Gov. Palin at http://www.defenders.org/resources/publications/programs_and_policy/w ildlife_conservation/imperiled_species/wolf/alaska_wolf/scientist_and_wil dlife_professional_letter_to_ak_gov._palin.pdf. Accessed 2/13/2012.

592) Williams, Ted. "Kill, Baby, Kill.: Incite. *Audubon*. Vol. 111, No. 4; July-August 2009. http://www.audubonmagazine.org/incite/incite0907.html.

593) This essay was first published in the Fall 1983 issue of *Alaska Fish Tales & Game Trails*. It is part of a memoir, *The Stars, The Snow, The Fire*, published by Graywolf Press in St. Paul, MN. The author, a long-time Alaskan, presently makes his home in Helena, Montana. http://www.wildlife .alaska.gov/index.cfm?adfg=trapping.hearts.

594) U.S. Geological Service, Northern Prairie Wildlife Research Center, in North Dakota. Furtakers Educational Manual. http://www.npwrc.usgs .gov:80/resource/mammals/furtake/beaver.htm.

595) Muth, Robert M. et al. 2006. Unnecessary Source of Pain and Suffering or Necessary Management Tool: Attitudes of Conservation Professionals Toward Outlawing Leghold Traps. *Wildlife Society Bulletin*: October 2006,

Vol. 34, No. 3, pp. 706-715. http://pinnacle.allenpress.com/doi/abs/10.219
3/0091-7648percent282006percent2934percent5B706percent3AUSOPASp
ercent5D2.0.COpercent3B2?journalCode=wbul. Accessed 12/5/2010.

596) Vucetich, John A. and Nelson, Michael P. 2007. What are 60 warblers worth?
Killing in the name of conservation. *Oikos* 116: 1267_1278, 2007. doi:
10.1111/j.2007.0030-1299.15536.x. http://forest.mtu.edu/classes/fw4260/
pdfs/VandN2007.pdf. Accessed 5/4/2010.

597) McComb, Karen et al. 2001. Matriarchs As Repositories of Social Knowledge
in African Elephants. *Science.* 20 April 2001: Vol. 292. no. 5516, pp. 491 – 494;
DOI:10.1126/science.1057895. http://www.sciencemag.org/cgi/content/abs
tract/292/551 6/4911. Accessed 10/12/2009.

598) Hutchins, Michael. A response in the Letters section to an article (Perry and
Perry, 2008), and a response to Hutchins by Perry and Perry, both given the
same title, Animal Rights and Conservation. *Conservation Biology.* Volume
22, No. 4. 2008.

599) Perry, Dan and Perry, Gad. Improving Interactions between Animal Rights
Groups and Conservation Biologists.
Conservation Biology, Volume 22, No. 1, 27–35. DOI: 10.1111/j.1523-
1739.2007.00845.x. http://www.neighborhoodcats.org/uploads/File/Res
ources/Articles/Animalrights&Conservation2008.pdf. Accessed 11/02/2009.

600) Scully, Matthew. *Dominion / The Power of Man, the Suffering of Animals, and
the Call to Mercy.* St. Martin's Press. 2002. Quoting Douglas H. Chadwick in
The Fate of Elephants. San Francisco: Sierra Club Books, 1992. (p. 343)

601) Allendorf, Fred W. and Hard, Jeffrey J. 2009. Human-induced evolution
caused by unnatural selection through harvest of wild animals. *PNAS.* June
16, 2009. Vol. 106/ suppl. 1. (p. 9987–9994). www.pnas.org_cgi_doi_
10.1073_pnas.0901069106. Like domesticated species, heavily hunted
wildlife species have a much higher rate of mortality than they would if
hunted by nonhuman predators alone. It is an entirely different evolutionary process that these biologists say needs to be incorporated into
wildlife management. ... "... the frequency of elephants (Loxodonta africana)
without tusks increased from 10 percent to 38 percent in South Luangwa
National Park, Zambia, apparently brought about by poaching of elephants
for their ivory. Similarly, trophy hunting for bighorn sheep (Ovis
canadensis) in Alberta, Canada caused a decrease in horn size because rams
with larger horns had a greater probability of being removed from the

population by hunting."

602) Prugh, Laura R. et al. 2009. The Rise of the Mesopredator. *BioScience*. October, 2009. Vol. 59 No. 9. (p. 779-791). doi:10.1525/bio.2009.59.9.9.

603) Prugh, Laura R. et al. 2009. The Rise of the Mesopredator. *BioScience*. October, 2009. Vol. 59 No. 9. (p. 779-791). doi:10.1525/bio.2009.59.9.9.

604) Prugh, Laura R. et al. 2009. The Rise of the Mesopredator. *BioScience*. October, 2009. Vol. 59 No. 9. (p. 779-791). doi:10.1525/bio.2009.59.9.9 "Why are apex predators more effective than humans at controlling mesopredators? Emerging studies of behavior mediated interactions indicate that it is exceptionally difficult to replicate the full ecosystem effects of apex predation (Peckarsky et al. 2008). In a review of intraguild predation, Palomares and Caro (1999) noted that interactions between predators result not only in direct killing but also in avoidance behavior and defensive group formation. Fear of predation can therefore have an even stronger impact on food webs than the killing itself (Brown and Kotler 2007)." ... "Why are apex predators more effective than humans at controlling mesopredators? Emerging studies of behavior-mediated inter-actions indicate that it is exceptionally difficult to replicate the full ecosystem effects of apex predation ... interactions between predators result not only in direct killing but also in avoidance behavior and defensive group formation. Fear of predation can therefore have an even stronger impact on food webs than the killing itself ..."

605) Scales, Helen. "Shark Declines Threaten Shellfish Stocks, Study Says." *National Geographic News*. 3/29/2009. http://news.nationalgeographic .com/news/pf/76004165.html. Accessed 3/4/2012.

606) Lovgren, Stephan. "Million Sharks Killed Accidentally Off Africa Yearly." *National Geographic News*. 4/17/2007. http://news.nationalgeographic .com/news/pf/3173711.html. Accessed 12/16/ 2007.

607) Naomi A. Rose, E.C.M. Parsons, and Richard Farinato. The Case Against Marine Mammals in Captivity, 4th Edition. 2009. The Humane Society of the United States and the World Society for the Protection of Animals. http://www.humanesociety.org/assets/pdfs/marine_mammals/case_against _marine_captivity.pdf. Accessed 8/5/2012.

608) Grimm, David. "Are Dolphins Too Smart for Captivity?" *Science* 29 April 2011: Vol. 332 no. 6029 pp. 526-529. DOI: 10.1126/science.332.6029.526. http://www.sciencemag.org/content/332/6029/526.summary. Accessed

3/04/2012.

609) Naomi A. Rose, E.C.M. Parsons, and Richard Farinato. The Case Against Marine Mammals in Captivity, 4th Edition. 2009. The Humane Society of the United States and the World Society for the Protection of Animals. http://www.humanesociety.org/assets/pdfs/marine_mammals/case_against _marine_captivity.pdf. Accessed 8/5/2012.

610) http://ceta-base.com/lugalogue/deceasedlugas/deadlugas_pdza.html. Accessed 7/13/2011.

611) http://orcanetwork.org/captivity/LolitaMSQFactsflyer.pdf. Accessed 2/14/2011.

612) From Wikipedia: "The fusion of cognitive science and classical ethology into cognitive ethology 'emphasizes observing animals under more-or-less natural conditions, with the objective of understanding the evolution, adaptation (function), causation, and development of the species-specific behavioral repertoire.' – (Niko Tinbergen 1963)." Links omitted. http://en.wikipedia.org/wiki/Cognitive_ethology. Accessed 1/17/2011.

613) Bekoff, Marc. Animal Passions and Beastly Virtues: Cognitive Ethology as the Unifying Science for Understanding the Subjective, Emotional, Empathic, and Moral Lives of Animals. *Human Ecology Review,* Vol. 13, No. 1, 2006. http://www.dancingstarfoundation.org/pdfs/bekoff.pdf. Accessed 12/5/2009.

614) Hatfield, Linda. "Report on Bowhunting." (Then) Executive Director of HOWL (Help Our Wolves Live). "This report summarizes twenty-four studies on bowhunting from across the country...." I believe this is NOT a peer reviewed published paper. http://www.animalrightscoalition.com /doc/bowhunting_report.pdf. Accessed 9/7/2009.

615) 13 percent = http://www.ubbc.ca/resources/documents/archive/retrieval _and_loss_rates_ofpercent20white-tailed_deer_bypercent20_minne sota_bowhunters.pdf ; 18 percent = http://www.seafwa.org/resource/ dynamic/private/PDF/Pedersen-31-34.pdf ; 50 percent = http://www. seafwa.org/resource/dynamic/private/PDF/Pedersen-31-34.pdf.

616) Krueger et al. 2001. Retrieval and loss rates of white-tailed deer by Minnesota bowhunters. The lead author is from the MN Department of Natural Resources using an address at the Archery Manufacturers and Merchants Organization. http://www.ubbc.ca/resources/documents /archive/retrieval_and_loss_rates_ofpercent20white-tailed_deer_byp

ercent20_minnesota_bowhunters.pdf. Accessed 9/5, 2011.

617) Ditchkoff, Stephen S. et al. 1998. Wounding Rates of White-tailed Deer with Traditional Archery Equipment. *Proc. Annu. Conf. Southeast. Assoc. Fish and Wildl. Agencies* 52:244-248. http://www.vex.net/~aac/deerpercent20-per cent20woundingpercent20ratespercent20deerpercent20andpercent20bowp ercent20hunting1998.pdf. Accessed 9/5/2011.

618) "Bow hunters shoot elk in Skagit Co. pasture; state agency closes season." *Skagit Valley Herald*. 12/28/2009. http://www.bellinghamherald.com/ northwest/story/1221692.html. Accessed 1/03/2010.

619) http://wdfw.wa.gov/do/newreal/release.php?id=dec3009a .12/30/2009. Accessed 1/03/2010.

620) Williams, Ross. Tough Questions for Hunters. KUOW Public Radio program, The Conversation. Aired 12/30/2009. 12:40 PM. http://www.kuow. org/program.php?id=19095. Accessed 1/03/2010.

621) Donahue, Debra L. *The Western Range Revisited /Removing Livestock From Public Lands to Preserve Biodiversity.* University of Oklahoma Press. 1999. (108)

622) USDA. APHIS. http://www.aphis.usda.gov/wildlife_damage/prog_data/20 09_prog_data/PDR_G_FY09/Basic_Tables_PDR_G/Table_G_FY2009_Short. pdf. Accessed 2/15/2011.

623) Washington State University Extension Service. http://www. extension.org/pages/Blackbirds#Brown-headed_Cowbird. Their source is Richard A. Dolbeer, Project Leader, Denver Wildlife Research Center. USDA-APHIS-Wildlife Services, Sandusky, Ohio. Site updated as of 2008. Accessed 2/16/2011.

624) Eisemann, John D et al. 2003. Acute and Chronic Toxicity of Compound DRC-1339 (3-Chloro-4-Methylanlline Hydrochloride) to Birds. Wildlife Damage Management, Internet Center for USDA National Wildlife Research Center - Staff Publications. University of Nebraska-Lincoln.

625) http://www.aphis.usda.gov/wildlife_damage/prog_data/prog_data_report _FY2008.shtml. Accessed 1/04/2010.

626) http://www.mayoclinic.com/health/kidney-failure/DS00280/DSECTION =symptoms. Accessed 4/30/2010.

627) http://www.pestoff.co.nz/msd/drc.pdf. Accessed 2/23/2011.

628) Knittl, Edward C. et al. Status of Compound DRC-1339 Registrations. Vertebrate Pest Conference Proceedings collection. Proceedings of the

Fourteenth Vertebrate Pest Conference 1990. University of Nebraska – Lincoln. "The most widely known product containing DRC-1339 is Purina Mills' Starlicide Complete®, a pelleted bait used to control blackbirds and starlings in feedlots," according to the paper, "Status of Compound DRC-1339 Registration."

629) http://www.aphis.usda.gov/publications/wildlife_damage/content/print able_version/WS_tech_note_sodium.pdf. Accessed 2/16/2011. "Results document that SLS causes mortality in European starlings, red-winged blackbirds, common grackles, and brown-headed cowbirds and may be useful as part of integrated wildlife damage-management programs designed to reduce local blackbird populations. Birds died as soon as 30 minutes after exposure to SLS."

630) Avitrol Corporation Closes Doors. Posted 11/1/2010. http://ovocontrol .com/avitrol-halting-further-sales/. "Unlike a poison, OvoControl only interferes with the reproduction of birds. When used according to label directions, the population of pigeons in the treated area declines at a predictable rate. Not limited to short-term effects, OvoControl represents a long-term and sustainable bird control solution for sites with too many pigeons. OvoControl is classified as an unrestricted pesticide ..."

631) Wildlife Services. M-44 Device for Local Predator Control. Factsheet. May 2010. http://www.aphis.usda.gov/publications/wildlife_damage/content/ printable_version/fs_m44_device.pdf. Accessed 2/16/2011.

632) Wildlife Services. M-44 Device for Local Predator Control. Factsheet. May 2010. http://www.aphis.usda.gov/publications/wildlife_damage/content/pr intable_version/fs_m44_device.pdff. Accessed 2/16/2011.

633) Wildlife Services. M-44 Device for Local Predator Control. Factsheet. May 2010. http://www.aphis.usda.gov/publications/wildlife_damage/content/ printable_version/fs_m44_device.pdf. Accessed 2/16/2011.

634) Eisler, Ronald. 1991. Cyanide Hazards to Fish, Wildlife, and Invertebrates: A Synoptic Review- U.S. Fish Wildl. Serv., *Biol. Rep.* 85(1.23). http://www.infomine.com/publications/docs/Eisler1991.pdf. Accessed 2/22/2011.

635) Eisler, Ronald. 1991. Cyanide Hazards to Fish, Wildlife, and Invertebrates: A Synoptic Review- U.S. Fish Wildl. Serv., *Biol. Rep.* 85(1.23). http://www.infomine.com/publications/docs/Eisler1991.pdf. Accessed 2/22/2011.

636) Connolly, G., Burnsy, R. J., Simmonsz, Gary D. 1986. Effects of sodium cyanide and diphacinone in coyotes (*Canis latrans*): Applications as predacides in livestock toxic collars. (Table 2 shows time to symptoms, then "going down" to death). Vertebrate Pest Conference Proceedings collection Proceedings of the Twelfth Vertebrate Pest Conference (1986). University of Nebraska - Lincoln Year 1986. Alternate Toxicants for the M-44 Sodium Cyanide Ejector. http://digitalcommons.unl.edu/cgi/viewcontent.cgi?ar icle=1014&context=vpc12. Accessed 2/22, 2011.

637) Medline. National Institute of Health. http://www.nlm.nih.gov/medlin eplus/ency/article/003195.htm. Accessed 2/18/2020.

638) http://www.pesticideinfo.org/Detail_Chemical.jsp?Rec_Id=PC34366#Sym ptoms. Accessed 2/18/2011.

639) Connolly, Guy, Burnsy, Richard J., Simmonsz, Gary D. 1986. Effects of sodium cyanide and diphacinone in coyotes (*Canis latrans*): Applications as predacides in livestock toxic collars. (Table 2 shows time to symptoms, then "going down" to death). Vertebrate Pest Conference Proceedings collection Proceedings of the Twelfth Vertebrate Pest Conference (1986). University of Nebraska - Lincoln Year 1986. Alternate Toxicants for the M-44 Sodium Cyanide Ejector. http://digitalcommons.unl.edu/cgi/viewcontent.cgi?article =1014&context=vpc12. Accessed 2/22, 2011.

640) Guidotti, Tee. MD, MPH, DABT. 2005. Acute Cyanide Poisoning in Prehospital Care: New Challenges, New Tools for Intervention. *Prehosp Disast Med*. 2005;21(2):s40–s48. http://pdm.medicine.wisc.edu/Volume _21/issue_2/guidotti.pdf. Accessed 12/16/2010.

641) Witmer, Gary W. and Fagerstoney, Kathleen A. 2003. The Use of Toxicants in Black-tailed Prairie Dog Management: An Overview. Wildlife Damage Management, Internet Center for USDA National Wildlife Research Center. http://digitalcommons.unl.edu/cgi/viewcontent.cgi?article=1288&context=i cwdm_usdanwrc. Accessed 2/22/2011.

642) Packer C, Kosmala M, Cooley HS, Brink H, Pintea L, et al. 2009. Sport Hunting, Predator Control and Conservation of Large Carnivores. *PLoS ONE* 4(6): e5941. doi:10.1371/journal.pone.0005941. http://www.plo sone.org/article/info:doi/10.1371/journal.pone.0005941. Accessed 3/04.2012.

643) 2008 CITES Report. Association of Fish and Wildlife Agencies. http://mafwa.iafwa.org/mem_com/CITES_rpt08. Accessed 1/10/2010. One look at their partners and sponsors, all hunting operations and businesses

excepting one (Nature Conservancy) and their strident policies that seek to exclude and demean the majority culture, says a lot. http://www. fishwildlife.org Accessed 1/13/2010.

644) http://www.thecovemovie.com/. Accessed 2/18/2011.

645) http://www.savejapandolphins.org. Accessed 9/8/2009.

646) History of Wildlife Management in West Virginia. West Virginia Conservation Agency. http://www.wvca.us/envirothon/w2.html. Accessed 7/14/2009.

647) Some of these phrases are quotes from History of Wildlife Management in West Virginia. West Virginia Conservation Agency. http://www. wvca.us/envirothon/w2.html. Accessed 7/14/2009.

648) Botkin, Daniel. *Discordant Harmonies / A New Ecology for the Twenty-First Century*. Oxford University Press. 1990. (p.8)

649) In Alaska, there is a prohibition of discriminating between extremely rural residents in the "bush," who are often indigenous people, and urban hunters looking to kill moose and other wildlife. Therefore, the state of Alaska has long carried out a program of aerial gunning down of wolves in large areas of the state to create more moose targets for hunters. They also increase the quotas for killing bears who depend upon moose calves in the Spring. Representing Greenpeace Alaska, I testified against the initiation of this aerial hunt at the originating Alaska Board of Game hearing in Fairbanks this program began. They said it would be a temporary action. I easily said it would not. One board member said to me during my testimony that he would like to see my head on his wall. We still see this current human ecology today, most famously represented by Governor Sarah Palin who fights endangered species protections for polar bears and belugas and avidly supports aerial wolf killing and opening the Alaska National Wildlife Refuge to oil and gas development.

650) Mallonée, Jay S. and Joslin, Paul. 2004. Traumatic Stress Disorder Observed in an Adult Wild Captive Wolf (*Canis lupus*). Journal of Applied Animal Welfare Science. 7(2), 107–126.

651) Giant pandas suffer post-quake trauma. China View. 2008-07-14 18:08:39. http://news.xinhuanet.com/english/2008-07/14/content_8544436.htm. Accessed 4/2/2010.

652) Aguirre, A.A. and Gómez, A. 2009. Essential veterinary education in conservation medicine and ecosystem health: a global perspective. *Rev. sci. tech.*

Off. int. Epiz., 2009, 28 (2), 597- 603. http://www.ecohealthalliance
.org/writable/publications/veterinary_education_in_conservation_medicin
e_and_ecosystem_health.pdf. Accessed 3/4/2012

653) http://www.rachelcarson.org/. Accessed 2/16/2011.

654) http://earthday.envirolink.org/history.html. Accessed 2/16/2011.

655) Inger Egede, in a speech given at the Inuit Circumpolar Conference, 1995, as quoted in Poisoned Food: Cultural Resistance to the Contaminants Discourse in Nunavik. O'Neil, John D. et al. *Arctic Anthropology*. Vol. 34, No. 1, pp. 29-40, 1997. http://www.jstor.org/pss/40316422. Accessed 3/04.2012.

656) Gelbspan, Ross. *ORION* magazine. July 7, 2004. (p. 11)

657) Our Creative Diversity. Report of the World Commission for Culture and Development, UNESCO. 1995. (pg.16) http://unesdoc.unesco.org /images/0010/001016/101651e.pdf. Accessed 9/09/09.

658) O'Neil, Dennis. World Diversity Patterns. Copyright © 1997-2006. http://anthro.palomar.edu/ethnicity/ethnic_5.htm. Accessed 9/09/2009. "Just how many different societies, cultures, and ethnic groups make up the world's population is not certain. This is due, in part, to the fact that these social entities are not always distinct enough to clearly warrant their being considered as separate groups. For instance, Canada and the U.S. are separate nations but culturally and linguistically similar almost to the point of not being distinguishable by outsiders (except for French speaking Quebec Province). Contributing to the problem of counting the number of societies, cultures, and ethnic groups is not only the overlapping nature of many of these groups but the fact that they are now changing rapidly as mass media and relatively inexpensive long distance travel increasingly blur cultural differences. We are experiencing culture change on a scale and at a pace that is unprecedented in human history."

659) UNESCO. http://www.unesco.org/bpi/eng/unescopress/2000/00-120e.s html. Accessed 9/15/09.

660) The Linguistic Society of America. How Many Languages Are There In the World? http://www.lsadc.org/info/pdf_files/howmany.pdf. Accessed 9/09/2009.
"The most extensive catalog of the world's languages, generally taken to be as authoritative as any, is that of the *Ethnologue* organization (http://www.ethnologue.com), whose detailed classified list currently includes 6,809 distinct languages."

661) Townsend, Patricia K. *Environmental Anthropology / From Pigs to Policies.* Second Edition. Waveland Press.2009, 2000. (p. 21)

662) http://www.worldatlas.com/nations.htm. Accessed 9/15/2009.

663) Olson, David M. et al. 2001. Terrestrial Ecoregions of the World: A New Map of Life on Earth.
BioScience, Vol. 51, No. 11 (Nov., 2001), (p. 933-938). http://www.jstor.org/stable/1313989. Defined by the authors as "relatively large units of land containing a distinct assemblage of natural communities and species, with boundaries that approximate the original extent of natural communities prior to major land-use change."

664) Spalding, Mark D. et al. 2007. Marine Ecoregions of the World: A Bioregionalization of Coastal and Shelf Areas. *BioScience*. July/August 2007 / Vol. 57 No. 7. (p. 573-583). www.biosciencemag.org.
The authors state, "Ecoregions are the smallest-scale units in the Marine Ecoregions of the World (MEOW) system and are defined as follows: Areas of relatively homogeneous species composition, clearly distinct from adjacent systems.

665) Wilson, Edmund O. *The Future of Life.* Borzoi Book/Published by Alfred A. Knopf. 2002. (p. 94)

666) Grim, John A. "Native North American Worldviews and Ecology." In *Worldviews and Ecology / Religion, Philosophy, and the Environment.* Tucker, Mary Evelyn and Grim, John A., editors. Ecology of Justice Series. Catholic Foreign Mission Society of America. Maryknoll/Orbis Books. 1997. (p.41)

667) Perkins, Sid. "Is Agriculture Sucking Fresh Water Dry?" *Science* Magazine. February 13, 2012. http://news.sciencemag.org/sciencenow/2012/02/is-agriculture-sucking-fresh-wat.html. Accessed 2/17/2012.

668) Lauk, Christian and Erb, Karl-Heinz. 2009. Biomass consumed in anthro-pogenic vegetation fires: Global patterns and processes. *Ecological Economics* 69 (2009) 301–309. doi:10.1016/j.ecolecon.2009.07.003. http://www.uni-klu.ac.at/socec/downloads/6_2009_LaukErb_fires_EE69_53.pdf. Accessed 3/4/2012.

669) Hiskes, Jonathan. "Can Human Rights Be the Climate Movement's Moral Guide?" *Grist.* May 29, 2009. http://www.grist.org/article/2009-05-29-can-human-rights-be-guide. Accessed 1/05/2010.

670) Milton, Kay. "Cultural Theory and Environmentalism." *The Environment in Anthropology.* Nora Haenn and Richard R. Wilk, editors. New York

University Press. 2006. (p. 353)

671) MacDonald, Christine. *Green, Inc. / An Environmental Insider Reveals How a Good Cause Has Gone Bad.* Lyons Press/Imprint of Globe Pequot Press. 2009. (p. 195)

672) Timiraos, Nick. "The Race Where Horses Die." *Wall Street Journal.* August 2007. http://online.wsj.com/article/NA_WSJ_PUB:SB118678342614494614 .html. Accessed 7/31/2010.

673) http://www.nativepeoples.com/article/articles/102/1/Rodeo-Cowboys-in-Indian-Country/Page1.html. Accessed 7/31/2010.

674) All Indian Rodeo Cowboys Association website: http://www.aircarodeo. com/content.asp?CustComKey=314275&CategoryKey=314276&pn=Page& DomName=aircarodeo.com. Accessed 7/31/2010.

675) Merchant, Carolyn. *The Columbia Guide to American Environmental History.* Columbia University Press, publisher. 2002. (p. 5)

676) Naess, Arne in "The Ecology of Wisdom / Writings by Arne Naess." Alan Drengson and Bill Devall, editors. Counterpoint Press. Berkeley, CA. 2008. (p. 101)

677) Naess, Arne in "The Ecology of Wisdom / Writings by Arne Naess." Alan Drengson and Bill Devall, editors. Counterpoint Press. Berkeley, CA. 2008. (p. 113)

678) Oxfam International Media Briefing. November, 2010. Ref. 08/20/10. http://www.oxfam.org/sites/www.oxfam.org/files/oxfam-cancun-media-briefing-2010.pdf. Accessed 12/5/2010.

679) Rifkin, Jeremy. *The Empathic Civilization / The Race to Global Consciousness In a World In Crisis.* Jeremy P. Tarcher/Penguin, publishers. 2009. (p. 436)

680) For example: Pelly Amendment —Title 22. Foreign Relations and Intercourse; Citation: 22 USC 1978. Summary: Restriction on importation of fishery or wildlife products from countries which violate international fishery or endangered or threatened species programs. http://www animallaw.info/statutes/stus22usc1978.htm. Accessed 9/14/2009.

681) Ereira, Alan. The book: *The Elder Brothers.* Tairona Heritage Trust, publishers. 2009. The original VHS video release: *From the Heart of the World: The Elder Brothers Warning.* Director: Alan Ereira. Available to be viewed online as of 9/15/2009 at: http://www.onlinedocumentaries4u.com /2008/05/kogi-from-heart-of-world-elder-brothers.html.

682) "Greenland Aboriginals Abusing Whaling Quota." Reuters. June 17, 2008.

http://www.reuters.com/article/idUSL16792620080617. Accessed 1/05/2010.

683) "Greenland Whaling Is Not All Subsistence." *ECO: The Environmental Voice at the IWC.* Volume LXI No. 4 Madeira, Portugal Thursday June 25, 2009. http://www.earthisland.org/marinemammal/index.php/eco2009. Accessed 1/05/2010.

684) http://iwcoffice.org/conservation/catches.htm#aborig. Accessed 1/13/2012.

685) PROPOSED SCHEDULE AMENDMENT (IWC 64) (Greenland Catch Limits) Submitted by Denmark; IWC/64/12. http://iwcoffice.org/_documents/commission/IWC64docs/64-12.pdf. Accessed 6/16/2012.

686) E.J. Milner-Gulland et al. 2003. Wild meat: the bigger picture. *TRENDS in Ecology and Evolution.* Vol.18 No.7 July 2003. doi:10.1016/S0169-5347(03)00123-X. http://www.iccs.org.uk/papers/Milner-Gulland2003TREE.pdf. Accessed 10/19/2009.

687) Clapham, Phil and Van Waerebeek, Koen. 2007. Bushmeat and bycatch: the sum of the parts. *Molecular Ecology.* Volume 16, Number 13, July 2007, pp. 2607-2609(3). DOI:10.1111/j.1365-294X.2007.03378.x. http://onlinelibrary.wiley.com/doi/10.1111/j.1365-294X.2007.03378.x/full. Accessed 3/4/2012.

688) Milner-Gulland, E.J. et al. 2009. Wild Meat: the bigger picture. *TRENDS in Ecology and Evolution.* Vol.18 No.7 July 2003. doi:10.1016/S0169-5347(03)00123-X. http://www.iccs.org.uk/papers/Milner-Gulland2003TREE.pdf. Accessed 10/19/2009.

689) E.J. Milner-Gulland et al. 2009. Wild Meat: the bigger picture. *TRENDS in Ecology and Evolution.* Vol.18 No.7 July 2003. doi:10.1016/S0169-5347(03)00123-X. http://www.iccs.org.uk/papers/Milner-Gulland2003TREE.pdf. Accessed 10/19/2009.

690) Pittman, Todd. Associated Press. "Monkey meat: It's what's for dinner." *Seattle-Post Intelligencer.* 6/16/2004. A news that describes how bush meat is flown in by airplane to the city of Kinshasa, Congo. Overall, in Africa, "'A few thousand commercial bush meat hunters supported by the timber industry infrastructure will illegally shoot and butcher $2 billion worth of wildlife this year, including as many as 8,000 endangered great-apes,' according to the California-based Bushmeat Project."

691) McRae, Michael. "Road Kill in Cameroon." *The Environment in Anthropology.* Nora Haenn and Richard R. Wilk, editors. New York University Press. 2006.

692) Cameroon Officials Stage Successful Bushmeat, Poaching Raid. World Wildlife Fund Update. May 8, 2009. http://www.worldwildlife.org/

who/media/press/2009/WWFPrescongobushmeat.html.
Accessed 12/5/2009.

693) "Future for Gorillas in Africa Getting Bleaker." Press Release. CITES. 3/24/2010. http://www.cites.org/eng/news/press/2010/20100324_gorrilas.sh tml Accessed 4/20/2010.

The Rapid Response Assessment report, entitled *The Last Stand of the Gorilla – Environmental Crime and Conflict in the Congo Basin*, says militias in the eastern part of the DRC are behind much of the illegal trade that may be worth several hundred million dollars a year. ... Christian Nellemann, a senior officer at UNEP's Grid Arendal centre who was lead author of the 2002 report and who has headed up the new one, said the original assessment had underestimated the scale of the bushmeat trade, the rise in logging and the impact of the Ebola virus on great ape populations. ... . "With the current and accelerated rate of poaching for bushmeat and habitat loss, the gorillas of the Greater Congo Basin may now disappear from most of their present range within ten to fifteen years," said Mr. Nellemann."

694) Nunez-Iturria, Gabriela et al. 2008. Hunting reduces recruitment of primate-dispersed trees in Amazonian Peru. *Biological Conservation*. 141 (2008) 1536-1546. http://www.uic.edu/labs/howe/pdfs/Nunez-IturriOlsson Howe08.pdf. Accessed 3/4/2012.

695) Peterson, Dale. *Eating Apes*. University of California Press. 2003. (p. 25, 31, 41, 50, 54, 63, 65)

696) Kinver, Mark. "Illegal bushmeat 'rife in Europe." BBC News Science and Environment. 17 June 2010.

"In total, 11 species were found - including two types of primates, two kinds of crocodiles and three rodent species - four of which were listed as protected species." http://www.bbc.co.uk/news/10341174. Accessed 12/5/2010.

697) VegFam: http://www.vegfamcharity.org.uk/ . Accessed 11/27/2010.

698) http://www.vegfamcharity.org.uk/ ; http://www.hippocharity.org.uk/ ; http://www.ffl.org ; http://hkffl.org ; http://www.malnutrition.org/.

699) http://awellfedworld.org/. Accessed 2/18/2012.

700) For a general overview, see http://www.unesco.org/education/tlsf/ TLSF/theme_a/mod02/uncom02t05.htm.

701) World population estimates vary. A summary of estimates published by the

U.S. Census Bureau suggest that in 1825 there were roughly 1.2 billion people on Earth. http://www.census.gov/ipc/www/worldhis.html. Accessed 4/15/2010. Others feel this population was not reached until about 1850: http://geography.about.com/od/obtainpopulationdata/a/worldpopulation.htm. Accessed 3/4/1012.

702) Ridgeway, James. BP's Slick Greenwashing. 5/4/2010. http://motherjones.com/mojo/2010/05/bp-coated-sludge-after-years-greenwashing. Accessed 5/04/2010.

703) MacDonald, Christine. *Green, Inc. / An Environmental Insider Reveals How a Good Cause Has Gone Bad.* Lyons Press/Imprint of Globe Pequot Press. 2009. (p. 155) Refer to the TerraChoice site for their latest work. TerraChoice helps businesses market their products. http://www.terrachoice.com/.

704) James, Shauna. "Graze Anatomy." *Seattle Metropolitan.* July, 2007.

705) King, Anna, reporter. Spring Lambing Is Nearly Chaos In Northwest Farm Country. April 8, 2010. http://news.opb.org/article/7071-spring-lambing-nearly-chaos-northwest-farm-country/. Accessed May 5, 2010.

706) Food and Agriculture Organization of the United Nations (FAO). http://www.fao.org/ag/magazine/0612sp1.htm.
Most of my reliable, mainstream sources use 26 percent as total global grazing land use. One recent study pegged it at 22 percent: Ramankutty, N., A. T. Evan, C. Monfreda, and J. A. Foley (2008), Farming the planet: Geographic distribution of global agricultural lands in the year 2000, *Global Biogeochem. Cycles*, 22, GB1003, doi:10.1029/2007GB002952.

707) Sonesson, Ulf et al. 2009. Food Production and Emissions of Greenhouse Gasses / An overview of the climate impact of different product groups. Swedish Institute for Food and Biotechnology. Swedish Presidency of the European Union.

708) Sedorovich, D.M., Rotz, C.A., Richard, T.L. 2007. Greenhouse Gas Emissions from Dairy Farms. Proceedings of the American Society of Agricultural and Biological Engineers International (ASABE). Paper No. 074096, St. Joseph, MI: ASABE. http://www.ars.usda.gov/research/publications/publications.htm?SEQ_NO_115=210471. Accessed 2/21/2011.

709) Fleming, Nic. "Beware of 'Bluewash': Which Fish Should You Buy?" *NewScientist.* January 12, 2010. Issue 2742. http://www.newscientist.com/article/mg20527425.000-beware-of-bluewash-which-fish-should-you-buy.html?DCMP=OTC-rss&nsref=online-news. Accessed 1/13/2010. "There

is little consensus on what constitutes a 'sustainable' fishery. Jacquet [Jennifer Jacquet of the University of British Columbia Fisheries Centre in Vancouver, Canada] points out that while most schemes agree on high-profile species such as the Atlantic bluefin tuna, six organisations rank Atlantic halibut as a species to avoid, while Friends of the Sea and the Monterey Bay Aquarium recommend it as sustainable. ...They conclude that governments, not consumers, should take the lead to protect fisheries by legislating on the amount of seafood used in animal feed..."

710) Bluefin tuna main course of CITES world conference. CITES Press Release 2/05/2010. http://www.cites.org/eng/news/press/2010/20100205_cop15.sht ml. Accessed 4/20/2010.

711) http://www.bbc.co.uk/news/world-asia-pacific-16421231. Accessed 1/14/2012.

712) Benjamin White dedicated his life to a brilliant and self-sacrificing path few have equaled. An arborist by training, Ben risked all to work tirelessly for our social justice and the rights of other species in arenas that ranged from the Convention on International Trade in Endangered Species (of Wild Fauna and Flora—CITES) and the International Whaling Commission (IWC) to the waters of Japan where he freed dolphins from nets. Ben origi-nated the symbolic cardboard turtle costumes worn by protesters at the World Trade Organization (WTO) meeting in Seattle.

713) Bonne, Karijn and Verbeke, Wim. 2008. Religious values informing halal meat production and the control and delivery of halal credence quality. Citing (Sack, 2001: 218). *Agriculture and Human Values* (2008) 25:35–47 DOI 10.1007/s10460-007-9076-y. "Most religions forbid certain foods (e.g., pork and not ritually slaughtered meat in Judaism and Islam, pork and beef in Hinduism and Buddhism), with the notable exception of Christianity, which has no food taboos." https://biblio.ugent.be/input/download?func =downloadFile&fileOId=590500&recordOId=409105. Accessed 3/4/2012.

714) Gregory, N.G. et al. 2010. Time to collapse following slaughter without stunning in cattle. *Meat Science*. Vol. 85, Issue 1. May 2010. Pp. 66-69. Abstract. http://www.sciencedirect.com/science/article/pii/S03091740090 03854. Accessed 1/21/2012.

715) Waller, Sarah. Sound Focus. Interview of Scott Meyers of Sweet Grass Farm. National Public Radio, KUOW, Seattle, WA. http://www.kuow.org/program .php?id=14228.

716) Denn, Rebekah. "It's A Pig's Life." *Seattle Post-Intelligencer*. 4/12/2006. Section D. Life and Arts. http://www.seattlepi.com/local/.

717) Clement, Bethany Jean. "Burning Beast Three: The Beastening / A Report from the World's Best Beast Feast in a Field." *The Stranger*. July 15, 2010. (p. 23)

718) Pollan, Michael. *In Defense of Food*. The Penguin Press. New York. 2008. (introduction)

719) Hamilton, Lisa M. "The Carnivore's Dilemma: Responsible meat eaters belly up to the offal truth." *Conscious Choice* . (Seattle) November, 2007. http://www.lime.com/magazines?uri=seattle.consciouschoice.com/lime/2007/11/offaltruth0711.html. Accessed 11/19/2009.

720) Book review and excerpt. http://life.gaiam.com/article/why-our-ancestors-were-not-vegetarians. Accessed 1/19/2012. *The New Evolution Diet* . Arthur De Vany, PhD. Rodale, Inc. 2011.

721) Rubin, Peter. "Guess Who's Coming As Dinner?" *Good*. Issue 009. March/April 2008. http://www.good.is/post/guess-whos-coming-as-dinner/. Accessed 1/19/2012. *Good* magazine describes itself: "Good is for people who give a damn. It's an entertaining magazine about things that matter."

722) Jones, Dena. "Crimes Unseen, The dark story of America's big slaughter-houses, and the effort to make their grim work more humane." *Orion*. July/August, 2004. http://www.orionmagazine.org/index.php/articles/article/144/. Accessed 1/19/2012.

723) Houston, Jason. "Shortening the Food Chain." *Orion*. July/August 2004. www.orion.org.

724) Pinkowish, Mary Desmond. "Not the Same Old Drive-Thru." *Ode*. April, 2008. http://www.odemagazine.com/doc/52/not-the-same-old-drive-thru/. Accessed 11/25/2009.

725) In Jeffrey Moussaieff Masson's book, *The Face on Your Plate: The Truth About Food*, W.W. Norton Company. 2009. He writes about a blog written by chef Tamara Murphy who to *The New York Times* about "the betrayal" she felt in raising and then slaughtering several pigs. She called this meal a celebration of the pigs' lives. This was widely reported and at about the same time I was questioning Tamara via email about her strange beliefs. But she was resolute in her understanding of her role, and that of the pigs. Masson has a lot to say about denial and betrayal.

726) Watson, Lyall. *The Whole Hog / Exploring the Extraordinary Potential of Pigs*.

Smithsonian Books / Profile Books, publisher. United Kingdom. 2004. (p. 17, 192)

727) Watson, Lyall. *The Whole Hog / Exploring the Extraordinary Potential of Pigs.* Smithsonian Books / Profile Books, publisher. United Kingdom. 2004. (p. 192 – 193)

728) Capper, Judith L. 2011. Replacing rose-tinted spectacles with a high-powered microscope: The historical versus modern carbon footprint of animal agriculture. *Animal Frontiers.* July 2011, Vol. 1, No. 1. p. 26. doi:10.2527/af.2011-0009. http://www.agron.iastate.edu/courses/agron515/ Historical%20vs%20modern%20footprint.pdf. Accessed 1/21/2012.

729) Friedman, Thomas L. *Hot, Flat, and Crowded / Why We Need A Green Revolution – And How It Can Renew America.* Farrar, Straus, Giroux. 2008. (p. 205)

730) *The Sun*, June 2009. Issue 402. www.thesunmagazine.org.

731) Speth, James Gustave. *The Bridge at the End of the World / Capitalism, the Environment, and crossing from Crisis to Sustainability.* A Caravan Book. 2008. (p. 204)

732) Rifkin, Jeremy. *The Empathic Civilization / The Race to Global Consciousness in a World in Crisis.* Jeremy P. Tarcher / Penguin. New York. 2009. (p. 616)

733) Terbough, John. *Requiem for Nature.* Island Press/Shearwater. 1999/2004 (p. 142-143, paperback).

734) Goodland, Robert and Anhang, Jeff. Livestock and Climate Change: What if the key actors in climate change are...cows, pigs, chickens? *WorldWatch.* November/December 2009. (p. 10-19) http://www.worldwatch.org/files /pdf/Livestockpercent20andpercent20Climatepercent20Change.pdf

735) Harrington, Jennie M., Myers, Ransom A., Rosenberg, Andrew A. 2005. Wasted fishery resources: discarded by-catch in the USA. *Fish and Fisheries.* 2005. 6, 350–361. Not including marine mammals, birds, and turtles, "Overall, our compiled estimates are that 1.06 million tonnes of fish were discarded and 3.7 million tonnes of fish were landed in USA marine fisheries in 2002. This amounts to a nationwide discard to landings ratio of 0.28, amongst the highest in the world." http://www.globalcitizen .net/Data/Pages/1435/Papers/2009051213286579.pdf. Accessed 3/12/2011.

736) Baroni, L. et al. 2006. Evaluating the environmental impact of various dietary patterns combined with different food production systems. *European Journal of Clinical Nutrition.* (2007) 61, 279–286. http://tier-im-

fokus.ch/wp-content/uploads/2009/09/baroni07.pdf. Accessed 2/24/2011.

737) Masson, Jeffrey Moussaieff. *The Pig Who Sang to the Moon / The Emotional World of Farm Animals.* Ballantine Books, publisher. 2003. (p. 104)

738) Ziegler, Jean. UN Rapporteur on the Right to Food, speaking in *We Feed the World*, an Alegro film. 2005.

The Index can be found at

www.ThisIsHopethebook.com

EARTH

BOOKS

Earth Books are practical, scientific and philosophical
publications about our relationship with the environment.
Earth Books explore sustainable ways of living; including green
parenting, gardening, cooking and natural building. They also look at
ecology, conservation and aspects of environmental science, including
green energy. An understanding of the interdependence of all living
things is central to Earth Books, and therefore consideration of our
relationship with other animals is important. Animal welfare is
explored. The purpose of Earth Books is to deepen our understanding
of the environment and our role within it. The books featured under
this imprint will both present thought-provoking questions and offer
practical solutions.